*To my mother and father,*
*and to the fun we've had finding, restoring,*
*and selling treasures of all sorts.*

## About the Author

For much of his adult life, **Greg Holden** has been hunting down and reselling collectibles, oddball items, and antiques of all sorts. In his younger days, he assembled an old sports car from pieces of three different sports cars. He bought and restored a century-old townhouse. Now, he hunts down fountain pens, watches, and other items online. Greg has written 30 books on computers and the Internet, including *How to Do Everything with eBay* and *The Collector's Guide to eBay,* both published by McGraw-Hill/Osborne, as well as *eBay PowerUser's Bible, Internet Auctions for Dummies,* and *Cliff's Notes Guide to Buying and Selling on eBay,* all published by Wiley Publishing. His lifelong interests in literature and writing and the history of Chicago recently culminated in the book *Literary Chicago: A Book Lover's Tour of the Windy City,* published by Lake Claremont Press. He lives in Chicago in the house he restored along with his two daughters and an assortment of pets.

## About the Technical Editor

**Lisa Suttora** is the owner of WhatDoISell.com, a membership web site that specializes in teaching online auction sellers creative, professional strategies and techniques for selecting products to sell on eBay, locating legitimate suppliers, and effectively selling in the eBay Marketplace. WhatDoISell.com is an eBay Certified Services Provider. Lisa is also a contributing editor for Creative Online Selling Strategies to Entrepreneur Magazine's E-Biz Radio Show (**http://www .wsradio.com/ebizshow/**) and has been a featured guest on eBay Radio's Product Sourcing Segment (**http://www.wsradio.com/ebayradio/index.htm**). An eBay PowerSeller, Lisa provides consulting services for individuals who are building an eBay business and for companies that are interested in adding a new channel of revenue from eBay into their existing business model. Lisa may be contacted via her web site at **http://www.whatdoIsell.com**.

# How to Do *Everything* with Your

# eBay® Business

## Second Edition

### Greg Holden

**McGraw-Hill**/Osborne

New York   Chicago   San Francisco   Lisbon
London   Madrid   Mexico City   Milan   New Delhi
San Juan   Seoul   Singapore   Sydney   Toronto

The McGraw·Hill Companies

**McGraw-Hill**/Osborne
2100 Powell Street, 10th Floor
Emeryville, California 94608
U.S.A.

To arrange bulk purchase discounts for sales promotions, premiums, or fund-raisers, please contact **McGraw-Hill**/Osborne at the above address. For information on translations or book distributors outside the U.S.A., please see the International Contact Information page immediately following the index of this book.

### How to Do Everything with Your eBay® Business, Second Edition

1234567890 CUS CUS 0198765

ISBN 0-07-226164-1

| | |
|---|---|
| **Vice President & Group Publisher** | Philip Ruppel |
| **Vice President & Publisher** | Jeffrey Krames |
| **Acquisitions Editor** | Marjorie McAneny |
| **Project Editor** | Janet Walden |
| **Acquisitions Coordinator** | Agatha Kim |
| **Technical Editor** | Lisa Suttora |
| **Copy Editor** | William McManus |
| **Proofreader** | Francesca Ferrie |
| **Indexer** | Claire Splan |
| **Composition** | International Typesetting and Composition |
| **Illustrator** | International Typesetting and Composition |
| **Series Design** | Mickey Galicia |
| **Cover Series Design** | Dodie Shoemaker |
| **Cover Illustration** | Tom Willis |

This book was composed with Adobe® InDesign® CS.

# Contents at a Glance

# Contents

# Acknowledgments

Whether you are writing books for a living or selling on eBay either part-time or full-time, much of your work seems to be done alone. But the truth is that you're never really alone. There are plenty of people sitting at *their* computers who are depending on you, who are waiting for you, who are rooting for you to be a success.

Any successful sale on eBay depends on help and cooperation from lots of people, from the individual who provided you with the item to sell, to the companion who helped you carry it home, to the shippers who made sure it reached its destination. Trust and cooperation make online auctions work. I've often been struck by the fact that the most successful auction sellers are also the most generous with their time and experience. They have taught me that the more helpful you are, the more successful you'll be in return.

In the same way, writing a book about selling on eBay depends on a community of individuals you might never meet face to face. First, I want to thank the eBay sellers who took the time to talk to me either on the phone or by e-mail and share their knowledge. Thanks go to Gary Pitts, Chad Gibbons, Jo Stavig, Buddhachick, Bob Kopczynski, Don Colclough, Jon and Steve Brothers, decoray, Shiela Schneider, Dana Titus, Kevin Boyd, Tom Hergert, Carol Hearn, Mike Morin, and Andy Noise.

I also want to acknowledge my own colleagues who helped me with research and editing, Ben Huizenga and Pam Parrish.

I have been impressed with the enthusiasm and encouragement I have received from all the folks at McGraw-Hill/Osborne, starting with Margie McAnerny, who got the ball rolling (and kept it rolling smoothly); acquisitions coordinator Agatha Kim; Janet Walden, who served as project editor; technical editor Lisa Suttora; copyeditor Bill McManus; and publicity manager Bettina Faltermeier.

Thanks also to my agent, Lynn Haller, and everyone at Studio B Productions. Last but not least, thanks to my mother and father, who instilled the love of giving new life to someone else's castoffs—a practice that carries over perfectly to the new electronic flea market, eBay. Bargain hunting is an art I'm now passing down to my two daughters, Zosia and Lucy, as their sharp eyes are becoming ever more skilled at finding just what they're looking for at thrift shops and garage sales. Sharing so many adventures with them puts fun in my life, especially when they allow me to share their ever-widening circle of loving friends and pets.

# Introduction

Just a few years ago, it seemed like everyone (including yours truly) was describing the Web as the new Wild, Wild, West for businesspeople—a place where they could strike out on their own, stake a claim, open up their own storefront, and start to do business for the first time. Well, the bloom is off the rose, as far as e-commerce on the Web is concerned, but eBay remains a thriving destination for anyone who wants to make a few extra bucks or even start a new career as an auction seller.

eBay has quickly become a part of everyday life rather than a novelty enjoyed by a few. Now that eBay has been around for several years, it has become more reliable and easier to use. It has also inherited both the good and bad aspects of the free market—the people who are trustworthy and community minded, as well as those who don't follow through with transactions and actively try to swindle other people. Luckily, the first group of eBay users far outnumbers the second. eBay's network of trust still makes it a great place to realize the highest possible profits on online sales and start up your own online business. It's also giving a new lease on life to antique dealers and small business owners who have suddenly found a worldwide market of eager bidders to add to the local people who drive or walk to their stores. Lately, eBay Stores specializing in wholesale items and general consumer goods are becoming more and more popular.

This book is especially for people who want to sell regularly on eBay—those who want to run a business selling on eBay. "Running an eBay business" can mean a variety of things. It might mean you sell full-time on eBay, as some experienced and successful sellers do. It might mean you make small but regular part-time income selling after work or on the weekends. Or it might mean you sell a handful of items on eBay each month. This book assumes, though, that you want to sell regularly on eBay, and that you want to be a successful seller. It assumes that you're already familiar with eBay, at least as a buyer. Part I, "Get Started with eBay," starts at the beginning—deciding what you want to sell, how you want to sell it, and who you want to sell it to. You also get suggestions for how to do the kind of strategic buying that will keep your business flowing smoothly rather than having fits and starts simply because you've run out of merchandise to sell.

Part II, "Improve Your Competitive Edge," seeks to take you beyond being a casual eBay seller who completes transactions once in a while, to someone who sets up a system for selling on a regular basis. In Chapters 4 and 5, you learn the importance of building an initial positive feedback rating to build your credibility as a seller, as well as how to make your auctions stand out from the crowd and build goodwill with potential bidders by providing complete, honest descriptions of your sales merchandise. In Chapter 6, you learn how auction management software and online services can streamline the process of getting sales online and storing images, and provide you with records that are sure to come in handy at tax time. In Chapter 7, you learn about different options for promoting your eBay sales by creating web pages, such as eBay's About Me page and eBay Stores, as well as your own web site. In Chapter 8, you explore the ins and outs of one of the most important ways to attract bids: providing good images of your merchandise.

Part III, "Business Practices for eBay," takes a look at the "back end," indispensable business operations that can take your eBay sales business to a new level. Chapter 9 focuses on different ways to serve your customers, including answering questions, sending out e-mail responses promptly, and accepting payments. Chapter 10 focuses on two essential operations that you might overlook otherwise—packing your merchandise and shipping it out safely. Chapter 11 explores ways to be a participating member of the eBay community, by leaving feedback, using e-mail effectively, and making use of eBay's extensive selection of discussion forums.

Part IV, "Sell Specialty Items on eBay," examines the wide variety of auction venues that make up eBay's auction world, and that you might overlook in your zeal to get conventional auction sales online. These chapters examine how to sell vehicles ranging from motorcycles to airplanes and yachts on eBay Motors; how to trade business goods and services; how to sell fixed-price items on Half.com and through eBay Stores; and how to use the live format, traditional auction system, eBay Live Auctions.

Part V, "Keep Your eBay Business Running Smoothly," covers strategies for streamlining your eBay business once you've gotten it off the ground. In Chapter 16, you learn how to protect yourself and your customers' security. In Chapter 17, you get advice on how to fulfill your accounting and tax requirements. In Chapter 18, you are introduced to legal considerations that can keep you from getting in trouble. In Chapter 19, you learn how to deal with the common sorts of difficulties that eBay sellers occasionally confront. Some of these are commonsense approaches, while others take advantage of various problem-solving mechanisms that eBay has put in place for individuals just like you.

I didn't write this book with the intention that you would read it from beginning to end like a story. Like the Web itself, you should be able to skip around from chapter to chapter to find the information you need to know immediately. Plus, you'll find special elements to help you get the most out of the book:

- **How to...** These special boxes explain, in a nutshell, how to accomplish key tasks. Read them to discover key points covered in each chapter.

- **Notes** These provide information that's often very important to gain understanding of a particular topic.

- **Tips** These tell you how to do something smarter or faster.

- **Cautions** These point out potential pitfalls that you need to steer around so you can keep operating smoothly.

- **Did you know?** Here I address topics that are related to the subject at hand and that illuminate it in a new way.

- **eBay Bestsellers** These profiles of real-world eBay sellers give you tips and human-interest stories that will inspire you and make you a better seller.

Within the text, you also find words in special formatting. New terms are in italics, while specific commands you need to choose or type yourself are in boldface.

Along the way, you'll read comments and tips by individuals who sell on eBay on a daily basis, and who are generous enough to share their expertise with you. The information isn't all just coming from me, but I've compiled it with the help of these online experts. Don't get upset if a web page or a piece of software isn't exactly where it's described in the book. eBay's site changes all the time, as does the rest of the Web. That's part of the fun of doing business online. If a web page isn't where the book says it should be, try entering only the site name (such as **www.ebay.com**) or use a search engine to search for the topic you're looking for.

I wish you happy selling on eBay. Relax, have fun, and enjoy being an online merchant; tell me your own experiences and whether this book has helped you by dropping me a line at **greg@gregholden.com**.

# Part I

# Get Started with eBay

# Chapter 1

# Become an eBay Auction Expert

## How to...

- Establish your goals for selling on eBay
- Decide whether to be a full- or part-time eBay seller
- Get the big picture of how eBay works
- Understand what hardware and software you need
- Follow the eight steps to start selling on eBay
- Calculate and pay your eBay sales fees

The phrase "working at home" used to be a contradiction in terms. Way back in the twentieth century, when you worked at home, you wore different clothing than you did in the office. You had more relaxed mannerisms and habits. But these two scenarios have changed. Offices have casual dress days, and working at home means much more than padding around the kitchen in your bathrobe and slippers and talking on the phone.

Working at home can mean that you run a full- or part-time business in which you conduct transactions with customers from around the world, thanks to the Internet. One of the most exciting and potentially lucrative ways to work from home is to sell merchandise online with the biggest and most successful online auction site: eBay. eBay is known as a place where you can sell or buy at auction: you put an item up for sale by publishing a description and (usually) a photo of it on eBay's web site. Prospective buyers find your item for sale and submit bids by filling out a form right on the auction page. The person who has the highest bid when the auction ends is the winner. In addition, eBay allows you to sell items for a fixed price through stores you create yourself, and has special areas for selling vehicles, business services, and high-end antiques, each of which is described in this book.

Whether you should sell on eBay full- or part-time depends on your needs and the amount of time you have available. If you've been laid off and need to make some extra income during the time between jobs, you have lots of time to devote, so selling full-time on eBay is a viable possibility. If you already have a full-time job and are trying to make some extra money, and you're limited to off-hours such as evenings and weekends, part-time eBay selling makes sense. If you already run a business and are looking for new customers, you can find a worldwide audience by devoting part of your available time to selling online. An eBay business is flexible enough to handle each of these situations. First, you need to decide what you want to accomplish.

# Set Goals for Your eBay Business

The first step in starting up any business, whether it's on eBay, on your own web site, or in the offline, brick-and-mortar world, is to set your goals and objectives and then develop strategies for attaining them. In the traditional business world, this step is called coming up with a business plan. A business plan requires you to ask yourself some basic questions of the sort that apply to your eBay business, too:

- *Why do you want to sell on eBay?* This question is deceptively simple. It forces you to focus on your goals for your eBay business. Do you want to sell full-time? Do you want to find new customers for a sales business that you already operate, either on the Web or through a storefront? Do you need to expand an e-commerce business that's flagging? Or do you just want to make some extra money each month to help with expenses?

- *What do you want to sell?* This question is also important: since you're going to spend many hours per week on your business, you need to make sure that you're working with merchandise you know well and hopefully enjoy buying and selling.

- *Are there enough buyers for what you want to sell?* This question involves market research: make sure there aren't a thousand people already selling what you want to sell on eBay. If the market is already flooded, you'll have a hard time breaking in. Switching merchandise or sales categories can help you find more bidders (see "Decide What to Sell" later in this chapter).

- *How do you define "success"?* This question is essential: envision how you want your eBay business to function ideally once it's up and running. What will make you happy—being able to leave the office and work at home? Being able to help your spouse out with some extra expense money or "fun money" while taking care of the kids? Or just being able to pay the bills at the end of the month? Defining success will help you design your business and encourage you to feel satisfied when you reach your goals, too.

## Jump-Start a Brand-New Business

Selling on eBay is a terrific way to start up your first business. That's because eBay provides you with a well-established framework in which to operate. It has rules that sellers and buyers alike have to follow, and an elaborate system of feedback that helps keep people honest. Once you get used to buying and selling on eBay, the move to running an online business is not that dramatic. It's probably easiest to start out selling a limited number of items each month before you consider trying to handle the 50, 100, or even 200 items a week that some busy sellers put online.

## Selling on eBay Part-Time

You don't have to sell on eBay as your full-time "day job" in order to generate a steady income. Far from it: one of the busiest sellers I know, Bob Kopczynski (User ID: maxwellstreetmarket), has a full-time job. His wife and various relatives and neighbors help him put as many as 20 to 30 items up for sale each day. Chad Gibbons (User ID: boomer1967) works on eBay about ten hours a week. Despite ongoing health problems, he manages to put 100 to 200 sales online each week for himself and several individuals whose items he sells on consignment.

## Selling on eBay Full-Time

Few things are as rewarding—and as exhausting—as working on your own full-time from home. I know whereof I speak. I worked in an office for many years and dreamed of being able to stay at home and raise my children while writing. When I was able to make the move to being a full-time freelancer, that's when the hard work really began. The moment you make the decision to support yourself full-time, you've got to be prepared for long hours. It's the same with selling on eBay. When it becomes a full-time business, you've got to develop a schedule; the things that were simply an enjoyable hobby before, like scouring garage sales and flea markets, become work. You might develop a schedule like the one in Table 1-1. (It starts on Thursday because that's when most garage and estate sales start.)

At the same time, it's hardly all work and no play. You've also got to be prepared for freedom—for being able to run your own schedule, work when you want, and spend time with your family or friends when you want. You can sleep until 10 A.M. and work from 1 P.M. to 9 P.M. if you want. You can accompany your kids on field trips or hit the golf course in the morning and work on getting your sales online in the afternoon.

# Find Customers Worldwide

A number of the sellers I interviewed while writing this book used to operate, or still operate, storefronts where they sell antiques or other general merchandise. eBay has revolutionized life for such sellers. On one hand, they had to start selling online just to keep up with the competition. On the other hand, once they did start to sell at auction, they found a new and dramatically wider audience for what they have to sell.

| Day of the Week | Morning Tasks | Afternoon/Evening Tasks |
| --- | --- | --- |
| Thursday | Estate sales | Unpack, schedule more sales for weekend; post office at 3 P.M. |
| Friday | Estate sales | Unpack, research items, prepare descriptions |
| Saturday | Flea market | Personal time |
| Sunday | Personal time | Check sales that are ending today; send out end-of-sale notifications |
| Monday | Send out more end-of-sale e-mails; contact wholesale distributor (if you have one) to order new stock | Take photos for new sales; ship and pack; post office at 3 P.M. |
| Tuesday | Take photos, prepare descriptions | Get sales online; ship and pack last week's sales; post office at 3 P.M. |
| Wednesday | Get more sales online | Look through classifieds and find estate sales, or visit your wholesaler; answer e-mail inquiries; ship and pack last week's sales; post office at 3 P.M. |

**TABLE 1-1**    Sample Schedule for Full-Time eBay Sellers

Many auction enthusiasts are savvy shoppers who need to save money on things they purchase, either for personal or business use, and do not have the time to spend searching for them in conventional sales outlets. They're actively seeking rare items to add to their collections, or specialty items they can't find in their local stores. They don't have time to schlep around the country for months or years visiting antique stores, flea markets, and retail venues to find them. They're happy to find something they want on eBay and have the chance to obtain it from the comfort of their own homes. If you're a seller, your adrenaline starts to rush when you anticipate having two bidders who will offer you far more than you ever expected for what you have to sell—or when someone instantly pays the fixed price you want for the item you have put up for sale.

## Give Yourself a Financial Cushion

One reason for selling on eBay is to get a source of extra income that you can put aside for a rainy day. Some eBay sellers use their sales revenue for their children's tuition. Others use it for vacations. The fact is, once you have a system set up that enables you to sell, you can adjust how active you are based on your needs. You're not required to sell the same number of items every week. I know at least one eBay seller who sold full-time for several years, then decided to take a full-time office job. She still sells on eBay, but not nearly as often as she did before. The important thing is that it's nice to have that extra income to call on when you need it.

 ## eBay Keeps Some Businesses Afloat

The other day, I stopped in Pitts Antiques Shops, an antique store in Batavia, Illinois run by Gary and Louise Pitts. Gary (User ID: pitts-antiques) spoke to me from behind the counter; his computer and digital camera were on the table beside him, along with an antique pen he had just put up for sale on eBay. I knew that eBay had made life difficult for many brick-and-mortar antique and collectible dealers. But Gary surprised me by saying that eBay helped keep his storefront afloat.

"eBay is keeping us in business," he said. "Once you realize you can't beat 'em, you join 'em." Several other antique stores that used to be located in his area closed because the owners were afraid of selling on eBay, he added. Gary estimated that he had made $5000 in sales in the last two months on eBay. He uses his expertise as a longtime antiques dealer to evaluate what to put up for sale both at auction and in his eBay Store, a type of sales outlet described in Chapter 14.

Gary advises selling good-quality merchandise with brand names and no damage. (The brand-name items are more easily found by dedicated collectors searching for them online.) He also adds a $2 handling charge to each of his sales, to ensure that he makes at least a small profit on even the least expensive items. It pays off: when he purchased a box of 500 old postcards for $50, he put one or two of them up for auction on eBay each week for a starting bid of $0.99. Many sold for $8 or $9 each on eBay, and one sold for more than $70. Needless to say, he made a tidy profit on his original investment.

## Uncover Collectors and Specialty Buyers

One seller I interviewed, Don Colclough (User ID: mrmodern), found an artificial leg at an estate sale. He had no idea whether anyone would want such a thing on eBay, but he put it online anyway. He ended up selling it for more than $100. eBay attracts collectors and bargain hunters from all walks of life, many of whom are passionate about what they want and will pay anything to get it, provided you have the right item. You've probably heard about the Florida woman who managed to sell (for $28,000) a ten-year-old, partially eaten grilled cheese sandwich that supposedly bore the face of the Virgin Mary. You never know who's going to pay for what you have. eBay's Chatter newsletter reports about the 1941 beer can that sold for $19,000 (see Figure 1-1), and the fishing lure (item number 2708468802) that sold for an astonishing $31,857.50.

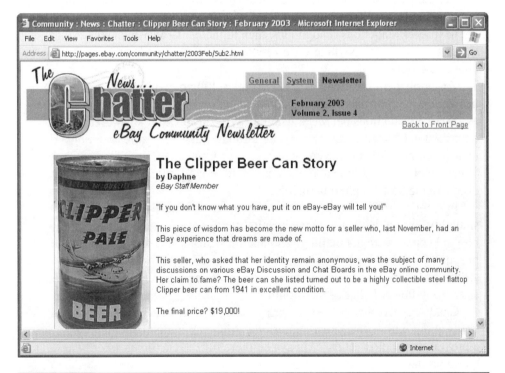

**FIGURE 1-1**    This beer can's seller never dreamed someone would bid $19,000 for it.

## eBay Bestsellers
## eBay Gave Him a "Reason to Get Up in the Morning"

It's often said that eBay has the potential to change your life. I've met many sellers whose careers have been changed by eBay. But I don't think I've met anyone to whom eBay is more important than Chad Gibbons.

Chad, 25, lives in Windsor, Ontario, and goes by the User ID boomer1967 on eBay. Like many young men, he has collected sports cards since childhood. He first started using eBay in 1999, in fact, to trade cards. "I started selling cards because there were many that I didn't really want, so I sold them off to buy more."

In 1999, Chad was diagnosed with kidney failure. He had to take a medical leave from his regular job. The three years while he was waiting for a kidney transplant were difficult.

"When I was sick for those three years eBay helped me by making me get up in the morning. I *had* to get up: I had to mail stuff out and do e-mails and get next week's auctions ready to go, then to the bank to cash checks. All those things that needed to be done were keeping me preoccupied and not thinking about how sick I was."

To supplement his income, Chad started selling on consignment for other people. He now has up to four consignment customers, and he conducts as many as 100 to 300 auctions per week using eBay's Turbo Lister software, which is described in Chapter 6. Amazingly, he estimates that he is able to conduct that many auctions while only spending ten hours a week on eBay-related activities. "I have met lots of people and made a few friends from eBay. The people on eBay are the best people imaginable."

In August 2002, Chad received a kidney transplant. Everything went smoothly, except that being in the hospital for two weeks made it difficult for him to keep up with his mailings and auctions. Just a few months out of the hospital, Chad had his best sales month to date, selling 477 out of 530 items and grossing $2,656. He's now sold more than 8500 items and has been highlighted as an eBay Power Seller of the Month.

Chad suggests that when you are planning your own eBay business, sell items about which you know something. Also sell items for which there is a proven demand on eBay. "Always be there for the customer, to answer questions and concerns."

# Know How eBay Auctions Work

eBay's auction site is complex, and has its own tricks and quirks. On top of that, many of the individuals who buy and sell regularly on eBay have been doing so for years and are well acquainted with how the system works. Don't start placing items up for sale without knowing what's involved first. Be sure you read eBay's User Agreement (**http://pages.ebay.com/help/policies/user-agreement.html**) so you know what you can and can't do. The following sections provide you with some more rules of thumb.

## Set a Time Limit

Time plays an important role in eBay sales. First of all, eBay is located in California, so the advertised time when auctions begin and end is in Pacific Standard Time. eBay calls this "eBay Time," and you can check the current eBay time at **http://cgi1.ebay .com/aw-cgi/eBayISAPI.dll?TimeShow** (see Figure 1-2).

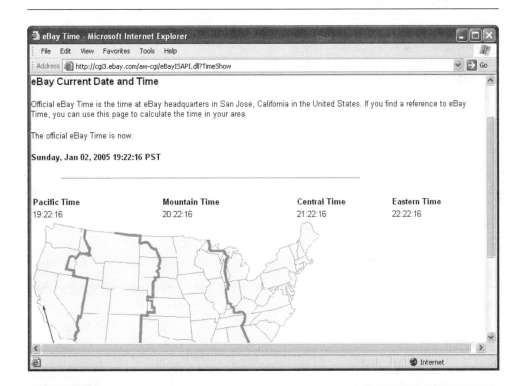

| FIGURE 1-2 | eBay time is an important consideration when scheduling auctions. |

In most cases, you get auction descriptions online by filling out the Sell Your Item form (see Figure 1-3). You access this form by clicking **Sell** in the eBay navigation toolbar that appears on virtually all eBay pages. Page 3 of the Sell Your Item form allows you to schedule your auction and select how long the sale will last.

Auctions can begin at one of two times:

■ The exact moment they appear online, which is the moment the auction description is posted on one of eBay's servers.

■ A time you schedule, if you are willing to pay 10 cents to schedule the auction.

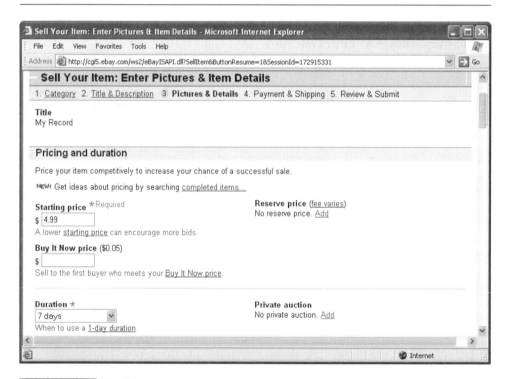

**FIGURE 1-3**    The Sell Your Item form is the basic way to get sales descriptions and photos online.

The reason why you need to pay attention to when a sale starts is that the starting time controls the ending time. For instance, if you start an auction at 6:05 P.M. on a Thursday and you specify that the auction should last three days, the auction will end at 6:05 P.M. the following Sunday. Most sellers believe that it's best to have sales end on a weekend, when the largest number of bidders has time to shop and bid online. This might not always be true: if you are selling household or baby care items that would appeal to stay-at-home parents, you'll have the best results by ending your sales during the week. Business buyers looking for supplies and equipment are more likely to shop during the week than on weekends. Scheduling sales to meet the needs of your likely customers is important.

The Duration drop-down list on page 3 of the Sell Your Item form enables you to choose the length of your auction. You have the following options:

> NOTE *If you sell multiple items, you can streamline your work significantly with special auction software and online auction services, some of which enable you to schedule sales so they all go online at specified times. See Chapter 6 for more details.*

- **1 day**   One-day auctions are unusual, but they work if you are selling tickets to concerts or other time-sensitive items. You have to meet some requirements to be able to hold a one-day auction; see the explanation at **http://pages.ebay .com/help/sell/1-day.html**.

- **3 days**   Three-day auctions work best for things that bidders are wild about because they're the newest got-to-have-'em item. Three-day sales also work well around holiday time when shoppers are in a hurry to have items shipped to them.

- **5 days**   Five day auctions are also useful at holiday times when people are in too much of a hurry to buy at a seven-day or ten-day auction. They might also work well over holiday weekends such as Labor Day or Memorial Day. The only real advantage to a five-day auction is that it gives you a little more time to gather bids than the three-day variety.

- **7 days**   Seven-day auctions are the "classic" and most popular variety on eBay. By letting a sale go on for seven rather than three or five days, you give yourself time to get more bids and hopefully a higher price. Seven days gives buyers the opportunity to track a sale during the week and then place their final bids over the weekend, if you schedule it to end then.

- **10 days** Sometimes, one weekend is not enough for a sale. Many eBay sellers advocate the ten-day sales period even though it does incur an extra 20-cent fee.

- **Buy It Now** Whenever you list an item for sale, you are given the option of specifying a fixed price for it. Anyone who wants to pay that fixed price can buy the item at any time, no matter what the length of the sale is supposed to be. Rather than letting the market determine how high the price should go, you effectively put a limit on your profits by specifying a Buy It Now price. On the other hand, you can use a Buy It Now price to encourage bidders to buy an item immediately at a profit to you.

*Buy It Now prices and auction bids don't mix, so there's no chance that someone will "outbid" your Buy It Now price. On a reserve price auction, the Buy It Now price disappears as soon as the first bid is placed that meets your reserve. On an auction without a reserve price, the Buy It Now price disappears when someone places the first bid. In either case, you might end up with a final purchase price that's higher than the original Buy It Now price you specified.*

## Build Customer Trust

In any kind of e-commerce, the seller needs to build trust and confidence in buyers who never meet them in person. The one-on-one contact that the Internet provides can do a lot toward building such confidence: quick e-mail responses, speedy shipping, and honest descriptions all encourage buyers to check out your sales in the future and keep bidding.

When it comes to encouraging bids initially, the single best way you can develop trust is to develop a good feedback rating. That can only be done over time, by making a commitment to follow through quickly and honestly on all of your transactions, whether you are purchasing or selling. Any buyer can check your feedback rating by clicking on the feedback number that eBay lists next to your name. Your eBay ID card appears. Your goal is to have the same sort of feedback, as shown in the following illustration, as boomer1967, who is profiled earlier in this chapter.

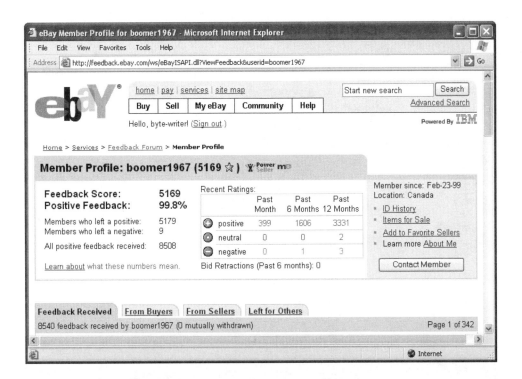

When it comes to gaining good feedback through selling, the two most important things you can do are things you might overlook at first: packing your merchandise carefully and shipping it out quickly. Because these two tasks are so important, I've devoted extra attention to them in Chapter 10.

## Provide Clear Images

The online equivalent of placing your auction merchandise on a table so prospective customers can preview it before bidding is to open a digital version of the image in your web browser window. The clarity of the image you see depends on the clarity of your computer monitor and the quality of your computer's video card. (I discuss these and other hardware requirements for participating in Internet auctions in Chapter 2.)

Because the image is broken down into tiny segments of digital information called *pixels*, and the visual details are compressed into special graphics formats used on the Web in order to get them online, you don't get a perfect representation of the image when you see it online. If you can provide more than one image, so much the better. eBay's own Picture Services lets you post one image for free and

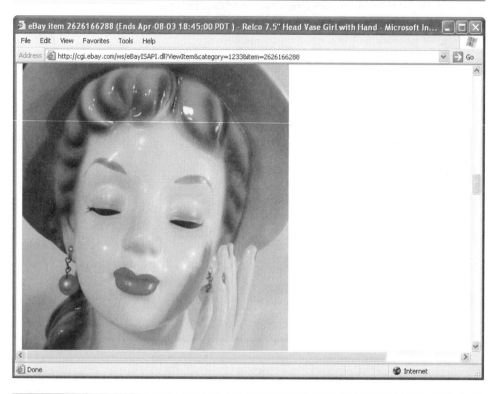

**FIGURE 1-4**    eBay sales depend on good descriptions and digital images displayed online, supplemented by research.

charges a nominal fee for each subsequent image. There's really no excuse not to present multiple views of an item when the item warrants it, since digital cameras make photography so easy. For example, an eBay seller (User ID: decoray) profiled in Chapter 10, took five separate images of the head vase shown in Figure 1-4. Each image was sharp and well-lit and taken from a slightly different angle. The last image was of the label at the bottom of the vase.

## Write Clear Descriptions

No matter how clear the images are, there's no substitute for your own knowledge, much of which is provided by or augmented by research. Part of the fun of creating auction listings, in my opinion, is taking the time to find out something about what you want to sell—how old it is, how rare it is, and what makes it special. You can do your research at web sites that describe the type of merchandise you sell, for instance. These web sites range from consumer electronics publications to collector's groups. One of the best and easiest places to do research, though, is on eBay itself. Just go to the Search page (**http://search.ebay.com/ws/search/AdvSearch**), enter your search terms, check the box next to Completed Listings Only, and click the Search button (see Figure 1-5). You can search through past auctions for similar items.

The main thing about your auction descriptions is that they need to be complete and honest about any flaws or shortcomings in what you're selling. You don't want to get in a dispute with a buyer about a chip or crack in something that the buyer doesn't discover until the package is unwrapped. Be honest up front, and you'll avoid such surprises while building trust among your customers. (Besides, if a buyer really wants what you have to sell, chances are a few minor flaws won't discourage them from bidding anyway.)

**FIGURE 1-5**    Research completed sales on eBay to find out more about the items you want to sell.

TIP    *Read what other auction sellers have said about their items. You might be able to benefit from their research. Many sellers reuse parts of other sellers' descriptions in their own auction listings—but make sure that you rewrite the text to fit your own sales and don't copy the text outright. Is it a violation of copyright? It may be, technically, but sellers don't seem to mind because so many of them rewrite one another's descriptions.*

## Decide How You Want to Be Paid

Watching bids come in on your item, exchanging chatty messages with other sellers in the eBay Café or the other eBay message boards, and researching your sales items can be so much fun that you forget about the real purpose of why you're starting an eBay business. Why, you're in this to make money, of course. Remember?

The simplest and most effective way to accept payments from your customers is by letting them pay with a credit card. Your high bidder or buyer (for a Buy It Now item) submits a credit card number, either to you or to a payment service, the funds are transferred in a matter of minutes, and you can ship the item out immediately. When it comes to accepting credit cards, you have two general options. Most eBay sellers sign up for an account with eBay's own payment service, PayPal. PayPal streamlines the process of accepting credit card payments: buyers tell PayPal to debit their credit card accounts, and PayPal receives the payments, subtracts its transaction fees, and forwards the money on to you. If you accept PayPal transactions, you get to add a standard logo to your auction listings, like the one shown in the following image:

On the other hand, some sellers don't like PayPal because of the fees that it charges. If you have a PayPal personal account, you pay a lower fee for a transaction, but your payment options are limited to accepting checks or money orders from your customers. This process takes longer because you depend on the mail to get the money. A PayPal Premier or Business Account enables customers who also have PayPal memberships to pay you instantly (see Chapter 9 for more information) by making a deduction from their credit card or debit card account. If a personal check is involved, you're safest if you delay shipping until the check actually clears the bank.

Otherwise, if you're planning to be in business for the long haul, you can establish a credit card merchant account, either with your own bank or with a company that specializes in providing such accounts.

# Get the Hardware and Software You Need

Before you can step up to the auction block, you need to connect to the Internet, and to do that, you need some basic computer hardware and software. Buying and selling through auctions, like other types of electronic commerce, doesn't require a super-fast connection to the Internet. Nor do you have to spend thousands for a computer with the latest multimedia bells and whistles. A detailed description of hardware and software you *do* need is presented in Chapter 2, but here is an overview of the kinds of things you need to get started.

## Buy the Right Computer and Monitor

The good news is that buying and selling on eBay doesn't require much computing overhead. In other words, if you can get on the Internet and surf web sites, and if you have enough memory to run an image editing program as well, you should be able to sell successfully on eBay. However, the speed and quality of your computer, monitor, and other hardware *can* affect your auction experience.

Hard disk storage space isn't an issue for most new computers, which come with hard disk drives that store one or more *gigabytes* (GB) of data. (A gigabyte is a thousand megabytes [MB].) Any hard disk that is capable of storing a gigabyte or more should be fine for your needs. (Many new computers come with hard disks of 10, 20, or more gigabytes these days.) If you're buying a used computer, beware: don't take home a computer with less than a gigabyte of storage space, or you'll run out of room before you know it.

Going online, using a web browser, and shopping for auction treasures doesn't require huge amounts of memory, but if you plan to put up goodies for sale, you need some additional software, and each program requires RAM. For example, you may want to do one of the following (all of which require RAM):

- **Create a web page**    A web page or web site can help advertise you or your business, if you have one (see Chapter 7).

- **Capture digital images**    You're likely to get more bids if you provide a clear, computerized image of your items by scanning them or using a digital camera (see Chapter 8). Saving the images on your hard disk can quickly consume storage space unless you delete the image files as soon as the sale ends. Running a good image editing program like Adobe Photoshop or Photoshop Elements does require a lot of RAM, however.

The cost of RAM keeps going down, so you should load your computer with as much as you can in order to streamline the process of creating auction listings, not to mention listening to Internet radio, downloading video clips, and the many other multimedia events that are increasingly popular parts of the online user experience.

## Pick a Scanner or Digital Camera

Hardware requirements for auction sellers are a bit more extensive than those for buyers. You need a way to take images of the merchandise you want to sell and capture those images as digitized computer files. Including a clear, sharp image on your web site greatly increases your chances of selling your product or service. You have several choices for digitizing:

- Take photos with a digital camera and save the image files on your computer.

- Take photos with a conventional camera and then scan them into your computer.

- Take conventional prints or slides and then have a photo lab send them back to you on CD-ROM or post them online so that you can copy or reuse them.

After you have an image in the form of a computer document, you can transfer it to a web site to let potential buyers take a look (see Chapter 8).

## Install Web Page and Auction Software

For the most part, the software you use to conduct transactions on eBay is the same as the software you use to view sales, bid on items, surf web sites, and exchange e-mail with others. You don't need special software to get your sales online, format auction listings or web pages that describe you or your business, or edit photos—but special software can help, especially when your sales activity increases.

In addition, software that enables you to keep track of your financial activity so you can prepare your taxes more efficiently, apply for loans or merchant accounts, or perform other tasks can make your business life much easier as well. You'll find out about web page software in Chapter 7, digital image editors in Chapter 8, auction listing software in Chapter 6, and accounting programs in Chapter 17.

## Become a Power E-Mail User

Aside from the web browser that you use to create auction listings, e-mail is probably the single most important tool you have as a seller. E-mail is what you use to answer questions, notify bidders that they have won, tell bidders that their item has shipped, and remind buyers when they are slow to follow through on their commitments. When you sell at auction, it's important to use all aspects of e-mail fully. These include:

■ **Signature files**   A signature file is a bit of text that you can append automatically to each of your outgoing e-mails. Such a file tells others your User ID, the name of your web site if you have one, and any other contact information you want to provide. It's a great way to get free marketing for your auction business.

■ **Attachments**   Sometimes prospective bidders who are particularly interested in an item will ask you for more information and possibly more detailed photos. Although you should post such additional images on the auction listing itself, you might also want to attach them to e-mails you send to interested buyers.

■ **Checking your e-mail**   Get an e-mail account that you can access from the Web; also consider getting a wireless device that you can use to check your e-mail, such as a web-enabled cell phone or a handheld device, so you can get those messages as soon as they arrive.

■ **Vacation notices**   If you're going to be out of town, make sure your sales don't end while you are gone. Be sure to put a vacation notice on each of your auction listings that tells bidders when you'll be back.

TIP    *For more about using e-mail, see Chapter 11.*

# Follow the Eight-Step eBay Sales Plan

As long as you're at least 18 years old, whether you are a student, the CEO of eBay (yes, Meg Whitman is reported to have sold her college textbooks on Half.com), or a trash collector—you can still sell on eBay. You don't need any experience in business. You just need to follow the rules, gather good feedback by being honest and responsive, and sell items that people want—the kinds of things that merchants have depended on throughout the ages.

First, you need register as an auction seller. eBay makes you register as a seller even if you are already a registered eBay buyer. You can use the same username and password; the main purpose is to verify your identity. (See Chapter 2 for more details.) The following steps give you an abbreviated version of the process described in detail in subsequent chapters so that you can begin the process of selling on eBay.

## Decide What to Sell

Sometimes, it seems like you can sell anything on eBay. Some people certainly *try* to sell oddball, weird, tasteless, or even illegal materials. eBay quickly removes the most offensive things. (See Chapter 16 for descriptions of items that eBay considers offensive or illegal.) But if you are trying, as this book assumes, to develop an ongoing eBay sales effort, you need to identify materials that eBay customers are actually going to bid on and buy on a consistent basis. Based on what I've learned and been told by longtime sellers, you need to choose items that:

- **You like to sell**   Choose things that you know and love, and that you know well enough that you can come up with reasonable reserve and Buy It Now prices. You'll be working with these items for years at a time; don't sell clothing if you are really interested in sports equipment and collectibles, for instance.

- **People actually want**   Shop around on eBay and see which items get bids and which don't. Don't waste your time buying, and then reselling, merchandise that just isn't desirable to begin with.

- **Are easy to ship**   Keep in mind that you'll not only be buying merchandise and hauling it home, but also photographing it, packing it up, and probably hauling it to a shipper (unless you pay extra for pickup; see Chapter 10). Be sure the types of items you sell are ones you can pack and ship safely.

- **You have room to store**   Sellers who deal on eBay on a regular basis soon need to buy merchandise on a regular basis, too. The question of where and how to store that stuff can become a problem. Sellers have given up their basements, garages, and eventually rented warehouse space just to store the merchandise they're planning to sell in the future.

In my experience, the items that sell best on eBay are ones that are offbeat or hard to locate. Items also are more likely to sell if you include more than one good-quality photo and if you write honest descriptions.

## Choose One or More Categories

What you sell also involves decisions about where to sell—which one of eBay's hundreds of auction categories is right for your particular item. If you decide to specialize in a particular type of item, you might find that certain categories become places that you frequent on a regular basis. Getting to know the category in which you're going to deal is a good idea—get to know who the big players are in a category, and study what they sell and how they describe what they have. Don't try to copy what they do—rather, pick items that are slightly different and put your own personal spin on your descriptions so you can attract your own customers.

*You can list items in two categories rather than just one in order to gain extra exposure. You pay double the listing fee, but the small extra expense can be worthwhile. See Chapter 5 for more information.*

## Enlist the Help of Friends and Relatives

What to sell, and how many items to sell, also depends on whether you are going to do the work yourself or develop a team of assistants. Selling on eBay is ideal for two or more people—two spouses, two domestic partners, two friends, or two relatives. You're sure to have some nieces, nephews, or cousins around who can help you with packing and shipping—or photographing or doing other computer work with which you're uncomfortable.

Collecting and then selling dolls, action figures, cards, or other goodies can be a great family activity. Your kids can keep you company and help you shop for the most desirable collectibles and keep you informed about the latest trends. Even if you're dealing in general wholesale merchandise rather than collectibles, your family members can help look up addresses, affix labels, and relieve some of the burden of shipping things out.

## Set the Price

You don't always need to worry about setting a fixed or maximum price for an item that you want to sell on eBay. It depends on how you decide to sell. I go into more detail on starting bids and reserve prices in Chapter 3, but here's a quick rundown of the kinds of prices you might need to consider:

- **Starting bid**    This is the price at which bidding starts.

- **Reserve price**    This is the lowest price at which you will commit to sell something. If bids don't reach the reserve price, you don't have to sell. Usually, the reserve price is secret, but some sellers do reveal the reserve price of an item right in its description.

- **Buy It Now price**    If you want to sell something at a fixed price, you can specify it, either in addition to placing the item at auction or as an alternative to an auction.

- **eBay Stores price**    If you have enough positive feedback, you can set up an eBay store: a page where you list items on eBay for a fixed price for 30, 60, or an indefinite number of days. It's a great place to unload items that you tried to sell at auction but didn't sell the first time or to find another way to sell stock from your brick-and-mortar store if you have one (see Figure 1-6). Find out more at **http://stores.ebay.com**.

> **NOTE**    *Setting a minimum bid as the least amount you are willing to accept often discourages buyers who need to feel they are getting a bargain for something. Many such sales end with no one placing any bids.*

Many auction sellers don't worry about reserve prices at all. They simply put a starting bid of $1 or so on an item and let the marketplace determine the price. The risk, of course, is that you might lose money on what you sell without a reserve— you could conceivably pay $10 for a lamp and sell it on eBay for a high bid of $6 if you don't put a reserve of, say, $15 on the item. On the other hand, items that are advertised as having no reserve price do tend to attract more attention than those with a reserve, because bidders are attracted by the certainty that the item will sell and the possibility that it will sell at a bargain price. If the seller loses a few dollars on one particular item, he or she will probably make it up on others that are sold without reserve and that attract lots of bids.

> **TIP**    *The pricing strategy you choose is up to you, and it doesn't have to be applied to every item you sell, either. You can put a set of items up for auction with no reserve and see how they sell, while putting others up for sale with a reserve.*

**FIGURE 1-6**    You can sell merchandise at a fixed price by establishing an eBay Store.

## Provide Good Online Photos

As much as I would like to think that words are the most persuasive medium around, I have to admit that photos are probably the most important sales feature you can include with your merchandise. Items that are put online without any photos just aren't going to get as many bids as they could. There's no excuse not to include photos, either, because the range of options for capturing digital images is growing all the time. Digital cameras and scanners are growing more affordable, too.

Don't be stingy with creating and posting photos of your sales items. Often, bidders will ask you for more photos if you haven't included enough to begin with. You'll get to know how many you should include. There's no rule about how many photos you should include of a particular object; as a general rule, however, two to

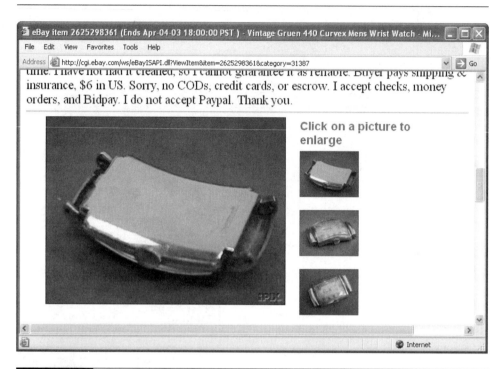

**FIGURE 1-7** Include multiple images of an item, especially if it is detailed or intricate.

six photos taken from different angles is a good range. Often, wristwatches need multiple photos in order to show all the different features (see Figure 1-7). See Chapter 8 for more information about capturing digital images of your sales items and putting them online.

## Pile On the Information

If you run a brick-and-mortar business, you'll probably be surprised by the important role descriptions play in making sales on eBay. After all, in a store, you place your items in the window or on a shelf and put a tag on them. Perhaps the tag identifies the item and provides some basic information about it, perhaps not.

On the Internet, shoppers decide whether or not to buy something based in large measure on how much information you provide about it. Yes, the price matters, and yes, the experience and level of trust the seller inspires is also important. But when several similar items are available on eBay, many placed up for auction by reputable sellers, the ones with more information are more likely to get the most bids. A good description is

- **Concise**   Good descriptions don't have to be long. They describe sizes, dates, colors, and other characteristics.

- **Upbeat**   Selling means telling prospective buyers why an item is exceptional and desirable and why they need to have it.

- **Complete**   Along with the good points, be up-front about any cracks or flaws the item has. Also be sure to include model numbers and serial numbers for consumers who are very knowledgeable and are looking for specific items.

The best descriptions engage a bidder's imagination and get him or her to envision how the merchandise might be used, or (if it's a used item) how others used it in the past. See Chapters 3 and 4 for more about creating good descriptions.

## Give Good Customer Service

Customer service on eBay is a little different from customer service in a retail store or on an e-commerce web site. On eBay, a substantial amount of customer contact takes place before a sale is made, and it mostly takes the form of answering questions posed by people who have either bid on your items or are considering placing a bid. In addition, you might be answering questions from individuals who don't turn out to be your actual customers. After all, a single item can have only one high bidder or buyer, but you might receive 6, 10, or even (if you're lucky to get this much interest) 20 questions from bidders before the sale ends. Customer service on eBay, to a large extent, is a matter of checking your e-mail and responding to it in a professional and prompt manner.

After a sale, customer service means making sure the merchandise is sent out quickly and that it arrives in good shape, as described in the next section.

## Process Those Sales

Once a sale is completed, you need to communicate to your high bidder or buyer that you are competent and in charge. Send them an e-mail message to notify them that they are the winner and congratulate them on making such a good purchase. Auction management software of the sort described in Chapter 6 can automate such e-mails for you. Restate the shipping information that is already presented in your listing, and ask them to respond as soon as possible. Once you receive payment, you need to pack your items carefully. Many sellers include notes or extra gifts with their items; you don't have to do this, of course, but it helps build goodwill. It's more important to include bubble wrap or other materials in the package to protect what you're sending, and to get it out to the post office or shipper in good time. See Chapter 10 for more information on this important aspect of building an eBay business.

## Pay Your eBay Fees

Everyone has to pay the piper for the services they receive, and eBay is no exception. After you sell something on eBay, it's time to pay the fees charged not only for selling items but for listing them. eBay calls its listing fees *insertion fees*, and the fee charged when you actually sell something a *final value fee.* You have to pay your insertion fee whether you sell your item or not. The insertion fee is based on the higher of two amounts: your starting bid or your reserve price. For instance, if you sell something with a starting bid of $1 and a reserve price of $40, your insertion fee is $1.10; if you have no reserve price and your starting bid is $1, the insertion fee is $.30. (See eBay's schedule of fees at **http://pages.ebay.com/help/sell/fees.html** for tables that show how the fees are calculated.)

If your item sells, you then have to pay a final value fee; for reserve price and no reserve auctions, the "final value" is the final bid. On a reserve price auction, the final value fee is only charged if the reserve is met. If the final value is, for example, $100, the final value fee is about $3.38.

eBay makes it quite easy to pay your fees; you are sent an invoice once a month. You receive a rebate on these fees if you follow eBay's recommendation and have the fees automatically deducted from your PayPal account. You can also configure your seller's account so that you pay by check, money order, credit card, or checking account debit. Find out more about configuring your seller's account at **http://pages .ebay.com/help/sell/payfees.html**.

## Deliver the Goods

The final step in becoming an eBay auction expert is shipping out your merchandise quickly and safely. You've got to find good shipping boxes, pack your items safely with plenty of packing material if necessary, and get the package to the mailer quickly. You've got to provide your customers with different shipping options. You'll get to know your local postal employees and mailing services well. The professionalism with which you ship has a direct impact on the amount of positive feedback you receive. Shipping is sometimes overlooked by eBay sellers when they start out, and that's why I've devoted a whole chapter to the subject: see Chapter 10 for more detailed information.

## Where to Find It

- **eBay User Agreement**
  **http://pages.ebay.com/help/policies/user-agreement.html**
  Rules of what you can and can't do on eBay's site as far as listing auctions for sale and bidding on them.

- **Current eBay Time**
  **http://cgi1.ebay.com/aw-cgi/eBayISAPI.dll?TimeShow**
  A page that verifies the current time in eBay's home location (in other words, Pacific Standard Time) and other time zones in the U.S.

- **eBay's Help page on Seller's Fees**
  **http://pages.ebay.com/help/sell/fees.html**
  An overview of the fees eBay charges sellers, including tables to help you calculate them.

- **eBay Stores**
  **http://stores.ebay.com**
  Home page of a section of eBay's site where merchants can sell items at a fixed price for 30 or 60 days or on a "Good 'Til Cancelled" (GTC) basis.

# Chapter 2

# Start Selling with eBay

## How to...

- Learn the ins and outs of selling on eBay

- Decide how you want to sell on eBay

- Choose the categories in which you'll sell

- Build positive feedback by bidding and buying

- Set up a seller's account

- Make sure your computer equipment is up to speed

Before you start selling on eBay, you need to know the secrets and the tried-and-true approaches that can make your auction business a success from the start. You're joining a well-established business community, and one that is proving to be popular and resilient despite (or perhaps, because of) the ups and downs of the economy. To stand out from the crowd and make sales, you have to know how to compete on an equal footing with individuals who have auctioned off hundreds, even thousands, of items over a period of years.

You've also got to gain the attention, as well as the trust, of bidders from all walks of life and all levels of computer experience. Some are wary of purchasing at auction because they've heard stories about sellers who take bidders' money and never ship what they've sold. To build trust, you need to present your sales items—and yourself—in a professional, businesslike manner and give the impression that you are an expert seller even though you're just starting out. That's what this chapter will do: give you a head start so that you can jump right in and sell like a pro.

# Learn the Culture of eBay

When you're only a bidder, eBay is all fun. You can shop, find bargains, compete with other bidders, and enjoy the thrill of being the high bidder when the auction ends. When you make the move to being a seller, you have to change your perspective. Selling on eBay can still be fun, of course. In fact, it adds a new dimension to your interactions with the other members of the eBay community. And it can certainly be fun to have extra money around at the end of the month to pay bills or treat yourself to some presents.

By *changing your perspective*, I mean that you need to regard your selling activities as a business, and treat them as such. You're going to have to do a lot of hard work, whether it means getting up early on a rainy Friday morning to hit the local estate sales, hauling your wares into and out of the house, packing your merchandise carefully and taking stacks of boxes to the post office, or waiting in line to ship everything out to your customers. You need to be dedicated and keep your ultimate goal in sight: generating a regular source of income through selling on eBay. The following sections help prepare you for what's in store so that you can hit the ground running and start selling (a process described in Chapter 3).

## Use eBay's Own Educational Programs

When it comes to learning how things work, I'm a big proponent of reading books, but as a book author, I'm not exactly an unbiased authority on the subject. One good way to learn all about eBay quickly is to read a book like this one and supplement your learning with some live events and tutorials provided by eBay itself. That way, you'll get the very latest information about changes in eBay's procedures for sellers, and you'll get to meet some other sellers in person.

TIP     *eBay's Learning Center area includes links to tutorials for sellers, seller workshops held on the message boards, and instructions on how eBay works in general. You'll find the Learning Center at **http://pages.ebay .com/education/index.html**.*

### eBay University

You can pick up advanced tips and meet some experienced sellers and eBay staff people alike by attending one of the live workshops eBay sends around the country. The cost to attend is nominal, and you can learn a huge amount in a short period of time. These and other eBay-sponsored education options fall into three categories:

- **Online courses**   If you're just starting out, you can take eBay University's online courses on selling basics—though after you read this book, you'll probably be ready to take the Beyond the Basics course. Both cost $19.95.

- **Local instructors**   eBay has a network of Education Specialists who are located around the country and can provide you with individual instruction or scheduled classes. Search for one in your area at **http://www.poweru .net/ebay/student/searchIndex.asp**.

- **Classes**   If you don't have a lot of time to spend, look for a series of in-person classes held in an area. Classes are held in different cities every two or three weeks. You can see if one is going to be held in your own location by clicking one of the Register Now! drop-down lists at **http:// pages.ebay.com/university/classes.html** (see Figure 2-1).

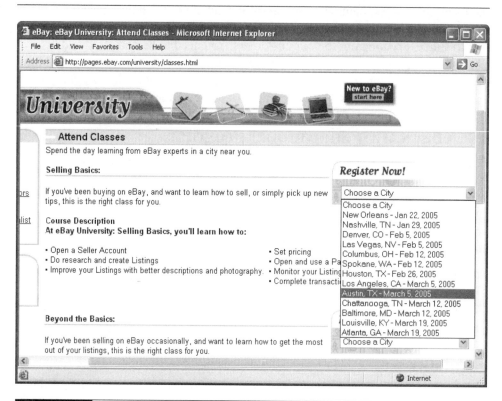

**FIGURE 2-1** When a live eBay workshop comes to your area, strongly consider attending.

 *eBay's upcoming schedule of education programs, including the community event held once a year, can be found at **http://pages.ebay.com/university**.*

## Power Sellers and Workshops

If you can't attend a live event in your area, you always have access to one of the best ways to learn about eBay—online workshops held by experienced sellers. You'll find a list of eBay's upcoming online seller workshops at **http://pages.ebay .com/community/workshopcalendar/current.html**. When I checked, the titles of upcoming seminars all seemed useful for sellers:

■ Building an eBay Brand

■ Sell with Efficiency

- How to Ship Large and Delicate Items

- Listing Designer (how to make your descriptions more professional, add character, and have fun)

- Outlet Malls—Catalog Returns and Overstock

These, too, are held on specific days. If you're present online during the workshop, you can ask the hosts questions by posting them on a message board, and the hosts will respond to you with an answer while the workshop is going on.

However, you don't have to be present at a workshop to benefit from it. The workshops are archived so that you can review past discussions any time. Just click the **Archives** link on the left side of the Workshop Calendar page (see Figure 2-2) and then scan the list of archived workshops for a subject that interests you. (You can also reach past workshops at **http://forums.ebay.com/forum.jsp?forum=93**.)

FIGURE 2-2    Online workshops are held by sellers, and you can view archived events any time you wish.

# Be Encouraged by Success Stories

As I write this, eBay is one of the few parts of the world of e-commerce that not only are doing well but are continuing to grow by leaps and bounds. More and more individuals are taking to selling on eBay part-time, to get a little extra money, or have even moved to making eBay their sole source of income. The amazing thing to me is that people figured out on their own that they could make a living by selling solely on eBay or supplementing other sales with eBay auctions. eBay didn't market itself as a place where you could create your own eBay business; eBay sellers figured that out by experience. They realized that no matter how offbeat or unusual the item, they could find a buyer for it somewhere around the world. They also discovered that, with a worldwide pool of buyers available, they were likely to get a far higher price online than they could selling through an antique store, flea market, or garage sale. Read the stories of the people I interviewed for this book, whose profiles are presented in various chapters:

- Bob Kopczynski sells as many as 600 items a month and doesn't even do it full-time. He works part-time selling on eBay, but his wife works full-time and various family members and neighbors help out.

- Don Colclough decided to close his antique store and sell full-time on eBay when he realized he could make his own hours, save on travel time, and get more buyers online than ever came through the front door of his store.

- An eBay seller (User ID: decoray) sold an antique photo of a tavern for more than $700; he estimates that he's sold as many as 6000 separate items on eBay, shipping as far away as Africa.

- Sheila Schneider has had a hard time finding regular employment as an interior designer in Portland, Oregon, but she's been supplementing her income nicely through eBay.

- Carol Hearn retired early from a government job and ran an antique store before it closed; eBay allows her to keep in business and make some extra income in her retirement.

Need more inspiration? eBay regularly features its own sellers on the Community Member Spotlight page, **http://pages.ebay.com/community/people/spotlight.html**. You'll also find member profiles in the eBay newsletter, the Chatter, **http://pages .ebay.com/community/chatter/index.html**, shown in Figure 2-3.

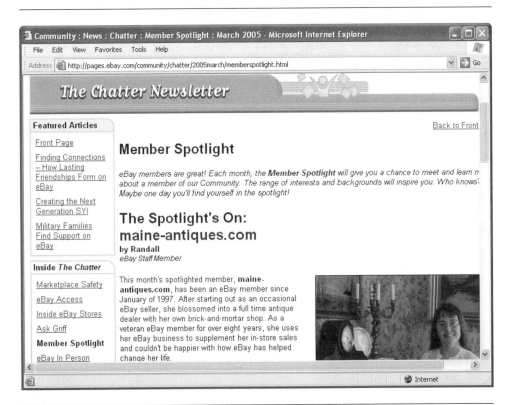

**FIGURE 2-3**    eBay's own newsletter can inspire you with profiles of successful sellers.

## Beware of eBay Scams and Shams

This book doesn't present a glowing picture indicating that selling on eBay always goes smoothly and that problems never occur. On the contrary, eBay's very popularity attracts an assortment of swindlers, cheats, and outright crooks who seek to victimize buyers and sellers alike. If you're aware of the potential pitfalls and know how to avoid them, chances are you'll run into very few problems during your career as a seller.

When you hear about eBay in the news, you usually hear about the weird, often illegal, things that people put up for sale on the auction site. The more notorious items are quickly removed by eBay itself. You should avoid breaking the law or eBay's own rules for sellers by reviewing the lists of questionable and prohibited items described in Chapter 16.

That's not to say you can't put odd, quirky, or downright weird things up for auction on eBay. A check of the odder eBay categories, such as Slightly Unusual, Really Weird, Totally Bizarre (which are under the Weird Stuff category, which is under the Everything Else category), or the Other subcategory under the Metaphysical category will cure you of that notion right away. The important thing is that you should watch out for typical scams that plague eBay buyers and sellers alike, such as:

■ **Deadbeat bidders**    These are individuals who refuse to pay for what they have bought. You run into these folks far less often than you might think, however.

■ **Scam artists**    eBay members regularly get junk e-mail from individuals who claim to be representatives of eBay or the payment service PayPal, and who try to trick members into giving them their passwords or other confidential information by requesting that they click a link in the e-mail and fill out a fake form. The perpetrators can then "hijack" the user's eBay account.

■ **Shill or fake bidders**    Some of the bidding activity on your merchandise may be fishy. An article on the AuctionBytes web site (**http://www .auctionbytes.com/pages/abn/y02/m04/i05/s01**) reported on programs that reward customers for clicking through to the eBay web site, registering, and bidding on auctions. *Shill bidding* is a prohibited and dreaded practice (not to mention illegal in some areas) conducted by some disreputable eBay sellers who agree to run the price up on auction items so high bidders have to pay more than they would otherwise.

You'll find more detailed descriptions of the kinds of problems you can run into as an eBay seller, and some suggestions for overcoming them, in Chapter 19.

# Do Your Research

Before you start selling on eBay, do your homework. Know which kinds of sales attract lots of bids and which turn out to be duds. Scan the message boards to get an idea of the kinds of problems sellers tend to confront, so you can watch out for them yourself. In order to succeed, any business needs to come up with a business plan, and online businesses are no different. A business plan doesn't have to be an elaborate production. The most important things are to make sure what you want to sell, determine where you want to sell it, and verify that there's a market of buyers for the kinds of merchandise you want to put up for auction. The sections that follow provide you with some other tips for planning your eBay business.

## eBay Bestsellers
## Making the Move from Bidder to Auctioneer

Like many eBay sellers, Jo Stavig (User ID: vintagevisionjo) is no stranger to antiques and collectibles, or even to putting her wares up for sale. She rented space in an antique mall in Chicago for many years, but she wasn't happy with the 10 percent commission the mall's owners charged on each sale, and things just weren't selling fast enough. When she cleaned out her mall space, her home became filled with boxes full of twentieth-century memorabilia. With the holidays coming, she became convinced that it was time to make the move from being a buyer on eBay to starting to sell.

"I had some silver, crystal, and glass items that I was nervous about taking to the mall because I didn't have a locked cabinet there (you had to pay extra for that)," says Jo. "I had some inventory left over when I moved out of there, and now I had the problem of where to put it all. It seemed that eBay would be a more cost-effective way to sell and reduce my collection."

Even though she had sold merchandise, and was used to buying on eBay, Jo still found the process of becoming a seller "somewhat intimidating." She had to make a series of decisions about how to ship, whether she would ship internationally, how to accept payments, and whether she would accept returns. Next came the issue of how to take photos, and where to store them online. Then the technical preparation—where to load your photos from, how to take photos. Her husband, Steve, helped by taking photos with his mini DV (digital video) camera, then touching up the images using the sophisticated graphics program Adobe Photoshop. "I put together a couple of backdrop fabrics on a drawing table, and I have a couple of clip-on lights that I can manipulate," Jo explained.

Jo signed up for PayPal, one of several payment methods that enable eBay businesspeople to sell internationally. She decided to take personal checks. Finally, she was ready to go online with her first sales. "It was exciting. I found it more exciting as a seller than as a buyer. At the end of an auction, watching a new bid suddenly come up, was really something. My first really exciting sale was a set of six silver plates and forks that I bought at a rummage sale for 10 cents each. They went for $78. I knew they were good, but I didn't think they were *that* good!"

"I have not come up with a bad-check policy. I haven't gotten a bad check yet." Jo uses U.S. Postal Service (USPS) Priority Mail for most of her shipping, and orders boxes through the USPS web site. She emphasizes the importance of packing and shipping with care. "You can never use too much packing material. I thought I knew packing really well, because I worked in an art gallery, but found out I did not. There was a breakage on something that arrived in two pieces. I refunded part of the sales price. The buyer didn't send it back. If something gets broken, filing a claim with the post office is really difficult."

In Jo's first four months as a seller, she has sold about 100 items, including "bunches and bunches of Christmas ornaments. I've been spending quite a lot of time doing it. I've been doing freelance interior design, and other types of consulting, so it definitely helps with bills."

Jo's main piece of advice: "It's worth spending some time as a browser and a buyer first before you sell. I purposely tried to accumulate some feedback as a buyer and got a feedback rating of 30 before I went out there as a seller."

The biggest benefit, she concludes, "is being able to get rid of all that stuff all around the house! Also, being able to sell things in a more timely manner, things that would have been sitting around in the mall for months without a buyer. I've enjoyed the contacts with buyers, which can seem amazingly personal. In mall space, other people were selling for me, and I had no contact with my customers. Now, on eBay, people will write me back, saying things like 'I love the way this looks; this is better than it could possibly be.' That's been an unanticipated benefit of it for me."

## Learn by Bidding

Few, if any, people start out selling on eBay without having bid on some items first. You *can* open an account and start selling without any other experience on the auction site, but I don't recommend it. The best way to get a feel for how transactions proceed and are completed is to bid on and purchase something yourself from a reputable seller.

Perhaps the biggest benefit of bidding and buying before you start selling is the fact that you are able to accumulate positive feedback simply by following through with payment in a timely manner. You get some stuff you need or want, hopefully at a bargain price, and you get the feedback that you can then use to help you attract bidders when you start to sell. When you get to a feedback level of 10 or 20, people can tell you've used eBay for a while and are likely to be a reputable seller. At that point, you can start putting your own items up for auction.

## Pick Items That People Want

It doesn't do any good to put items up for sale that no one wants, that don't get any bids, and that only consume the time and energy required to photograph and list them. For example, rather than trying to sell new dolls that were distributed at fast-food restaurants a few months ago and that aren't hard to find, try to sell older, limited-edition dolls, preferably in their original packaging. Take a few minutes to look through the categories in which you have chosen to list your merchandise to see not only what's desirable, but what items turn out to be dogs on the market. You might be better off giving the undesirables away to charity through eBay Giving Works (**http://pages.ebay.com/sell/givingworks/index.html**) or on eBay's Giving Board (**http://chatboards.ebay.com/chat.jsp?forum=1&thread=59**).

Even if you decide to sell merchandise that is readily available to general consumers and is sold by other eBay sellers, such as electronics or computer equipment, you can distinguish yourself from the crowd. Take more photos; include more details in your description; provide potential buyers with an About Me page so they can find out more about you; or build up your positive feedback rating so you seem more trustworthy than the competition.

> TIP    *eBay's Seller Central area puts out a number of publications for buyers and sellers in especially popular areas, and they contain tips on what constitutes a good sales item. Check out the Sell by Category section of Seller Central at* **http://pages.ebay.com/sellercentral/sellbycategory.html**. *Click on one of the* **Seller's Edge** *links under a category to find more detailed tips.*

## Pick the Category in Which You Want to Sell

eBay started out with only a handful of categories in which to sell items. It's since grown to about 8000 different categories. Yes, it's true, bidders usually find what they're looking for through keyword searches that bypass the category system altogether, but it still matters where you sell your merchandise. Combine relevant keywords in your descriptions with a good location. Do a search of eBay's current or completed auctions to find items that resemble what you have to offer, and see what categories they were listed in.

Because there are so many possible categories, it's quite possible that what you want to sell could fit in one or more categories. If that's the case, you have to spend only a few dollars more for the extra listing fee that enables you to list something in more than one category.

"If you're not sure which category is best, or if an item has two groups of collectors, try to sell it in two categories," suggests eBay seller "decoray". Although the fee for listing an item in two categories is twice the fee for listing it in one category, the extra investment is worth it. It pays to think the way your prospective customers think, he recommends.

# Get Registered

Just as you had to register with eBay when you started to buy, you have to register to become a seller as well. Even if you already have an eBay User ID and password and have accumulated feedback as a buyer, you still need to create a Seller's Account. That way, eBay is able to maintain a record of your contact information so that its employees can contact you if necessary. eBay also requires you to put your credit card name and number on file so that it can deduct Final Value Fees, listing fees, and the other fees that go along with getting your auctions online.

## Pick a Good User ID

Perhaps you already have a User ID that you use for bidding on eBay. Even if you do, when you start an eBay business, you might want to consider changing it or choosing a new User ID just for selling. Why? Your name is part of your identity, and therefore it's part of your business identity as well. Names that are frivolous, silly, or potentially offensive might turn away bidders. Whether you are creating your first User ID or thinking about changing an existing one, consider the following:

- Make your ID reflect your business. If you sell buttons, for example, try to work the word "button" into your name.

- Don't use your e-mail address. For one thing, you don't need to, as buyers and sellers can find you by clicking **Ask seller a question** from one of your auction listings. I made the mistake of using my e-mail address as my User ID, and I was flooded with junk e-mail.

- Don't use the @ or & symbol—other letters, numbers, and symbols are okay.

- Don't use blank spaces; if you need to separate two words, use a single underscore character (created by pressing SHIFT-HYPHEN).

- Don't use a URL as your User ID.

- Don't try to use the word "eBay" in your User ID. eBay does not allow this.

Many sellers use separate User IDs for buying and selling: this allows them to go "incognito" when they're bidding on items. When you create a new User ID, you get an icon that looks like a miniature pair of sunglasses next to your name. The icon tells other eBay users that you changed your User ID or obtained a new User ID sometime within the past 30 days. Remember that, if you ever have second thoughts about a User ID, you are allowed to change it 30 days after you create it.

## How to ... **Create a Seller's Account**

To start the process of becoming a seller, go to the Create a Seller's Account page and follow the appropriate steps based on whether you are new to eBay or already an eBay user. You can access the Create a Seller's Account page in a few ways:

- Type **http://cgi4.ebay.com/ws/eBayISAPI.dll?SellerSignIn** in your browser.

- Go to the Help page entitled Creating a Seller's Account at **http://pages.ebay.com/help/sell/seller_account.html** and click the Create a seller's account link.

After you have completed either of these options, follow these steps:

1. When the Create a Seller's Account sign in page appears, type your User ID and password and click Sign In Securely.

2. When the Sell Your Item: Create Seller's Account page appears, click Create Seller's Account.

3. Enter your credit or debit card information and click Continue.

4. Enter your checking account information and click Continue.

5. Choose your preferred payment method for your eBay fees (credit card or checking account) to finish setting up your account.

The requirement to enter your credit card information, checking account number, and your billing address might seem a bit off-putting, but don't worry: eBay uses this information only to charge you when it comes time to pay your seller's fees—not when you register.

NOTE    *Changing your User ID doesn't mean you lose your accumulated feedback. eBay carries your feedback from your previous ID to your new one.*

## Create a Secure Password

Passwords are the most basic level of security on the Internet and, when used by themselves and not protected by encryption or other means, one of the least secure. You can improve the inherent security of the eBay password you create by following a few simple principles:

- *Don't use a word in the dictionary.* Some hackers use password-cracking software that looks up all of the words in a dictionary to try to uncover just this sort of password.

- *Don't make it too short.* Hackers also try to crack passwords using "brute force" attacks that generates a vast quantity of random characters and submits them to the computer at very high speed. Keep your password between six and nine characters.

- *Don't make it too long and complicated.* You won't be able to remember it, or you'll easily mistype it.

- *Don't make it easily recognizable.* For example, think of a familiar or common phrase, like My eBay Auction Business, and then use the initials MEAB. Mix the characters into upper- and lowercase: mEAB. Add a number that is meaningful, such as your street address: mEAB1553.

> **TIP** *Some easy-to-use software programs are available to help you manage not only your eBay password but the many other passwords you probably use to get online, read your e-mail, and register to use other web sites. Look into Whisper 32 (**http://www.ivory.org/whisper.html**), and PassKeeper (**http://www.passkeeper.com**). PasswordWallet is available for Macintosh users (**http://www.selznick.com/products/passwordwallet/index.htm**).*

# Get the Computer Equipment You Need

Making the move from only buying on eBay to selling on a regular basis is like moving from being a backup player on a sports team to a starting player. You become a full participant. Accordingly, you need to make sure your Internet connection and your computer equipment are up to snuff. This section provides some tips on what you need to put your sales listings together.

Remember, when you shop for memory or other computer hardware, save your receipts. You may be able to record and deduct all these purchases as business expenses on your tax return if you make money selling through auctions (and you will!).

> **NOTE**
>
> *If you're satisfied with your Internet connection and equipment or if you sell on consignment, you can skip this section. This section is for those of you who are eager to start wheeling and dealing but aren't sure what equipment you need. Keep in mind that I'm examining the ins and outs of running an eBay business. I'm not talking about selling something once a month or a few times a year. For occasional selling, you can use any computer equipment that gets you on the Internet. For regular sales that generate part or all of your income, though, it pays to get the best equipment and Internet connection you can afford.*

## Internet Connection

In theory, you can create and upload auction listings from a computer at your public library or at a relative's house, but when you start selling, you're going to need to check your e-mail regularly for inquiries from prospective bidders. You'll also want to experience the end-of-auction excitement as bids go up on your items. You really need your own Internet connection so that you can get on eBay any time of the day or night.

Chances are your computer has a modem built into it that you can use to connect to the Internet. A *modem* is a hardware device that translates your computer's digital data to signals carried over other types of electronic cables. A conventional analog modem translates the digital computer information into analog data that can be sent over ordinary phone lines. People who make a phone call to their Internet Service Provider (ISP) to connect to the Internet are said to have a *dial-up modem connection*. These days, most analog modems operate at a speed of 56 kilobits per second (Kbps), which is a minimal speed for using the Internet.

Because of the relatively slow speed of dial-up modems, Internet users are increasingly turning to higher-speed solutions. I highly recommend that you look into a Digital Subscriber Line (DSL) or cable-modem connection, if one is available in your area. These are *direct lines*, which keep you connected at all times, rather than just for the length of your modem's phone call. Besides freeing up a phone line, a direct connection is typically light years faster than a dial-up modem connection. Cable modems receive data from the Internet through a cable TV company's existing underground fiber optic cable and may be available from one of your local cable providers. DSL is a cost-effective type of direct connection to the Internet that uses conventional telephone lines to transfer data at very high speeds. You may be able to get a DSL connection from your local phone provider or an ISP such as Earthlink (**http://www.earthlink.com**).

If you do use a phone line to get online, probably the most important telephone- or connection-related decision you can make is to install a second phone line for your online buying and selling. Having a second line is pretty much a necessity if you plan to do business online regularly, especially if your children or significant other uses your existing phone line even on a semiregular basis.

*If you have a "day job" in addition to your eBay sales, don't get in the habit of putting merchandise up for sale or checking your auction listings from your office computer. You can easily get in trouble for misusing company resources. To stay out of the doghouse, set up your own system at home.*

## Computer

Buying and selling on eBay, like other types of electronic commerce, doesn't require a machine with the latest super-fast processor and multimedia bells and whistles. Nevertheless, the speed and quality of your computer, monitor, and other hardware can affect your auction experience. If your machine is slow and your modem a crawler, it could take an inordinate amount of time to get multiple sales items online. If you can't inspect a detailed screen image of your image as it appears on eBay, you might not be able to correct or retake it if you need to. Make sure you have, at the very least:

- *A reasonably fast computer.* In other words, one with (at the very minimum) a 500 or 600 MHz processor. The speed at which a processor operates is measured in megahertz (MHz). Most new computers run at much faster speeds, of 1 or 2 GHz (that's gigahertz, or 1000 megahertz) or more.

- *Lots of random access memory (RAM).* Along with browsing the Web and checking e-mail, you're likely to be operating scanning and image editing software, which can be memory-intensive. Get a minimum of 128MB of RAM, and more if you can afford it.

Where better to buy computer equipment, if you need it, than eBay's own Computers & Networking category? You might find a bargain, and if you pay up quickly, you'll get another positive feedback mark as well (see Figure 2-4).

*If you need to find out more about computer hardware terms and descriptions of what to buy, check out* PC QuickSteps *by Guy Hart-Davis (McGraw-Hill/Osborne, 2004).*

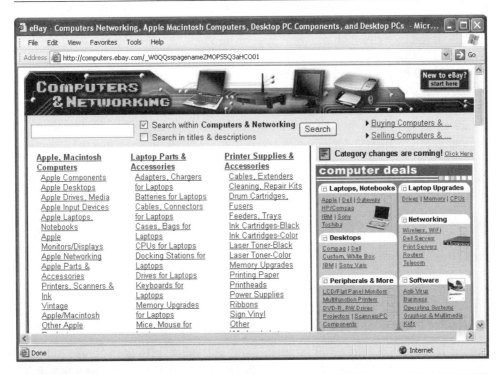

**FIGURE 2-4**    Improve your auction experience by shopping for computer equipment on eBay itself.

## Monitor

Your monitor is the window through which all the action on eBay occurs. A clear, sharp monitor can help you verify that your images are of good quality. A monitor that's especially spacious (say, 17 or 19 inches or more) enables you to open to several browser windows at a time, so you can monitor multiple sales as they come down to the wire.

When it comes to buying online, a good monitor and a video card are two of the most important investments you can make. In order to know whether an item is exactly what you want, you have to be able to see it clearly. Sometimes, too, the only reference you have for an item's quality is an onscreen image.

It's tempting to scrimp on computer monitors, especially if you're a bargain hunter like me. You can find cheap monitors for $100, or even less if you buy a used one. Because monitors are so important to your auction experience, though, don't scrimp on this important component. Monitors are inexpensive enough that you should definitely purchase a 17-inch or bigger monitor instead of a smaller variety. Even an extra inch makes a huge difference, whether you're looking at word-processing documents or web pages.

Computer monitors display graphic information that consists of little units called *pixels*. Each pixel appears in a computer image as a small dot. The pixels are so small that they're hard to see with the naked eye unless you magnify an image to look at details close up. The higher the resolution, the better the image appears. A monitor *resolution* of 1280×1024, for example, refers to the number of pixels that the monitor displays. Another important point to consider when shopping for monitors is the maximum refresh rate at the monitor's resolution. Anything less than 75 Hz produces visible flashing in the image, which is guaranteed to be annoying.

*Features like refresh rates don't apply to LCD monitors. LCD stands for liquid crystal display, a way of displaying images on a monitor in which back light shines through liquid crystals on the screen. LCD enables the use of flat-panel displays by laptops and other computers.*

## Software You'll Need

For the most part, you can sell on eBay using the same software you use to buy: your web browser and your e-mail software. However, when you start to sell, you'll probably start to use those tried-and-true programs in some new ways. Plus, you might want to install some auction-specific software.

### E-Mail Software

Although a web browser provides you with a port of entry for getting involved with auctions, e-mail often seals the deal. E-mail communication is essential for exchanging both pre-sale and post-sale information between buyers and sellers. You can, and should, ask sellers for background information about items in which you're interested.

As far as obtaining e-mail software, this isn't usually something you have to worry about. You'll probably use the e-mail software that comes with your web browser: Outlook Express for Internet Explorer or Netscape Messenger for Netscape Communicator, or America Online's e-mail client. All of these programs handle the quoting and attaching features mentioned next.

After the sale, you need to provide shipping information and answer bidders' questions through e-mail. It pays to be proficient with some of the finer points of e-mail communication, such as the following:

- **Quoting**   Almost all e-mail programs let you quote from a message to which you're replying so that you can respond easily to a series of questions and remind the sender what he or she said earlier.

- **Attaching**   Attaching a file to an e-mail message is a quick and convenient way to transmit information from one person to another. For instance, it's common to e-mail a photo of an item that isn't displayed on the Web. If you do this, be sure to send the image in a common graphics format that your recipient can view, like GIF, JPEG, TIFF, or PCX.

You might also want to attach a signature file to the end of your e-mail messages that describes who you are and provides the name of your eBay business (if it has a name), your User ID, and other contact information, as described in Chapter 11.

NOTE   *When it comes to keeping in touch, one of the best ways to get your e-mail when you're on the road is a cell phone that has web and e-mail capabilities. My own provider charges about $8 a month for e-mail and web service, and it's well worth the expense. You can, in theory, browse eBay on your cell phone and check on auctions, but I find it time-consuming and impractical. E-mail, however, works well by cell phone, and gives you a great way to keep up with customers and inquiries.*

## Web Browser

When it comes to using Internet auction services, your tried-and-true web browser will see you through. However, when you sell, you have to run this familiar software through a few more paces than usual. You need your browser to do the following:

- Display sale items you want to buy or sell after you put them online, so you can make sure the listings and images look the way you want.

- Preview any personal web pages you create, such as an About Me page or an eBay Store (see Chapter 7).

- Support some level of Internet security, such as encryption or secure transactions, so you can register, place bids, or change your seller's account information if you need to.

In addition to having an up-to-date browser with the latest features, having more than one kind of browser installed on your computer is often a good idea so that you can test the way your auction sales look, if you use HTML formatting like colors or headings. For example, if you use Microsoft Internet Explorer simply because that's what came with your operating system, be sure to download the latest copy of Netscape Communicator as well.

*eBay provides a free add-on browser toolbar that makes it easier to search, sign in, and receive alerts: find out more in Chapter 6.*

### Image Editing Software

You need a graphics editing program either to create original artwork for your web pages or to crop and adjust your scanned or digitally photographed images. The software you need to adjust or crop photographic image files almost always comes bundled with the scanner or digital camera, so you don't need to buy separate software. I discuss auction images in Chapter 8, but the two image editing programs I use the most are Paint Shop Pro by Jasc Software (**http://www.jasc.com**) and Adobe Photoshop Elements (**http://www.adobe.com**).

### Auction Software

If you plan to present lots of auction items for sale on the Web and envision a full-fledged online business that includes customer service options and online purchases, you may want to look into software specially designed to help you present items for sale, track bids, or even set up your own auction service. One of the most popular programs is eBay's own Seller's Assistant (**http://pages.ebay.com/sellers_assistant/ index.html**). Virtual Auction Ad Pro by Virtual Notions also gives you a user-friendly way to create auction listings (**http://www.virtualnotions.com**) and is a program that I've personally found easy to use.

*Other software that helps you manage multiple sales at once is described in Chapter 6. The Auction Software Review site (**http://www .auctionsoftwarereview.com**) contains links to a wide variety of auction-related tools.*

## Image Capture Device

A good photo is pretty much a must-have for attracting bids on your merchandise. A picture is worth a thousand megabytes of information, in online terms. The photos that appear on eBay auctions need to be digitized—in other words, they need to be in the form of computer files rather than the paper photos you normally get back from your photo processor. You have a variety of options for obtaining digital images of your sales items:

- Take photos with a digital camera and save the image files on your computer.

- Take photos of your merchandise with a conventional camera and have your photo processor return them to you on CD or store them online so you can retrieve them.

- Get conventional photos back from your photo processor and scan them into your computer using a device called a *scanner*. The most common type of scanner is a flatbed scanner, which resembles a miniature photocopier. It is primarily used for scanning paper items, but can be used for some small three-dimensional objects, with varying degrees of quality. I've even seen them priced on eBay for $50 or less.

Scanning is the process of turning the colors and shapes contained in an image such as a photographic print or slide into digital information (that is, bytes of data) that a computer can understand. You place the image in a position where the scanner's camera can pass over it, and the scanner turns the image into a computer document that consists of tiny bits of information called *pixels*.

Unless you already have a scanner at home and know how to use it, chances are you're better off with one of the first two options. Buying your own digital camera and learning how to use it is ideal and cost-effective because it saves you photo-processing costs. The advantage of using a digital camera is that it's portable and convenient. A digital camera connects directly to your computer, so you can save images right to disk. You can get photos online in a matter of minutes without spending money or time having them processed and printed conventionally. Not so long ago, digital cameras cost thousands of dollars. These days, you can find on eBay good digital cameras in the $100 to $200 range that provide a resolution of 3.0 megapixels or above and are made by reputable manufacturers like Nikon, Fuji, Canon, Olympus, and Kodak. You have to make an investment up front, but this particular tool can pay off for you in the long run. Not only can you use the camera for your auction offerings, but with the addition of a color printer, you can even print your own photos, which can save you a pile in photo lab costs.

However, if you're a technophobe and are most comfortable with your conventional camera, let your photo processor save the photos in digital format for you.

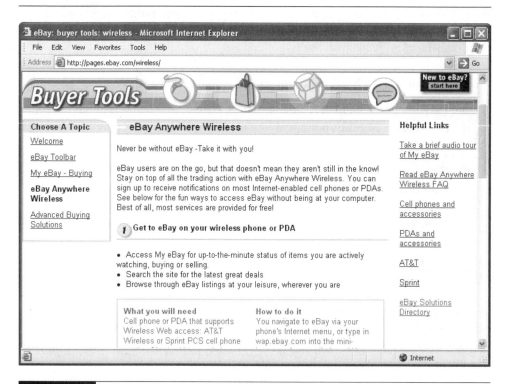

**FIGURE 2-5**   Use your web-enabled cell phone or handheld device to check on your auctions while you're away from home.

## Handheld Device

This is a pretty high-tech option, but it's worth noting that if you use a cell phone or handheld computing device that can browse the Web, you can use it to check out your eBay auctions while you're on the road. Find out more on the eBay Buyer Tools: eBay Anywhere Wireless page (**http://pages.ebay.com/wireless/**), as shown in Figure 2-5.

## Protect Your Investment

Remember, when you run an eBay business, your computer isn't just a toy for playing games or a tool your kids use to do their homework. It's business equipment. Be sure to protect your investment by taking steps to guard against damage or data loss.

Be sure your computer has antivirus software installed that is configured to automatically scan your incoming e-mail for virus attachments as you download your messages.

Protect your equipment against electrical problems that can result in a loss of data or substantial repair bills. A *power surge* or *spike* (a sudden increase in voltage) can damage your equipment. Electrical storms can damage ungrounded equipment, and blackouts can put you offline and prevent you from getting work done, which can hit you in your pocketbook.

At the very least, make sure that your home office has grounded three-prong outlets. (Even if the rest of your house has old-fashioned outlets, pay an electrician to upgrade the line to your office.) Upgrading doesn't just mean changing the outlets themselves, however; it means using a three-wire cable to bring electricity to the outlet. The third wire, the ground wire, should literally connect to the ground. Usually, electricians do this by burying a copper spike in the ground near your house. This causes shorts or lightning strikes to go into the ground rather than into your computer equipment.

Another must-have is a *surge suppressor*, a device that guards your equipment against power surges and other electrical problems. A common variety is a five- or six-outlet strip with a built-in protection device. You can find surge suppressers at hardware and computer stores.

Be sure to back up your data on a regular basis in case your computer is lost or stolen (if you use a laptop, this is a real possibility) or is damaged by fire, coffee spills, floods, or other natural disasters.

## Where to Find It

- **eBay Learning Center**
  **http://pages.ebay.com/education/index.html**
  Links to tutorials for sellers and workshops conducted on eBay's message boards.

- **eBay University**
  **http://pages.ebay.com/university/index.html**
  A list of upcoming road shows and workshops held around the country.

- **eBay Workshop Events**
  **http://members.ebay.com/aboutme/workshopevents**
  Links to excellent tutorials and workshops for sellers held on eBay's message boards and archived online.

■ **eBay Community Member Spotlight**
**http://pages.ebay.com/community/people/spotlight.html**
Profiles of eBay users presented by eBay itself in brief question-and-answer format.

■ **The Chatter**
**http://pages.ebay.com/community/chatter/index.html**
eBay's own community newsletter.

■ **eBay Buyer Tools: eBay Anywhere Wireless**
**http://pages.ebay.com/wireless**
Instructions on how to retrieve auction data on your cell phone or PDA.

# Chapter 3

# Become an eBay Auctioneer

## How to...

■ Get your eBay business up and running, step by step

■ Choose the right eBay sales format

■ Choose the right types of auctions for your needs

■ Apply some add-on features to gain extra attention

■ Use eBay's Listing Designer to boost graphic interest

■ Get sales online with the Sell Your Item form

■ Know how to manage sales while bidding is still open

■ Procure inventory so you can keep your business running smoothly

It's time to get down to business—e-business, eBay style, for e-entrepreneurs, in other words. Any business endeavor requires at least a little advance planning. Happily, setting up a sales operation on eBay is far simpler than starting a brick-and-mortar operation. You don't have to purchase or rent a store or office space, and you don't have to install lots of furnishings or equipment. You don't have to hire employees (at least not yet).

In fact, if you are already online and bidding on eBay, you've got most of what you need to get started. At this point, you just need a little bit of confidence, and you need to make a few choices. In fact, you can break down the process of starting an eBay business by making a series of decisions in response to the following questions:

■ What kind of eBay business do I want to run?

■ What kind of sale is the best choice for what I have to sell?

■ How am I going to take and store photos?

■ How am I going to accept payments?

■ How am I going to ship?

Each of those decisions will be covered, in varying levels of detail, in the following sections. Later in the chapter, you will find out how to conduct your first auction and how to keep your store well stocked.

# Decision 1: Custom-Design Your eBay Business

There are any number of different ways in which you can sell on eBay. Just because you settle on one option to begin with doesn't mean you have to stay with it all the time, either. Some sellers start by selling part-time, and then quit their day job and sell on eBay full-time. Others fall into selling on eBay as their sole source of income after they lose their job; they sell full-time for a while to make ends meet, then move to selling part-time when another job shows up. The beauty of eBay is that you can tailor the type of selling to fit your needs. The various options are described in the sections that follow.

## Sell Part-Time on eBay

You can easily fit eBay auction sales activities around your full-time work schedule. Plenty of people do so, from those who sell only a handful of items a month to people who put 20 items online each day. Bob Kopczynksi, who has an active eBay auction business profiled in Chapter 4, works full-time at another job, but his wife devotes all of her working hours to eBay, and they have several other staff people on call as well.

You should, in fact, set a moderate goal for your initial sales on eBay. Starting out by selling perhaps five or six items will help you to ease into the system and get used to how it works. It depends on the amount of time you have available, the number of items you have to sell, and your level of ambition.

## Become a Full-Time Auctioneer

When you sell on eBay full-time, you make all of your income through eBay. It's not clear how many people actually do this, but the fact is that individuals all across the country and around the world are selling regularly through the auction site. To get an idea of just how many full-time sellers there are, do a web search for Trading Assistants in your area code (go to the URL given in the "Having Someone Do the Selling for You" sidebar). You're likely to find lots of individuals with very high feedback, many of whom are probably selling either full-time or on what might be called a "most-of-the-time" basis.

When you sell full-time, you have to make a substantial commitment. You'll be checking your e-mail, putting up auction descriptions, packing and shipping items, and taking photos on a regular basis. You'll want to establish an eBay Store, which enables you to have items for sale round-the-clock. (See Chapter 14 for more information on eBay Stores.) You'll probably benefit by coming up with a regular schedule that calls for you to visit the post office or shipping store at certain times of

# Having Someone Do the Selling for You

One of the easiest ways to start selling on eBay, especially if you aren't sure whether you want to sell online at all, is to have someone do the selling for you and see if you like the process. It can be exciting to watch your items sell. My friend Pam does this, in fact; she has been placing her silver dinner sets and other treasures with her friend, an experienced eBay seller named Jo Stavig. Pam expressed great excitement at being able to clean out some of the clutter in her house while not actually having to do the work of taking photos and creating auction descriptions.

If you're interested in having some experienced eBay sellers, called *Trading Assistants,* sell your items for you, go to the Trading Assistants home page (**http://pages.ebay.com/tradingassistants.html**), shown here:

Expect to pay a fee that ranges anywhere from 10 to 40 percent of the sale; the exact terms depend on the individual seller. Some sellers charge a flat fee for each sale; others purchase the items from their owners and sell them online, collecting all of the proceeds. It pays to shop around. Look for someone in your local area so that you can take your items to the seller, who can then photograph them for you and ship them out when bidding ends.

One of the fastest-growing ways to sell on eBay, in fact, is the eBay drop-off store—a brick-and-mortar outlet where individuals can drop off their merchandise so that the store's proprietors can put them up for auction on consignment. Whether you choose a Trading Assistant or a drop-off store, you should take advantage of the opportunity to learn a lot about what it takes to sell on eBay. Ask questions, and make note of how experienced sellers handle your items. You may just get bitten by the eBay sales bug and decide to start selling on your own.

the week, answer e-mail queries at certain times, take photos at certain times, and so on. You'll also need to come up with a way to accumulate items to sell, because you'll be running out of them eventually and you'll need to replenish your inventory. If you sell general consumer goods rather than unique items like antiques and collectibles, you'll probably want to find wholesale suppliers so you have a steady stream of stock.

When you set up an eBay business, there are also tax and accounting implications, which are addressed in Chapter 17. Some of the financial implications, such as business deductions and payments to contractors, come into play if you hire employees. You can do all the work of selling on eBay by yourself, but you'll benefit greatly if you have someone to help you divide the labor involved in shopping, selling, packing, shipping, and e-mailing. Chances are this will be a spouse, relative, or significant other.

## Supplement Web Site Sales

Lots of online businesses supplement their web site sales with eBay auction sales. They use their web sites to advertise their businesses and give their customers a way to contact them. They put some of their merchandise up for sale there, but they also use eBay to get top dollar for especially desirable items. The Bruce Hershenson site, shown in Figure 3-1, claims to have sold more than 80,000 items on eBay.

**FIGURE 3-1** eBay can supplement the sales on your web site, if you have one.

## Boost Brick-and-Mortar Sales

Companies that do business traditionally sometimes sell on eBay in order to empty out excess inventory or simply make some extra profit. In the "excess inventory" category, no less an entity than the U.S. Postal Service has used eBay to sell off unclaimed items under User IDs such as usps-mrc-everythingelse, usps-mrc-books, and so on, according to a story on the AuctionBytes web site (**http://www.auctionbytes .com/pages/abu/y202/m05/abu0070/s02**). I've seen plenty of antique dealers who have brick-and-mortar storefronts sitting at their computer terminals behind their cash registers, checking on their eBay sales. Arena Leather Shop of Cookeville, Tennessee

# eBay Bestsellers
## When Selling Online Is Fun

A friend of mine whom I'll call Buddhachick (not her real User ID) sold full-time on eBay for several years, selling as many as 20 to 50 items each week. When she recently took a full-time job, she had to cut back considerably on her sales activities, and now sells only a handful of items at a time. Nevertheless, she still regards selling on eBay as an enjoyable and even creative activity, one that has enabled her to meet plenty of nice individuals from all over the world.

"I sell only vintage and antique stuff," she says. "I basically spend a lot of time combing the newspapers for estate sales and antique auctions, sometimes in my local area and sometimes not so local; every Thursday night, I'm checking Internet newspaper sites for garage sales. Sometimes, I have to get there at 6:30 or 7 A.M. to wait in line so I can find some treasures. My mother was an antique dealer, and my boyfriend's father was in the business. For me, the fun of it is selling stuff I really love.

"It's a little like gambling for me, in that if you find something really valuable, it can be really exciting. One time there was a 1970s belt buckle I bought for $1. It had the words 'Jesus Christ Superstar' on it. It looked like it was from the original 1970s musical. I sold it for $40. Another time, I helped a woman who bought estates empty the house. She said I could have anything that was left. I laughed because it seemed there was nothing left. I stood on a chair and looked up near the ceiling in the basement. I pulled out all this junk. Way in the back there was a cigar box full of fishing lures. I sold one really rare one for $1000. It was my biggest sale."

Buddhachick had some suggestions about how to handle problems that might arise during and after the sale, though she emphasized that such problems don't occur often. "I do watch my auctions while they are going on. Sometimes people ask me to end the auction early. I never do. A new seller has to do what they think is right. Only once has the offer been higher than the eventual sale price. I just say, "Thank you for your offer" and try to be as courteous as I can, even when I know they are trying to rip me off.

"When an auction ends, I also have a standard end of auction e-mail that I send out. I also have one that says, 'I haven't gotten your payment yet. Thank you for bidding. Here are the details of how you can pay, and the shipping costs, and the price.' About 5 percent of my high bidders have turned out to be deadbeats. It hasn't been a huge problem."

Buddhachick has been able to put her skills to good use when writing descriptions. "One thing I learned is that I have marketing skills I didn't think I had. I got a degree in creative writing in college, and I put it to work. I think the art of writing the description is important. I have a lot of friends who watch my auctions because they like the way I write my descriptions, and it really makes a difference."

What makes a good description? She says she learned a lot from reading the descriptions created by other sellers. "Someone wrote, 'I have no doubt the bidders would be thrilled with the condition of this item,' and I thought, that's a really good way of saying that the condition is really good. So I try to say things like that, too. If something has a stain on it, I use the word 'mark' or 'spot.' I don't say 'stain.' If it's a tablecloth, I say, there are a few spots where someone must have dribbled coffee. That way the stain is part of the interesting history of the item. I don't go over the top. I try to be honest but creative.

"Another time I had this old Barbie doll in a really tight dress. It was one of the first Barbies. It looked like a 1950s nightclub singer. I said, 'You'll have your Barbie sing "Happy Birthday, Mister President," in an outfit that's great for serving mint juleps.' Writing creative descriptions keeps me interested, too. If you're doing 20 or 30 descriptions in a day, you've got to keep yourself interested."

Taking photos is not a big production: she tapes a one-color piece of cloth against the wall, and photographs the item on a table. If the item is a light color, she uses a dark background, and vice versa. Buyers who refuse to follow through with payment aren't a big deal, either. "If you have any kind of business, you'll run into those kinds of things. I don't hold it against people. I've never had a check bounce, and I have more than 1000 feedback."

As far as shipping, Buddhachick uses the U.S. Postal Service. "I like going to the post office; people there know me, and it's convenient. I myself hate to pay high shipping costs when I buy, so I keep the shipping cost down. I offer Priority Mail or parcel post. I don't charge a handling fee.

"I have a lot of friends on eBay, and we'll swap information from time to time about what sells and what doesn't," she concludes. "I don't do this full-time now, but I think I spend more than 40 hours a week on it. Still, it doesn't seem to take that much time when you are having fun."

**FIGURE 3-2**   eBay sales can be part of a sales program that includes a brick-and-mortar store and web site.

regularly sells on eBay (User ID: idoleather) as well as through its brick-and-mortar outlet and its web site (see Figure 3-2). In addition, well-known retailers like Sears and KitchenAid are using eBay as a marketing tool as well as an additional sales channel.

# Decision 2: Pick the Auction That's Right for You

eBay resembles a virtual ice cream store for auction buyers and sellers. Sales come in many different varieties—flavors, you might say. You can add additional interest to the sales you pick by featuring them so they stand out from other sales—you can make the listings bold or highlight them in a color, or you can feature them in a special category. Which one is the right one for your needs? The following are some quick points to consider based on my experience.

■ Remember that eBay charges you for setting a reserve price (see "Reserve Price Auction," later in this chapter, for a rundown). For that reason, many sellers set a starting bid that is the minimum price they want to receive for the item. In essence, this performs the same function as a reserve bid. A starting bid of, say, $100 basically tells bidders that the seller has set a reserve price of $100. High starting bids used to turn bidders away automatically, because they felt that they weren't going to get a bargain. Many bidders still feel that way—items with high starting prices are more likely to go unsold than those with low starting prices. However, since eBay started charging a fee for setting a reserve price, the practice of setting a high starting price is becoming more widespread and more accepted.

■ Do some research by going to the local library and looking up the item's value in a price guide; or search eBay's Completed Auctions to see what similar items have sold for on the auction site.

■ Consider going with no reserve price for some items—not necessarily the ones you have paid a lot for, but ones that weren't expensive to begin with. Sales with no reserve set tend to get more bids than others (though this isn't a hard-and-fast rule). To make your reserve price sale more likely to attract bids, consider saying something in the description that gives bidders an idea of whether they are close to the reserve, such as "The reserve is half of the retail price on this item."

■ If you have a number of items to sell that are exactly the same and that don't constitute a set, such as six jazz albums you uncovered in the bargain bin at a music store, consider a Dutch auction format (see "Dutch Auction," later in the chapter).

In general, a good item will sell no matter what reserve price, starting bid, or Buy It Now price you put on it. Over and over, you find people who were astonished to find that they had surprisingly valuable items, such as a beer can from the 1940s that sold for more than $16,000, for example. (See Uncle Griff's web site, **http://www.unclegriff.com**, for this and other success stories.) Don't agonize too much over these details; just put your items out there and give them a chance to sell through a good description and clear images.

## Review Your Auction Options

Real estate sellers have always known that location counts for a great deal. Locating your sale in the right part of the eBay auction world can make the difference between making your sale a hot item or a dud. Whether you're a full-time or a sometime trader, one of the first steps to mastering eBay is simply understanding the different kinds of auctions that are available to you. The following sections give you an overview of the various auction categories on eBay.

## Regular Online Auction

The classic type of eBay auction, the one you see most of the time, enables sellers to sell to the highest bidder after a fixed length of time. Auctions can list 1, 3, 5, 7, or 10 days (real estate auctions can run for 30 days). eBay simply calls this a "regular" auction. Within the category of regular auction, there are variations depending on whether you are auctioning off an item, offering it at a fixed price, or both. These variations are described next.

NOTE    *Ten-day auctions will cost you an extra 10-cent listing fee. This fee does not apply to three-, five-, or seven-day auctions.*

**Reserve Price Auction**    A reserve price auction is the same as a regular auction in that it lasts for a fixed amount of time, and the sale goes to the high bidder—the difference is that the high bidder only wins if his or her bid meets or exceeds an amount the seller has designated as a *reserve price.* A reserve price protects a seller against selling something for less than what it's worth. If a seller simply won't part with something for less than $50 because that's what it cost in the first place, the seller puts a reserve of $50 on the item. Bidders only know that there is a reserve price; the auction listing makes it clear whether or not the reserve price has been met. The actual reserve price is kept secret. See "When to Use Reserve Auctions" later in this chapter for more information.

Reserve prices protect you against losing money, but they discourage some customers from bidding, because they think they won't get a bargain on an item with a reserve. Reserve prices also cost you money. If the item sells, you are charged the following:

- $1 if the reserve price is $49.99 or less

- $2 if the reserve price is $50 to $199.99

- One percent of a reserve price that is $200 or more

For items with a costly reserve price, the fee can add up. If you are selling a valuable watch with a reserve of $2000, for example, the reserve price fee is $20. Add that to the insertion fee of $4.80 and the final value fee of $43.12 (on a sale of

$2000), and you begin to see why eBay is making so much money. (Of course, if the item doesn't sell at all, you aren't charged any of these fees.)

**Online Auction with Buy It Now Price**    You can also sell an item for a fixed price, called a Buy It Now price. However, if you choose the regular auction format, the Buy It Now price disappears when the first bid is placed—that is, if you have set a starting bid and no reserve. This is the most common way to combine an auction with a Buy It Now option. For instance, you might sell something that has a starting bid of $8.99 and a Buy It Now price of $24.99. If someone pays $24.99 immediately, the sale ends. If someone bids, say, $12, the Buy It Now option disappears. It's less common to mix a reserve price with a Buy It Now option; see "How to Use Reserve Auctions" later in this chapter for more information.

 *The problem with setting a Buy It Now price is that, to be successful, you must make an accurate estimate of how much an item is really worth in a worldwide marketplace full of collectors whose tastes and pocketbooks you can't really predict. You never know if the item you sell at a Buy It Now price of $20 might really have sold for $200 to someone who was looking for an item to fill out his or her collection.*

## Fixed Price

A fixed price sale isn't really an auction: you offer something for sale at a fixed Buy It Now price and you don't allow people to bid on the item. People can buy it at any time during the sale for a fixed price. Don't overlook the Buy It Now sale, even though it costs you an extra 5-cent fee. It's becoming increasingly popular, especially as eBay becomes more popular and bidding wars grow more intense. A Buy It Now sale is quick and convenient for both buyer and seller.

 *You can also sell at a fixed price through an eBay Store—a web site that you can set up on eBay after you have accumulated a feedback rating of 20 or more, have had your identify verified through the ID Verify program, or have a PayPal account. Things can be for sale for 30, 60, 90, or 120 days at a time. See Chapter 14 for more about setting up an eBay Store.*

## Dutch Auction

A *Dutch auction* is one in which the seller puts two or more identical items up for sale. The seller then specifies the minimum successful price for each of those items, as well as the number of items available. Potential buyers can buy at or above the minimum for the number of items in which they are interested. At the close of the auction, the highest bidders purchase the items at the lowest successful price (that is, the lowest bid that is still above the minimum price).

An example should make this easier to grasp. Suppose you uncover a box full of ten Chuckles the Cat Bean Bag Babies at a garage sale. You put all ten up for sale at the same time in a single Dutch auction. You specify a minimum bid of $20 for each cat. Eighteen separate bidders place bids: one bids $30, two bid $25, three bid $24, two bid $22, two bid $21, and the rest bid $20. The ten highest bidders win: these are the individuals who bid $30, $25, $22, and $21, respectively. However—and this is the confusing part—in a Dutch auction, they all purchase at the *lowest* successful price, which is $21. Those who bid $20 lose out because there are no more than ten cats available.

## Fixed Price (on Half.com)

If you have surplus items available for sale, such as books or electronic equipment, and you are at all anxious about auction sales, Half.com provides an attractive and straightforward alternative. Sellers put up items for a fixed price; there is no bidding. There's also little or no chance for fraud; buyers pay Half.com, which then turns around and pays the seller. See Chapter 14 for more details about selling on this unique alternative to eBay.

## Real Estate Auctions

You would be amazed at how many individuals put up real estate for sale through eBay. The system works particularly well if you have property for sale that might appeal to a wide variety of bidders throughout the world—such as a time-share in the Bahamas, for instance. Your ad can appear for 30 days or 90 days in eBay's Real Estate section (see Figure 3-3).

## Business Services

Most of eBay's categories allow you to auction off tangible items, whether they are as tiny as beads or as sizeable as yachts. But one category, Professional Services, gives professionals a place to auction off their services to other businesses. If you have talents as a graphic designer, a writer, or other professional, you can register and bid on projects. eLance Online has partnered with eBay to bring businesses and service providers together in a manner similar to the want ads or employment agencies; find out more about this innovative auction service in Chapter 13.

Real estate can sell well when it appeals to a worldwide audience.

*The information contained in this section changes all the time. You can get the latest list of eBay's auction options at **http://pages.ebay.com/help/sell/ ia/formats.html**.*

## Club99 Auctions

A group of eBay users has created its own auction category within the eBay auction universe. The home-grown auction, called Club99, takes place the second Saturday of every month. Merchandise is offered at an opening price of 99 cents with no reserve price. The auctions last a week. You won't find exotic Italian sports cars or Babe Ruth autographed baseballs here. The typical Club99 auction is a single object such as a book, CD, alarm clock, shirt, or another household or personal item. Find out more about this special Saturday event at **http://members.ebay.com/ws/eBayISAPI .dll?ViewUserPage&userid=club99**.

# How to Use Reserve Auctions

Many of the auctions you find on eBay are reserve price auctions. A reserve price is a way you can protect your investment: it's a price you set that represents the lowest price at which you are willing to sell an item. Usually, your reserve price isn't disclosed to bidders, so they are encouraged to bid as high as they wish. If someone's bid goes above the reserve price you have specified, you are required by eBay to sell it to that high bidder. On the other hand, if the bids that have been placed fail to meet your reserve price, you aren't required to sell to anyone.

> **NOTE**  *Just because no one meets your reserve price, it doesn't mean you can't sell. If you use the Second Chance Offer option, you and the high bidder can negotiate a sales price. You can send an e-mail saying, "My reserve price was $_____ and I'll sell it to you for that much," for instance. Or, if you think you'll have better luck trying again, you can relist your item in a couple of weeks.*

Here's an example. Suppose you find a doll from the 1960s at an estate sale for $20. Naturally, you want to sell the doll for at least $20 plus your listing fees and any expenses you have incurred in obtaining the item. (Expenses might include the gas, time, and effort in obtaining the doll, and the time involved in creating the auction listing. Remember, when you run a business selling on eBay, time is literally money—the more time you have, the more items you can sell.) You put a reserve price of $25 on the doll when you create the auction listing. You also set an initial bid—a bid at which you want the auction to start—of as low as 1 cent, but more commonly, about $1. You do this in the Sell Your Item form (see Figure 3-4).

> **NOTE**  *You have an additional option to consider—whether you want to give bidders the option to stop the sale and buy the item for a fixed price that you consider reasonable. Suppose, for the doll in question, you've done some research through doll catalogs and completed eBay auctions and you have determined that it must be worth $100. You put a Buy It Now price of $100 on the doll, which gives bidders the opportunity to buy it immediately. If a bidder is willing to pay the Buy It Now price, you save some time and trouble, and you sell to someone you can be reasonably sure is going to follow through with payment.*

The prevailing wisdom about starting bids is that, the lower the starting bid, the more likely you are to attract bids. Higher starting bids scare off bidders who are afraid that the bidding will go too high and they'll never win. As stated earlier in the

FIGURE 3-4 A reserve price protects your investment, but remains concealed from bidders while the sale is going on.

chapter, many sellers now use a starting bid instead of a reserve price to avoid paying the extra fee, so starting bids aren't much more acceptable than they used to be.

There's another consideration about setting the starting bid, however: the lower the starting bid, the more bids are required to meet your reserve price. This can work to your advantage, however: a sale that attracts 30 bids or more is designated as a "hot item" and eBay adds a matchstick icon to its listing. This tells bidders that the item is especially desirable and is likely to attract more attention.

A small percentage of eBay sales mix a reserve price with a Buy It Now option. In this sort of sale, the Buy It Now option disappears only when the reserve price is met. For instance, if you have an item you paid $10 for and you think (and hope) it's worth $20, you can put a reserve price on it of $10, and an initial bid of $1. Additionally, you can put a Buy It Now price on the item of $20 in the hope that someone will purchase it immediately at the price you consider ideal.

# When to Use Featured Auctions

Chances are you've spent a considerable amount of time finding, hauling, photographing, and describing your merchandise. You can go a step further and make your sale items appear exceptional by placing them in special featured locations. Featuring an item in these locations costs extra, and items offered for sale in those categories tend to cost more, too. But the merchandise in these featured categories generally is unique and hard to find.

## Featured Auctions

Featured Auction listings appear at the top of the main Listings page, which is accessible from the menu bar at the top of every page on eBay. Additionally, some Featured Auction listings are randomly selected to appear on the eBay home page. However, there's no guarantee when or whether a certain item will appear in this well-traveled, highly popular location.

To create a Featured Auction, you need to meet certain requirements. You must have ten or more positive feedback comments, and the merchandise listed can't include adult items or things that eBay judges to be "illegal, illicit, or immoral." Find out about Featured Auctions and Category Featured Auctions (more information on these in the next section) at **http://cgi5.ebay.com/ws/eBayISAPI.dll?PromoteItemLanding**.

## Featured Plus! Auctions

Sellers must have a feedback rating of at least ten to list items as Featured Plus! Auctions, but they aren't subject to the other restrictions that apply to Featured Auctions (see the previous section). Featured Plus! Auctions appear at the top of the first web page for the eBay category in which they fall.

Paying the extra $19.95 listing fee is a good way to get attention for an exceptional item, particularly if the listings in its category run to 30, 40, or even more web pages. As with Featured Auctions, the seller decides whether an item is special enough to fall into this category.

 *Featured Auctions or Featured Plus! Auctions don't have to be more unique or notable than other auction listings. In fact, they might be items that need a little extra attention in order to attract bidders.*

## The Gallery

Another way to gain extra attention for your merchandise is to include a photo of it in the category in which it is listed. Such photo-enabled descriptions are called Gallery Listings. They carry an additional 25-cent listing fee. The eBay Gallery

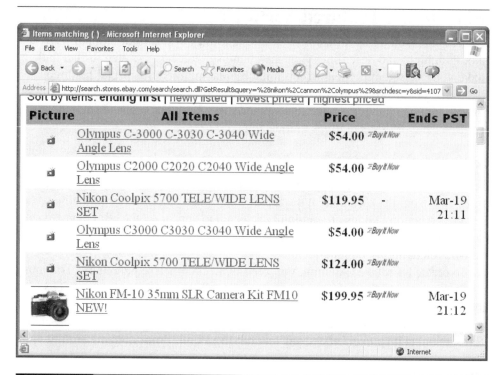

**FIGURE 3-5**    Gallery listings use photos to make your merchandise stand out from the crowd.

used to be a separate photo album of its own; now, the Gallery appears right in the category. When people see your listings in the category, they appear with a photo next to them (see Figure 3-5) and stand out from other listings that have no Gallery photos. In fact, eBay estimates that listings that include Gallery images are 76 percent more likely to get bids than those that don't.

eBay visitors can also click on the Gallery View link in the View box on the left of a listing page to see only Gallery items in that category (see Figure 3-6).

To add your image to the Gallery, simply save your image in JPEG format and check the appropriate box when you list your item. If you want something to really stand out, you can pay an additional fee of $19.95 to sell it in the Gallery Featured format. Such items appear in a special Featured section above the Gallery; Gallery Featured photos are twice as big as other photos.

TIP    *Find out more about JPEG, GIF, and other image-related alphabet soup in Chapter 8.*

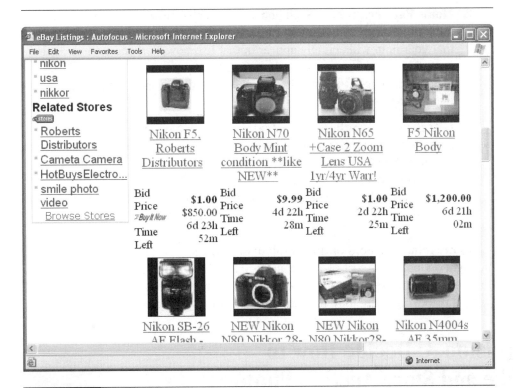

**FIGURE 3-6**    Gallery listings also appear on this page for viewers who like to shop by catalog.

## Other Featured Categories

Imagine that you've shown up at the local flea market at the crack of dawn, hoping to get the best place for your table full of sales merchandise. How do you get the most attention? You place yourself near the entrance, or near a frequently visited facility such as the refreshment stand. You arrange your space with eye-catching merchandise.

Similarly, eBay provides you with a variety of other ways to get more attention for your merchandise in a long page full of listings. Examples include:

- ■ **Bold**   Such formating is added to an item's title for an additional fee of $1.

- ■ **Highlighting**   Such listings have a border (a line of color around the edges in the shape of a box) for $3 or a highlight (a band of color) for $5.

- **Home Page Featured** Such items "have a chance" that they will appear in a list of items that appears on eBay's home page. eBay doesn't guarantee that your item will actually appear in that list, however, and a single listing costs $39.95 and two or more items in a Multiple Item listing cost $79.95. (The Home Page Featured items are also listed on a special page full of featured items.)

- **Gift Services** Sellers pay an extra dollar to have a gift icon included along with their listing title and to have the items included in a special gift category. Such gifts are supposed to be suitable for gifts for Mother's Day, birthdays, or other occasions. Gift sales also allow buyers to find your items if they check the box next to Gift Items on the Advanced Search page (**http://search.ebay.com/ws/search/AdvSearch?sofindtype=1**).

To my mind, the bold option is relatively inexpensive; the "band of color" highlight option is less cost-effective and will stand out only if surrounding listings don't use the same option. If your item is noteworthy and someone who really wants it is looking for it, they'll find it whether or not you spend money to feature it.

# Decision 3: Decide How to Take and Store Auction Photos

Everything that appears on the Web is stored on a computer called a web server. A web server is connected to the Internet 24 hours a day and is equipped with special software that makes files available to anyone with a web browser. When you create an auction listing, it is stored on one of eBay's web servers.

When you capture images of your items, you have some options. You can move your files from your computer to one of eBay's Picture Services sites and store them there. eBay lets you store one image per sale for free; the rest are subject to charges. Because of the cost (and image quality considerations, which I explain in more detail in Chapter 8), you might want to find another home for your image. You may, for instance, choose one of the auction management services mentioned in Chapter 6. These services come with their own storage space for auction images. Or you can use the storage space that comes with your Internet access account.

Before you can find a home at all, you have to have some images to put there. Are you going to have a friend or relative take photos for you? Or are you going to buy a digital camera and do it yourself? In any case, you need to decide how you're going to take good-quality digitized (in other words, computerized) images, because good photos are critical to sales. See Chapter 8 for a run-down of the options.

*You might hear the techy sounding term* upload *in connection with storing images and creating web pages. When you download a file, you copy it from a web server to your computer. When you upload, you move a file in the opposite direction, from your computer to a server online.*

3

# Decision 4: Figure Out Your Payment Options

Transferring payment for something that's purchased online, whether it's through an auction or through an e-commerce web site like Amazon.com or Landsend.com, is one of the most nerve-racking things you can do with your computer. The big danger, from a seller's standpoint, is that you'll run into a high bidder who changes his or her mind or backs out of the deal for some other reason—you'll never get paid, and you'll be forced to relist what you sell. Buyers, for their part, have the great fear that they'll hand over payment to a seller who will take the money and run without ever bothering to ship what's been purchased.

These things do happen, unfortunately, but my experience indicates that they occur less often than you might think. A number of options for getting payment from buyer to seller have been used with success by thousands of eBay users, and while they're described in some detail in Chapter 9, here is a brief summary of the kinds of choices you need to make now, before you start putting up items for sale.

## Should You Use a Payment Service?

Brief answer: Yes. A *payment service* is a company that serves as an intermediary between someone who provides goods or services and someone who pays money in exchange for those goods and services. Instead of sending a check or money order to a seller directly, the buyer pays the service, which transfers the payment to the seller. Depending on the service, both the seller and buyer have to have accounts with the same payment service.

One payment service, PayPal, is widely used on eBay, and in fact was purchased by eBay not long ago. If you have a PayPal Premier or Business account, you have a big advantage: you are able to accept payments that have been funded by credit card, without having to apply for a merchant account from a bank or lending institution. Sellers who accept credit card-funded payments generally sell more merchandise for higher prices. Buyers, too, are likely to spend more if they can pay by credit card. There is a per-transaction fee charged for Premier and Business PayPal accounts, but the cost is small in comparison to the benefits derived from being able to accept credit card-funded PayPal payments.

But PayPal charges fees that make some sellers unhappy. Other services such as BidPay (**http://www.bidpay.com**) are also popular, too. The point is that payment services make buyers feel more secure about bidding, and you need to use at least one service in order to sell on eBay. Keep in mind that PayPal and BidPay only offer minimal protection for buyers or sellers. Although PayPal does verify the IDs of charge card users in the United States, credit card fraud still occurs. And BidPay offers no protection at all.

> TIP
>
> *The escrow service Escrow.com offers a more secure environment for buyers and sellers than BidPay or PayPal. Escrow.com withholds payment to sellers until after the buyer has received the merchandise and approved it. The service also verifies payments by credit card, so sellers are protected against fraud. But because of the fees associated with Escrow.com, it's generally only used for purchases of $500 or more. (Other escrow services that aren't affiliated with eBay may not protect you adequately.)*

## Should You Accept Checks?

Short answer: Yes, with qualifications. Many sellers accept checks for years without encountering any that turn out to have rubbery qualities (in other words, that are returned for lack of funds). Even if you do run into bad checks, that doesn't mean you should penalize all of your buyers by refusing to accept checks altogether. Just put a note on your auction listings that puts buyers on notice that if they send you a check, you will wait ten days to two weeks for the check to clear before you send shipment. The veteran seller (User ID: decoray), who is profiled in Chapter 10, includes an extensive note about checks with each of his auction listings (see Figure 3-7).

There's no hard-and-fast rule about holding checks for ten days or more before they clear. Many sellers decide how to handle the check-clearing question on an individual basis. For buyers with good feedback ratings, most sellers don't wait for the check to clear. For a buyer with a zero feedback rating and warning signs, such as a low check number, you should wait for the check to clear, especially in the sale of an expensive item.

## Should You Accept Credit Card Payments?

Quick answer: Not yet, unless you already accept credit cards through a brick-and-mortar store or an e-commerce web site. Enabling yourself to accept credit cards is typically an involved process, as is the matter of verifying credit card information and dealing with chargebacks—the cost of purchases removed from someone's account if their credit card was used fraudulently. You need some sort of hardware or software to process the credit card data your buyers send; you need to pay fees to the banks or merchant account companies that actually process the payments. Get yourself well established as an eBay seller before you tackle this one.

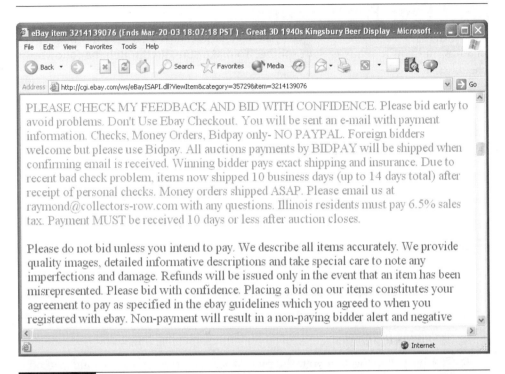

FIGURE 3-7    Tell buyers up front that you'll accept checks but won't ship until they clear.

# Decision 5: Pick Your Shipping Options

Whether you get your merchandise where it's supposed to go, quickly and safely, is one of the things that buyers note when they leave feedback for sellers. And at this early stage, accumulating positive feedback should be one of your big goals (along with generating income, of course). Therefore, you need to determine—now, before you start making sales—how you're going to pack and ship your merchandise.

First, you need to pick a shipper. Most eBay sellers choose the United States Postal Service (USPS), United Parcel Service (UPS), or Federal Express (FedEx). USPS's Priority Mail is especially popular because it offers delivery times as short as two days and provides free, high-quality boxes, labels, and other shipping materials. But FedEx's Ground and Home Delivery options are competitively priced, especially for heavy items. In any case, you'll need to start accumulating large quantities of boxes, bubble wrap and other packing material, packing tape, labels, and other goodies. See Chapter 10 for more details.

# Conduct Your First Auction

Let's say you've made the decisions you need to get started. You've got your ducks in a row and you're ready to start selling. To make sure, go through the following checklist:

- You've signed up for a seller's account with eBay and submitted your credit card information.

- You have accumulated some positive feedback through bidding and buying at auction.

- You've determined the general type of eBay business you're going to run.

- You've accumulated the merchandise you're going to sell.

- You've purchased a digital camera or figured out another way you're going to capture digital photos of your merchandise.

- You've picked some categories in which you're going to sell your merchandise.

- You've signed up with a payment service and decided on other methods of accepting payment.

- You've gotten together your shipping materials and picked a shipping method.

At last, you're ready to get some sales online and start getting bids. The following sections describe how to get started.

## Gather Your Materials

Pull together the items you plan to sell first. Don't start with too many items at once; for starters, just try a few so that you can get used to the process gradually. Get a good-quality digital camera, and consider assembling a "photo studio," including auxiliary lights and solid-colored backdrops you can use for photos.

Come up with a *boilerplate* text that you can use with all of your auction listings—standard text that you include with each of your descriptions and that applies to all of your items. Buddhachick, the seller profiled earlier in this chapter, has a particularly friendly boilerplate:

I take personal check, PayPal, and money orders.

SORRY MICHIGAN BUYERS, PLEASE ADD 6% SALES TAX!

Please do not be alarmed if it takes me a day or two to send you your total. I have several jobs and can only close out sales three days a week.

It is my goal that all buyers will have a pleasant experience doing business with me. I am reasonable, honest, and I make every effort to describe each item accurately. If shipping is not quoted in description, I will charge actual shipping only. Clothing and textiles are sold as is, directly out of estates unless otherwise noted. I do not take responsibility for uninsured items. I will contact you by sending you an "eBay Checkout Invoice." Thanks for looking and HAVE FUN!!

You might say something about your payment options and about your policies as a seller. Save this document as a text file that you can paste into the Sell Your Item form whenever you create an auction listing.

## Do Your Product Research

It's always a good idea to treat selling on eBay as a pleasant, creative experience. You are creating miniature sales campaigns, one for each item. Telling the story of how you found an item and describing how it looks can be fun (at least, it is for someone like me, who enjoys writing and describing things anyway).

At the very least, take a few minutes to look around at search engines, at web sites related to the merchandise you want to sell, and at auction descriptions of similar items, as well as some price guides in the library, to find out exactly what you've got and what you might be able to get for it. You just might discover that you have a real treasure once you do a little research with a respected resource such as the popular Kovels price guide. The Kovels web site (**http://www.kovels .com**), shown in Figure 3-8, contains more than 340,000 items in its database.

## Pick the Right Auction Category

Once you prepare to sell items on eBay, you take a different perspective to categories than you do as a buyer. Your goal is to find the category (or categories) in which people who are interested in bidding on or buying what you've put online are most likely to search. You want to find those ideal buyers who not only like what you're offering but who've simply got to have it. These are people who probably know more than you do about your item, who collect similar items as well. Do a search for items that seem similar to yours and note in what categories they appear.

You aren't limited to listing your item in one category. In fact, if you think your item could fit well in two different categories, you'll find it cost-effective to list in two places. You pay two listing fees as well as any upgrade fees such as Bold or Gallery. (You can't list real estate in two categories, however.)

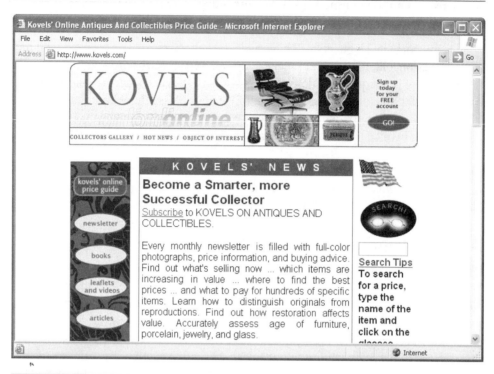

FIGURE 3-8    Do some research so you can create compelling descriptions of your merchandise.

If you are at all apprehensive about putting something up for sale, do a test. You'll notice that one of the categories in the list is simply called Test. This enables you to put your sale online without having other users bid on it. It's a place where you can make sure your images appear the way you want and that you have used the Sell Your Item form correctly.

*You'll find a complete list of categories, plus the number of items currently up for sale in each one, at **http://listings.ebay.com/**.*

## Create Your Descriptions

Once you've gathered details about what you're selling and taken some photos (see Chapter 8), you can begin filling out the Sell Your Item form and actually creating auction listings. You only need to click the Sell button in the toolbar that appears on nearly all eBay pages to access the form. (You may be prompted to sign in with your User ID or password first, unless you're already logged in.) The form itself contains tips on how to provide good information. But just for good measure, here are a few more tips.

## Your Auction Title

The title of your auction listing is critical. When shoppers conduct searches on eBay and come up with lists of auction items, they'll come up with your title as well as others. Make your title no longer than five or six words. Be sure to pack as much relevant information in those five or six words as possible. The more information you can put in, the better your chances of selling. Don't waste valuable space using tired terms such as L@@K or !!Wow!!, which are overused and have no effect on buyers. Try to put in dates and brand names if you can: rather than saying "Beautiful Pottery Vase," say "Pink Roseville Pottery Vase 1934."

Also, remember to be honest: if something is a reproduction rather than an antique, don't bury that fact at the bottom of a description. Lack of forthrightness will turn buyers off; they may never look at your auctions again.

## Item Subtitle

A relatively new feature—one that can get extra attention for your sale and help it stand out from others on a page of search results or category listings—is a subtitle. A subtitle is a heading that appears beneath the main title of your description and that provides additional information about the item. Subtitles cost an extra 50 cents, but they give potential buyers additional information that might persuade them to click on an item and find out more about it. Adding a subtitle helps make the item stand out from others by highlighting key selling points.

 *The text included in the subtitle will not be searchable when buyers conduct a "basic search" of titles. However, the subtitle will be searchable if the buyer searches in "titles & descriptions."*

## Category

As I mentioned, eBay presents you with hundreds of different categories. Look for items that are similar to yours. Also, try to imagine the kind of person who might want what you have to sell, and try to envision how it might be used. This might suggest the category where such an individual might look for it.

## Picture URL

URL stands for Uniform Resource Locator, a standard address that enables anyone with a web browser to locate an object or web site that's on the Internet. You get the URL for your image from the site where you have stored your image.

This can be eBay's own Picture Services or another photo hosting service. See Chapter 8 for more details about adding images.

## Minimum Bid

A minimum bid is a starting point. It's like the auctioneer in an auction saying, "Bidding will start at one dollar. Do I hear two dollars?" It's generally a good idea to pick a small minimum bid, such as $1, for the starting point. Many sellers set as the minimum bid an amount that represents the very least they're willing to accept for an item. It's not at all uncommon to see items that start at $100. Choosing a high starting bid helps sellers avoid the reserve price fees mentioned earlier. But you'll often notice that such auctions attract no bidders at all. Sellers are likely to turn some bidders off by setting a sizeable minimum bid. Let the bidders feel they're getting a bargain when they start out; you set a reserve price to ensure that an item won't sell for less than a certain price.

## The Description

On the Internet, to a degree that's different than with other media, detailed information about an item helps to sell it. The more you can say about a sales item, the more likely you'll generate interest in it. The most experienced sellers try to create descriptions that engage the viewer's imagination—that induce viewers to imagine what that pair of gloves might feel like, or how they might use that automatic juicer, or how that old Ford Thunderbird would look in their driveway.

 *Don't be reluctant to point out any flaws in what you are selling. You don't want bidders to discover flaws when they unpack the item. You want them to know exactly what they're getting—and to know that you're an honest seller whom they can trust.*

## Use Listing Designer

A feature that appeared as I was writing this book, Listing Designer, is accessed from page 3 of the Sell Your Item form. It's an interactive utility that lets you pick a theme and a layout for your item (see Figure 3-9). There is an extra charge of 10 cents for each item for which you use Listing Designer. However, many sellers will find this a bargain, because Listing Designer has one big plus: it shields sellers from having to know Hypertext Markup Language (HTML). HTML is the set of markup instructions that lets you create web pages.

**FIGURE 3-9**    eBay's Listing Designer lets you format auction listings by adding themes.

*You can find out more about Listing Designer at **http://pages.ebay.com/sell/designer%2Dlandingpage/**.*

## Monitor Your Sales Activity

Once your sale goes online, you'll probably want to keep an eye on it just to see when the bids come in, and to check out exactly who bids on it. This is when all your hard work pays off. You'll need to check your e-mail or your My eBay page in order to field questions from interested customers. If you receive several questions that are in a similar vein, you may want to edit your description to include the answer as additional information. Even while your sale is ongoing, you can change the item's category or add additional text or photos any time you want.

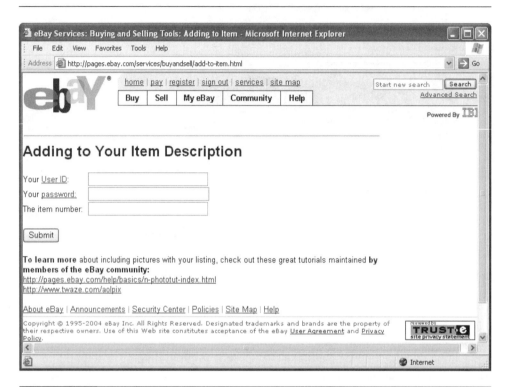

FIGURE 3-10    You can add photos after your sale has started.

If you want to add photos or details to your auction descriptions (for instance, in response to questions posed by your bidders), use the Adding to Your Item Description page, shown in Figure 3-10 (**http://pages.ebay.com/services/buyandsell/add-to-item .html**), and fill out the form.

## Close the Deal

When the sale ends, in some ways a new round of work begins. In this case the work ends with a couple of big rewards, however: you receive payment, and you get positive feedback for your good customer service. In order to get those rewards, you need to begin by contacting your high bidder or buyer promptly—within the hour after the sale ends, if you can, but at least within a day.

eBay sends the buyer a stock e-mail notification that the sale has ended and that they are the high bidder. You should follow quickly with your own e-mail, in which you congratulate the winner and provide them with directions for paying you. You'll need to find out how the buyer wants the item shipped (if you offer two different shipping options, such as Priority Mail and Parcel Post). You'll also need to know where the buyer lives so that you can calculate the exact shipping cost—virtually all shippers charge based on weight, the size of the package, and the distance to be shipped.

If you have a seller's account with PayPal, it's even easier to seal the deal. You can send an invoice automatically by PayPal. The invoice can be customized by adding information such as your address, your eBay Store name, or other information. Shipping costs are calculated based on the information you set up with your listing. If you use calculated shipping rates, the rates are determined automatically based on your buyer's shipping address.

After payment comes in, before you celebrate, send out an e-mail acknowledgement to your bidder to let them know that you have received the check, money order, PayPal account transfer, or credit card payment. More importantly, you need to tell the customer when you're shipping out the merchandise—and then ship it out as quickly as you can. It's a good business practice to send out your merchandise the same day that the payment arrives, or the day the payment clears your bank. (Most banks will let you know if a check is cleared either by phone or in person.) Try not to wait more than a week until after the payment clears, or you risk having your buyer leave you negative feedback.

## Resell an Item

Hopefully, most of the items you put up for sale on eBay will actually go to a bidder or Buy It Now buyer. However, you'll probably put up some items that don't attract any bids at all. That doesn't mean you need to give up selling the item. You attract more (or higher) bids at a later date by providing better images, changing the title or description, or going with no reserve—removing the reserve price altogether. You can relist your item if the following applies:

- You didn't receive any bids on a regular auction and you did not hold a Dutch auction.

- Fewer than 30 days have passed since the closing date of the first auction.

- You didn't receive any bids that met your reserve price if you originally held a reserve price auction.

eBay does charge you a second insertion fee if you relist your item, but if your item sells the second time you put it up for sale, eBay will refund you the second insertion fee. (But if it doesn't sell the second time, you still need to pay the second insertion fee.)

## Make a Second Chance Offer

If you don't want to relist an item right away, you have an alternative: a Second Chance Offer. You can make such an offer when the winning bidder fails to pay, no one met your reserve price (if you specified a reserve), and you have an identical item for sale but you didn't choose to list the multiple items in the Multiple Item auction format. You can make a Second Chance Offer up to 60 days after the end of the sale. The offer can be made to any of the underbidders—not just the second-highest bidder. The offer that's sent is a Buy It Now price equal to the winning bid of the original high bidder.

To make a Second Chance Offer, go to the auction description page for your closed sale and click Bid History. Then click the User ID for the bidder you want to approach. Alternately, you can go to My eBay, click Sold under All Selling, click the Action menu, and click Send a Second Chance Offer. Second Chance Offers are offered by eBay's Buyer Protection Program, so underbidders might be happy to have the opportunity to get the item they wanted. For sellers, eBay doesn't charge a second insertion fee to make the offer.

NOTE    *You can't make a Second Chance Offer after a Multiple Item auction ends.*

## Paying eBay's Seller Fees

How does eBay make the money that made it one of the most successful e-commerce operations in recent years? It makes money from people like you who sell items on its site and who are charged fees. You need to pay a fee before the sale, called an *insertion fee*, just to list an item for auction. You must pay the insertion fee whether or not the transaction is successfully completed. The insertion fees in place as this was written are listed in Table 3-1.

| Opening Value/Reserve Price/Buy It Now/Minimum Bid | Insertion Fee |
|---|---|
| $0.01–$9.99 | $0.30 |
| $10–$24.99 | $0.55 |
| $25–$49.99 | $1.10 |
| $50 and up | $2.20 |

**TABLE 3-1**    eBay Insertion Fees

| Sale Price | How to Calculate Final Value Fee | Example Final Bid | Final Value Fee |
|---|---|---|---|
| $25 or less | Multiply sale price by .0525. Round the number to the nearest penny. | $23 | $23 × .0525 = $1.2075<br>Final value fee = $1.21 |
| $25.01 to $1000 | Take $25 of the sale price and multiply it by .0525. Multiply the sale price minus $25 by .0275. Add the two calculations. | $800 | $25 × .0525 = $1.31<br>$775 × .0275 = $21.31<br>$1.31 + $21.31 = $22.62 |
| $1000.01 and higher | Follow steps for a sale of 25.01 to $1000 but take the amount over $1000, multiply it by .015, and add that to remaining amounts. | $2500 | $25 × .0525 = $1.31<br>$2475 × .0275 = $68.06<br>$1500 × .015 = $22.50<br>$1.31 + $68.06 + $22.50 = $91.87 |

**TABLE 3-2**    Calculating Final Value Fees

After your item sells, you pay eBay a commission called a *final value fee*. The final value fee isn't a flat fee, but rather is calculated based on the final sale price or the type of item sold. Table 3-2 indicates how to calculate final value fees.

How do you actually pay eBay's insertion fees and final value fees? You have three options:

- Use eBay Direct Pay, in which eBay automatically deducts fees from your bank account each month if fees apply.

- Have eBay charge a credit card.

- Have eBay invoice you, and pay by check or money order.

If you sell only occasionally, it makes sense to pay invoices as they arrive.

 *eBay's current selling fees are listed at **http://pages.ebay.com/help/sell/fees.html**.*

# Keep Your Store Well Stocked

When you're selling on eBay only occasionally, you can sell whenever you find something at a yard sale or secondhand shop. If you want to create an eBay business that provides you with a steady source of part-time or full-time income, acquiring inventory that you can then sell on eBay becomes a major part of your operation. You'll do better if you can do strategic buying: buying good items at an economical price that you can then auction off at a profit on eBay. How, exactly, do you do strategic buying? The following sections provide some suggestions.

## Know Your Field

There's a store not far from me that specializes in clothing and memorabilia from the 1960s and '70s. The owners, a husband and wife, head over to the local resale shop every morning when the store opens at 11 A.M. They are among the first customers, and they find plenty of inventory over there. I know because I often go there myself. The difference is that, while I'm not looking for anything in particular, they know exactly what they want and what their customers are looking for: cool "retro" clothing and bric-a-brac that they can wear to parties or add to their collection of nostalgia.

You can learn a lesson from these folks, and from the many eBay sellers, whether they deal in collectibles or general consumer merchandise. Pick the type of item you want and study it well. When you go out shopping, know what you're looking for. The better you know what's valuable, the better your chances of uncovering a hidden treasure.

## Know Where the Good Stuff Is

When you're shopping for inventory, it pays to look where you are likely to find quality merchandise. The Chicago area where I live is known as a particularly good source of secondhand collectibles and wholesale merchandise. But some areas within the area, such as the suburbs north of Chicago where many high-income people live, yield better results than others. Look for garage and estate sales in such neighborhoods in your own area. Often, local newspapers that cover individual towns or groups of towns contain more listings for estate sales and garage sales than major metropolitan newspapers. The area I mentioned is covered by a chain of newspapers that lets you browse through its garage and estate sale listings online, as soon as they come out. You can scour the classifieds (see Figure 3-11) and plan your Friday or Saturday shopping activities accordingly.

Once you have an area in mind and a general sense of what you're looking for, you can shop through the typical venues where collectibles and valuables are sometimes found:

- Garage sales
- Secondhand stores
- Auction sales

**FIGURE 3-11**    Look through classified ads online to plan shopping trips.

In addition, you might find inventory by buying at local retail or wholesale outlets that are having closeouts or that sell merchandise at reduced prices:

- Discount club stores
- Dollar stores
- Going-out-of-business sales

No matter where you shop, another tried-and-true tip for finding bargains is "buy off-season." You'll find the best prices on Christmas decorations in July, not in November. Similarly, winter is a great time to stock up on sports equipment, croquet sets, badminton sets, barbecue equipment, and other outdoor merchandise.

Many of the people who scour eBay looking for auction bargains aren't collectors at all, but dealers in antiques and collectibles who are looking for inventory. While it's unlikely (though not impossible) that you'll find someone buying a bargain item on eBay that he or she will later attempt to sell for a profit on eBay, you do find people who buy on eBay to stock their antique stores or to provide stock they can sell at a flea market or a show.

## Where to Find It

- **Trading Assistants Directory**
  **http://contact.ebay.com/ws/eBayISAPI.dll?TradingAssistant&page=main**
  Search page where you can locate eBay sellers who will sell on consignment.

- **Sell Your Item form**
  Click the **Sell** button in the eBay toolbar (no URL)
  A form you fill out to get your auction sales online.

- **Selling Formats page**
  **http://pages.ebay.com/help/sell/formats.html**
  List of current eBay sales formats, with fees if applicable.

- **All Categories page**
  **http://listings.ebay.com/**
  Long list of eBay sales categories and subcategories, plus the number of items currently being offered in each one.

- **Adding to Your Item Description page**
  **http://pages.ebay.com/services/buyandsell/add-to-item.html**
  Form you can fill out to add more details to the description of an item you currently have up for sale.

- **Selling Fees page**
  **http://pages.ebay.com/help/sell/fees.html**
  List of eBay's current fees for listing and selling items.

# Part II

# Improve Your Competitive Edge

# Chapter 4

# Tips and Strategies for Online Sellers

# How to…

- Set a goal of turning your hobby into a long-term business

- Build knowledge in an area of interest to develop potential customers' confidence in you

- Create honest and complete product descriptions that encourage bids

- Solve problems and get inside tips by networking with other sellers

- Attract bids by selling without a reserve

- Handle problems in a businesslike manner

- Shop for bargain merchandise you can resell at a profit

- Gain attention for your auctions by linking and advertising

You've learned the basics of buying and selling on eBay. You've even put that old cuckoo clock that used to clutter your attic or that old Mickey Mantle baseball card up for sale. You've started to accumulate some positive feedback. You're thinking to yourself: "I can do this. This auction sales thing is actually fun!" In other words, you've been bitten by the eBay selling bug—the eBug, you might call it.

Now it's time to take your auction sales to the next level. You need to turn what's currently an occasional thrill into a regular routine. Once you come up with a system for selling on eBay, you can begin to boost your sales income and develop a system for marketing many different things. The mechanics of buying and selling individual items on eBay are relatively simple. Turning your eBay sales hobby into an eBay business is more involved. In many ways, it's a matter of changing your perspective—of making the eBug work for you.

In this chapter, you'll get some insider tips—tips I've gleaned from my own experience, and from talking to eBay sellers, about how to change your sales perspective. You'll learn that you need to keep the long-term establishment of a successful business as your ultimate goal, which might mean writing off quick profits or occasional problems. You'll learn how to work with the eBay community rather than operating as a "lone wolf." You'll learn how to boost sales by selling with no reserve and by letting the market determine the final price. Finally, you'll learn how to find inventory, implement some marketing tricks, and drum up free advertising so that you stand out from the competition.

# Work for the Long Term

People are what make eBay run well, but when it comes to making sales, you need to look to the numbers. Certain numbers may induce shoppers to place bids: the number of items you have for sale at one time, which tells bidders that you're likely to be a professional and not a "fly by night" seller; the reserve price and opening bid prices you set; and your feedback rating, which is the most important number because it directly affects your sales. eBay sellers who are able to earn a steady supplemental income or who sell on eBay full-time tend to be the ones with high feedback ratings. And those who are able to maintain positive feedback and a steady income over several months attain the highly coveted status of Power Sellers; if you can become one, your chances of attracting bids are even better.

## Go Retail

What, exactly, constitutes a high feedback rating these days? As eBay grows and becomes more established, the amount of feedback displayed by the Power Sellers goes up as well. According to the sellers I interviewed for this book, there's a threshold in the 1000 to 1200 feedback range. If you have feedback in the range of 200 to 1000, you are certainly doing well, and customers are certain to know that you are an experienced eBay merchant. But when you reach 1000, something happens.

"I call it 'going retail,'" comments Bob Kopczynski, a longtime eBay seller who is profiled later in this chapter. At the time this chapter was written, his feedback rating was nearly 7500. "When my feedback rating went over 1000, I started getting more bids and higher prices for what I was selling. It was like people recognized me as a retail businessperson, not just a part-time seller. It's the difference between someone who has been running a brick-and-mortar store for ten years and someone who just opens a store down the street. The store that's been established is going to get the most business."

I'm not suggesting that you need to shoot for a feedback rating of 1000 specifically before you can be a successful eBay businessperson. Not at all; however, this is a book about running an eBay *business*, not just selling on eBay once or twice a year. A feedback rating of 100 or 200 is great in its own way. If, however, you want to make all or part of your regular income through selling on eBay, you need to set your sights higher—the higher your sights, the wider your perspective will be, and the better your chances of success.

# Build That Feedback

How do you build your feedback ratings? It takes time, effort, commitment—and a systematic way of completing transactions and shipping out merchandise. Do everything you can to build your feedback by putting up lots of no-reserve sales and shipping them out promptly to your high bidders or buyers.

The eBay feedback ratings at the time I was writing this book are described at **http://pages.ebay.com/help/feedback/reputation-stars.html**, and are shown here:

As you can see, a rating of 1000 isn't that high, relatively speaking. Suppose you sell 20 items a week—you'll get to 1000 in a year, provided that all of your responses are positive and all of your customers actually leave feedback, which doesn't always happen. Come up with a plan for how you can get to 20 sales per week: you need to obtain merchandise by following a system. Many sellers obtain wholesale merchandise; they buy directly from manufacturers, liquidators, or wholesalers. The alternative is to scour flea markets, auctions, or garage sales; consider enlisting the help of friends and relatives who can assist you with packing and shipping.

Create a weekly schedule and stick to it. Such a schedule would call for you to get your sales online, say, on Monday morning; end your sales on the following Monday; get a new batch of sales online late Monday; respond to bidders Monday night or Tuesday morning; ship out on Thursdays and

Fridays; and so on. (In reality, you might prefer to ship on a daily basis to get merchandise to your customers more quickly.) Also remember to remind your customers, after they have received the goods, to leave a feedback comment. Otherwise, they might well forget to do so. In fact, you should expect to have to remind your buyers to leave feedback: a large proportion don't bother to do so on their own.

## Go By the Numbers

You need to establish a long-term "numbers goal" for your eBay sales. The moment you declare to yourself, "I'm going to have an 800 feedback rating by the end of the year," or "I want to be making $1000 a month on eBay by the end of the year," your perspective changes. Individual sales become less important than your cumulative sales figures. Turning sales around quickly and keeping your customers satisfied becomes the top priority, even if you only make a dollar or two of profit on a sale. Rather than focusing on this or that individual sale, you start thinking of coming up with a system, and building volume, with the ultimate goal of building profits.

## Develop a Good Reputation

Most consumers have needs that are pretty straightforward. They want a reason to buy from you as opposed to all of those other sellers that populate eBay's auction listings. They want to feel they can trust you; they want to get what they pay for quickly. Above all, they are usually looking for a bargain (a few might also be looking for a specific model number or a particularly good selection of items). To some extent, you can't control whether they get a bargain or not. You put an item up for no reserve, or you set a modest reserve, and the market takes care of the rest.

You can, however, control how much trust your bidders may place in you. In many professions, service providers go to school to add some significant letters to their names, such as Ph.D., M.D., J.D., or C.P.A. You can do the same in auction sales. Bob Kopczynski, who's profiled later in this chapter, went to school and became a licensed auctioneer. You don't have to do that, yourself, but you can demonstrate that you know something about what you're selling. You can

■  Operate a web site or online store devoted to your area of interest. Bob Kopczynski, who goes by the User ID maxwellstreetmarket on eBay, also has a Maxwell Street Market web site (**http://www.maxwellstreetmarket .com**), shown next.

- Moderate a discussion group (popularly called a newsgroup) devoted to what you buy or sell. You can create your own group on eBay Groups (**http://groups.ebay.com/index.jspa**), as described in Chapter 11. It's relatively easy to set up a newsgroup in the Alt category in Usenet (the Internet's system of newsgroups), whereas groups in other areas of Usenet are difficult to establish and maintain. The web page editor Microsoft FrontPage helps you set up a discussion group on your own web site.

- Answer questions on eBay's message boards.

- Answer questions in Internet newsgroups about your area of interest.

If you have written any essays or books about the type of merchandise you typically sell, so much the better. Even if you don't do any of the foregoing, you can still create an About Me web page that tells visitors something about you and what you do, and your commitment to customer service as well. Here, too, Bob Kopczynski provides a good example. His About Me page (see Figure 4-1) is as extensive as they come; it includes a history of his eBay business, a link to his web site, a list of employees, a phone number, and terms of sales.

## Prove You Are a Professional

You can boost your sales if you are able to show people that you are professional in your manners and your behavior. Being professional doesn't mean you need to sell on eBay full-time, or that you need to run your own online business. Rather, it has to do with how you communicate—how quickly and completely you respond to questions from bidders, how well you deal with problems, and how promptly and carefully you pack and ship what you sell.

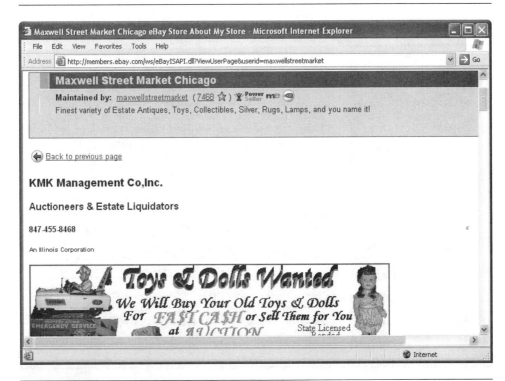

FIGURE 4-1    An About Me page can be used to build your credibility as an eBay businessperson.

## Be Honest, Be Thorough

The more information you provide about your auction item, the better your chances of getting bids.

Honesty is certainly the best policy when it comes to selling online in any venue, including eBay. At the very least, it lets buyers know about any defects or flaws your merchandise has before they even bid, so they won't be surprised when they actually receive what they've purchased. Accuracy shows your customers that you are making every effort to be honest and up-front with them. Some sellers go into a lengthy bit of detail about defects in their sales items, especially for items that they know are desirable in and of themselves. Once again, you can look to Bob Kopczynski's listings. The description shown in Figure 4-2 is honest about defects, but plays up the parts of the package that are in exceptionally good condition, too.

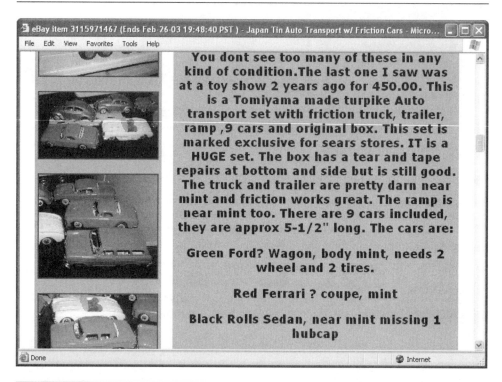

**FIGURE 4-2** Don't be reluctant to describe any defects so that purchasers won't be surprised.

*Keep in mind that many of the individuals who buy your eBay items are professionals themselves: they might be business buyers, retailers, or experienced collectors. Often, they're experts who buy your type of merchandise often or who hope to resell your wares in their own stores. You can't fool people who are in business or "in the trade," nor should you try to.*

## Attract Bids with Information

The more information you include with your auction descriptions, the more likely you are to make a sale. That doesn't mean you have to spend acres of valuable computer screen real estate getting around to the point. You need to state, in the very first sentence, what it is you are selling and what qualities make this item stand out from the crowd. Be sure to mention, if applicable, that it is a one-of-a-kind piece, in perfect condition, or in a rare color. Try to get a one- or two-word mention of the item's most desirable quality in the auction title, if you can.

Auction bidders are in a hurry. They might stop in at your sale only for a short period of time before moving on to your competitors' wares. Suppose you're trying to sell something that might not seem desirable at first, like a pair of used sneakers. How, you ask, could you make sneakers seem attractive? Here are a few suggestions:

■ *Lead with a hook.* Hook your bidders' attention with some quick statements that show why your item is exceptional, such as "Rare 1967 Chuck Taylor Converse All-Stars, Size 12."

■ *Be a historian.* Describe your item's provenance—which, in auction-speak, means the history or origin of an item. Tell where you got the object, how old it is, who used it, and so on: "These classic high-top Chuck Taylors, in the hard-to-find red color, had only one owner—the seller's cousin. They show very little wear and even come in the original box."

■ *Don't overlook the downside.* Once you've gotten everyone interested by gushing about the item's good points, be sure to avoid surprises or misunderstandings by describing any problems: "Although thoroughly dry cleaned, a subtle basketball odor remains. Some wear on right heel; laces have been replaced."

■ *Finish on a high note.* Don't end on a problem note; provide a closing sentence that reminds people why they should be buying this wonderful item. You might even provide a note about payment options or shipping costs, or restrictions (you don't take personal checks, or you won't ship internationally, for instance).

You'll find some of these approaches in the brief sales description shown next. Notice how the description starts with a good mention, then describes some flaws ("brassing" means the gold overlay has worn off), then finishes on a positive note.

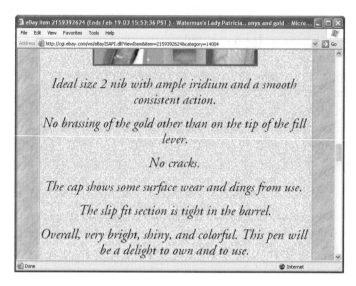

The same sort of salesmanship applies to general consumer goods. Suppose you want to sell a like-new pair of snow skis. You should mention the flaws and end on a high note the same way:

Men's Rossignol Downhill Skis

Up for auction is a high-quality pair of Rossignol Equipe skis.

Skis have been used and have a few scratches.

Skis are in the desirable 195-cm length and have the Vibration Absorbing System that Rossignol is famous for!

The important thing, whether you are selling new, like new, consumer, or collectible items, is to be up front about any flaws or condition issues, but emphasize the desirable points that apply to your merchandise.

 *Attempts to get attention for auction listings by using the @@@ or !!!! keys multiple times are overused. I don't think they grab anyone's "eye space" because so many others use them. And no one will search for an auction using @@@ or !!! as keywords. Let your description speak for itself.*

## Build Your Volume

What does it mean to build a lot of sales? How do people build the volume that enables them to earn a steady income on eBay? You can find indications on eBay itself. Just find a seller you regard highly who has a high feedback rating, and look

## Throw in a Lagniappe

When I was in New Orleans, I went to some garage sales in the French Quarter and became acquainted with the wonderful local custom of the *lagniappe* (pronounced "lan-yap")—something extra that's thrown in along with the sale. Nothing builds goodwill with your customers like an extra touch you can add to your item(s) when you ship them out.

At least one of the sellers I interviewed, Don Colclough (who appears in Chapter 5), occasionally adds an extra item if one is available. "Sometimes we will sell a set of six glasses," he told me. "You can only sell them in groups of six. Even if you have seven of them, people just won't bid if you try to sell them all. If we sell a set of six, we will throw the seventh one in for free." If you sell dozens or even hundreds of items at a time, it might be impractical to throw in an extra gift with every sale. But if you can, consider doing so. You'll go a long way toward keeping your customers happy—not to mention getting some glowing feedback.

up the sales that have been conducted recently by that seller. For instance, to look up the completed sales by Bob Kopczynski, do the following:

1. Go to the eBay Basic Search page (**http://search.ebay.com/ws/search/ AdvSearch?sofindtype=13**).

2. Click **Items By Seller**.

3. Enter the seller's User ID (maxwellstreetmarket) in the Enter Seller's User ID box.

4. Click the Include Completed Listings check box and then choose from the drop-down list next to it the option that describes the number of auction sales you want to retrieve: Last Day, Last 2 Days, Last Week, Last 2 Weeks, or Last 30 Days.

5. Click the Search button. You are presented with a list of auctions recently completed by this busy seller, as shown next.

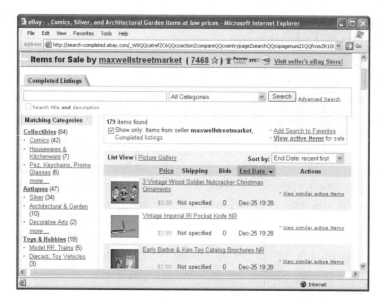

6. For instance, when I checked Bob's sales, I found that he frequently completed anywhere from 20 to more than 50 sales per day. Most of these sales attracted bids; a few ended without attracting any bids, as indicated in Table 4-1.

## Get Help from Family and Friends

Very few of the eBay auction sellers that I know do all the work themselves. Often, two people divide up the tasks: the buying, the carrying, the photography, the publishing, the shipping, and the bookkeeping.

The moment you start to think in terms of selling hundreds or even thousands of items each year, you've got to think about getting assistance. Look first to your family: enlist your kids, your brothers and sisters, anyone who has time and is willing to help. Many sellers employ neighbors or college students who are home for summer vacation. Don't try to do it all yourself. Distributing your workload will enable you to ship purchased items out quickly and remain courteous with your customers.

| Date | Sales Completed That Day | Sales with No Bids |
|------|--------------------------|--------------------|
| 12/22/04 | 12 | 3 |
| 12/21/04 | 43 | 21 |
| 12/20/04 | 2 | 0 |
| 12/19/04 | 22 | 5 |
| 12/18/04 | 6 | 3 |

**TABLE 4-1**    Bob Kopczynski's Sales Record

## Use an Auction Manager

When you're trying to sell multiple items at once, it can be invaluable to enlist the help of an auction service: a business that assumes the responsibilities of managing your auctions for you. A program like AuctionHelper (**http://www.auctionhelper .com**) sends notices and invoices to high bidders and maintains records of your sales so that you can add up totals at tax time. You can find out more about using such services in Chapter 6.

 *The eBay Services: Seller Central Resources page (**http://pages.ebay.com/ sellercentral/resources.html**) contains the link Seller Tools, which leads to services that can help manage your sales, such as Selling Manager. UK Auction Help (**http://www.ukauctionhelp.co.uk/sitemap.php**) provides a web page full of tips for auction buyers and sellers alike, including suggestions on how to manage auctions and build volume.*

# Schedule Your Sales

Experienced sellers know that if they have an especially desirable item, it's likely to sell no matter when the auction ends. However, they also know that auctions that end when the majority of bidders are available are more likely to gain the highest prices. When you create a sales description, whether you use eBay's own Sell Your Item form or another auction tool like Turbo Lister, you have the ability to schedule when you want the sale to end. Here are some suggestions for when to schedule your auctions:

- Sales that end on weekends are more likely to get bids because many more bidders have the time to shop.

- Sales that end on Sundays—particularly, Sunday nights—tend to get more attention at the end of the sale if what you are selling is targeted at a general audience, not a specific type of individual.

- Some sellers start sales on Thursdays and schedule them to last for ten days: that way, they'll end on a Sunday, and bidders will have two weekends to shop and place bids.

- If you are selling to a business audience (for instance, in the Business & Industrial category), be sure to end your sale during the conventional 9 A.M. to 5 P.M. hours during the week, when most business users will be online.

- If you are selling baby clothes or other items that appeal to stay-at-home moms or dads, be sure to end the sale during the week, when your audience will be at home and the kids are hopefully napping.

## eBay Bestsellers
# Recapturing the Spirit of the Chicago Entrepreneur

Chicago, which is my home town, has a rich history as a center for manufacturing and commerce. Those of us who love to buy and sell treasures of all sorts benefit from that history. We fondly remember a place called the Maxwell Street Market, a huge open-air flea market where you could find virtually anything for sale, and which lives on in a smaller (not to mention cleaner) form every Sunday morning.

As a child, Bob Kopczynski used to visit Maxwell Street with his father. Today, he and his wife, Katy, keep a little bit of Chicago history alive with his eBay business, which goes by the User ID of maxwellstreetmarket. Bob, who works full-time as a construction manager and runs his eBay business in his off-hours, first became interested in eBay when he was looking for computer equipment and souvenirs related to the rock group Van Halen. Then, on a whim, he decided to sell a pair of tickets he had to the original Woodstock music festival held in 1969. "I said to myself, I'll put 'em for sale up there on eBay, and we'll just see what happens." Bob was immediately clued in to the promise of selling on eBay when the tickets, which normally would have sold for $30 or $40, fetched a whopping $150 online. He convinced Katy to start selling on eBay, put up $250 to get started, and the rest is history.

"When Don [Don Colclough, who is profiled in Chapter 5] and I started out, we were ridiculed," laughs Bob. "People thought we were crazy." Today, maxwellstreetmarket is very much an eBay business. Katy left her job as a schoolteacher three years ago. Now she works full-time at the business, handling bookkeeping and answering questions from buyers. Bob handles purchasing by scouring estate sales and flea markets and does photography. A neighbor, Nancy Armstrong, makes sure the sales go online. At least five Kopczynski family members help with crating, packing, cleaning, and the many other duties that are required to sell anywhere from 20 to 50 items per day on eBay.

The business has expanded along with the Kopczynskis' suburban Chicago home. First, Bob and Katy worked out of their basement. They made enough on eBay to build a pool and a deck. Then they had to build a garage just so they could store their eBay inventory (Bob calls it "the garage that eBay built"). Now, they rent warehouse space in several locations.

The Kopczynskis put a premium on credibility and customer service. They have built a steady income by putting customers first. "I have a goal to make people feel comfortable," Bob explains. "Eighty percent of people are still not comfortable with buying online, even though they love auctions. The big hurdle is, why would I send someone I don't know money? I set a goal to become a licensed state auctioneer; I have to take classes and pay $500 every year to keep my license. I sometimes do auction off high-end items like cars or boats on site, but 99 percent of my auction business is on eBay. I mention that I am a licensed auctioneer in my eBay listings, and I think that tells people they can rely on me. It's well worth the expense because it tells people I am well established."

The family's eBay operation is a business in many other ways. For one thing, it's part of KMK Management Co, Inc. Auctioneers and Estate Liquidators, a company of which Bob is President and CEO. Bob says one reason he decided to incorporate was liability; the corporation has limited liability if a customer decides to sue for some reason (see Chapter 18 for more on incorporating). "I pay a CPA to do our taxes, we do collect sales tax charged to Illinois residents. Besides that, we pay our employees' payroll taxes, too."

The businesslike emphasis pays off in customer relations. Bob and Katy don't run into too many deadbeat bidders. They estimate that only 2 to 3 percent of their customers fail to follow through with sales. More than 99 percent of the feedback they receive is positive. When they do run into problems with customers, they don't make a big deal about it. "We're not going to chase you if you don't pay us. We'll send you couple of reminders, and then we tell eBay to pursue you. Then, we just wait 10 or 14 days and relist it."

The matter-of-fact approach to the business applies to sales, too. Bob has a policy of selling everything on a no-reserve basis—even highly desirable items for which he may have paid $100 or more. "I'll put up a Tiffany lamp at a starting bid of $1.99 with no reserve. Almost all of our auctions are conducted that way. The no-reserve policy quickly eliminates competition that sets an opening bid. My items tend to sell higher than ones with a reserve. Personally, when I'm shopping on eBay, I pass up any auction that has a reserve. You don't always get your cost back. You don't always make money on everything you sell. But it's a matter of volume and turnover—that's what counts. If you pay $200 for something and if it sits on a shelf for six or eight months, it's no good. Volume is the magic—better to get the money quickly and build up lots of sales."

Bob doesn't specialize in one particular type of item, although he personally collects vintage toys, radios, and musical instruments. He says he is "continually surprised by how much some things will bring. We even sell empty toy boxes—people who know what they are and who collect toys will pay for them."

Bob estimates, in fact, that a high percentage of his own customers are antique and collectible dealers who buy on eBay and resell items in their own brick-and-mortar stores. "I would like to have 90 percent collectors and dealers as my customers because they will pay a higher price, and they're not likely to turn out to be deadbeats."

In order to turn around 600 to 700 items a month, Bob uses an auction management service called AuctionHelper (**http://www.auctionhelper.com**). "The auction management service does the shipping. They send an e-mail to the high bidder that says, 'Click here to get your invoice and your seller's address.' The buyer has a printable invoice with all of the details printed right on it."

Bob's number one tip to would-be eBay businesspeople? "Don't get hung up on making a ton of money on every single item," he says. "You have to let it go. Not everybody makes money on every investment. If you had a brick-and-mortar store, you'd run into losses too—something might get damaged, or your employees might take stuff. It's the same on eBay. You just have to let it go and move on to other sales."

Beware of any holidays like Memorial Day and Labor Day that might take place near the end of your sale: people who are traveling won't be able to bid, and you might not get as much attention for what you're selling. But on the other hand, holidays might be a good day to end a sale; devoted sellers with time on their hands might be shopping for bargains and hoping for less competition than usual on a holiday. If you are going to be in town, try to end your sale on a holiday if possible.

CAUTION    *Be sure not to end the sale at a time when eBay is down for maintenance. Frequently, eBay goes offline between 1 A.M. and 3 A.M. PST on alternate Friday mornings. (You'll find announcements of such system shutdowns at **http://www2.ebay.com/aw/announce.shtml**.) If you attempt to end your sale then (this is more likely for international users than those in the United States), you should get a notice from eBay advising you to pick another time. Instead, you should be aware of the occasional maintenance and avoid Friday morning endings.*

# Be Community-Minded

Why has eBay continued to grow and prosper while other online auction sites (not to mention a host of e-commerce retailers) have gone to that great Recycle Bin in the sky? It's not the ups and downs of the economy, which are always present. It's because of the strength of eBay's user community, and eBay's ability to build that community.

The eBay community isn't simply a place where you can submit feedback and view feedback of other users. It's the best way (along with books like this) to get inside information from other experienced sellers—tips you'd need weeks or months to learn otherwise. You can also find out who your competition is by talking to other users and searching the message boards—and devise ways to stand out from the crowd—by being a group participant.

## Share Information

You learn a lot about selling on eBay by talking to the entrepreneurs who already sell there. That might sound obvious, but working at a computer tends to be a solitary operation. (I'm speaking from experience.) After a few successful sales, you think you can do it all yourself, without anyone else's help.

You are likely to be cured of this notion the moment you scan the current messages on the eBay Café or on the product-specific message boards. You'll regularly find such seller-specific questions as "What do I do about this deadbeat bidder who…," "My bidder showed up and refused to pay for the ___ when he saw it," or "How do you handle 40 or 50 sales per week?"

In many ways, the best source of information about specific problems or situations you encounter on eBay is by consulting your fellow eBay users. You might also encounter eBay sellers while waiting in line at an estate sale, or in a crowd at an auction.

*Consider creating a name tag that says "eBay User" instead of your "real" name. Wear it to sales events such as auctions or flea markets. You just might meet some fellow eBayers with whom you can share tips and experiences.*

## Know Your Competition

Why is it that when a gas station appears on one corner of a busy intersection, another one appears right across the street? They don't necessarily take business away from each other. In fact, they tend to draw people to the same area, and both outlets get more business than they otherwise would.

It's the same with auctions. Sure, you'll see others selling the same things you are in the same categories. Be happy for the crowded activity. If you were all alone in a category, would you get as many bids? Probably not.

How many times have you seen pages full of the same kinds of sales items, often with nearly identical descriptions? It can be instructive to look at how the sales are presented and to analyze which get the most bids—or any bids at all. For example, many vintage gloves go up for auction without getting any bids. Which of the listings in Figure 4-3 would you investigate if you were a buyer?

This isn't a scientific analysis by any means, but the gloves up for auction like those shown in Figure 4-3 seem to get bids if:

- A good thumbnail Gallery photo appears next to them.

- Descriptive keywords are included in the auction title, such as "women's vintage leather gloves."

- You make full use of the 55 characters available to you in the title and add terms like "Sexy" or "Red Hot."

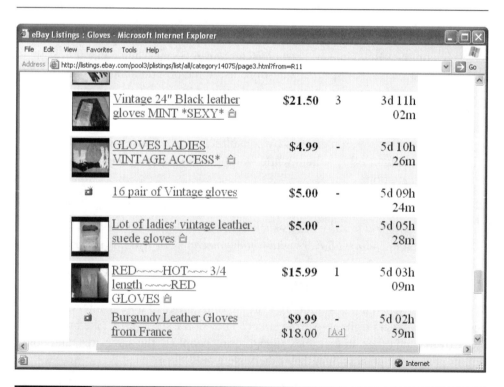

**FIGURE 4-3**    Study other sales and try to learn sellers' "trade secrets."

Another benefit of visiting the message boards on a daily basis is that you get to know other sellers. It also pays to scout around the other sales in your area of interest after your sales go online, not only to make sure your sales are presented correctly and all of your images appear clearly, but to know if anyone is selling the same things you sell—and doing a better job of it than you are.

# Relax, It's Only a Sale

When you begin to think in terms of making hundreds of sales rather than individual sales, and of selling on eBay for years to come rather than on a week-to-week basis, you don't take each sale so seriously. You'll benefit in the long run by not getting bogged down in problems and details, as described in the sections that follow.

## Shed Your Reserve (Price, That Is)

You probably know from your own eBay buying that "no reserve" (usually designated NR) auctions get more attention than those with a reserve. Does that mean you should sell everything without a reserve? Different sellers take different approaches. When you're starting out, your impulse is to protect your investment with a reserve price on all your sales. Many sellers go no reserve for all sales except their most expensive. When my mother asked me to sell some of her antiques at auction, she insisted that I put a reserve price on them so she could be sure to recover what she had originally paid for the goodies.

However, when you're dealing in volume and turning your eBay sales activities into a business, it only makes sense to go with no reserve as often as possible— that is, for all sales except those items for which you originally paid a substantial amount.

Time and time again, auction sellers have told me that they get the most interest and the highest prices for items that they offered for little or no reserve. I once wrote about a woman who found a Depression glass coaster at the bottom of an auction box full of other items. In other words, it cost her almost nothing. She put a reserve of $10 on it and an initial bid of $1. She ended up with more than 20 bids and the glass sold for more than $200.

## Control When Your Auction Ends

Suppose that valuable porcelain lamp you just put up for sale takes a tumble off the shelf and shatters in bits on the concrete floor of your basement. Or suppose that your aunt, who gave you that painting to sell, suddenly decides to donate it to an art museum instead. In such cases you can cancel your sale. eBay provides

## Set a Starting Bid, Not a Reserve Price

For eBay's first several years, sellers weren't charged for specifying a reserve price. Then eBay changed this policy and began charging a reserve price fee. The fee is only $1 for a reserve of $49.99 or less. But for high-priced items like autos or boats, a high reserve can cost you a reserve fee of hundreds of dollars. You lose twice: the reserve price discourages bids, and you have to pay extra for it, too.

More and more sellers are abandoning reserve prices. Instead, they set a reasonable starting bid to ensure that they'll recoup their purchase price and make a profit. For instance, if you find an old radio at an estate sale for $10 and you want to make a minimum profit of $10 or $15, set a starting bid of $25 on the radio and no reserve price. Better yet, set a starting bid of $24.99: that way, you'll have to pay an insertion fee of only 60 cents rather than $1.20.

you with a form that allows you to explain the reason for ending the sale early. The form lets you choose between canceling all bids or selling to the high bidder and canceling all other bids. After you fill out the form, an e-mail message is automatically sent to any bidders explaining that the sale was ended early.

On the other hand, you can also extend the end of your auction—if your item has not yet received any bids. Sometimes, when sellers conduct a three-day auction and their item does not receive any bids during those three days, they extend the auction by one day. The moment a bid comes in, either the auction must end at the currently advertised time or you must cancel it. Some sellers will list for three days, and if they get no bidders will extend the duration one increment at a time until they reach ten days (this is done via the **Item Revision** link on the description page).

## Control Your Emotions

You're bound to run into problems during your time as an eBay businessperson. Someone will e-mail you and leave negative feedback because they're not happy with what they purchased. Or the item you sent will get lost or delayed in transit and your customer will (understandably) be displeased. What's the best way to respond to such problems? Longtime sellers know it's best not to get emotionally

4

involved. Even though you are involved in a person-to-person sale, this is a business transaction. If a buyer has failed to follow through with payment, use eBay's Unpaid Item Process. Keep cordial at all times when you're communicating with someone who is unhappy. If someone has violated eBay's user policies or is harassing you, file a complaint by filling out the the Contact Us form (**http:// pages.ebay.com/help/contact_inline/index.html**) and let eBay pursue those bidders who turn out to be deadbeats. Other than that, try to resolve disputes yourself in an effort to avoid negative feedback. Consider coming up with a stock response when you run into an unhappy camper. That way, bidders will get some money back, you keep your positive feedback, and you dodge a dispute. The following is a sample stock response:

> My Auction Company, Inc., puts customer service first and is committed to keeping you happy. If you are unhappy with what you have purchased, we will refund your purchase, less a shipping fee.

You can't give a refund to everyone who complains, of course—nor should you. I'm only saying that, sometimes, it's better to resolve disputes yourself and write off a moderate financial loss.

NOTE    *You can cancel someone's bid if you notice that they have received substantial amounts of negative feedback and have not followed through with other sales. If a bidder contacts you and asks to be taken out of the sale, or if he or she is located internationally and your description clearly states you will not ship internationally, you can also cancel a bid. When you do so, you should e-mail the individual to explain the reason for the cancellation. The bid cancellation form is located at **http://pages.ebay .com/services/buyandsell/seller-cancel-bid.html**.*

## Resell Items When You Need To

If something doesn't attract any bids, or you had to cancel your auction early, or the bidders didn't meet your reserve price, simply wait a week or so and then relist the item. You can relist by returning to the completed auction results page and clicking the link **Relist item**. You get a small bonus the first time you relist: If your item sells the second time around, eBay refunds your insertion fee. If it doesn't sell the second time, however, you have to pay the insertion fee.

*Don't simply repeat the original auction description when you relist something. Look around at other eBay sales descriptions of similar items and try to identify some adjectives that might generate excitement, or add some phrases that suggest how people might be able to use what you are trying to sell. Be sure to pay attention to sales that ended with high winning bids rather than sales that attracted lots of visits on an auction counter but failed to attract a buyer. Consider going no reserve, or lowering the opening bid price when you relist.*

# Buy Strategically So You Can Resell

Once you've got the routine of selling down to a regular system, the big challenge isn't actually making sales on eBay. Rather, the challenge is finding merchandise you can resell. Many of the sellers I spoke to spend a considerable amount of time each week gathering merchandise at garage sales, flea markets, estate sales, auctions—wherever they can find it. As anyone who has tried to make a purchase at a conducted sale (a sale of someone's possessions that is conducted by a professional dealer rather than the homeowner) knows, such sales are likely to have great bargains, but the competition for them is fierce. Often, you have to stand in line for hours before the sale opens just so you can have a chance at finding treasures. If a sale opens at 9 A.M., for instance, you might have to get in line at 6 A.M., 5 A.M....who knows?

There aren't many tricks to obtaining inventory you can resell online. It requires a lot of commitment and "sweat equity." Here are a few suggestions I've discovered in my own bargain hunting over the years and from talking to eBay sellers:

- *Don't do it alone.* If you work as a team, you can find more merchandise than you could alone. You'll also have help hauling away what you buy. Some sellers hire college students to go to sales before the sun is up and wait in line for them; they show up at a more reasonable hour, ready for the hunt.

- *Buy off-season.* Often, resale shops have plenty of winter clothes in spring and fall, and summer clothes in winter, for the simple reason that most people don't need them at that time. Buy off-season and store your inventory so you can sell it at a time when most of your customers will actually want it.

- *Become a dealer yourself.* If you become a licensed auction seller or if you are an antique dealer, put out advertisements suggesting that people who are retiring or moving out hire you to conduct their house sale. You never know—you might be able to find a bargain or two for yourself.

■ *Try dollar stores.* One of the most interesting trends in the world of bargain hunting is the proliferation of stores that sell all, or most, of their wares for a dollar or less. All too often, the shelves are full of junk, but once in a while, you can find pop culture memorabilia or good books that you can pick up for a bargain.

■ *Join a warehouse club.* Costco, Sam's Club, and other warehouse stores deal in volume; sometimes you can find DVDs or computer games at two-for-one promotions at these brick-and-mortar discount warehouses.

■ *Look for bargains online.* Some discount outlets hold their own online auctions, and you should definitely check them out. The Sam's Club auction page shown in Figure 4-4 (**http://auctions.samsclub.com**) is a great place to find bargains you can resell on eBay. You can shop online at Costco (**http://www.costco.com**) and at other bargain outlets like the 99¢ Only Stores web site (**http://www.99only.com**).

**FIGURE 4-4**   Shop online at warehouse clubs to find bargains you can resell.

- *Find a wholesaler.* One of the best sources of general consumer inventory is a wholesale supplier who will sell you a large quantity of items at a bargain price; you can then mark up the items and sell them through your store or at auction.

- *Visit trade shows and gift shows.* Where do you find a wholesaler or a line of consumer goods you can sell? Trade shows and gift shows that are held in your area give you an excellent chance to check out different lines of merchandise and talk with distributors who might become suppliers.

TIP *Know when the garbage pickup days are for your own neighborhood and any neighborhoods where people who are well-off live. Be sure you start scouring alleys either the night before or early in the morning on garbage day. I, personally, am not above "garbage picking" or "dumpster diving" in order to uncover bargains that others are discarding. For a primer on this popular activity, read the online diary "Dumpster diving: an Introduction" at http://www.kuro5hin.org/story/2003/1/29/215523/088.*

## Drum Up Some Free Advertising

Everyone who sells online needs to drum up business by doing some form of marketing and advertising. By choosing to sell on eBay, you take a big step toward getting lots of attention for you and your merchandise. You can go even further by marketing your eBay sales.

For example, you might include links to your eBay Store, your About Me page, or to a specific sale in a posting you leave in an Internet newsgroup that's related to what you are selling. That's how I first found out eBay even existed, back in the mid-1990s. I subscribed to a newsgroup for individuals who collect and sell antique fountain pens. In the course of reading postings, I frequently saw listings by dealers that contained links to pens they had up for auction on eBay. I clicked one of the links, and instantly became an eBay junkie.

## Link to Your Web Site, and Vice Versa

If you have a web site, whether it catalogs the members of your family or the items your business has for sale, use it to promote your eBay auction listings. Selling on eBay is a remarkably personal activity. Buyers remember sellers, and if they have a good experience with you, they are quite likely to check you and your sales out once in a while to see what you have to offer. Many eBay sellers include links to their eBay auctions on their web sites, in the posters they put up in supermarkets, and in their e-mail signature files, and also include in their auction listings or eBay Stores/About Me pages links back to their web sites. (But be sure you don't link from a page that's stored on eBay, such as an eBay Store or About Me page, to a site that advertises products for sale outside of eBay.)

*If you have a business card, include it with the items you ship out, and make sure it includes your web site URL as well as your e-mail address and other contact information.*

## Where to Find It

■ **eBay Services: Tools for buying and selling**
**http://pages.ebay.com/services/index.html**
Links to services that can help you manage multiple sales listings, and to pages where you can revise your item description, cancel an auction, cancel a bid, or relist an item.

■ **UK Auction Help**
**http://www.ukauctionhelp.co.uk/sitemap.php**
A web page full of tips for auction buyers and sellers alike.

■ **eBay System Announcements board**
**http://www2.ebay.com/aw/announce.shtml**
Announcements of times when eBay will be offline for maintenance.

# Chapter 5

## Spruce Up Your Auction Presentation

## How to…

■ Create a sales template so you can produce multiple auctions quickly

■ Attract bids with engaging, imaginative descriptions

■ Research your merchandise so you can describe it accurately

■ Check your spelling so you don't look unprofessional

■ Take time with your presentation to build bidders' interest

■ Format auction listings with HTML to grab more attention

■ Add a counter to your auction listing

■ Choose design templates with eBay Seller's Assistant

Unlike personal or family web pages, auction listing pages aren't primarily about you. They don't need to be graphically eye-catching. You don't need to impress anyone with your design sense or even your sense of coolness. Your primary goal is to induce people to bid—as often as possible—and to eventually make a sale. Yet, a few well-chosen words and some good images can make the difference between zero bids and a number of 1 or more in the Bids column.

Auction listings are a little like personal ads in their presentation. You want to stand out from a crowd through good photos, quick descriptions, and a few choice words. You need to attract shoppers by giving them enough information in your auction title to engage their imaginations, by giving them just enough information to get them to discover a little more about what's being advertised. Then, you want to give them all the information you can in your description.

You can also use your auction presentations to create an identity for your eBay business. Just as you try to build credibility through a good feedback rating and professional handling of sales, you can brand your business on eBay through your choice of colors, the name of your business, and a consistent presentation. This chapter examines ways to give your eBay auction pages some "razzamatazz" while streamlining the process of getting your auctions online.

# Create a Sales Template

When you use eBay's Sell Your Item form, you are essentially filling in the blanks. You're putting standard information into a standard format so you can get the basic information online.

There's nothing wrong with using the Sell Your Item form to create an auction listing, but a successful eBay business is built on volume and efficiency. Suppose you get to the point where—like many of the sellers I profile in this book—you need to get 20, 30, or even more items online every day. If that's the case, you need to come up with a system—or rather, a *template.*

A template is commonly used to prepare a publication that appears periodically, such as a newspaper or a magazine. It's a preformatted set of items that appears the same from issue to issue. A template saves time, and it lets readers know what to expect. After a while, they use the standard elements in the template to process information more quickly.

Many eBay sellers create an auction template in the form of a Hypertext Markup Language (HTML) web page. The template contains the name of their business (if they have one), their shipping and payment policies, and any other phrases that apply to all of their auctions. I've taken the liberty of altering one of the auction listings of eBay seller "mrmodern", who is profiled in this chapter, and showing it in Figure 5-1.

The beauty of a template is that your auction listing is actually half-complete before you even start. After you've taken your photos (see Chapter 8) and researched your item (see "Do Your Research" later in this chapter), simply paste the material that is unique to each sales item (the name, the description, and the links to images) into the template. You simply upload the pages, reopen their original template file, and paste in the descriptions that apply to the next sales item.

> **NOTE** *eBay has a service called Seller's Assistant that streamlines the process of creating templates. See "Use eBay Seller's Assistant" later in this chapter for more information.*

In Figure 5-1, I've drawn a big X to mark the spot where the unique description and photos should appear in the template. mrmodern's template has another formatting trick: it's been formatted as an HTML table, a container that allows web page contents to be arranged in the form of rows and columns. In this case, the table serves two functions. First, it keeps the auction listing at a fixed width so that it's easier to read; it takes up a single column in the middle of the page. Second, the table divides the information into two rows. The first row sets the Mr Modern logo apart from the text beneath it. Tables are useful ways to organize the contents of web pages and gain some control over how they turn out.

> **TIP** *One of the first tutorials on HTML is still one of the best. A Beginner's Guide to HTML (**http://archive.ncsa.uiuc.edu/General/Internet/WWW/HTMLPrimerAll.html**) includes information on tables and how to use them to design web pages.*

First row of table      Second row of table        Company logo

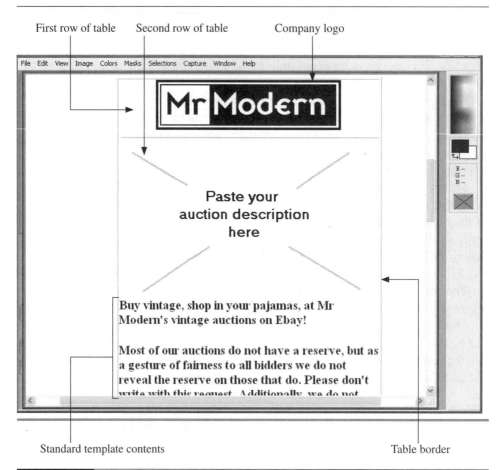

Standard template contents                                Table border

**FIGURE 5-1**    A template lets you create auctions quickly in "cookie cutter" fashion.

## Consider Getting Some Design Help

The Web was made for do-it-yourselfers. You can publish your own photos, text, and web pages in no time. But just because you *can* do something on your own doesn't mean that it's a good idea. When you're just starting out with an eBay business, it pays to spend a little time (and possibly a little money) designing a template.

Since you're going to be online for years, and you're probably going to sell hundreds or perhaps even thousands of items, a few hundred dollars paid to a designer at the beginning will pay off in the long run. The single best investment you can make is the few hundred dollars it will probably cost to create a logo for your business. You can use it not only on your auction pages but on business cards and stationery you have made.

It's worth securing the services of a professional designer for this purpose. The designer can create a consistent look for your business, which includes the look of your auction listings. The look of your logo and your use of color and other design elements can complement what you sell and tell people that you are committed not only to customer service, but to obtaining quality items. The Silk Road Trading Concern's auction listings, one of which is shown in Figure 5-2, are a perfect example.

The business name shown in Figure 5-2 is a textual logo, which is accompanied by a graphic logo that complements the business name. It's difficult to create such a textual logo without the help of sophisticated graphics software like Adobe Photoshop (**http://www.adobe.com**). It might be difficult to tell from Figure 5-2, but each Silk Road auction listing has a background image that seems to "float" behind the text and images. Such background images are another feature of HTML that you can use in your eBay auction listings. This particular auction listing uses an HTML table that the page designer has configured to have invisible borders for the layout, but it does include prayer flags and other designs that complement what's being sold. A consistent, professional appearance like this has a direct bearing on how many bids you get.

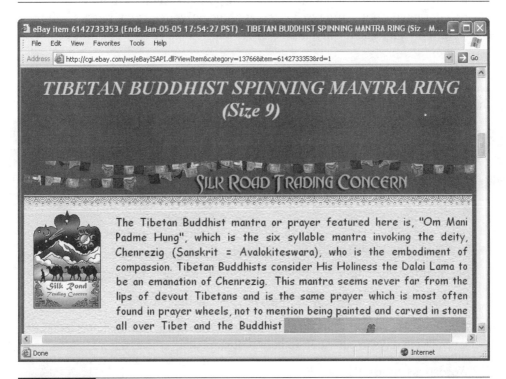

**FIGURE 5-2**   Your use of color and type can complement what you sell at auction.

*Many of the graphic designers who advertise their services on the eBay-affiliated site eLance Online (**http://www.elanceonline.com**) specialize in creating logos and developing graphic designs for businesses.*

## Pick Standard Items

Once you have come up with a "look and feel" for your auction listings—one that might include a background, colors, graphics, and a logo—you need to add the parts of the template that you want to be the same from listing to listing. In the world of publishing, this sort of content is called *boilerplate*. This text might include:

- The name of your business

- Your shipping options

- Your payment options

- Your contact information

- Any additional statements about your policies, such as money-back guarantees, not selling to bidders with negative feedback ratings, not shipping internationally, and so on

Create your listing and save it as a text document so you can simply copy and paste the contents from auction to auction. Your auction boilerplate might look like the following:

Higher Grounds

Coffee Collectibles for Cost-Conscious Collectors

[REPLACE WITH AUCTION DESCRIPTION]

Buyer to pay $7.50 for shipping via USPS Priority Mail.

Ground shipping also available on request.

International customers will pay extra air mail shipping charges.

Payment must be received within ten days of auction closing.

Money orders and personal checks accepted, but please note that checks take seven to ten days to clear before item will ship.

We also accept BidPay and PayPal.

Illinois residents will be responsible for an additional 8.75% sales tax.

Feel free to e-mail us with questions. We will be happy to provide additional information as needed.

If you decide to use HTML formatting to present your auction, include the necessary HTML commands (which are called *tags*) right in the body of the listing. (See "Dress Up Your Descriptions" later in this chapter.) You can also use a program that gives you the option of editing the visible contents of web pages as well as the HTML code, such as Macromedia Dreamweaver or Microsoft FrontPage.

## Add the Description

Once you have a template and boilerplate, you need to come up with what you might call the "silverplate" part of your listing: the actual description that applies to the merchandise itself. You do this by opening the Sell Your Item form, as follows:

1. From just about any part of the eBay site, click the **Sell** button in the navigation bar at the top of the page.

2. Sign in as a seller and create a seller account if you need to (see Chapter 3).

3. When the Sell Your Item form appears, fill it out. Paste your template into the Description box in the form (shown in Figure 5-3). If you want to paste some HTML you have already prepared, click the Enter Your Own HTML tab; otherwise, use the Standard tab. Then add the details specific to the item you are listing, and put your sale online. You can use some tricks when you're creating the contents of your description to make your sale more attractive to bidders, such as imaginative words and good images, as described in the sections that follow.

TIP    *Auction listings don't have to be completely unique. Although it's not a good idea to completely copy someone else's description and paste it into your own listing, you can use good descriptions as a "starting point" for creating your own if you are tired or in a hurry. Auction descriptions, like other web publications, are protected by copyright, as described in Chapter 18. However, the truth is that plenty of eBay sellers "reuse" one another's descriptions as a shortcut even though it's technically a violation of copyrigtht. You can at least shop around other descriptions to get inspirations and tips for their own listings.*

# Create Reusable Inserts

Each of the standard items identified in this section is a bit of text that you reuse from listing to listing. For the most part, the information contained in each segment remains the same. You don't have to retype and then insert such reusable elements from sale to sale. Instead, you can have eBay store the text for you in the form of "inserts."

Inserts are standard bits of description information that sellers need to use in all of their sales. The idea of a user-created template became so popular and widespread that eBay decided to make the Sell Your Item form more functional by enabling you to save such inserts online.

Suppose you have a statement like "Illinois residents must pay 8.75 percent sales tax" that you want to insert in each of your sales listings. You can turn this into a reusable insert by accessing the Item Description box on the Sell Your Item form and doing the following:

1. Click the Inserts menu near the top of the Item Description box and choose Create Insert.

2. Type your insert and save it with a name that will help you recognize it more easily on subsequent visits, such as "sales tax note."

3. When you return to the form later on, prepare your description, then choose your insert from the list of saved inserts that appears in the Inserts menu.

Is it better to use the Inserts feature or to save your own inserts on your hard disk and cut and paste them from your own template file? If you want control over your own material and don't trust eBay to save your information, use your own file. At any rate, it's a good idea to save a copy of the inserts you create with the Inserts feature, in case you need them—for instance, if you use auction listing software such as that provided by Andale, SpareDollar, or Marketworks and that may or may not have its own Inserts feature.

**FIGURE 5-3**    Paste your auction template into the Description box in the Sell Your Item form.

# Fine-Tune Your Descriptions

A picture may be worth a thousand words, and good images are perhaps the most important elements you can use to grab someone's attention and get them to click that all-important Place Bid button. The way you describe your sales item is important, too. You can take a lesson here from the big, traditional auction houses such as Sotheby's. Staff people at such institutions often painstakingly research the history of what they're selling and present detailed descriptions both in their sales catalogs and in their live auctions. An example is shown in Figure 5-4.

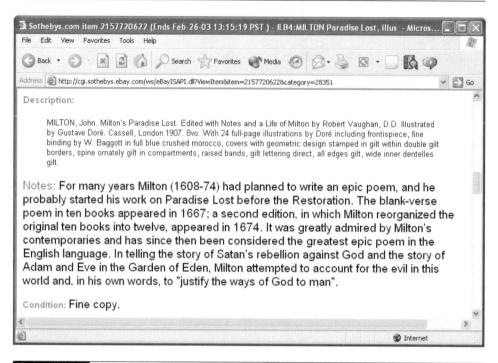

**FIGURE 5-4** Some history and background on what you're selling can attract bidders' interest.

The example in Figure 5-4 shows that descriptions don't have to be long to be effective. Rather, a little background about what you're selling and a few telling details count for a lot. Some ways to spice up your own descriptions are presented in the sections that follow. All it takes is some research, some imagination, and some attention to detail.

## Craft a Compelling Title

The title of an auction description is what initially attracts potential buyers to investigate your sale. It's vitally important to take the time to craft a title that is attention-getting and that makes full use of the 55 characters available to you. An estimated 90 percent of buyers look for products by doing a keyword search. Therefore, it's essential that your listing titles contain searchable keywords.

Without searchable keywords, potential buyers may never find your merchandise. For example, consider the following title:

```
Beautiful Ikea Wooden Desk
```

This title is adequate, but it won't attract as many potential buyers to your listing as one that contains specific keywords, like this:

```
NEW Ikea Grontaal Computer Desk MGT-786 Beech Hutch 78" H
```

You don't have to "re-invent the wheel" when it comes to titles. Do your research on eBay and look at completed listings with the highest final sales price. What keywords did those sellers use in their title? Evaluating what keywords are pulling in buyers to other listings is a good starting point in determining what keywords you should use in your listing title. Always take advantage of the 55 characters allowed in the title—the more searchable keywords that you use, the more traffic you will get to your listing, which will translate directly into more sales.

## Do Your Research

Occasionally, you'll run into bidders who know far more about what you're selling than you do. The merchandise practically sells itself because this is what your customers have been looking for. You might be able to sell an empty toy box for hundreds of dollars if it's the box to a toy that someone needs to fill out his or her collection.

Most often, though, your sales need a little "push" from you in the form of information. Information sells on eBay. Before you put something up for sale, do some research online and find out everything you can about what you're selling. Tell people when the item was made, whether or not it is considered rare, and anything else you can uncover.

The eBay seller mrmodern, who is profiled later in this chapter, told me he keeps one computer screen open to prepare his auction listings, and another open to the search service Google (**http://www.google.com**). While he creates his auction listings, he can find out details about what he's selling and pass them along, as indicated earlier in Figure 5-4.

## Generate Excitement

If you can generate some excitement among shoppers and get them to visualize how they might use or enjoy something, you're more likely to gain bids. This isn't just something that's well known on eBay. Some online catalog sites (in particular,

Lands End, **http://www.landsend.com**) let customers virtually "try on" clothing on a 3-D model they make of their own bodies. Put yourself in your bidders' shoes (or gloves, as you'll see in a moment), and encourage them to want to wear, use, or simply enjoy what you have to sell.

Your goal as an auction seller is to capture, in a few sentences, what makes your object unique or interesting. I admit, you can't do this for every single item you try to sell. (How exciting can you make a matched set of drawer handles, for instance?) But if you can pick a few choice descriptive words for some of your sales, you'll do better overall. Suppose you turn up a set of old bathroom lights that you want to sell. How can you make them seem interesting? Here's how mrmodern described them:

> Here is a great pair of Streamline Art Deco chrome and milk glass bathroom wall sconces. The lights are made to mount on either side of a mirror and each have an outlet on the bottom. The chrome backplates are 15" long by 2.5" wide. The milk glass tubes are 12" long by 2" in diameter. Both tubes have the chrome ring cap. Good chrome throughout...One tube is perfect, but the other has a chip and crack 1" up from the end. Turned to the back, the chip cannot be seen. Best bet is to have them shortened 1" so the chip and crack will be gone. The shades will still extend ¼" beyond the top edge of the backplate...Either way they are a great pair of original 1930s wall lights.

The thing I notice about this description is that some effort has been put into suggesting how the lights can be used, what can be done with them, and where they might go in a house. It's not just a straight description of what the items are and how big they are. When I last looked, the lights had attracted a bid of $101.

## Use Your Dictionary

Buyers on eBay are often wary of sellers to begin with. Unless they know you and trust you, they might doubt that they can rely on you to follow through with your end of the deal. Anything you can do to make yourself look more professional helps your chances of getting more bids. For that reason, you should spell check your auction descriptions before you put your sale online. It's easy enough to do so: eBay itself provides a spell check form on the Sell Your Item form and on Turbo Lister, as well as forms you fill out when you revise or relist an item. You could even have a web browser window open to the dictionary web site, Dictionary.com (shown in

Figure 5-5), so that you can look up troublesome words while you are doing the work. Check your spelling.

There's another, more obvious reason for proofreading your description before your sale goes online: you don't want to get facts and figures wrong. You don't want to turn $250 into $2500 or 25$0, for instance. A spell-checker won't catch a numerical error like this, so there's no substitute for proofreading your description carefully before it goes online. Read it out loud so you can slow down and catch errors more easily.

Finally, if you misspell a word in your title, it can cause bidders to not find your sale in their keyword searches, which can cost you money.

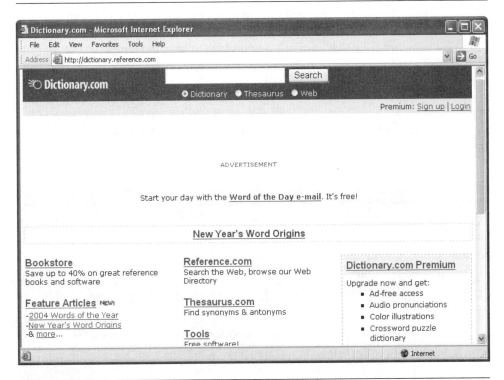

**FIGURE 5-5**    If you don't check your spelling, you might appear unprofessional or careless.

# Dress Up Your Descriptions

Part of calling attention to your auction items is the ability to direct the eyes of busy, hurried shoppers toward the most important parts of your sales descriptions. That's where web page formatting with HTML comes in. HTML is the set of commands that's used to format all of the pages you enjoy not only on eBay but on the rest of the World Wide Web. By using HTML to format headings in bold or large type, you can call attention to the name of an item or an especially important feature, such as its age or condition.

You've got a couple of options for formatting your descriptions with HTML. The first option is the simplest: let the Sell Your Item form do the work for you.

To format your auction descriptions in HTML, you simply click the Enter Your Own HTML tab and then type the HTML commands in the Description box in the same Sell Your Item form you use to create your auction. If you use a template to present lots of auction listings, you can format the template using HTML and paste it into the same form. In that case, it's a good idea to save the template as a text file with the HTML commands included, so you can copy the contents and paste them into the form. An example is shown in Figure 5-6.

 *eBay's Help page that describes how to use HTML in auction listings is located at **http://pages.ebay.com/help/sell/html_tips.html**.*

```
eBayISAPI[1] - Notepad
File  Edit  Format  View  Help
<center>

<table border="0" cellspacing="0" width="100%">
<tr>
<td align="center" width="100%">
<font face="Arial, Verdana, Helvetica, sans-serif" size="2" color="#000000"><a
href="http://listings.ebay.com/aw/plistings/list/category91/index.html?from=R1
1">Pottery &amp; Glass:Pottery &amp; China:Pottery:Shawnee</a></font>
</td>
</tr>
</table>
</center><img src="http://pics.ebay.com/aw/pics/dot_clear.gif" width="1"
vspace="2" border="0" alt="Spacer"><center>
<table border="0" cellpadding="0" cellspacing="0" width="100%">
<tr>
<td width="13%" rowspan="30" valign="top" align="left"><a href="#DESC"><img
```

**FIGURE 5-6**    Save your template in text format so you can copy and paste the contents.

## HTML: The One-Minute Version

This isn't a book about HTML and formatting web pages—there are many other books on those subjects, not to mention web sites, tutorials, classes, and videotapes—so I'm not going to go into great detail on what HTML is or how to format a web page using HTML. I will, however, give you a one-minute overview so you know what I'm talking about in this chapter.

> TIP *If you want to learn more about HTML, consult one of these McGraw-Hill/Osborne books:* HTML QuickSteps, *by Martin Matthews (2004);* How to Do Everything with HTML & XHTML, *by James H. Pence (2003); and* HTML & XHTML: The Complete Reference, *by Thomas Powell (2003).*

Hypertext Markup Language (HTML) is the set of commands (called tags) that is used to *mark up* text or images so they can be displayed on the Web. Using HTML commands, a web browser will be able to display the following text as bold:

```
<B>This text is bold.</B>
```

The following text will be displayed in Heading 1 format:

```
<h1>This is a web page heading</H1>
```

You can make a reference to a JPEG image using the following HTML so that a web browser can display it on your page:

```
<IMG SRC="image.jpg">
```

How, exactly, do you create all of these nifty HTML tags? You have two options: the hard way and the easy way. The hard way is to enter all the tags by typing them manually into a text document. This requires you to actually learn HTML or, at least, to copy the tags from a book or web site and apply them to your own purposes.

The easy way is to use a software program called a *web page editor.* Such a program shields you from having to create or actually see the HTML commands you create. Rather, you click buttons, choose menu options, and make use of other graphically friendly elements to format web pages. Two of the best programs are Dreamweaver by Macromedia Inc. (**http://www.macromedia .com**) and Microsoft FrontPage (**http://www.microsoft.com/frontpage**).

The problem with using such web page editors, from the standpoint of eBay, is that you eventually have to look at the raw HTML commands when you paste them into the Sell Your Item form. Even if you create and format a nice template using one of these programs, you'll need to choose a command such as View Source or View Code to view the HTML commands, copy them, and paste them into the auction description form.

Of course, you don't have to use HTML at all to format your auction listings. But if you want to create a business identity and stand out from the crowd, a little formatting is all you need.

*An easy-to-use and reliable program called Virtual Auction Ad Pro by Virtual Notions (**http://www.auctionadpro.com**) will also help you generate formatted auction ads without having to learn HTML.*

# Make Your Auction Count with a Counter

One of the most popular features that eBay sellers add to their auction listings (besides images and text, that is) is a *counter*—a utility that records the number of visits that are made to that auction listing. A counter sits on an auction page (or on any web page) and records the number of times the page has been viewed. It doesn't tell you who is viewing those pages, or whether each of the visits recorded is by a unique viewer. A counter that has recorded ten visits, for example, might have recorded visits by only two individuals—one who has seen the page nine times and one who has visited just once.

A counter that indicates to visitors that a page has been visited a high number of times indicates to people that there must be a lot of interest in the item, and suggests that they may want to place a bid themselves. On the other hand, if a counter has a low number, it may turn people away. If it has a high number of visits but just a handful of bids, it might even suggest that there's something wrong with the item being sold—or that bidders are biding their time and preparing to bid at the very last minute.

To my mind, counters only have limited value, whether on an auction page or a regular web page. They're more of a curiosity than a marketing tool. A type of counter that makes sense to me is a *private counter* or *hidden counter*—one that doesn't actually appear on the auction listing itself but is only visible to the auction seller. A hidden counter gives you the advantage of knowing how many people have looked at your description, but it prevents buyers from being turned off by a low number. The easiest way to get either a private counter or a visible one is to choose an option from the counter options at the bottom of page 3 of the eBay Sell Your Item form. Other private counters are available from a number of different sources, and many of them are free. Of course, you have to sign up with the auction service that provides the counter to you, and that includes the one provided by ManageAuctions.com and shown in Figure 5-7.

You can go a step further and install a counter provided by Andale.com that provides detailed information about when your auctions were viewed each day and how many times they were viewed. During the process of registering to use the counters, you can uncheck a box so that you won't receive unsolicited e-mail from Andale.com. You can go to **http://www.andale.com/corp/products/track.jsp** to find out more about installing Andale.com's counters.

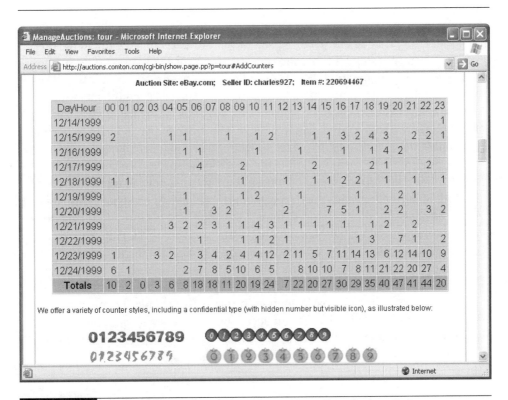

**FIGURE 5-7**   A private counter is visible only to the seller who installs it.

# eBay Bestsellers
## Making a Good Presentation

Image is important to Don Colclough (User ID: mrmodern). For one thing, he wants his eBay customers to know that he will solve any problems that arise, and that customer service is paramount to him. Don Colclough and Lisa Polito have gained control of their own lives through selling on eBay. They are able to set their own schedules thanks to their eBay business. They don't have to commute to work, they can work on their own schedule, and they run their own work space too.

"I've been selling on eBay since April 1999," says Don. "By September of that year we had sold our antique store and moved out. It was beating a dead horse." He and Lisa found a 3000 square foot space in a former bank building in Oak Park, just west of Chicago, where they set up their full-time eBay business. That's where Don and Lisa store their inventory and work on their three-computer network, keeping a regular business routine even though they don't work the conventional 9 A.M. to 5 P.M. schedule.

"We go to work five days a week, from 1 P.M. to 9 P.M.," says Don. "Every day at 4 P.M. UPS picks up our outgoing shipments. At 4:30 I make a run to the post office. We mostly ship UPS because it's simpler for the delivery guy to simply load everything on the truck. But for smaller items we use the post office. Then we take a break to eat. After that we work from 5:30 to 9 P.M., putting items up for sale on eBay. Lisa writes all the sales tickets and does all the paperwork. During the summer, we have young men in college who work for us and help us writing auctions."

Besides the time spent in their office-warehouse space, Don and Lisa, like many other eBay sellers, spend countless hours waiting outside estate sales and hauling home the treasures they've gathered. You have to run your eBay sales like a business in order to build volume, Don advises. "We closed 200 auctions this past month, and we have six months' worth of inventory stored up at any one time. There are times when we buy an item at 7 o'clock in the morning and we have it up for sale that same afternoon."

The businesslike system applies to the way sales are presented online. Initially, Don developed a basic auction format with a standard choice of type fonts and colors, and standard statements about payment and shipping. Once the basic format was set, he and his coworkers only had to type up individual descriptions and paste them into the preset format.

With regard to different styles of writing descriptions, Don states, "When I write an auction, I am pretty cut and dried about it. I just give the size, general condition, rarity. If it is something special, I will do a little research to find out some of the history of the item, and tell bidders something about it. When Lisa writes an auction, she caters to the Martha Stewart crowd, and she tends to be a bit more decorative and descriptive; she tells people how they might use a particular item. It stimulates the brain of the reader, and encourages them to make a bid."

Photos are an essential part of any auction description. "I'm not averse to putting 15 pictures online," he says. "We keep photos pretty small, perhaps a quarter of the size of the average computer screen. We try to include a range of photos, showing every aspect of an item, from every angle."

Don and Lisa specialize in twentieth-century furnishings, household items, and collectibles of all sorts. He fondly recalls the unusual items he has sold—such as a prosthetic leg for $430—but the most unusual sale was that of a complete pharmacy. The pharmacy, which was located at Elston and California Avenues in Chicago, was sold by Don and his friend Bob Kopczynski (who is profiled in Chapter 4). "We sold the complete pharmacy for $13,000 to a man who was opening a gift store in Jackson Hole, Wyoming," says Don. "It wasn't a bad deal for him, considering that it might cost as much as $200,000 to outfit a complete store from scratch. We had to work back and forth a bit with the buyer to arrange the shipping; it cost $3500."

Don's biggest tip to new eBay sellers is the importance of following through quickly when sales are completed. "Don't delay the shipping. There's no need to delay, especially when you use PayPal. Try to get the merchandise out the next day. People are often flabbergasted at how fast our shipping is. If someone sends us a personal check and we see that they have 500 feedbacks and they are all positive, we won't wait until the check clears to ship, either."

It's a strategy that's kept the amount of negative feedback to a minimum (at this writing he and Lisa had 3269 positive feedback comments and 26 negatives). In general, Don reports, all his dealings with eBay users tend to be positive—only 2 or 3 percent of his sales turn up deadbeat bidders.

"First, give us the opportunity to resolve the problem. We will resolve it. We made a form that we include with every completed auction. It says, 'We hope you are happy with your item. If you are not happy, here is our toll-free number—give us a call.' We give them a money-back guarantee, too."

The high level of service has a direct result in repeat business. "I know people check us every day to see what we put online," he says happily.

5

> TIP
>
> *CQ Counter, which comes both in a free version that requires banner ads to be displayed on your site and in an ad-free version that costs $49.95 per year, goes a step beyond simply recording the number of times your page has been viewed. It reports on the sites that your visitors come from before they view your pages, how many times your pages have been reloaded, and the IP addresses (an identifying series of four numbers that is assigned to every computer connected to the Internet) of your visitors' computers. Find out about it at **http://cqcounter.com**.*

# Use eBay Seller's Assistant

Many of the approaches to making your auctions stand out from the crowd that I've already described in this chapter are included in two utilities provided by eBay itself. These utilities, Seller's Assistant Basic and Seller's Assistant Pro, are designed to help you get your photos online and give your auction descriptions graphic interest.

> NOTE
>
> *Seller's Assistant Pro does carry a higher monthly fee than Seller's Assistant Basic (which is deducted from your eBay seller's account), but it provides you with some useful features that will make managing multiple auctions a lot easier, including the ability to track your inventory, print shipping labels, and create sales reports. These features are discussed in Chapter 6 along with other software that helps you manage multiple auctions.*

From the standpoint of graphic presentation, Seller's Assistant Basic and Pro both provide you with a variety of templates you can use to present your sales items. Each template has its own graphic design. Unfortunately, you can't get a look at these designs without subscribing to the monthly service. You can try out either the Basic or Pro versions free for 30 days, but after that eBay begins charging you ($4.99 per month for Basic and $15.99 for Pro) unless you cancel. Just follow these steps:

1. Go to the eBay Seller's Assistant page (**http://pages.ebay.com/sellers_ assistant/index.html**) and click **Subscribe Now** at the bottom of the page.

2. When the Seller's Assistant Subscription page appears, fill in your User ID (if necessary; it may already be filled in) and password, and click **Sign In Securely**.

3. When the eBay Seller's Assistant Subscription page appears, click **Subscribe** next to the version of Seller's Assistant that you want.

4. Read the User Agreement, and then click **I Accept**.

5. Click **Download Seller's Assistant Basic** (or Seller's Assistant Pro, depending on the version you have chosen).

6. When the File Download box appears, click **Open**. The file downloads to your hard disk.

7. When the download is complete, the InstallShield Wizard opens automatically. Follow the steps shown in the wizard to install Seller's Assistant.

8. Start up Seller's Assistant by clicking Start | Programs (All Programs on Windows XP) | eBay | Seller's Assistant Basic (or Pro).

9. When the License Agreement window appears, read the License Agreement, then click **I Agree**. You may have to insert your original Microsoft Office CD-ROM in order to update the software.

10. The Seller's Assistant program leads you through a series of initial setup tasks. When you're done, the program window opens (see Figure 5-8).

Click here to spell-check your description

Choose a theme from this list

**FIGURE 5-8** Seller's Assistant lets you choose a graphic theme and spell check your listings.

Seller's Assistant comes with a set of 20 built-in themes; you preview them by clicking the Edit button next to the drop-down list of themes in the Seller's Assistant window.

## Where to Find It

- **ManageAuctions.com**
  **http://www.manageauctions.com**
  A variety of useful services for auction sellers, including counters you can add to your sales pages.

- ***A Beginner's Guide to HTML***
  **http://archive.ncsa.uiuc.edu/General/Internet/WWW/**
  **HTMLPrimerAll.html**
  Basic tutorials and instructions on the most common HTML tags.

- **eBay Seller's Assistant**
  **http://pages.ebay.com/sellers_assistant/index.html**
  Links to eBay Seller's Assistant Basic and Pro.

# Chapter 6

# Manage Multiple Auctions

## How to...

- Use eBay's own software for managing and scheduling multiple auction listings

- Automate eBay auction listings with third-party software you can install yourself

- Sign up with an auction service for better management

- Track your eBay sales with eBay's browser toolbar

- Manage your eBay activities with a My eBay page

- Use Seller's Assistant to create multiple auction listings quickly

Henry Ford knew the value of automation. So does the McDonald's restaurant megachain. Once you get the hang of selling at auction, you're likely to jump in the game with both feet and start to sell lots of items at once. As your eBay business grows and you can prepare sales more quickly, the more you'll want to automate tasks that are repetitious. Why? The more time you save, the more sales you'll be able to list, and the greater the revenue those sales can generate. At the same time, you'll be able to focus on the parts of your eBay business that really interest you: creating and describing merchandise, finding merchandise you can sell, completing transactions, and other good things.

This chapter discusses ways you can speed up your business and run it more efficiently so as to reduce stress and boost your productivity. You can automate the processes of publishing photos online, keeping records of your sales income, and maintaining data about your sales. These are ambitious goals, but they are ones you need to shoot for if you want to make a steady living on eBay.

# Start with eBay's Management Tools

The logical place to start is with the tools eBay provides its own sellers, which are described in Table 6-1 and in the following sections. If you need help or have questions, you can access the message boards for any of these programs and services and get help from other users and eBay staff people who monitor discussions.

eBay provides a variety of options for creating groups of sales listings, formatting them with user-friendly design elements, tracking sales while they're online, and even sending automated e-mail responses and printing out labels in

| Tool | Main Features | Cost | Pros and Cons |
|---|---|---|---|
| Turbo Lister | Lets you create multiple listings and format them without using HTML; you can schedule listings to go online at specific times; you can track your remaining inventory. | Free | You are required to have 20MB of free disk space and at least 64MB of RAM to run the Windows-based software; you either have to download it or obtain a CD-ROM version. |
| Selling Manager | Enables you to relist items but not to create or upload new listings. Lets you track sales online, print labels, and send preformatted e-mails. | Free for first 30 days; $4.99 per month thereafter | You don't have to download and install software; you access the service from eBay's web site. It's similar to Seller's Assistant Basic, but includes relisting and label-printing features that Seller's Assistant doesn't have. |
| Selling Manager Pro | Enables volume sellers to do bulk listing and manage inventory. | Free for 30 days; $15.99 thereafter | Similar to Selling Manager, but enables you to create sales listings and automate feedback and e-mails. |
| Seller's Assistant Basic | Provides you with 20 templates for designing sales listings; allows you to upload listings in bulk. | Free for 30 days; $9.99 per month thereafter (you can also subscribe to Selling Manager for no additional charge) | Very similar to Selling Manager, but you need to download and install the Windows-based software, and you have the ability to upload sales auctions based on other sales. It will eventually be replaced by Selling Manager. |
| Seller's Assistant Pro | Enables you to create your own macros so you can repeat a sequence of steps; leave automated feedback in bulk; use multiple User IDs. | Free for 30 days; $24.99 per month thereafter | Many of its features are provided more cheaply (or for free) by Turbo Lister or Selling Manager. |
| My eBay | A Selling tab gives up-to-date information on sales that are pending, sales that are completed, and unsold items. | Free | A convenient place to track all of your sales in one location, though you can't perform any management functions. |

**TABLE 6-1**   eBay Tools for Auction Sellers

6

order to complete transactions in a more streamlined fashion. In fact, choosing between the eBay sales tools can be somewhat confusing because their functions overlap in some respects.

## Speed Things Up with Turbo Lister

Turbo Lister (**http://pages.ebay.com/turbo_lister**) is software with a wizard-like interface that eBay provides to sellers for free. It's the successor to a utility called Mister Lister that enabled eBay sellers to put dozens of auctions online at once. With Turbo Lister, you can sell lots of items at the same time, and design those sales by means of templates that enable you to format descriptions without having to know HTML. Finally, you can manage the items you create with Turbo Lister— scheduling them to all start and end at a specified time, or duplicate sales details so you can use them over if needed.

You can download the 18MB Turbo Lister software directly from **http://pages .ebay.com/turbo_lister/download.html**, which provides a full set of system requirements as well. The software does not work on Macintosh systems, however; it's supported by Windows 98, Me, NT, 2000, and XP. You need 20MB of free hard disk space to use the software. If you'd rather use a CD-ROM to install the software, you can obtain it for a $2.99 handling fee from The eBay Shop, eBay's online store (**http://www.theebayshop.com**).

TIP      *If you have questions about Turbo Lister or have problems using the software, check the Turbo Lister Discussion Board (**http://forums.ebay .com/forum.jsp?forum=34**). You can see if someone else has encountered the same problem, or ask a question if you need help.*

 **Install and Use Turbo Lister**

1.   Start up Internet Explorer and go to the Turbo Lister Download page (**http://pages.ebay.com/turbo_lister/download.html**).

2.   Click **Turbo Lister Web Setup**. If a Security Warning dialog box appears, click Yes to proceed with the download.

3.   After the Turbo Lister Setup application downloads, the InstallShield Wizard application opens. Follow the steps presented by the wizard to download the full set of Turbo Lister software.

4. Once installation is complete, the Turbo Lister application should open automatically, and the Welcome To Turbo Lister screen should appear, with the heading "What would you like to do?"

5. You could choose Open A Sample Turbo Lister File to see how a finished file might look. For this example, choose Set Up A New Turbo Lister File, then click Next.

6. In the next screen, enter your eBay User ID and password, then click Next.

7. In the next screen, click **Connect Now** and Turbo Lister will connect to eBay to retrieve your account information. Once your account information has been retrieved, click File | New | Item from the Turbo Lister menu bar to open the Create A New Item wizard.

8. Choose the country you want to sell in, and choose a format for your sale—an auction, a store, or a real estate advertisement. Click Next.

9. Enter a title for your item in the Item Title drop-down list.

10. Either enter the category number, if you know it, in the Category box, as shown here, or click Find Category. If you click Find Category, the Select A Category dialog box opens.

**11.** Click the plus signs next to the categories to pick the category where you want to sell the item. Highlight the category and click OK.

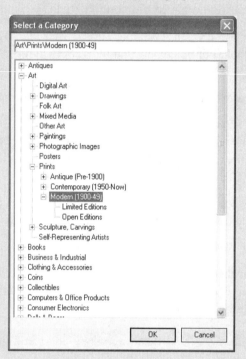

**12.** Click the Add/Change button near the bottom of the Create A New Item page to enter item specifics if you want to. Then click OK.

**13.** Click Next. The Enter Your Description screen gives you a user-friendly HTML editor, as shown next, that enables you to choose a design template for your auction listing. Even if you don't use Turbo Lister for bulk auction listings, it's worth installing the software just to get this feature. In the Themes box on the left side of the screen, choose a design from the Themes list. In the Layout section, choose a layout for your item's photos. You can specify that they appear to the left of the description, to the right, at the top, at the bottom, or as a series of images called a Slide Show.

14. Insert a photo by clicking one of the boxes labeled Click Here To Insert a Picture. When the Insert Picture—eBay Picture Services dialog box opens, click the Look In drop-down menu to locate a photo on your hard disk that you want to include with the description. Click Insert to add the image. Then click in the text box (the box enclosed by dashed lines) to position the text cursor so you can type your item description or paste it from a text file. Click Preview to make sure your layout looks the way you want. Then click Next.

15. Click Next to open the Format Specifics wizard page, where you add specific details about your listing such as the duration of the sale, the starting bid, and the reserve price. When you're done, click Save. You return to the Turbo Lister main screen, where

this auction and any others you have created are listed, as shown here:

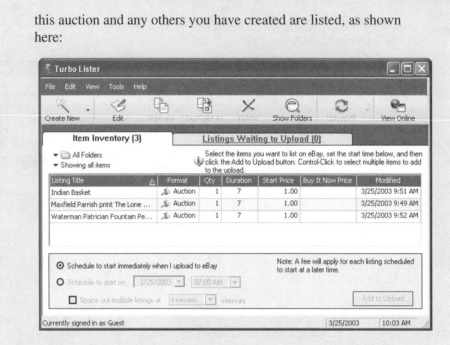

16. When you're ready to start your sales, select them from the list and click Add to Upload. If you want to schedule your sales to go online automatically, select them, then click the Schedule to Start On radio button and enter a date or time in the corresponding drop-down list box.

## Use eBay's Selling Manager

Turbo Lister is a terrific selling tool, but it does require some overhead—after all, you have to download and install the program before you can run it on your computer. Another sales management tool that eBay provides, Selling Manager, is one that you don't download at all. Rather, you access it at **http://pages.ebay.com/selling_manager**. You sign up to use the service free for 30 days; if you decide to keep using the service, eBay charges you $4.99 per month.

Selling Manager lets you relist multiple sold and unsold listings at once. eBay provides Turbo Lister so that you can create groups of auction listings and get them online; it gives you Selling Manager so that you can manage your sales once they're online, and complete transactions in a more automated fashion.

> **NOTE**   *You can use Selling Manager to keep track of your sales on all areas of eBay except the fixed-price sales you list on Half.com (see Chapter 14). You need Internet Explorer 4.0 or later, Netscape Navigator 3.0 or later, or AOL Web Browser 3.0 or later to use Selling Manager. However, because it's a tool you access online rather than run on your own computer, you don't need to worry about special memory and processing requirements.*

Selling Manager is built into another eBay feature that is normally of interest primarily to auction buyers—a starting page called My eBay that lets you track items you've bid on and items you've purchased. When you subscribe to Selling Manager, your My eBay page's usual Sell "view" is replaced by Selling Manager, where your pending auction listings are listed. Selling Manager also gives you seven preformatted e-mail messages that you can use to answer questions from prospective bidders and complete transactions after an auction ends.

One thing to keep in mind is the fact that the original My eBay page (which is free) already has a Selling section that lets you track sales. I suggest that you try the free version of My eBay before you move up to Selling Manager, which is really useful only if you begin to sell dozens of items a month.

## Create a My eBay Page

My eBay is a useful tool that you can use whenever you're buying or selling on the auction site. It's a web page that eBay provides to keep track of things you have bid on. There's also a Selling page that you can use to keep track of your current sales.

My eBay isn't something you have to set up or subscribe to use. Any time you want to access My eBay, click the **My eBay** link at the top of the eBay navigation bar that appears on just about every eBay page. A page like the one shown in Figure 6-1 appears.

> **TIP**   *Many sellers make their My eBay page their home page—the page that appears when they first open their web browser, and that appears when they click the Home button in the Internet Explorer toolbar. Open My eBay, select the URL in the Address box of your browser, and press CTRL-C to copy the URL to your clipboard. Choose Tools | Internet Options, make sure the General tab is selected, click in the Address box in the Home Page section, and press CTRL-V to paste the URL. (If you use Internet Explorer 6, you can simply click Use Current to make the currently displayed web page your home page.) Click OK to make the page your home page.*

FIGURE 6-1    My eBay lets you track your sales and other auction activities online.

## Use Seller's Assistant

Seller's Assistant is software that enables you to create and manage your sales. At the time of this writing, it comes in two versions, Basic and Pro.

### Seller's Assistant Basic

The Basic version's features are mainly covered by a newer product, Selling Manager. If you haven't yet chosen any sales tool, I advise you to pick Turbo Lister and Selling Manager, which let you create and manage sales items with just about all of the functionality of Seller's Assistant Basic. Or, take advantage of eBay's offer to use Seller's Assistant Basic for $9.99 per month along with a free subscription to Selling Manager.

## Did you know?

# Tabs and Links

My eBay contains a variety of useful links to web pages and utilities that can help you buy or sell more efficiently on eBay. The My eBay Views column on the left side is divided into six separate "views," or ways of viewing your eBay activities. Each has its own contents and options. The views are My Summary, All Buying, All Selling, My Messages, All Favorites, and My Accounts.

The All Selling view gives you a place to track sales. It's broken into the following sections:

- **Selling Reminders**   Reminders about items you might want to relist or resell in the future

- **Scheduled Items**   Items that you have scheduled to go on sale at a future date

- **Selling Totals**   The number of sales you have made in the past month

- **Items I'm Selling**   Sales you already have online

- **Items I've Sold**   Sales you have completed recently

- **Unsold Items**   Sales that failed to attract high bidders or buyers

You can change the number displayed in the Period box on the right-hand side of each section to have the page present as few as 24 hours' worth of sales up to a maximum of 60 days. But My eBay only enables you to see what's been sold, how many bids have been received, and so on. You can't use the page to upload or schedule sales, but you can use it to relist items or resell items as part of an eBay Store's inventory. You need to use Turbo Lister or Seller's Assistant to create and upload sales and use Selling Manager or Seller's Assistant to perform management functions.

# eBay Toolbar

You may already be familiar with browser toolbars such as the ones offered by Google and Yahoo! that you can install and add to your browser's default set of toolbars. eBay has its own browser toolbar, too. The eBay Toolbar's features mostly help you search and track items you're bidding on or selling, no matter what web site your browser happens to be displaying at the time. But it also contains a link to My eBay and other critical eBay pages, plus an Account Guard feature that alerts you when you connect to fake eBay pages. The basic eBay Toolbar controls are shown here:

You can also click Watch Alert to alert you to the progress of any sale on eBay, including one of your own. (Watch Alert doesn't appear on the eBay Toolbar by default; click Customize to move Watch Alert into the list of available toolbar buttons if you need to.) Since, as a seller, you may very well shop on eBay, the toolbar can be useful for obtaining inventory, too. Once you download and install the toolbar by clicking the Install Toolbar button on the eBay Toolbar page, a search box and set of options appear:

Downloading the toolbar is easy. Just go to the eBay Toolbar home page and click the Download eBay Toolbar Now button. When a download dialog box appears, click Open. A setup program is downloaded and begins to run automatically; the program automatically closes Internet Explorer. Click the Toolbar Setup application button in your Windows taskbar, then click Next. In the course of installation, you are presented with the opportunity to protect your eBay and PayPal passwords with the Account Guard feature, which gives you a visual warning if you connect to a fake eBay site and attempt to enter one of the passwords. I suggest that you fill out this screen, shown next, then click Save and follow the instructions on subsequent screens to install the toolbar.

**Account Guard**

## Protect your eBay and PayPal Passwords!

Account Guard Password Protection can protect your eBay and PayPal account by warning you when you are entering your eBay or PayPal password into an unverified site **even if it looks like eBay or PayPal**

*Protect your eBay and PayPal passwords by entering them here (optional):*

eBay Password:

| •••••••• |

PayPal Password  (if you don't have a PayPal password, please leave blank):

| •••••••• |

Need more information?  Learn more about Account Guard

[ Save ]  [ Skip This Step ]  [ Cancel ]  [ Help ]

Once the toolbar is installed, the setup program closes and Internet Explorer automatically restarts. The eBay Toolbar appears beneath your other default toolbars.

> TIP
>
> *You can find out more about the eBay Toolbar and download it at **http://pages.ebay.com/ebay_toolbar**. The eBay Toolbar only works with Windows 98 or later systems, not the Mac OS. It also requires you to have Microsoft Internet Explorer 5.01 or later, not Netscape Navigator.*

## Seller's Assistant Pro

Seller's Assistant Pro is a souped-up version of Seller's Assistant that is designed for eBay sellers who sell all the time and need to automate tasks such as leaving feedback for many customers at once or printing sales reports for tax purposes. Plus, you can create *macros* (a recorded series of steps that you perform on an application) so that you can repeat just about any task you perform on eBay with your web browser. These are three features the program performs that aren't covered by the other eBay software mentioned earlier in this chapter.

The question you need to ask yourself is this: do these advanced features make Seller's Assistant Pro worth $24.99 a month? Is it also worth downloading the 20MB file and installing the program on your computer?

One advantage of using Seller's Assistant Pro (or Basic, for that matter) is the number of templates from which you can choose. Turbo Lister, the free software tool described earlier in this chapter, provides you with only about ten templates. The Seller's Assistant packages come with 20 different designs (see Figure 6-2). Another advantage is the fact that both versions of Seller's Assistant include a spell-checker so you can make sure your auction descriptions don't contain any obvious typos.

If you don't like a particular typeface or color that's included with one of the Seller's Assistant templates, you can always click the Edit button and customize a template so it looks just the way you want.

6

TIP    *You can find out more about both Seller's Assistant Basic and Pro at*
*http://pages.ebay.com/sellers_assistant/index.html.*

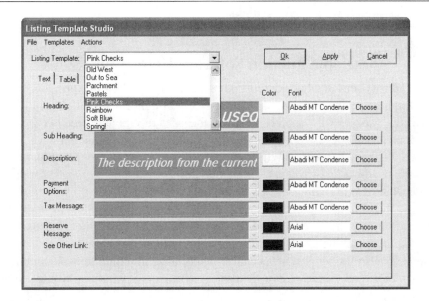

**FIGURE 6-2**    Seller's Assistant gives you great flexibility in designing auction listings.

# Find a Third-Party Auction Manager

Not so long ago, you had to hire an outside auction management service to perform slick sales-type functions like sending out automated e-mail announcements to each of your high bidders after a sale ends, or scheduling your sales to go online while you're not even at your computer. eBay has since come up with Turbo Lister and Selling Manager so that advanced sellers can accomplish such automated tasks.

On top of that, a wide variety of outside firms have jumped on the eBay bandwagon and are offering their own affordable solutions for creating listings and managing inventory and sales. You still might want to install third-party software (software that's made for managing eBay sales, but provided by a company other than eBay) like the popular Marketworks (**http://www.marketworks.com**) or the more affordable alternative SpareDollar (**http://www.sparedollar.com**). Or you might want to secure the services of a company that will manage your eBay sales for you so you can concentrate on answering e-mail, finding new inventory, or shipping out items you've sold. Both options are described in the sections that follow.

## eBay Bestsellers
### Affordable Auction Software Helps Build Sales

Dana Titus (User ID: tahoeskier2005) began selling on eBay in April 2003. "The first thing I sold was a dress that I impulsively bought for myself, but quickly realized it wasn't really 'me.' Having lost the sales receipt and already clipped the tag, a friend suggested I list it on eBay. I had bought on eBay but never sold before. Without knowing anything about selling, I took a few pictures of me wearing the dress and wrote a brief auction description. The dress sold for nearly twice what I paid! That was it, I was hooked."

Just three months later, Titus gained Power Seller status. She has been able to maintain that status even though she sells on eBay part-time. She also has a part-time consulting job. How does she sell so efficiently? For one thing, she has a good supplier for her area of specialty: "I specialize in selling sexy clothing for women of all shapes and sizes—the typical item I sell is what you would see on a woman in a dance club."

Another key to selling in quantity and with regularity is having an eBay Store, which allows a seller to keep merchandise up for sale for weeks at a time. In Titus's case, her store—which is called Bootywear—helps her to sell on eBay while raising her two young children.

"My sales definitely increased with the opening of my store," she says. "It's a great deal. For $9.99 you get a storefront where you can showcase your items. I get many compliments on my store logo. Without an eBay store, you are unable to display a logo on your seller's page; the buyers will only see a list of your items for sale." The logo and store are shown here:

Another big factor in Titus's success is her choice of auction management software: "I'm very frugal, so I use SpareDollar. I looked at all the auction management programs and many are expensive. My husband encouraged me to keep my expenses as low as possible—he told me that many small businesses fail because they overspend on bells and whistles that are really not needed to operate the business. With this in mind, I chose SpareDollar because it costs only $5 per month. For this fee you have a place to host your pictures and you can also schedule listings. I can schedule my listings for free. (eBay charges a premium for this service.) I can also add as many pictures as I want to my listings at no additional charge; again, eBay charges a premium for adding more than one picture. I would highly recommend auction management programs for anyone who has an eBay store or for anyone who lists on a regular basis."

All of these tools enable Titus to list 25–50 items per week and to achieve an amazing "sell-through" rate of 95 percent: in other words, 95 percent of the items that she lists result in sales. Titus offers this advice to aspiring eBay sellers: "The best suggestion I can offer people who are trying to start up an eBay Store is to think about how marketable your product is and give a lot of thought to pricing. eBay is no different than any other type of retail selling—in order to be successful, you have to offer a product that people want at a fair price. Many sellers make the mistake of thinking that just because they list it on eBay, the item will sell. eBay gives that impression to sellers as part of their marketing strategy. Actually, the average sell-through rate on eBay is something like 40 percent—this means that less than half of the items listed on eBay result in a sale. Try to avoid racking up huge listing fees because you listed an item that people do not really want at a price that is too high."

TIP    *You'll find a list of third-party auction applications that is several pages long on eBay itself. Go to the eBay Solutions Directory (**http://cgi6.ebay .com/ws/eBayISAPI.dll?SolutionsDirectory**), scroll to the bottom of the page, and click **see all Selling Solutions** to browse through the list.*

## Auction Services

A managed service is functionality that is provided online, and that you usually access by connecting to the service with a web browser. Rather than having to download and install software that needs to be updated on a regular basis, you subscribe to the service for a monthly or yearly fee. It's up to the service provider to update the software and make sure it works correctly.

Managed auction services—companies that provide services online that you can use to create auction listings, get your sales on eBay, upload and store images, and manage sales—are even more plentiful than software programs. Such services give you a number of advantages:

- **Image hosting**    After you post one item image online, eBay charges you for each subsequent image per item. By paying a flat monthly fee to a managed auction service, you can access its other auction features, including image hosting. In the long run, you can save money by using the outside service.

- **Auction statistics**    Some auction services report on statistics such as the number of visits your auctions have received in a particular day or even a specified hour in the day. They can tell you how much money your auctions have generated over the past several weeks.

■ **Complete management**   If you run a large-scale business and you hope to sell a substantial portion of your inventory on eBay, you can sign up with a company such as Channel Velocity (**http://www.channelvelocity.com**), which handles everything from strategizing and market analysis to shipping and returns.

Auction services also perform the functions covered earlier in the discussion of Selling Manager, Turbo Lister, and Seller's Assistant Pro, such as automated feedback, printing mailing labels for each sale, and leaving feedback automatically. Some of the best-known auction management services are described in Table 6-2.

| Service | URL | Fees |
|---|---|---|
| AuctionHelper | **http://www.auctionhelper.com** | 1.95% of gross sales ($0.15–$1.25 per item) plus a $0.02 eBay fee per each sold item |
| Marketworks | **http://www.marketworks.com** | 2% of each sale ($0.10 minimum, no maximum) or hosting fees of $14.95 to $99.95 per month |
| ManageAuctions.com | **http://www.manageauctions.com** | $0.06 per listing plus other charges ranging from $4.95 to $24.95 per month |
| Vendio Services | **http://www.vendio.com** | $0.06 per listing if you pay $250 for a year's subscription; $0.10 per listing if you pay $39.95 per month; $0.20 per listing if you pay $12.95 per month; $0.10 per listing and a 1 percent final value fee on the pay-as-you-go plan |
| ChannelAdvisor | **http://www.channeladvisor.com** | The least expensive plan for small businesses, charges $29.95 per month, which includes 500 completed listings (whether the item is sold or unsold) |

**TABLE 6-2**    Auction Management Services

TIP *You'll find an extensive (though not comprehensive) list of managed auction services on the AuctionBytes web site (**http://www.auctionbytes .com/cab/pages/ams**). You don't need to hire an auction service if you have the time and energy to do the work yourself, of course. But I think it makes sense to use a managed auction service if you offer a substantial number of sales each month (perhaps 50 or more, though this is not a hard-and-fast rule) and you don't have family or friends to help you create listings, send e-mails, and keep your accounting records.*

# New Management Platform Streamlines "Mpire" Building

Cutting and pasting goes only so far when it comes to selling on eBay. So does trying to keep track of sales, inventory, and e-mail manually. You can copy text from one sale to another, and manually check off an inventory item when a sale is made. But if you start to sell dozens or even hundreds of items each week, you'll quickly become overwhelmed.

In order to keep their eBay businesses growing and thriving, many sellers turn to an eBay Preferred Solutions Provider (PSP). A good PSP can streamline the process of selling in bulk while helping you track the actual costs and profits of each sale.

PSPs reduce the number of required steps to create and complete transactions. They do this, in part, by streamlining the software required. When you sell the occasional item on eBay, your primary tool is your web browser. When you are starting up a business with employees, accounting requirements, and inventory tracking and management, things get more complicated. You might have to install a variety of applications or subscribe to multiple services; for example, an auction management tool like Selling Manager, accounting software like QuickBooks, a photo hosting service, an account with a shipper so you can print labels and buy postage, and your browser. You might use your subscription with Andale to research prices, or with another software provider to place last-minute snipe bids. You could conceivably need six or seven separate application windows open at the same time to get everything done.

A new auction management service called Mpire intends to dramatically cut the software demands placed on sellers. Mpire (**http://www.mpire.com**) is an integrated suite of applications that puts many different functions at your fingertips. In a single browser window, you can manage inventory, track your sales, communicate with buyers, research prices, and handle shipping. You even get e-mail, chat, or customer service support 24×7—and anyone who has tried to contact eBay with an urgent technical support problem knows how unusual *that* level of access is.

Mpire helps you take care of tasks that are common to most PSPs, such as creating sales listings, keeping track of inventory, and automating the printing of shipping labels. Its advanced version also handles customer relationship management (CRM) and research on items you want to sell, among other advanced tasks. It's like your My eBay page, but with accounting information, image hosting, and ways to connect to the eBay community as well. Visit the Mpire web site to find out about this fully integrated end-to-end solution for eBay sellers.

**6**

## Category-Specific Services

The field of eBay selling software is so extensive that several companies have decided to focus their selling applications on specific areas of eBay. Here are just a few examples:

- **Auction123.com (http://www.auction123.com)**   This listing service specializes exclusively in eBay Motors listings. It's especially good for auto dealers that need to get a number of vehicles online quickly. The listing fee, not counting eBay's own fees, is $49.95 per vehicle.

- **Bandi.com (http://www.bandi.com)**   This company specializes in creating listings in the Business and Industrial category, including medical equipment, restaurant equipment, and tool and die machinery.

- **CARad (http://www.carad.com)**   This company also provides inventory management and listing tools intended specifically for eBay Motors.

- **EzRez (http://ezrez.com/)**   A solution for creating travel packages and selling them in eBay's Travel section.

You can find a more extensive list of category-specific selling solutions at **http://cgi6.ebay.com/ws/eBayISAPI.dll?SolutionsDirectory**.

## Where to Find It

- **Turbo Lister**
  **http://pages.ebay.com/turbo_lister**
  A page full of links that explain eBay's Turbo Lister feature and provide the software for download.

- **eBay Selling Manager**
  **http://pages.ebay.com/selling_manager**
  A page where you can learn about, and sign up for, a service that lets you automate relisting, e-mailing bidders, and completing transactions.

- **eBay Toolbar**
  **http://pages.ebay.com/ebay_toolbar/**
  A toolbar you can use to track sales and send alert notices at the end of a sale (including your own).

- **eBay Seller Tools**
  **http://pages.ebay.com/sell/tools.html**
  A page full of links to eBay's own selling software and services.

- **eBay Seller's Assistant**
  **http://pages.ebay.com/sellers_assistant/index.html**
  More eBay software tools for creating and managing auction listings.

- **eBay Solutions Directory**
  **http://cgi6.ebay.com/ws/eBayISAPI.dll?SolutionsDirectory**
  Third-party solutions for creating and managing eBay sales listings.

# Chapter 7

# Create Your Own Web Pages

# How to...

■ Tell buyers about yourself with an About Me page

■ Create your own web site with a free web host

■ Rent web space for free with your Internet Service Provider

■ Shoot the works with a full-featured web-hosting service account

■ Include the must-have features on your web site

One nice thing about eBay is that it allows you to start your own e-commerce business immediately, without having to build or stock a real brick-and-mortar store. But your eBay sales can be helped by the presence of a *virtual* customer service desk—a digital, text-and-image page on the World Wide Web such as an eBay Store or web site.

Chances are you've already got a web page out there somewhere in cyberspace. Maybe you use it to talk about yourself and your hobbies, or to show off photos of your family or your pets. Well, you can also use the Web to talk about your business.

If you've already created auction listings and completed transactions with satisfied customers, you've done much of the work involved in creating a business web site. You need to take only one more step: create a set of web pages devoted to your commercial activities. You've got plenty of options for creating pages:

■ Create a simple About Me page on eBay—after all, this is a web page like any other. You create it and edit it, but eBay is the web host that stores the image and text files on its servers.

■ Create an eBay Store (another set of eBay-hosted web pages).

■ Launch your own full-fledged web site.

As an entrepreneur, you owe it to yourself to take the next step and create web pages that boost your eBay sales even further.

You can take an extra step and set up an eBay web page or a full-fledged e-commerce web site that's hosted outside of eBay in order to back up your auction sales. But plenty of successful sellers never set up a web site at all; they let their sales descriptions and customer service do the talking. Starting up an e-commerce web site makes sense if you already have a business operation and your eBay sales are intended to supplement it. It's also a natural step forward if you are finding enough success on eBay that you want to sell through a web site as well. Whether you want to set up another sales venue through an eBay Store, or set up your own web-based catalog and shopping cart, you can use your eBay auction experience as a starting point for further development.

# MeBay: Create an About Me Page

If you sell on eBay, there's really no excuse not to create an About Me page. It only takes a matter of minutes—in fact, it's about as easy as creating your first auction listing. About Me is a feature that eBay offers free of charge to all of its participants; it also promotes the community atmosphere that eBay is continually touting. eBay's success really depends on people getting to know and trust one another.

By taking a little time to create a simple page that tells people a little about you, you increase the chances that people will bid on your merchandise. Not only that, but you get another cool icon placed next to your User ID as it appears on your auctions. If shoppers click your "me" icon (see Figure 7-1) they'll be taken directly to your

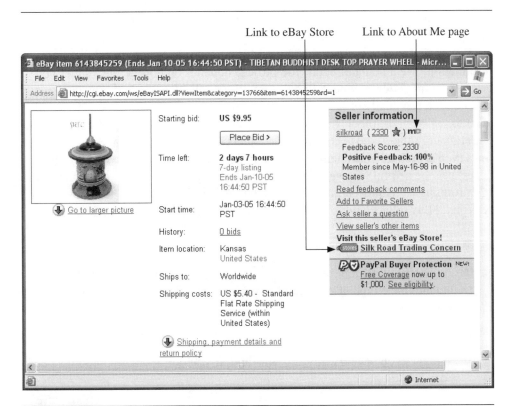

FIGURE 7-1    You advertise your About Me page in each of your auction listings.

About Me page. (An About Me page is the only place you can link to your web sites or other sites that are outside of eBay.)

As you can see in Figure 7-1, the seller known as silkroad—the Silk Road Trading Concern—has two links to web pages: an About Me page and an eBay Stores page. Not only that, Silk Road has all the bases covered by running a web site (**http://www .silkroads.com**). Each of these options is discussed in this chapter.

## Gather Your 411

The name *About Me* says it all: it's a place where you talk all about you personally— why you use eBay, what you sell, what you're interested in, or where you live. You can use an eBay Store or a web site to focus on your business rather than your personal side. Of course, these aren't firm dividing lines: you can use About Me to promote your business, and use your eBay Store to promote yourself and your business. For someone who runs a business on eBay, an About Me page is like a promotional brochure: it showcases what you do, what your customer service goals and policies are, and why shoppers should choose you rather than your competitors. No matter how you make use of these resources, however, they are sure to help drive people to your auction listings and the all-important Submit Bid button.

Before you start to create your About Me page, you just need to gather a little information. The amount of detail you provide depends on how active a seller you are, how many different kinds of items you sell or collect, and whether your page is about you personally or just about your auction activities. The best way to decide what to say on your About Me page is to search the About Me pages of other sellers. Unfortunately, there's no eBay page that gathers all the About Me pages in one set of links (you'd probably have tens of thousands of links in one place, which wouldn't necessarily be helpful). Rather, find a seller who's reputable and presents sales items in a professional manner, and click that seller's About Me link. You'll discover that, typically, eBay sellers tend to provide information that you can also include, such as:

- The name of your business.

- A mission statement: a few sentences that describe the purpose of your business, the type of merchandise you sell, and the kinds of customers you want to reach.

- Your names and the names of your partners or employees.

- Whether you sell on eBay full time and, if you don't, what you do for your "day job."

■ What makes your business distinctive or noteworthy. Don't be bashful; promote yourself enthusiastically. Tell people that you are committed to providing quality merchandise, excellent customer service, and the like.

■ Your most recent feedback.

■ Your background. If you're fortunate enough to have any honors, awards, or professional affiliations associated with your auction sales, by all means mention them.

■ A set of links to your current auctions. You might also include links to any other web pages or web sites you have created.

■ Contact information. Your web site needs to list all the ways in which buyers or prospective customers can reach you if they have a question or need some information. You don't need to publish your actual street address, of course; some eBay sellers prefer to use a post office box for extra security. But you should certainly include an e-mail address and possibly a phone number as well.

■ Optionally, you might also want to include photos of yourself or your employees, or an FAQ about your business.

That's quite a list. Frankly, if you have any more to say, you should create an eBay Store or a web site for yourself or your business. On the other hand, if you don't want to spend a lot of time on an About Me page, you don't have to create one, either. Sellers handle their own background information in different ways. Just consider some of the sellers profiled in this book. Each one has a different way of coordinating eBay auctions, a web site, and an About Me page:

■ Tom Hergert, who is profiled in Chapter 12, has a web site for his Tallzag Auctions business (**http://www.tallzagauctions.com**). That site has its own About page in which he talks about himself. Tom also has a similar About Me page under the User ID tallzagauctions.

■ Carol Hearn, profiled in Chapter 16, has an About Me page on which she describes her business, Wandering Creek Antiques, and spells out her shipping policy. She does not have a web site, however.

■ Dana Titus, profiled in Chapter 6, has an About Me page, but it's identical to the front page of her eBay Store, as is her web page (**http://www .bootywear.net**).

■ Mike Morin, profiled in Chapter 18, does not have an About Me page or an eBay Store—even though his feedback rating is more than 10,000. He does have a web page for his Wooden Nickel Trading Company (**http://www.wntconline.com**).

■ The PowerSeller glacierbaydvd has a detailed FAQ, contact information, and shipping policies on the About Me page at **http://members.ebay.com/aboutme/glacierbaydvd**.

> **TIP** *If you want to find someone's About Me page and you know their User ID, do the following: Click the **Advanced Search** link under the Search button, and click Find a Member in the Search pane on the left side of the page. When the eBay Search: Find a Member page appears, enter the User ID, click the About Me Page radio button, and click Search.*

No matter what you want to say on your page, it's good to know you have options for exactly how many web pages you want to create and how they link to one another. For now, just take a few minutes to think about and write down what you're going to say. Jot down some biographical notes and have a friend look them over, or suggest additional tidbits you can convey to the world.

> **TIP** *If you have more to tell the world about your hobbies, your family, your business history, or your thoughts about society in general, place a link on your About Me page that leads visitors to a web page that contains more information. (Try to avoid controversial subjects such as politics and religion, however.) You'll learn how to create such pages in this chapter.*

## Create Your Page

When you've got your content in order, follow these steps to get your About Me page online:

1. Make sure you're connected to the Internet, start up your web browser of choice, and enter the URL **http://members.ebay.com/aw-cgi/eBayISAPI .dll?AboutMeLogin** to go to the About Me login page.

2. Read the instructions, then click **Create Your Page**.

3. When the About Me: Choose Page Creation Option page appears, click Use Our Easy Step-by-Step Process, then click Continue.

4. Fill out the About Me: Enter Page Content form, which should look familiar if you have ever filled out the Sell Your Item form. Choose a title for your page

and add some information in each of the boxes. Also select the option that indicates how many eBay feedback comments you want the page to contain. The form allows you to create two paragraphs' worth of text about you or your business. You have the chance to display a graphic image such as a photo of yourself or a logo for your business. And you can enter some URLs to web sites that are related to your business—such as your own web site.

**CAUTION**   *Be aware that eBay's About Me Page Policy (**http://pages.ebay.com/help/ policies/contextual/listing-aboutme.html**) prevents you from making links to sites that "offer to trade, sell, or purchase goods or services outside of eBay."*

5.  On the About Me: Preview and Submit page, review the web page layouts that are available to you. Then click the button next to the arrangement you want: one-column layout (which is labeled Layout "A"), newspaper layout (Layout "B"), or two-column layout (Layout "C"). The three options are shown in Figure 7-2.

7

**FIGURE 7-2**   Choose the About Me layout option that matches your range of subjects.

**TIP**    *You might choose the two-column layout if you want to address a variety of different subjects, such as you, your family, your hobbies, and your business. The newspaper layout works well if you want to present various bits of information about the same topic (the different items you sell online, for instance). The centered arrangement is a good choice if your content—such as a brief description of your store—is short and sweet.*

6. The Preview and Submit page lets you see your page and make sure it looks the way you want. If you don't like your page's layout, click Back to try one of the other two options. Otherwise, if you're happy with your work, click Submit.

Once you click Submit, your page goes on the Web where everyone can see it. The Silk Road Trading Concern's About Me page is shown in Figure 7-3.

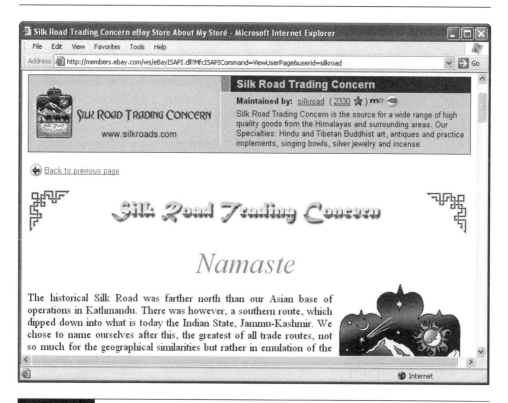

**FIGURE 7-3**    An About Me page can actually be About My Store.

Silk Road Trading Concern created an About Me page at the same time it created its eBay Stores page (see Chapter 14 for more information about creating an eBay Store). That's why it has the Stores logo at the top. If you create an About Me page through your eBay Store, you also gain the ability to add a logo that matches what you sell. (Such logos aren't made available if you follow the preceding set of steps from the About Me login page.) Tom Hergert added an automotive logo to his About Me page because he sells primarily on eBay Motors:

Most About Me pages don't contain the Stores logo. More typically, About Me gives an individual seller a place to talk about him- or herself. Chad Gibbons' About Me page, shown next, is more typical.

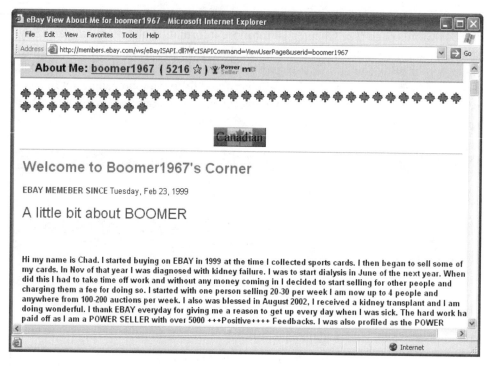

Typically, when you create an About Me page, you are assigned a URL that looks like the following:

http://members.ebay.com/aboutme/*Your User ID*

You can refer to this URL in your web pages or e-mail messages. Consider adding it to your e-mail signature file so people can find it more easily.

## Edit and Spruce Up Your Page

Suppose you have created an About Me page and you want to make some changes. Perhaps you've changed the focus of your business or started to sell a new line of merchandise. You only need to go to the About Me login page and click **Edit Your Page** to retrieve your current page and edit it. Just as when you create the page from scratch, you have the option of editing the raw HTML for your current About Me page (see "Dress Up Your Descriptions" in Chapter 5).

The nice thing about working with HTML is that you can do some spiffy formatting, such as adding images, creating headings and subheadings, and the like—provided you know what you're doing. The bad thing about working with HTML is that, well, you have to work with it at all. You might just prefer to re-create your page from scratch: use a web page editor to create the page, save the contents as a text file, and then copy and paste the HTML into the Preview and Submit section of the About Me page when you want to remake it. You're bound to find out about web page creation software when you decide to create your own personal or business web page, as described later in this chapter.

# Publish Your Own Web Site

About Me and eBay Stores are easy ways to promote your business. Another effective way to promote trust is to create your own set of interconnected web pages—a web site. On your site, you can talk about yourself and your qualifications in as much detail as you wish. You can also promote your business if you have one. An About Me page can be the glue that links an online business and an auction listing.

You don't *have* to provide a web site if you plan to sell at auction. For the most part, it makes sense to take this additional step if one of the following applies to you:

- You're in a business related to the items you're selling.

- You plan to make auction sales a significant part of your income.

- You plan to sell not only through eBay but through a catalog you present on your web site, so all the income from the sale (less sales tax) comes to you and not to your web host.

The first step in creating your auction web page is to decide where your page is going to "live" online. Your site needs to be hosted on a web server (a computer that is connected to the Internet all the time, and whose primary purpose is to make web pages available to anyone with a web browser) so others can view it. In other words, you need to find a hosting service—a company that functions like a virtual landlord, giving you space on a computer where you can set up shop. This is only the first step of a three-step process:

1. Pick your web host.

2. Create your web pages. Either use a user-friendly online tool such as a form you fill out to create a page, much the same as eBay's About Me feature, or purchase and install web page creation software and design your pages on your own computer.

3. Get your pages online. If you create your site using your host's online tool, you'll use another tool provided by that same host to move your files to the web server, where they can be seen on the Web by everyone. If you create your web pages yourself, you need to move the files from your computer to the web server. Sophisticated web page tools like Dreamweaver and FrontPage can do the file transfer for you. Otherwise, you have to use a special File Transfer Protocol (FTP) program to do the moving.

It's worth taking some time to pick the right host, because where your page is located can affect how you create it and how it looks. When it comes to finding a home for your web pages, you have several options:

- **A free hosting service**    There aren't too many free web hosts left; Yahoo! GeoCities is one of them.

- **Your own ISP**    If you have an account with a company such as America Online (AOL) or Earthlink, it'll usually give you space to create a simple web site as part of your monthly Internet access fee.

- **A company that doesn't function as an ISP, but only hosts web sites**    This is a business that hosts web sites, and that provides lots of handy tools and help for creating sites.

Your choice of host also has an impact on how you create your web pages. If you aren't technically minded and have no interest in the technical aspects of designing web sites, you'll enjoy using the simple forms-based web site creators provided by AOL, Yahoo! GeoCities, and Tripod: you fill out a form, and your web pages are created and automatically placed online. If you want to be in control and make everything look just the way you want, you'll probably prefer using a web page creation tool like Dreamweaver or Microsoft FrontPage and publishing your page yourself with your ISP or a web hosting service. These basic options are described in the following sections.

## Use a Free Web Hosting Service

If you want to create your own full-fledged web site (and possibly get a second e-mail address if you need one), sign up with one of the organizations that give anyone space on a web server where they can publish their own set of interconnected web pages. One advantage of signing up for an account with one of these organizations is that they are targeted at users who have little or no experience setting up web pages.

You'll find Help pages and other instructions to lead you through the steps in becoming a web publisher. Another advantage is that you become part of another community of web surfers. You can join clubs and interact with other users who also publish their pages on the site, just as you can with eBay community members. On the downside, you usually have to display ads on your site. Here are some sites to consider.

## Yahoo! GeoCities

Yahoo! GeoCities (**http://geocities.yahoo.com/**) is one of the oldest and most successful of the free online services. It not only provides users with a place on the Web for their personal home pages, but also supplies easy-to-use web page forms that format the web pages for you (see Figure 7-4), as well as programs that transfer (or, in technospeak, *upload*) the files from your home computer to GeoCities. Like eBay, GeoCities tends to be a world unto itself. Members identify themselves as being part of a "neighborhood" of individuals with similar interests.

7

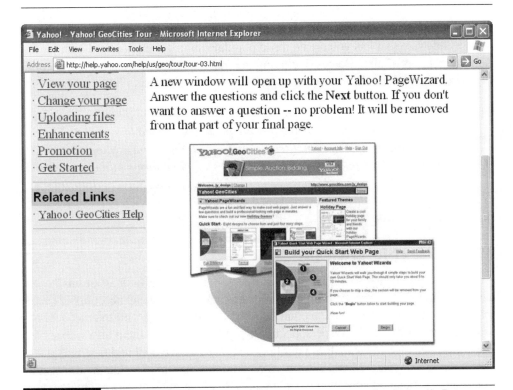

FIGURE 7-4    If you use GeoCities, you can create web pages using Yahoo!'s Page Wizard utility.

You can sign up for a free account with GeoCities which gives you 15MB of storage space. Considering that the typical web page only consumes 5K to 30K of disk space, not including images, this will let you store lots of material. But you'll have to show ads on your web pages. Plus, your URL (your web address) will have to take the form **http://geocities.yahoo.com/*your Yahoo! userid***. To move up to an easy-to-remember URL like **http://www.mysiteorbusiness.com**, you'd have to pay $8.95 per month for the GeoCities Pro hosting package. (GeoCities also offers a $4.95 per month hosting option, which frees you from having to display ads and offers 25MB of storage space.)

## Tripod

Tripod (**http://www.tripod.lycos.com**), which is owned by the Internet search service Lycos, also has an active site that hosts lots of individual web home pages. Members can chat and post messages on message boards. Like Yahoo! GeoCities, Tripod offers users a free web site hosting service that is ad-supported. Other ad-free hosting options are available, ranging from $4.95 to $19.95 per month.

Tripod is distinguished from Yahoo! GeoCities in that its free service includes 20MB of space (compared with 15MB for GeoCities), and its monthly fee packages include software that lets you create those popular running diaries called web logs (or *blogs*). Users of all packages (including the free one) also gain access to a library of clip art images that they can use to spice up their web pages.

TIP    *If you're looking for free web space and you don't mind displaying ads on your web pages, consider free hosting packages offered by companies such as Netfirms (**http://www.netfirms.com**), which gives you a whopping 25MB of server space plus the ability to create web page forms that are backed up by CGI (Common Gateway Interface) scripts. FreeServers (**http://www .freeservers.com**) gives you 12MB of space and a choice of web page creation tools as well.*

## Host with Your Own ISP

An Internet Service Provider (ISP) is a company that gives individuals or businesses access to the Internet. For the most part, ISPs give customers dialup accounts or cable-modem or DSL lines that let them connect to the Internet. Along with Internet access, most ISPs also let users create personal home pages and publish them on a web server. The advantage of using an ISP as your host is that it's convenient and free, and you get the service anyway. Most ISP web servers are fast and reliable. On the downside, you're pretty much on your own when it comes to obtaining software to create your web pages and then publishing those pages by moving them from your computer to the ISP's web server.

## America Online

America Online (AOL) is a wildly popular site for Internet access and, if you already have an account with AOL, you should certainly consider setting up a web page with it. If you have an account with AOL, you automatically gain 2MB of web server space where you can store your own web pages. This might seem like only a small amount of room, but it's more than enough for a moderately sized web site. Not only that, but each of the seven separate usernames you can create on AOL is entitled to 2MB of space, giving you a total of 14MB to work with. AOL's options for Web hosting are

- **My FTP Space**   This is AOL's catch-all term for a number of web page resources. One of those resources, 1-2-3 Publish, works like Yahoo!'s Page Wizard and eBay's own About Me feature: you create a web page by filling out a form with your web browser. You can use another web page design if you want to. You can only reach My FTP Space from within AOL's software, using the keyword My FTP Space.

- **AOL Hometown (http://hometown.aol.com)**   This is AOL's site on the Web where individuals can create web pages. You create the page using 1-2-3 Publish, and you locate it on AOL Hometown so that anyone on the Web can find it, not just AOL users. One difference between this and the preceding services is that this service is intended for business-oriented web sites. If you sell antiques on eBay, for instance, you might want to create a web site in the "neighborhood" called Furniture & Antiques, which is shown in Figure 7-5.

## Other ISPs

AOL isn't the only ISP in town, of course. Virtually all ISPs give their customers some web hosting space along with Internet access. I have some friends who have set up their web sites with Earthlink (**http://www.earthlink.com**), and I have created a couple of web sites with my own ISP, XO Communications (**http://www.xo.com**), as well. Earthlink gives you a pretty good deal: at this writing, it offers unlimited dialup access for $10.97 for the first six months and $21.95 per month thereafter. Users get 10MB of free web space and a web page creation tool called Click-n-Build, too.

**TIP**   *It's not hard to find ISPs. You can also peruse some lengthy and detailed lists of ISPs such as The List (**http://thelist.internet.com**) or Providers of Commercial Internet Access (**http://celestin.com/pocia**).*

7

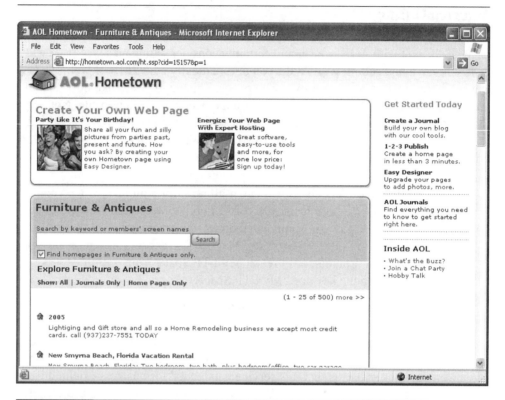

AOL gives you "neighborhoods" where you can locate web pages with
others who share similar interests.

When you use an ISP for web hosting, you save money. And you don't necessarily
need to go with the ISP's free web editor, either. You can easily download and install
the editor of your choice. By *web page editor,* I mean software that lets you format
web pages and then publish them on your web site. The advantage of creating your
own ISP-hosted web site is control: you can design your page by selecting your
own colors and page layouts, and adding as many images as you want. In contrast,
a simple web page feature such as that offered by eBay lets you select a basic page
layout that may or may not look the way you want. On the other hand, creating your
own web page and hosting it with an ISP is potentially complex: you're pretty much
on your own when it comes to selecting web page software and learning how to
publish your documents with the ISP. It's not all that difficult to learn some HTML,
of course, as you can see in the examples in Chapter 5.

*Some ISPs discourage individual users from setting up commercial web sites with the web space that comes with a personal account. If you want to set up a business site to supplement your auction sales, these ISPs want you to pay extra for a business web site account. Check with your own ISP to see what options are available.*

## Use a Dedicated Web Host

If you plan to run a full-fledged online business, I recommend that you pay a monthly fee and sign up for a full-featured account with a company that is primarily concerned with making web sites like yours available online. A dedicated web hosting service (one that does only hosting, and not Internet access) gives you more disk storage space, more services (such as statistics that report on the number of visits to all of the pages in your site, where your visitors are coming from, and so on), and customer service that is (or at least, should be) a cut above that provided by ISPs or free web hosts.

Typically, your account with a web host should enable you to get a "vanity" domain name (in the form **http://www.*mysite*.com**), anywhere from 50MB to multiple gigabytes of web space (depending on how much you want to spend each month), as well as multiple e-mail addresses. You may want to look for a hosting package that enables you to process web page forms by means of computer programs called CGI scripts. You might even get shopping cart software that enables you to set up an online sales catalog from which people can make selections. Your web host may be able to help you obtain a credit card merchant account as well (see Chapter 9). Each of these types of e-commerce features is a significant step up from a simple web hosting account, and each carries with it an additional degree of technical complexity. If you are interested in creating an e-commerce web site, be sure to find a hosting service that will lead you through the process in a user-friendly way without making you set up CGI scripts or other technical features completely on your own.

The following table sums up the web site alternatives covered in this chapter:

| If you want to... | Set up this web site alternative |
| --- | --- |
| Let your eBay customers get to know you better | An About Me page |
| Promote your business and build trust | An About Me page |
| Sell items for a fixed price | An eBay Store (see Chapter 14) |
| Have sales listings indexed by major search engines and be able to cross-sell products | An eBay Store |
| Have total control over your store and sales | An e-commerce web site |

7

*You'll find web hosting services among the many eBay Stores listed under Specialty Services | Web & Computer Services. The direct URL is **http://services.stores.ebay.com/Web-Computer-Services_Web-Hosting_ W0QQcatZ47106QQtZlw**. You can also register your domain name from within the Seller Manage Store area—from the eBay Stores home page, click Manage My Store, then Register Your Domain Name. Your browser is directed to a domain name registrar where you can obtain a domain name for your store.*

## Find the Right Web Site Creation Software

What software should you use to create your web pages? If you're on a shoestring budget and you don't want the trouble of choosing, purchasing, and installing software, consider using Netscape Composer, the web page tool that is built in with the web browser package Netscape Communicator. Composer is absolutely free, and it contains plenty of features for creating tables, forms, and other sophisticated web page elements (see Figure 7-6).

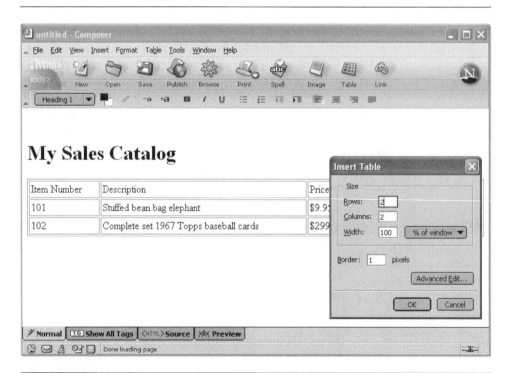

**FIGURE 7-6**   Netscape Composer is available for free with Netscape's web browser.

If you don't use Netscape's browser or if you would rather use a more powerful tool, consider Macromedia Dreamweaver (**http://www.macromedia.com**) or Microsoft FrontPage (**http://www.microsoft.com/frontpage**). These two high-powered programs give you all the tools you need to create web sites, and they enable you to move your web pages from your own computer to your host's site as well. Dreamweaver is shown in Figure 7-7.

## Regular Maintenance and Upkeep

On the Web, it's clear what's hot and what's not. One of the worst insults you can get in cyberspace is to be called the keeper of a *cobweb* page. Make sure your page is always fresh by updating it often. Add new features and remove dated material. Don't put up a page and leave it unattended for long periods of time. Don't include links to your outdated auctions on your regular web site; you'll have to update them constantly. Leave such links for an About Me page, where they'll be updated automatically by eBay.

**FIGURE 7-7**    Dreamweaver lets you monitor and organize entire web sites and publish them online.

An even better reason to update your web site is that you get the chance to rework and improve it. Don't be afraid to consider your site as being continually under construction and something you can always upgrade.

## Where to Find It

- **eBay About Me login page**
  **http://members.ebay.com/aw-cgi/eBayISAPI.dll?AboutMeLogin**
  A form you can fill out to begin the process of creating an About Me page on eBay.

- **The List**
  **http://thelist.internet.com**
  Detailed lists of ISPs organized by location and level of service, as well as lists of web hosting services.

- **eBay Stores that provide web hosting**
  **http://services.stores.ebay.com/Web-Computer-Services_Web-Hosting_W0QQcatZ47106QQtZlw**
  A set of eBay Stores that offers web hosting services, among other goods and services.

# Chapter 8

## Create Digital Images That Sell

## How to...

- Capture high-quality digital images of your sales merchandise
- Scan flat (or nearly flat) objects with a flatbed scanner
- Work with common web graphics formats
- Crop and edit images to optimize their onscreen presentation
- Assemble your own amateur photo studio
- Choose a service to host your digital images
- Link to your images to appear with your auction description

For many auction bidders, a good image is worth more than a thousand words of description. Many of the eBay denizens who scour auction categories searching for unusual, rare, or simply oddball items already know what they want. They scan the description primarily to determine an item's condition. They pay close attention to the images that accompany the auction listing, however. The more images you have and the clearer they are, the better your chances of getting bids.

Unless you're selling something that's so eagerly sought after that people will bid on it without seeing it, you've pretty much got to have one or more images to go along with its sales listing on eBay. There's really no excuse for not creating those images, even if you're the proverbial technophobe. eBay, after all, lets you post one image for free if you use its own Picture Services. Digital cameras are becoming more affordable and easy to use. You can also call on friends and photo labs to provide you with computer images if you need to. Digital imaging is well within your ability, however, and this chapter will show you how to create high-quality graphics that help you gain top dollar for what you want to sell.

# Capture Those Images

The term *capture* probably makes it sound like you need to go out and rope a wild animal. But obtaining images that you can publish on the Web is much easier than that. By "capturing" an image so that you can use it online, I mean that you have to create, save, or obtain the image in the form of a computer file—a digital image. Once you have a digital image in your computer, you can place it on your web page. In the process of capturing a digital image, a scanner or digital camera turns the image into very small squares, known as *pixels*. Each pixel in a computer image contains one or more bits of digital information.

Digital images that consist of pixels are called *bitmaps*. Bitmaps are images that have been saved in a format that makes them easy to display and transmit online. Scanned photos on all web pages, including auction listings, should be clear, small in size, tightly cropped, and compressed so that they appear quickly in a browser window.

NOTE

*TIFF (Tagged Image File Format), PNG (Portable Network Graphics), GIF (Graphics Interchange Format), and JPEG (Joint Photographic Experts Group) are all bitmapped image formats used in computer graphics. JPEG and PNG are used to present photos on the Web, so you need to save your digital photos in one of these two formats. eBay Picture Services only supports JPEG, however.*

Are you keeping all of these technical details straight? You won't be quizzed on them. The least you need to know is this: you need to get images of your sales items into your computer in JPEG or PNG format. How do you obtain (or "capture") digital images of your auction merchandise? You have four basic options:

8

- **Take a digital photo** The most practical and affordable option is to use a digital camera to take a photo of what you want to sell. The camera saves the image directly to computer disk. Digital cameras like the one shown in Figure 8-1 are becoming more affordable all the time (you can find one of sufficient quality on eBay for $50 to $100); you can take as many photos as your camera's memory will hold and transfer them to your computer in a matter of seconds.

- **Scan the image** Scanners like the flatbed model shown in Figure 8-2 are less expensive than digital cameras—you can find them at Buy It Now prices of $20 to $60. You can also rent time on a scanner at a branch of Kinko's. Or you can borrow a friend's scanning device. Simply take a conventional photo of an object with a camera and scan the image to convert it to the computer file.

- **Use a photo lab** You can take a conventional print or slide photo and have the photo lab return the images to you on a CD instead of as prints or slides. This might only cost a dollar or two more than just obtaining the film back and, if your roll of film contains 20 to 30 auction images, it's well worth the expense.

- **Capture a digital video image of the object** Digital video cameras like the one shown in Figure 8-3 take still images that you can save directly to disk. Plus, you can take high-quality videos of your family, too.

**FIGURE 8-1**  Digital cameras are an increasingly affordable option for auction sellers.

The option you should choose depends on how many auctions you plan to conduct, your budget, and your level of comfort with technology. If you only plan to put a few auctions online once in a while, you can take photos with a conventional camera and have a photo lab convert your images to digital files, but this can quickly get expensive. You can use a scanner, but these work best with flat objects such as magazines, and their size is limited by the size of the device's scanning area. Your most economical option is probably to use a digital camera, as described in the following section.

> TIP
>
> *eBay has its own photo tutorial that leads you step by step through the process of posting auction images to accompany your descriptions. Check it out at **http://pages.ebay.com/help/sell/photo_tutorial.html**.*

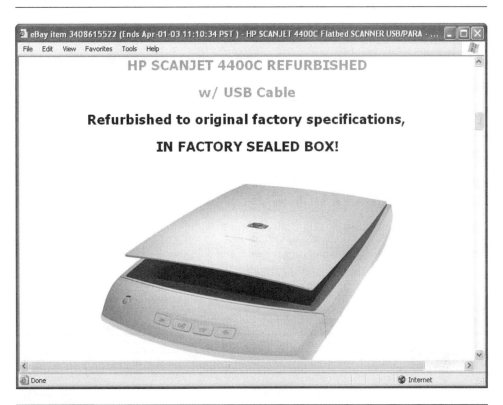

**FIGURE 8-2**    Flatbed scanners are inexpensive but designed mostly for scanning flat objects.

## Use a Digital Camera

Digital cameras bring a new level of convenience to capturing images that can be viewed and edited on a computer. My own experience tells me that this is how the majority of eBay sellers take their auction images. There are so many digital cameras on the market that this chapter isn't going to attempt to recommend which model is best for you to buy. Rather, it assumes that you already have a digital camera and you're looking for some tips on how to use it to capture auction images.

Most digital cameras give you two ways of composing images. You can look either through the viewfinder (the little window on the back of the camera) or the liquid crystal display (LCD, the miniature screen that lets you preview images).

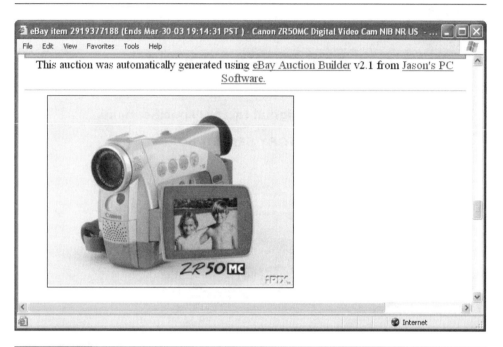

eBay item 2919377188 (Ends Mar-30-03 19:14:31 PST ) - Canon ZR50MC Digital Video Cam NIB NR US - ...

File   Edit   View   Favorites   Tools   Help

This auction was automatically generated using eBay Auction Builder v2.1 from Jason's PC Software.

Internet

**FIGURE 8-3**   You can use digital video cameras to capture still images of your auction items.

# Digital Cameras: Convenience Wins over Cost

When it comes to taking pictures for eBay or another web site, you don't need to get the latest and greatest camera available. Computer monitors are limited in the amount of digital information they can display at any one time, and a 9- or 10-megapixel digital camera will probably (depending on how you configure the resolution) produce files that are too large and slow to display. Not only that, but no matter what kind of digital camera you use, the graphics formats like JPEG in which your images are saved are going to result in a loss of information when images are compressed. And web browsers are unable to display fine nuances of color. The point is that if you are primarily interested in taking digital images for the Web, you may as well use a lower-megapixel camera.

Dana Titus, a PowerSeller profiled in Chapter 6, agrees: "I use a very basic digital camera for my listings. Many sellers go 'all out,' buying a top-of-the-line camera for taking pictures. This is a big mistake. I have a very expensive camera for my personal use, but for eBay auctions I use a Canon Digital Elph—a 3.1-megapixel camera. What many people do not realize is, for displaying pictures online you do not need high-resolution pictures. In fact, it's better to have lower-resolution pictures that will load instantly so the buyer does not have to wait very long to see your item. Having an easy-to-use camera that allows you to quickly upload the pictures is essential."

Dana has created a home studio with a partition as the background. She doesn't spend a lot of time adjusting color or brightness, however, "unless there is a need for cropping." In keeping with her general philosophy of making eBay auction descriptions affordable and simple, she uses the affordable auction service SpareDollar (**http://www.sparedollar.com**) to host her image files.

To my mind, the LCD is preferable because it's more precise. But don't depend on perfection from the little framing square that's supposed to indicate what's going to be in the final image. Leave some extra room around the edges when you frame your images (see Figure 8-4).

Digital cameras enable you to preview images and simply delete them and retake new images if they aren't the way you want. Virtually all digital cameras allow you to zoom in on your subject as well. As a general rule, the closer you are, the sharper your image. You should try to get as close as possible to your subject before taking the photo.

## Purchase a Scanner

If you consistently sell printed material such as postcards, stamps, or historical documents, you should use a device that's specially designed to capture those images in the form of computer files—a flatbed scanner. A scanner is computer hardware that digitizes a single object by moving an optical device much like a camera across it. There are different types of scanners around, but the most practical and easiest to use is a flatbed; its name reflects the fact that the bed on which the photo or other image is placed is flat.

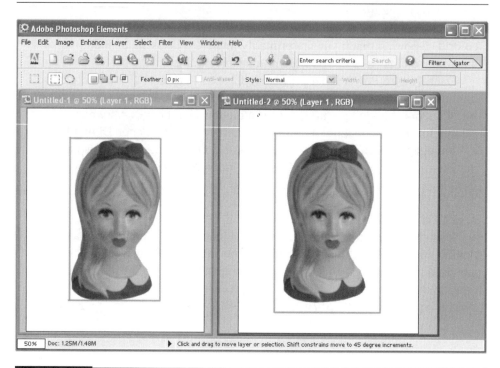

**FIGURE 8-4** The image on the left is too tight; the other is just right.

*Scanners are sometimes advertised as having very fine resolutions. While this is important if you intend to scan images for printed booklets, if you're scanning for eBay or the Web, you need a resolution of only 72 dpi (dots per inch), and any scanner can scan at that relatively coarse setting. But it's a good idea to scan at 144 or 300 dpi and then reduce the resolution using an image editing program in order to get better detail.*

## Scanning, Step by Step

After you buy a scanner and set it up, you won't find it that difficult to use. However, to ensure that your objects turn out clear and sharp, follow these guidelines:

1. Pick a good image. Remember that your images won't appear in print; they'll be seen on a computer screen. You have to account for those shoppers who have old, murky monitors. Select high-contrast images—images that have a clear difference between light and dark areas.

2.  Use your scanning software. All scanners come with some sort of software that lets you scan the images and save them in various formats. Sometimes, scanners come with programs that act as *plug-ins* (programs that work within another graphics program like Adobe Photoshop).

3.  After you install the software, following the instructions that come with your scanner, start up the program, turn on the scanner, and make a preview scan of your first image. A preview scan gives you a quick idea what an image will look like after you do the actual scan. Look for the button that says Preview, such as the one in the lower-left corner of the DeskScan II window, shown in Figure 8-5.

4.  Once you have the preview scan on screen, crop it. *Cropping* an image means that you select the part of the image that you want to appear in the final version and leave out the parts of the image that aren't essential.

**FIGURE 8-5**   A preview scan lets you crop or reduce an image before you make the final scan.

5.  Select an input mode. An input mode tells the scanner how you want the information in the image to be captured. For most auction images, you'll choose the Color option. However, if what you're scanning is a black and white photo, you can reduce the file size dramatically by choosing grayscale mode. On the other hand, if you're scanning line art, a signature, a cartoon, or another drawing, use line art mode.

6.  Set the resolution. Since you're scanning auction images for the Web, choose 150 or 300 dpi. Since computer monitors can display no more than approximately 72 dpi, reduce the resolution to 72 dpi in a graphics program.

7.  Make adjustments. All scanning software comes with brightness and contrast controls that you can move to see if the image improves. You can do this later using image editing software, but why not save yourself the work by making improvements at the scanning stage?

When you're done with all the preparation work, you can press the Scan button and finally scan your image.

TIP    *It's a good idea to calibrate your scanner before you start making scans. Calibrating means that you match the scanner to your monitor so that your image previews are accurate. The exact procedure differs from scanner to scanner, but in general, you make a test scan of an image and then use your scanning software's calibration controls. The exact menu options vary depending on the software used.*

## You Can Scan More than Just Paper

A scanner can be great for scanning flat objects for the Web, but you can also scan some three-dimensional items, like watches or almost-flat toys. Just drape some black cloth or clothing over the object so that it covers the glass, and you'll have a clean background behind what you're scanning. If a scanner is all you have, you can use it to scan items that are bigger than the scanning surface (such as LP-record albums) in pieces and then reassemble them using an image editing program (see "Choose a Graphics Editor" later in this chapter).

You can also find scanners that do more than just scan—they function as color copiers and fax machines as well. They, too, are becoming more affordable all the time and they regularly show up on eBay for Buy It Now prices under $100.

## Set Up Your Photo Studio

Most eBay sellers who take their own digital photos (in other words, most eBay sellers) set up a miniature photo studio in their home. It's easy enough to set one up, and not that expensive, either. Here's a shopping list for what you'll need:

- **Table**   Find a moderately sized table on which you can place and light your sales items. Things that are too large to fit atop the table can go in front of it.

- **Lights**   Make an effort to obtain professional studio lights, as discussed in the section on lighting that follows.

- **Tripod**   A tripod (like the one shown next that was sold on eBay) is a stand with extendable legs on which you can place your camera. A tripod isn't just to hold the camera still while you snap the shutter. In a photo studio, a tripod enables you to position the merchandise and the camera just right and adjust the lighting as well. Once you point your camera at your table, you can leave it there from photo to photo.

8

- **Power supply**   Instead of having to replace batteries every few days, purchase the rechargeable variety.

- **Display stand**   If you're selling jewelry and other items that consist of multiple pieces, you'll do well to purchase a display stand that includes a riser—something that makes the items stand up so you can photograph them better.

- **Background**   A solid, seamless background is a must-have for good photos of auction merchandise. Go to the local fabric store and get several lengths of four- or six-foot-wide fabric in several solid colors. Black is pretty much required for light items; also get a light neutral color such as white, gray, or beige so you can choose the color that makes the item look the best. Alternatively, for small items, you can buy a presentation board at your local office supply store and place it behind your objects.

## Give Your Piece a Chance

All the lighting, backgrounds, and even the best digital camera in the world can't make up for forgetting to do some basic things when you actually take your photo. For instance:

- **Whip out the Windex**   Be sure to take a towel and wipe off what you're selling. Brush the cat hairs off those clothes, polish that silver, and wipe the dirt smudges and fingerprints off those plastic slimline phones. But take care not to wipe too hard or use too strong a cleaner or you'll damage what you're trying to sell.

- **Move in for a close-up**   Most good digital cameras have powerful zoom lenses or macro (close-up) settings; use them to get nice and close on your item before you actually take the photo. If you're too far away, you'll lose detail and your item might even look out of focus.

- **Clean up the area**   A smudge on a wall or a stray toy on the floor can distract attention from what you want people to look at.

- **Clean your lens**   If you've been using your camera outdoors or if you have forgotten to put on the lens cap recently, wipe off the lens (with a clean, photo-quality lens cloth rather than a shirtsleeve or paper towel) so you don't obscure your image.

- ■ **Check your focus**   The autofocus feature on many digital cameras doesn't work perfectly all of the time. Take a good look through the viewfinder or LCD and adjust the focus manually, if necessary, before you click.

- ■ **Avoid the flash**   Find another light source than your camera's built-in flash, which creates bright spots and can distort the true color of what you're trying to depict.

One of the many nice things about digital cameras is that you can take as many photos as you want, delete the ones you don't like, and save only the best. Don't be reluctant to photograph an image from many different angles and with many different levels of zoom. You can publish as many photos as you want with your auctions—though I never seem to see more than six or eight at any one time. Don't limit yourself to one or two.

## Studio Lights

If you need to take lots of images, and you've been plagued by dim and deeply shadowed images, you might consider a drastic upgrade and buy studio lights for your eBay images. The problem is that the built-in flash on a digital camera comes from only one direction and is apt to leave shadows around the edges of what you're photographing. Two or three good studio lights with umbrellas to diffuse the light, like the ones shown in Figure 8-6, will do the trick.

## Let the Sun Shine

You may want to take your photos outdoors in order to avoid the problems caused by homemade backgrounds and shadows caused by indoor spot lighting. (As an alternative, you can place your item by a window that catches the sun and put a white cotton cloth or bedsheet over the window to diffuse the light.) It can be tricky to take photos outdoors, because the sun can produce shadows that actually make merchandise more difficult to see rather than easier. But on a bright cloudy day, the lighting outdoors is even and very good. Steve Brothers of Silk Road Trading Concern (User ID: silkroad) shoots all of his merchandise outdoors—in Nepal. He says: "We use a digital camera to photograph our items. I prefer to shoot outdoors in indirect light. Taking product photos is something one gets better at over time. The clients will guide you in terms of the necessity for auxiliary detail photos. We only ran one front view in the early days, and people would e-mail us asking for extra shots. We eventually realized that some items such as statues or paintings often require multiple shots—side views, back views, or close-ups."

**FIGURE 8-6**　Professional studio lights will pay off in the long run.

## Choose an Image Format

Whether you use a digital camera or a scanner to save your images to disk, you need to choose a file format in which to save them. The file formats that are especially designed to process photos on the Web, JPEG and PNG, process digital information in an image and compress files to make them consume less disk space. All web browsers can open and display files in these formats. Of these two, eBay recommends that you save your image in JPEG format.

NOTE　*Both GIF and JPEG images display correctly on eBay auction pages. JPEG, however, is generally a better format for photographic images with lots of colors, while GIF generally works better for line drawings.*

If you pay extra for a photo lab to create digital images for you, you can tell the service to save the files as JPEGs. Otherwise, you can do so yourself by using the software that comes with your scanner, digital camera, or other hardware device. Usually, you save in JPEG format by choosing File | Save from the program's menu bar and then choosing JPEG from the list of formats that are available. You also need to save the file with the filename extension JPG (or, on a Macintosh, JPEG).

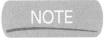

*JPEG compresses image files, but it provides you with several different levels of compression from which to choose. The higher the level of compression, the smaller the image file. At maximum compression, however, you lose some information in the image, and the image doesn't appear as sharp as it can if you use a lower level of compression. If you're not sure which level to choose, try High or Maximum compression to keep the file size as small as possible.*

## Create Images That Attract

You've got a snazzy new digital camera, you've read the instruction booklet, and you've even taken a few test images. You probably think all you need to do now is point, click, and upload to get your photos on the Web along with your auction descriptions. You *can* do that, and it's even possible that some of your photos will come out perfectly the first time. Remember, though, that I'm providing you with instructions for running a successful eBay business. An important part of consistently selling at auction is coming up with a system for creating good images that attract attention and help people decide whether what you're offering is a good match for what they need.

The fact is, most of the time, the images you take of your auction items are going to need some adjustments before you put them online. If you devote a few minutes to brightening and cropping your images, they'll show your objects in their best light (and I mean that literally). You'll separate your images from the ones I see on all too many eBay auctions that are too large, take too long to appear, and are dark and fuzzy to boot. You'll have another way to show your prospective customers that you are a professional and serious about selling on eBay.

### Choose a Graphics Editor

Often, images aren't good if you capture them straight from your scanner, digital camera, or other input device. Instead, after you save your image in JPEG or PNG format, you should edit (or, in photographic terms, *retouch*) the image in a graphics program to improve its appearance.

Personally, I like a program called Adobe Photoshop Elements, which, you'll be happy to know, comes bundled with many digital cameras. If you get this software along with your camera, you are getting a great deal. Here are the kinds of things you should adjust with Photoshop Elements or another graphics program:

- **Adjust contrast and brightness**    The *contrast* of an image is the degree of difference between its light and dark tones. *Brightness* refers to the vibrancy or energy of the colors or shades of color in the image. Images displaying adequate levels of contrast and brightness are easier to view on a monitor. Photoshop Elements' controls are shown in Figure 8-7.

- **Resize images**    Resize images so that they're smaller than originally scanned and fit well on the eBay auction web page. (Look through your graphics program's menus to find a Resize option.)

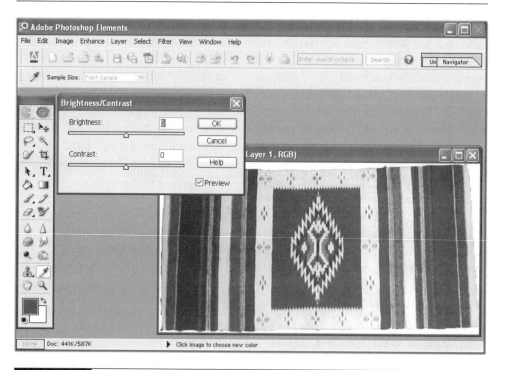

**FIGURE 8-7**    Graphics editors give you great control over an image's appearance.

## Other Graphics Editors

Photoshop Elements (and its "big brother" program, the professional graphics editor simply called Photoshop) is a terrific program, but it consumes lots of memory and disk space. Photoshop Elements 2 requires 128MB of RAM and from 150 to 350MB of hard disk space. I also like the simpler Windows program Paint Shop Pro, by Corel (**http://www.corel.com**).

If you are a Macintosh user and don't want to invest in a complex program like Adobe Photoshop Elements, Thorsten Lemke's GraphicConverter is a great shareware ($35) graphics program. You can download or purchase it from **http://www.lemkesoft.de/en/index.htm**. iPhoto is a free program that runs on any Mac that uses OS X: find out more at **http://www.apple.com/ilife/iphoto**.

*Generally speaking, an image that's two to three inches wide and perhaps four to five inches high is a good size. File sizes of 20 to 30K or less are also desirable.*

■ **Zoom in on what's important**   *Cropping* refers to the practice of cutting out unnecessary details and keeping a certain area of the image on which you want to focus. It makes the image size smaller so that the photo fits better in a web browser window. By making the image smaller, you also make the file size smaller. An image that's, say, 12K in size appears onscreen much faster than does one that's 100K in size.

## Keep File Size Small

You can't depend on your bidders to have relatively fast cable-modem, DSL, or other fast connections. You don't know whether they're viewing your images on an old, slow computer or on a new, speedy one. Your goal is to make your images consume as little memory as possible, so they appear in the browser window right away. These are simple tasks that you can perform in virtually any graphics editor to optimize your images for quick viewing.

## Crop Those Photos

Simply scanning an entire photo from edge to edge and putting the entire photo on your web page usually results in an image that takes up more space than it should—in

8

terms of physical size (height and width) as well as disk space. Cropping a photo does two things:

- Concentrates the viewer's eye on the most important area

- Makes the file size and the image size smaller

Cropping an image is important and you should do it whenever possible. The smaller an image file is, the quicker it will appear on your bidders' computer screens. You do this by clicking the cropping button, positioning your mouse pointer just above and to one side of the image, clicking and holding down your mouse button, and dragging your mouse down and to the opposite side of the image. Release your mouse when the subject of your photo is outlined with the marquee box.

Cropping photos whenever possible literally reduces the number of bits of information in the photo. A 550×250-pixel photo might contain 13K (13,000 bits) of information; reducing it to 300×139 pixels (approximately 4.75×2.25 inches) reduces the size dramatically. It's important to keep photos small in size to ensure that they fit within the smallest computer screens. Remember that, although a minority of web surfers have 21-inch flat-screen monitors, many others have 17-inch monitors with a viewing area that is actually only about 12 inches in width. Within that space, a user may configure a web browser window to be only seven to ten inches in width. Smaller photos aren't that hard to see clearly on web pages because people typically sit very close to their computer screen. Keeping your images three to six inches in width is a safe measurement that most people will be able to see in their entirety.

## Set the Resolution

Earlier in this chapter, I mentioned that scanned images are made up of little bits of information called pixels. Those dots are small, but they aren't always the same size. When you scan an image, you have the option of making the dots *really* small so that the image appears extra smooth. This is called setting the *resolution* of an image. The size of the dots is expressed in dots per inch (dpi). The higher the number of dots per inch, the smaller the dots are, and the finer the image will be.

Setting the resolution is a simple matter when you are preparing images for eBay. Scan at 300 dpi resolution, then reduce the resolution to 72 dpi when you edit the image in a graphics program.

TIP     *If the image seems dark or "muddy," adjust the brightness and contrast. In most scanning programs, the brightness and contrast controls are sliders that you can move either left or right. Try them out and see if the image improves. If you're happy with the image as is, leave the brightness and contrast set to zero.*

## Create Thumbnail Images

You can use a graphics program to create a *thumbnail* or miniature version of an image to a larger, more memory-intensive version. The smaller version (which takes up only a small amount of memory and appears onscreen quickly) gives the viewer a glimpse of what the full image will look like and the chance to decide whether to view the full image in greater detail. Clicking on the link brings a larger, more detailed version of the image to the screen (which is larger in size, and takes longer to appear onscreen).

## Take Time with Your Presentation

The way you present your merchandise has a big effect on whether people will pass it by or make a bid. If you have clothing to sell, or if you regularly sell watches or jewelry, by all means invest in some mannequins on which to mount them (see Figure 8-8). They'll be much more attractive if people can visualize how they look on a human body, rather than lying flat on a table. Where better to find mannequins than on eBay itself?

Don't be reluctant to include lots of clear photos with an item, no matter how "unpicturesque" it might appear. For instance, how many photos can you take of an old hat? eBay seller mrmodern included so many good close-ups in this listing that, if the hat would have fit me, I would have bid on it myself.

8

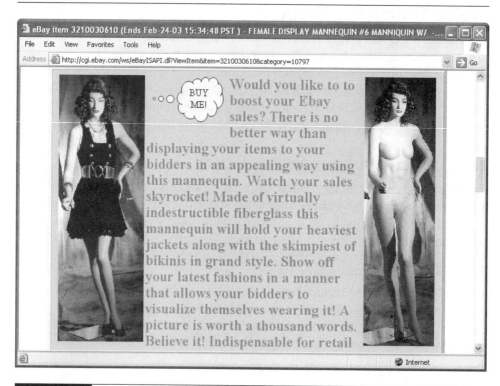

FIGURE 8-8    Display clothing or jewelry on mannequins or live models.

# Find a Home for Your Images

In order for images to appear on auction listings or other web pages, they need to find a home—a virtual home, that is, in the form of space on a computer that's connected to the Internet all the time, called a web server. You've got plenty of options for finding that home. Your ISP may provide you with storage space; you can send your photos to eBay's Picture Services; or you can sign up with a full-time photo hosting service. The options are described in the sections that follow.

## eBay Picture Services

eBay's own photo hosting services, eBay Picture Services (**http://pages.ebay .com/sell/pictureservices**), shown in Figure 8-9, is easy to use, and the quality is

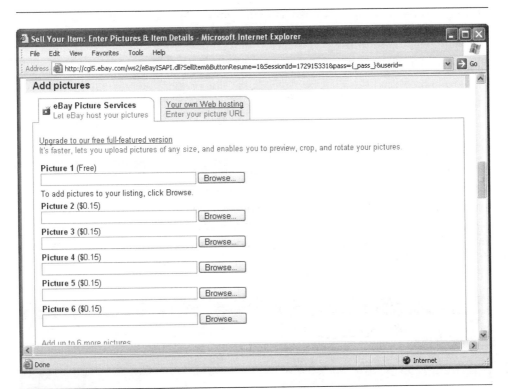

**FIGURE 8-9**    eBay Basic Picture Services

good—especially if you use the enhanced version that lets Windows users drag image files from their computer to the Sell Your Item form to get them online.

eBay Picture Services is fine if you are just starting out, but if you sell large quantities of merchandise on a regular basis, you still might want to shop around. Picture Services lets you include one image per item for no charge. You are charged a nominal fee (at this writing, 15 cents) for subsequent images of the same item. Suppose you sell 100 items per month, and you post an average of two images of each item. You could easily end up paying an extra $15 per month just for image hosting.

As an alternative to paying a per-image fee, you can subscribe to use eBay Picture Services on a monthly basis. For a flat monthly fee, you get storage space on one of eBay's servers. You can upload as many images as you want until you reach your storage limit:

■ For $9.99 per month, you get 50MB of storage space.

■ For $19.99 per month, you get 125MB of storage space.

■ For $39.99, you get 300MB of storage space.

It pays to at least know your options when it comes to finding a web server that can host your digital image file (that is, one that enables you to place the file in a directory on the server so that someone with a web browser can access it). If you sign up with eBay Picture Services, you also have the option to pay extra to display an image in a special way. For an extra 25 cents, you can present an image as a Picture Show, in which you present a series of views of the object in a box; as the following illustration shows, shoppers can click a button to move from image to image or just watch the series as they go by.

**Upload an Image**

1.  From any eBay page, click the Sell button in the toolbar.

2.  Choose the category in which you want to sell your item.

3.  Log in with your eBay User ID and password and click Continue.

4.  Fill out the Sell Your Item form. The Basic version of Picture Services appears by default (see Figure 8-9). Click Browse to locate the image file (or files) you want to add. Locate the file on your computer, click Open, and the image is added to the list of files to upload when you create your auction listing at the end of the form.

5.  However, if you use a Windows computer, click the link **Upgrade to our free full featured version** on the eBay Picture Services tab. If a dialog box appears asking if you want to download an ActiveX Control or Java Applet, click Yes. (You need these mini-programs to use the other version of Picture Services.) The Enhanced Picture Services appears.

6.  You can upload an image using Enhanced Picture Services in one of two ways: click on a box to select a photo file on your computer, or click on a photo file stored on your computer and drag the file to one of the picture boxes in the Add Pictures page.

 *Enhanced Picture Services works only with Windows computers; Basic Picture Services works with Macintosh or Windows. Also consider watermarking your photos—embedding a logo or mark in the image to make it harder to copy—as described in Chapter 18.*

8

For a 75-cent fee, you can include a "Supersize" version of your image. Shoppers can click on the Supersize link and view a close-up of the object you have for sale. A Picture Pack, which includes a Gallery image, extra images, a Picture Show, and a Supersize version, is also available for $1.

*eBay University includes an online tutorial that explains how to take digital photos and add them to your auction listings, located at **http://pages.ebay .com/education/tutorial/course2/photo_1.html**.*

## Other Photo Hosts

It pays to shop around when looking for a web server that your auction images can call home. After all, if your images don't appear reliably and quickly, your bidders might well leave your sale and bid on someone else's items. Another consideration is the software you use to get your images from your computer to the web storage space. You may have to use a special program that does the transfer by using a special set of instructions called File Transfer Protocol (FTP). Other services (such as AOL) provide such software for you. If you use one of the auction management packages mentioned in Chapter 6, you don't have to install special software, either; the transfer utility is provided as part of the service's user interface. The following list describes some of the types of web hosts that you can use to make your auction image files available online:

- **Your own ISP** The first place to turn is to the company that gives you access to the Internet: your Internet Service Provider (ISP). Providing users with access to the Internet and hosting web sites are two different functions, certainly, but the same organization may well perform them. Many ISPs provide you with use of at least 10MB of web site space at no additional cost to you.

- **America Online (AOL)** AOL enables subscribers to create and publish their own web pages or to place simple image files on the Web. (As mentioned in Chapter 7, you get as much as 14MB of web storage space with a basic AOL account.) AOL is quite popular with sellers on eBay and other auction services.

- **A web hosting service** The same web hosting service that publishes your web site gives you space that can be used for posting images and web pages alike. See Chapter 7 for suggestions. Click the Your Own Web Hosting tab in the Sell Your Item form to host your own photos. After clicking the tab, a field appears that prompts you for the URL of your hosted picture. You are also given the option to enter the URL for your Gallery photo.

- **An auction management service** Most services that help you manage your auction sales, such as ManageAuctions.com (**http://www.manageauctions .com**) and AuctionHelper.com (**http://www.auctionhelper.com**), make it easy to upload your image files.

■ **A photo hosting service**   A few web sites specialize in providing space where eBay and other auction users can publish auction images to accompany sales listings. PixHost.com (**http://www.pixhost.com**), for example, enables you to host two images on its site for free; after that trial usage, hosting images costs 50 cents each for 30 days, which is far more expensive than eBay's own Picture Services. However, you can upload files using your web browser, as described in the site's online tutorial (see Figure 8-10).

Other image hosting services are more affordable than PixHost.com or eBay Picture Services. Auction-Images.com (**http://www.auction-images.com**) gives you 1MB of storage space for free. A 10MB account is available for $5 per month. ProPicHosting.com (**http://www.freepichosting.com**) also enables you to store images for free or pay a monthly subscription fee.

**FIGURE 8-10**   An image hosting service gives you a way to upload image files with your browser.

*If you use Adobe Photoshop Elements 2, you can move files from your computer to storage space with the online photo service Shutterfly (**http://www.shutterfly.com**). You can even upload the files after you edit them in Photoshop Elements, without having to use a special file transfer program. Mac users can get 100MB of storage space through Apple's .Mac subscription service, which costs $99 per year after a free 60-day trial period.*

## Linking to Your Image

After you create a digital image and add it to your host site, you add that image to your sales description by specifying the URL for the image on the eBay Sell Your Item form. All ISPs provide customers with instructions on how to figure out their web page URLs. Call the Customer Service section of your ISP, or check the company's FAQ. A common convention is to assign a URL that looks like this (this example is for a JPEG image, which has the filename extension .jpg):

http://www.*yourISP*.com/~*yourusername*/*filename*.jpg

After posting an image online, verify that it actually appears on your page. The most common cause of a broken image or question mark icon appearing with your description instead of the image itself is an incorrect URL. If you're typing the URL from scratch, you must get it right exactly: a single blank space, capital letter, or typo in an URL can prevent a web browser from locating the image and displaying it onscreen.

## Upload Your Image to the Gallery

You can also specify whether to place any images that accompany your listing in the eBay Gallery in addition to displaying them on the auction web page itself. If you put a number of your images in the Gallery (at 25 cents per image), you can create your own photo gallery. If someone searches for your items and clicks Gallery View, they can see them all at once (see Figure 8-11).

The Gallery is a collection of small-scale thumbnail images that auction sellers submit of an item they're currently offering for sale. If you create a Gallery image (and you should), it appears next to the title of your auction item in search results and listings. Buyers also have the option to browse through all of your Gallery images in Picture Gallery format and click one in which they're interested; clicking the image takes them to the auction sales page where they can read a description and place a bid if they so choose. The Gallery doesn't display all the images that accompany auction listings—only the ones for which sellers pay the extra 35-cent fee for extra exposure

**FIGURE 8-11**    For an extra 25 cents, you can create your own photo gallery.

in the Gallery. (You can splurge and pay $19.95 to place your image in a featured area of the Gallery as well; it's called the Gallery Featured option.)

> **TIP**    *You can create a link to your own Gallery page and include it on your own web site or your About Me page (see Chapter 7 for more on creating and editing an About Me page). You need to use the following code, which serves as a link to your own Gallery page:*

```
<a href=http://search-desc.ebay.com/search/search.dll?MfcISA
PICommand=GetResult&query=eBayUserID&srchdesc=y&ebaytag1=
ebayreg&ebaytag1code=0&ht=1&SortProperty=MetaEndSort&sc=1&st=
2> Click here to view my Gallery auctions </a>
```

> *Clicking on the link causes the viewer's browser to perform a search of your sales and present the results in Picture Gallery format. Be sure to replace the eBayUserID string with your own user ID.*

# Where to Find It

- **eBay University How to Take Photos Tutorial**
  **http://pages.ebay.com/education/tutorial/course2/photo_1.html**
  An online tutorial that briefly explains how to capture and save images and
  get them online.

- **eBay Picture Services**
  **http://pages.ebay.com/sell/pictureservices**
  An overview of eBay's photo hosting service, plus links to an FAQ and an
  online tutorial on how to add a photo to your auction listing.

- **Photos/HTML Discussion Board**
  **http://forums.ebay.com/db1/forum.jsp?forum=99**
  Discussions about how to post photos on eBay and edit auction listings
  with HTML.

# Part III

# Business Practices for eBay

# Chapter 9

# Accept Payments and Serve Your Customers

## How to...

- Use e-mail to answer prospective bidders' questions

- Send out end-of-auction notices and reminders

- Respond to complaints and problems after the sale

- Accept checks and money orders safely

- Take advantage of payment services that streamline transactions

- Accept credit card payments

- Verify credit card purchasers' information

Putting your first sale online is exciting. Watching the bids come in is a thrill. Watching the action as the sale closes can make your pulse pound. But the really rewarding part—the real satisfaction—comes when you are paid for what you sold. All of your hard work pays off when you get a check in the mail or you have a notice that funds have been transferred to your PayPal or checking account.

Before you get to the payment stage, you need to interact with your customers at several critical stages. How you respond to bidders who make inquiries and to your auction winners has a direct bearing on the level of trust and professionalism you present online. Providing good customer service not only makes transactions go more smoothly, it also builds goodwill on eBay as a whole and has a tangible benefit in terms of the positive feedback you receive.

Sellers on eBay have an advantage when it comes to the end of the sale. They have lots of alternatives for receiving payment. The main problem is the deadbeat buyer—the one who never sends payment in the first place. Once people respond to your e-mails and send payment, it's likely that things will go smoothly. Yes, checks bounce once in a while. Yes, there is credit card fraud. But the overwhelming majority of transactions go smoothly, and most buyers are courteous and fun to deal with. That's why sellers keep coming back to put items up for sale. This is when eBay is really fun. This chapter spells out your options for receiving payment and maintaining positive interactions with your customers.

# Provide Customer Service

eBay grew to become so popular because people who use it are, for the most part, trustworthy. Encounters tend to be positive rather than negative. If transactions on eBay went badly more often than not, the marketplace's popularity would dwindle.

As a seller, you need to know how to handle your customers with care in order to preserve that atmosphere of goodwill.

Even if you don't own a brick-and-mortar store and don't manage a big corporate retail outlet, you need to provide good service to the people who buy from you, just like the big guys. In fact, because you're a lone seller, you can add a personal touch that big e-commerce retailers can't match. A pack of coffee included with a coffee maker, a few bags of tea delivered along with a teapot, and a quick and courteous answer to a question can build a good reputation as well as a dependable customer base.

## Become an E-Mail Expert

The best advice I can give to you as far as dealing with prospective bidders and buyers on eBay is to keep in constant e-mail contact, and keep your communications courteous and friendly whenever possible. Respond to inquiries quickly, and send out end-of-sale notices as soon as you can after a sale is made or an auction ends.

### Answer Questions

Responding to e-mail inquiries is one of the most practical and important ways in which you can build good customer relations. Try your best to answer questions posed by bidders as quickly as you can—within one day or less if possible. In your auction listings, be sure to include whether you plan to be out of town for a length of time so that customers will know that there might be a delay in your responses to their inquiries.

If you work in a brick-and-mortar store and meet customers face to face, you need to dress well and speak politely. In the same way, you need to make an effort to be professional in your communications with your online customers. What does that mean, exactly? It means spelling correctly, using correct grammar, and using salutations like Hello, Thanks, Best Wishes, or Sincerely. These little details are the substitute for the nuances of tone of voice, gestures, and facial expression that you can't express online. You'll get even more points if you thank people for writing:

> Thank you for your inquiry regarding the Sheaffer Scrip ink container. This is a display container that was probably used in pen shops. However, it does contain ink, and the ink appears to be liquid and useable (I haven't used it myself, however; I can't guarantee that you could actually write with it.) There are a couple of minor tears in the box and an ink stain on the bottom; otherwise the box is in excellent condition.

9

Don't forget to check my other auctions for fountain pens and other writing accessories that you might also enjoy.

Best wishes,
Greg Holden

 *Some of the best tips for dealing with eBay buyers and sellers in a courteous manner—even when they get mad at you for some reason— can be found on the web site of eBay's longtime seller and instructor Uncle Griff (**http://www.unclegriff.com**).*

## Send the End-of-Sale Notification

Many active eBay sellers sell multiple items every single day, and they need to use auction software of the sort described in Chapter 6 to send out e-mails in bulk to their winning bidders. If you don't sell quite so often and you have the time, however, you should take a few minutes to send out personal notifications to your high bidders once they have won what you're offering. The notification letter can still start out as a template with fields that you customize. You don't have to re-create the message from scratch for every sale. You might create a letter like the following that covers all the main points: the item sold, the shipping costs, the payment method, your address, and a time frame for payment.

I am happy to announce that you are the winning bidder for eBay item #122334455, the Sheaffer Scrip ink container. I look forward to a smooth transaction ending in positive feedback for both of us.

I accept payment by PayPal, a personal check, cashier's check, or money order. Please send the following within the next 7 days:

Winning bid amount: $29.95

Shipping (Priority Mail): $6.00

TOTAL Amount Due: $35.95

If you want me to ship by Express Mail, tell me and I will calculate a new amount for you. Please either include a copy of this e-mail address with your payment or write the eBay item number on your check. Send to:

Greg Holden
1234 Anywhere Street
Chicago, IL 60611

If you pay by personal check, your order will ship after a 14-day clearing period.

Thank you for your winning bid. I am happy to be working with you toward a smooth transaction.

Best wishes,
Greg Holden

If you want to make some extra points marketing your other sales, you can include a link to your About Me or eBay Store page or to another web site. But most buyers just want the facts, and if they're happy with the merchandise and the speed of the transaction, they'll search out your other sales eventually.

## Use eBay's Checkout Option

eBay uses the word "Checkout" to describe its quick payment system for buyers. Rather than having to calculate your shipping and handling totals in your end-of-auction e-mail message, you can expedite the transaction by entering the details in the Sell Your Item form when you prepare to put your sale online. That way, when a sale ends, your customer can click a Pay Now button to receive an invoice from you that automatically calculates the total and tells them how to pay (see Figure 9-1).

To make sure the Pay Now button appears in your sales listings, you need to activate Checkout, as described in the following sidebar, "Send Out an Invoice."

*The image shown in Figure 9-1 depicts shipping instructions that the buyer calculates based on his or her address; the Checkout process works if you prefer to charge flat shipping costs as well.*

## Send a Payment Reminder

Correspondence with customers gets less pleasant when you have to send a payment reminder to someone who hasn't yet paid for your auction items. However, that doesn't mean you need to lose your courteous, professional approach. Being nice when things aren't going perfectly is a sure-fire way to get positive feedback from grateful customers, in fact. Be businesslike and firm when you send your reminder; keep in mind that payment may have been lost in the mail, the high bidder may have fallen ill or gone out of town, the neighbor's dog may have eaten the check on the

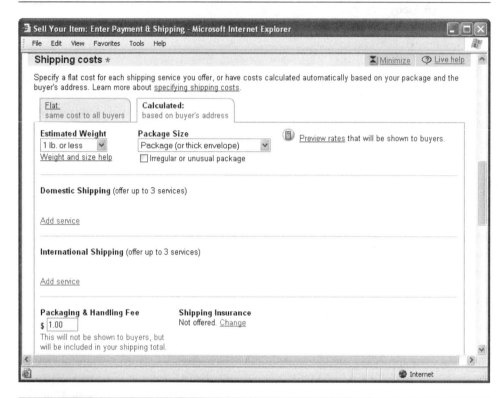

FIGURE 9-1    Help your customers by entering shipping and other charges when you create the sale.

way to the mailbox, or any number of legitimate reasons. Be sure to specify a time frame for receiving your response to the reminder e-mail:

Dear Buyer,

Last week you won a bottle of Scrip ink on one of my eBay auctions. The payment due date for this auction passed yesterday and I have not received a check or other payment notification. Perhaps the payment has gotten lost in the mail or you haven't been able to get to this matter yet.

I'd appreciate it if you could e-mail me within 24 hours to let me know what's going on, and whether you want to follow through with the transaction. Otherwise,

I would like to re-list the item if you don't want it anymore.

Best wishes,
Greg Holden

*You don't necessarily have to write each post-sale reminder from scratch. If you use eBay's Selling Manager software (described in Chapter 6), you can take advantage of templates that are provided for various types of post-sale communications, including payment reminders.*

 **Send Out an Invoice**

Giving your buyers the opportunity to click Pay Now and get their totals instantly is one thing. But if you don't want to depend on those buyers to click Pay Now and use the Checkout system, you have another option: send out an invoice.

The first step in being able to issue an invoice to your customers is to activate Checkout by following these steps:

1. Click My eBay in the eBay navigation bar.

2. In the My Account section of the My eBay Views column on the left side of the page, click eBay Preferences.

3. Scroll down to the Seller Preferences heading, and look at the bold words to the right of the Display Pay Now button item. The words "For all Items" should be visible. If they are not, move to Step 4.

4. Click Change, and when the Payment & Shipping Preferences page appears, click the Show the Pay Now Button in All My Listings choice.

5. Click Submit.

Once you have activated Checkout, follow these steps to issue an invoice to someone who has bought one of your items:

1. Go to your My eBay page and, in the All Selling section of the My eBay Views column, click Sold.

2. Scroll down to the Items I've Sold section and click the Send Invoice button located next to the User ID of the buyer you want to receive the invoice.

**9**

### Send a Shipping Notice

It's not technically necessary to send out a notice to a buyer from whom you have received payment stating that the item is being shipped out to them—but it helps. Tessa Hebert, a book dealer who has a page full of tips for sellers, sends a similar note. She told me that she also asks the buyer to confirm receipt of the book and satisfaction with the transaction. Such a note encourages the buyer to leave positive feedback for you after the item arrives—and many buyers need to be reminded to leave feedback.

The last step is to leave positive feedback for the individual after the transaction is complete. You don't need to receive feedback from someone in order to leave feedback for that same individual, of course. But if you want to build up your positive feedback rating, a reminder e-mail asking specifically for feedback can help.

*Tessa Hebert runs a mail-order book business called Book Dealers (**http:// bookdealers.home.mindspring.com**) with her partner Bill Fulkerson. Her tips for eBay auction sellers can be found at **http://www.mindspring .com/~bookdealers/help.html**.*

# Keep It Simple: Checks and Money Orders

The simplest kind of payment you can receive from bidders and buyers is in the form of a piece of paper—a check or money order. It's hard to beat these two options for simplicity and reliability. When you're just starting out, you should definitely include these methods of payment. Many sellers start out accepting checks and money orders. They soon move up to PayPal or another payment service, and a few move on to accepting some sort of credit card payment. (See "Accept Credit Card Payments" later in this chapter.) But this chapter will focus on the two basic forms of payment first.

## Accept Good Old-Fashioned Paper

Cyberspace is great, but even for those of us who have been online for several years, it's still comforting to receive a paper check in the mail. When you get to Step 4 of the Sell Your Item form (shown in Figure 9-2), the option for PayPal, the payment service that's affiliated with eBay, is checked, and you should make sure the options to accept checks and money orders are checked, too, in order to keep things easy and reliable for yourself and your customers.

**FIGURE 9-2**    This area of the Sell Your Item form lets you select checks, money orders, and other forms of payment.

## Cashier's Checks

Cashier's checks are probably the most secure form of payment that you can receive. As soon as the customer obtains one from a bank, the money is debited from his or her account. Nevertheless, cashier's checks can take several days to clear, and you should wait at least a few days after one arrives before shipping an item out. However, cashier's checks carry a service charge that ranges from $3 to $5, so you can't blame your customers if they don't want to send you a cashier's check. Be sure to provide other options as well.

## Money Orders

Money orders, too, usually carry a service charge when obtained from a bank. The fee can be anywhere between $1 and $3. However, money orders can be obtained less expensively from a wide variety of sources. You're liable to look around your

## eBay Bestsellers
## Put People First, Seller Advises

Lisa Suttora, an eBay PowerSeller (User ID: seattlemomsplace) and the owner of WhatDoISell.com (**http://www.whatdoisell.com**), an online auction education web site, regards customer service as centrally important to her eBay business. In fact, on the About Me page for her business, SeattleMomsPlace (**http://cgi3 .ebay.com/ws/eBayISAPI.dll?ViewUserPage&userid=seattlemomsplace**), she prominently states her policy: "At SeattleMomsPlace, old fashioned customer service *is* our business!"

"I knew when I started selling on eBay that it was important to establish a reputation for a high level of customer service right from the beginning," Lisa explains. "My goal was to make each eBay sale as personable as a face-to-face transaction. In fact, the name of my business, SeattleMomsPlace, came about because I envisioned a place where shopping online felt just like shopping from your favorite mom-and-pop corner store."

To achieve this goal, Lisa has implemented several customer service strategies designed to set her business apart from the competition. "First and foremost I answer every e-mail quickly and professionally. If you want to provide good service and present a professional business image, it is of the utmost importance that your e-mails are clear and concise, but also with an element of warmth."

Post-sale communications are also critically important. Using the customizable templates in eBay Selling Manager Pro, Lisa has created her own personalized templates that she sends out to customers to let them know the status of their transaction every step of the way.

"A customer should know when their payment has been received, when their item has shipped, and what the shipping tracking number is. If you do business with any major online retailer, this is standard operating procedure. Yet, I am always amazed at the number of eBay sellers who don't send any post-sales communications at all. In fact, I receive e-mails from my customers all the time who are thrilled with the fact that they get post-sales communications from me."

Lisa's other "Gold Star" customer service policies include:

- She ships on a daily basis within 24 hours of completed payment. Often, that means that items are shipped within hours of receiving payment.

- She ships worldwide: 40 percent of her business is international.

- She provides a 100 percent satisfaction guarantee. Studies have shown that such a guarantee translates directly into increased sales. "It is important to me that our customer is delighted with every purchase."

■ She uses excellent packaging so that the item has a gentle ride to the customer's home.

■ She provides the option for special gift wrapping services.

Most importantly, Lisa states her company's customer service policies in each listing. "Buyers should be able to find out everything they need to know about making their purchasing decision by easily scanning your listing. They should not have to click to your About Me page to see what your Customer Service policies are (although that information is available there as well). It is my job as an eBay seller to make it as easy as possible for my customer to click Buy It Now and make their purchase. On numerous occasions I have had buyers write to me to tell me that they are making the purchase from me rather than a competitor because of the service we provide."

She recalls a transaction that came in at 3:30 P.M. on a Friday afternoon. "I was just about to go to the post office to ship when a question came through from a potential buyer. He wanted to know if it was possible for him to buy a Spiderman Lego Pen for his little brother who was in the hospital. He was hoping to have it shipped that day." Even though this was a small-ticket item, Lisa knew that this was probably one of the most important sales she would ever make. "I wrote back to him and told him that I would be happy to ship the pen that afternoon. He then replied that he was creating a card and would send it to me via e-mail and asked if I would print it and include it in the package. While waiting for the card to come through, I wrapped the pen in brightly colored paper and put red ribbon and a big red bow on it. I wanted this little boy in the hospital to have a package he could unwrap. The card came through, and when I printed it, there smiling up at me was a picture of the customer's baby sending wishes to his uncle to 'Get Well Soon.' I went to the post office shortly thereafter."

"What most people don't realize about doing business online is that ultimately this is a business about people," says Lisa.

own neighborhood and find currency exchanges and stores that issue money orders. Some of the options—both virtual and brick-and-mortar—are listed in Table 9-1.

**TIP**    *Your customers don't have to go to the store or bank to obtain a money order. They can obtain one online through Western Union's BidPay.com service (**http://www.bidpay.com**), as explained later in this chapter—as well as the services listed in Table 9-1—or through Payko (**http://www .payko.com/index.aspx**).*

| Money Order Source | Fee for $20 Money Order | Fee for $100 Money Order |
| --- | --- | --- |
| Western Union BidPay.com | $2.95 | $5 |
| United States Post Office | $0.90 | $0.90 |
| Payko | $3.99 | $4.99 |

**TABLE 9-1** Options and Fees for Money Orders

## Personal Checks

You might ignore the check box next to Personal Check in Step 4 of the Sell Your Item form because personal checks seem much riskier than cashier's checks or money orders. It's true, money orders and cashier's checks are more secure; but personal checks are also less of a problem than you might think, and you should consider accepting them as well, while setting stringent conditions for your bidders.

One of your goals as an online businessperson should be to make life as easy as possible for your customers. If you decide to accept personal checks, you'll be giving them another option. You might save your buyers a trip to the post office or the 7-Eleven to pick up a money order. Also remember that you can (and actually *should*) specify in your auction terms that you will wait until a personal check clears before you ship out an item, even if this takes 7 to 10 days. Many sellers go through hundreds of personal checks without having one bounce. Of course, when

## eBay Bestsellers
## Bounced Checks Not a Big Problem, Says Seller

PowerSeller Kevin Boyd (User ID: preferreddiscounts) accepts PayPal, personal checks, money orders, and cashier's checks from his customers. He prefers PayPal, and says nearly all of his U.S. customers and 85 percent of his international customers make use of Checkout. "It's easier and better for everyone," he comments. "I receive immediate payment and the product is shipped immediately."

But personal checks aren't a problem, either, he adds. It's rare that a personal check actually bounces; he also doesn't always wait to ship out merchandise if the buyer indicates a personal check has been sent. "It depends on the amount and the customer," he explains. "It is very costly for a customer to bounce a check so it rarely happens on cheaper merchandise. Generally speaking, for anything under $50, I just ship the item. Anything between $50 and $100,

I double-check their feedback first, then ship if I don't see any problems. For anything over $100, I wait for the check to clear."

Nonpaying buyers are a bigger problem, Boyd says. "I think some people get buyer's remorse after they win an auction and then run and hide, don't return e-mails, and so on. This eats up my time trying to contact them, then waiting for payment, etc. I have found that in about 90 percent of the cases, if a customer does not pay within a week, he or she won't pay at all. So it is just best to use eBay's Second Chance Offer system and move the product out, rather than wasting time and effort running down the payment from the winning bidder. But these cases are rare."

Boyd, who owns Seattle-based Preferred Discounts, LLC, (**http://www .preferreddiscounts.net**), has been buying and selling on eBay for more than four years. Like many eBay sellers, it was first a hobby that grew into a full-time business. After 23 years in the corporate world, this former executive from the healthcare cardiology software industry was ready for a career change that provided better job satisfaction and complete control of his financial future. Kevin started an eBay-based, online business selling to businesses and consumers. He began with niche items that he was familiar with such as marine electronics, books, aquarium supplies, and smoking pipes, and then moved into other categories. Within four months he became a Silver PowerSeller.

"Many new eBay sellers want to sell the latest glitz products such as consumer electronics. My advice would be to forget mass market and go niche. The problem is the competition. You just can't compete with the big electronics stores or all the online competition and be profitable. You don't have the buying power they do so don't try to compete. Instead, think niche or accessories. Let the big stores sell the main units and you sell the accessories. For example, I just purchased a new cell phone and asked for a car charger. The store didn't carry them but the salesman said the best place to get them was eBay. So don't sell the phone, sell the car charger. Stick with niche items. What are your hobbies, interests, and area of expertise? Start there and sell products and accessories into those markets. Find what works, what doesn't, then expand from there."

Kevin recently became a Certified Education Specialist trained by eBay. He teaches seminars and consults eBay buyers/sellers and businesses around the Pacific Northwest. Kevin can be contacted by e-mail at **preferreddiscounts @comcast.net**.

9

one *does* bounce, it can be upsetting, and the experience has caused more than one seller to make auction terms even more restrictive ("I'll only accept personal checks if you have a positive feedback rating over 100," for instance).

### COD (Cash on Delivery)

Cash on delivery sounds sensible in theory. You rely on the delivery person to accept payment on delivering your merchandise. You don't have to wait for checks to clear, and you don't have to worry about credit card fees.

In practice, there are plenty of downsides to using COD. First of all, there are fees, and they can be hefty. UPS will collect payment but they will charge you $7 for the service, for instance. Suppose the driver attempts to make delivery and the individual isn't home. Then you have to wait days on end while delivery is attempted. You might have to exchange e-mails with your customer to arrange for alternate delivery; the item might simply be returned to you. You can easily wait weeks to receive your payment. It's far preferable to get a check or money order up front instead. If you insist on COD, consider using FedEx, which is flexible about delivery and pickup times, and will overnight the money to you using—surprise, surprise—FedEx.

 *It should seem obvious, but I don't recommend that you accept cash from your buyers because of the danger that it can be stolen from the mail. I know that some sellers do accept cash, however, especially from international customers who find it difficult to deal with payment services. And I have to admit that I have accepted cash from someone who insisted on it, and it arrived with no problem. But if something does happen and payment is lost, it becomes your responsibility to explain to the customer that the money never arrived, which can easily lead to a dispute that can put your all-important reputation in jeopardy. It isn't that difficult for customers, even those who are in other countries, to obtain a money order, and you should insist that they do so.*

## Offer PayPal and Other Payment Services

If you've never been in business before, you can be excused for feeling anxious about dealing directly with customers, even if they're sending you payment in the form of checks or money orders. Many sellers and buyers alike prefer to have a "middleman" accept the money and pass it along, and sellers don't mind having the service subtract a fee for doing so. A payment service does just that: it functions as an intermediary between someone who provides goods or services and someone who pays money in exchange for them.

For eBay transactions, payment services have two big advantages:

- **Security**   Payment is no longer a matter of trust when you use a payment service. The buyer knows you're going to get the money, rather than having to trust a shipper. The seller knows the payment is going to be received—and quickly, without having to wait for the mail to deliver it. (PayPal also offers fraud protection for its members.)

- **Credit card purchases**   Payment services like PayPal enable customers to pay you with a credit card even if you don't have a merchant account with a bank, a Point of Sale (POS) terminal, or payment gateway software. The payment service deducts the purchase price from the customer's credit card account and transfers it to you. You become an instant credit card merchant!

PayPal (**http://www.paypal.com**), which began as an independent company but was purchased by eBay in 2002, is by far the most popular payment service option used by eBay sellers. Most sellers welcome PayPal because it allows them to pay for purchases instantly with either a credit card account or checking account, so you should definitely include it among your options.

NOTE   *Sellers who don't use PayPal usually offer a service like BidPay (**http://www.bidpay.com**), which is described in an upcoming section. Other payment services include Moneybookers.com (**http://www.moneybookers.com**) and Escrow.com (**http://www.escrow.com**).*

## Accept Payment with PayPal

PayPal, the payment service that is now officially part of eBay (see Figure 9-3), has gained credibility simply because it is so widely used (it's reported to have more than 17 million customers). Simply put, many sellers expect you to give them the option to use PayPal to accept payment; if you don't, there's a chance they might not bid on what you have to offer (though if you're offering something they passionately desire, they'll have no problem sending you a check or money order for it).

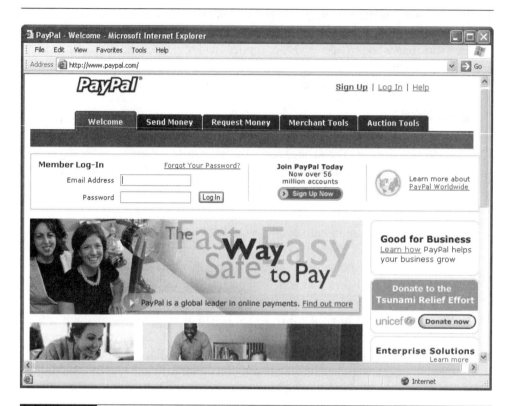

FIGURE 9-3 PayPal sellers can accept credit payments for auction sales on an e-commerce web site.

It's easy to set up an account with PayPal and start accepting payments; if you do so before you start selling, things will go smoother when the first payment comes in. When you register, you'll need to choose one of three accounts: a Personal account, Premier Account, or Business account. As a seller, you definitely want the Premier or Business account because Personal accounts may not receive credit card payments. In order to receive credit card payments, sellers are charged either a Merchant Rate or a Standard Rate. To qualify for the lower of the two, the Merchant Rate, both of the following criteria must apply:

- You have been a PayPal member in good standing for the past 90 days.

- You have received more than $3000 in payments in the previous calendar month.

If your monthly sales volume is $3000 or less, you are charged the Standard Rate. The difference between the Standard Rate and Merchant Rate fees at this writing is shown in Table 9-2.

As a Premier/Business account customer, you greatly increase the chances of attracting buyers because you give your customers the ability to make purchases with their credit cards. Plus, you can gain access to your PayPal funds with PayPal's ATM/debit card. If you have the debit card and indicate that PayPal is your preferred method of payment by choosing PayPal Preferred in your PayPal Selling Preferences, you may be eligible to earn 1.5% cash back for each purchase. To get this benefit, you need to meet several requirements, however; see PayPal's site for more details.

NOTE  *Keep in mind that PayPal's fees change from time to time and may be different by the time you read this. You can get the current fees at **http://www.paypal.com/cgi-bin/webscr?cmd=p/gen/fees-receiving-outside**.*

One particularly nice thing about PayPal is that it accepts credit cards such as Discover and American Express, which you may not be able to accept with a conventional merchant account. Normally, even if you obtain a conventional merchant account through a bank or other financial institution, you have to make arrangements directly through each of those two credit card companies to be one of its merchants.

You can configure your PayPal account so that your money is transferred directly to your checking account; transferred by check (there's a charge for each check); or held in your PayPal account. In addition, you can print invoices to send to your customers. The ability to print is especially easy if you use QuickBooks; PayPal has been integrated into the QuickBooks accounting system (see Chapter 17).

| Currency in Which You Are Paid | Standard Rate | Merchant Rate (For Monthly Income of $3000.01 to $10,000; Lower Rates Apply for Higher Monthly Income) |
|---|---|---|
| U.S. Dollars | 2.9% + $0.30 | 2.5% + $0.30 |
| Canadian Dollars | 3.9% + C $0.55 | 3.5% + C $0.55 |
| Euros | 3.9% + €0.35 | 3.5% + €0.35 |
| Pounds Sterling | 3.9% + £0.20 | 3.5% + £0.20 |
| Yen | 3.9% + Y40 | 3.5% + Y40 |

**TABLE 9-2**    Premier/Business Account Rate Fees

PayPal also protects both buyers and sellers in a number of ways:

- It checks a buyer's address against the credit card billing address. It confirms the buyer's address and, if you ship to that confirmed address in the U.S., you are not liable for chargebacks.

- Your account is insured up to $100,000 against unauthorized withdrawals.

- PayPal verifies credit card holders by having them submit the CVV2 identification numbers printed on the back of most credit cards; the numbers force the buyer to have the actual credit card rather than using a stolen credit card number.

- Premier/Business account holders can deny payment from any buyers who do not have confirmed addresses.

- The usual $10 fee that PayPal charges for any chargeback is waived if you fulfill the requirements in the Seller Protection Policy.

The Seller Protection Policy protects you against nonshipments, unauthorized credit card use, and chargebacks if you meet several requirements. You must have your address and checking account confirmed by PayPal with your bank, you must ship only to confirmed addresses, you must keep proof of shipping that can be tracked online, and you must ship to U.S., U.K., or Canadian buyers. Seller protection and address verification doesn't apply to international transactions—which is a sore spot with many eBay sellers who want to receive payments from other countries. In addition, PayPal's Buyer Protection program enables buyers to receive up to $1000 in fraud protection when they purchase from qualified sellers. If you are one of those sellers, you are likely to get more business.

NOTE *Some eBay users love PayPal for its convenience. Others dislike it for various reasons: the main one is cost. PayPal's fees aren't inconsiderable. Other services specifically advertise themselves as having fees that are lower than PayPal's. Another is the way PayPal handles disputes and user accounts. In fact, in September 2002 a class-action lawsuit was filed on behalf of more than 100,000 PayPal customers, alleging that the company responds slowly or not at all to disputes and complaints, thus freezing accounts for months at a time. You can read a* San Francisco Chronicle *article about the suit at **http:// www.sfgate.com/cgi-bin/article.cgi?file=/chronicle/archive/2002/09/07/ BU232114.DTL&type=business**.*

## Accept Payment with BidPay

One of the auction sellers I interviewed for this book, a gentleman with a feedback rating of more than 3400 whose User ID is decoray, specifies in his auction terms that he will not use PayPal at all. Rather, he accepts checks, money orders, and the Western Union–affiliated money order payment service, BidPay (**http://www.bidpay.com**).

BidPay is simple: sellers don't have to register with BidPay to receive money orders using the service. Registered sellers can set up accounts where they can review records of past orders and have their address verified by BidPay. You also need to set up an account if you want to receive an e-mail notification that a payment has been sent to you, or if you want a payment to be deposited directly in your checking account. However, buyers *do* need to register with BidPay to send money orders to you. Buyers use the BidPay.com web site to choose a credit or debit card to make payment. (BidPay does not accept MasterCard, however.) They add any shipping fees you have specified to the amount of the money order. They also pay transaction fees, some examples of which are listed in Table 9-3.

Once you get a confirmation e-mail from BidPay saying that the money order has been mailed to you, you have the option to either ship the merchandise immediately or wait until the money order actually arrives.

Money orders are shipped to sellers by first-class mail, and the shipping cost is included in the BidPay fees. However, buyers who are in a hurry to receive their merchandise can send you a money order by second-day air for an extra $8, and by next-day air for $15.

If you become a registered BidPay seller, you can add the BidPay logo to your auction listings (as well as other logos), as shown here:

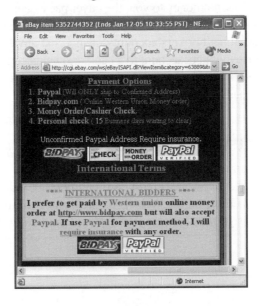

| Face Value of Money Order | Transaction Fee |
|---|---|
| $10 or less | $1.95 |
| $10.01 to $30 | $2.95 |
| $30.01 to $50 | $3.95 |
| $50.01 to $100 | $4.95 |
| $100.01 to $1000 | $4.95 plus 2.25% of money order amount |

**TABLE 9-3**    BidPay Transaction Fees

NOTE    *BidPay is not without its limitations. Sellers are limited to transactions of $1000 or less, including shipping fees, for one thing. For another, buyers can conceivably use stolen credit cards to purchase money orders. However, if this happens and you have not yet shipped the item, BidPay will notify you and ask you to cancel the transaction. If you have already shipped, BidPay "will typically honor the money order, absent unusual circumstances," according to its Frequently Asked Questions (**https://www.bidpay.com/ getPaidFAQProblems.asp#8**).*

## Accept Payment with Moneybookers.com

Moneybookers.com, a London, England–based payment service, enables buyers and sellers in a variety of countries to send payments to one another (see Figure 9-4). Both buyer and seller need to have accounts established with Moneybookers. It's free to establish an account, and free for the buyer to deposit money in his or her account from a bank account. To send money to you, the buyer pays 1 percent of the transaction fee or a minimum of €0.50. However, it's worth noting that, although having money transferred into your Moneybookers account doesn't cost anything, withdrawing money from your Moneybookers account to a bank or other account does cost money. You'll pay a flat fee of €3.50 (the U.S. equivalent at this writing is $4.65) to withdraw a check from your account.

# Accept Credit Card Payments

If you already run an antique store or other brick-and-mortar business, you probably know about merchant accounts and credit card payments. Credit card payments are ideally suited to transactions on the Web: you enter your card number and personal information in a web page form, click a few buttons, and you're done.

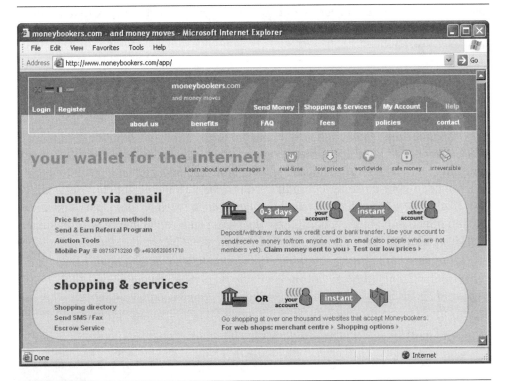

**FIGURE 9-4**   Moneybookers is especially good for international transactions.

Setting yourself up to accept credit card payments for your auction listings takes time and effort. Most beginning sellers will simply want to set up a PayPal account instead. But if you're planning to do business "offline" as well as online, you may well want to establish a conventional credit card account with a financial institution. If you plan to sell only on eBay and you want to give your high bidders and buyers another way to send you payment, look to a service like PayPal to do most of the work for you. Either way, you add a new level of convenience for your shoppers. Being able to add credit cards to the list of payment options in your auctions lets people know that you're truly serious about selling online and providing good customer service, too.

## The Conventional Way: Set Up a Merchant Account

A *merchant account* is a special account that a commercial operation (a merchant, in other words) sets up with a financial institution. The merchant account enables a business to receive credit card payments from its customers. Your financial institution processes the order, working with the credit card network to debit the customer's account and credit yours. Along the way, the financial institution charges fees for the processing.

## Traditional Bank-Based Merchant Accounts

The traditional way to obtain a merchant account is through a bank or other financial institution. You apply to the bank and provide documents that show that you are a legitimate businessperson. You also pay an application fee, which can amount to $300 or more. The bank's officers review your request for several weeks, after which time they hopefully grant you approval. You then purchase an input device that lets you send your customers' credit card numbers to the credit card network. This might be a Point of Sale terminal that lets you do "card swipes," plus a printer that can print out the receipts your customers sign. You can find inexpensive versions of such terminals on eBay for less than $50 (see Figure 9-5).

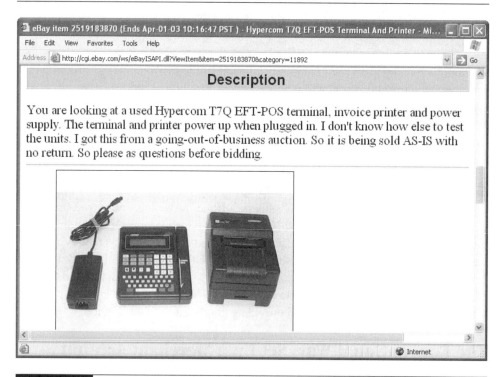

**FIGURE 9-5**    You need hardware like this or software to enter your customers' credit card data.

## Online Payment Gateways

In the online world, you don't need a hardware terminal to submit credit card purchase information to the financial network that does the processing. Instead, you use a software program that functions as a *gateway* to the network. One program that I'm familiar with is called PCCharge Express by Go Software (**http://www .gosoftware.com/index.htm**). Another is FreeCCS by Semaphore Corp. (**http:// www.semaphorecorp.com/ccs/ccs.html**).

Such software functions as a payment gateway: it allows you to add a Pay button to one of your web pages so that customers can send their payments to you. This means you need to set up a web site with a payment form where your auction customers can go to pay for what they've purchased. You also need to have a merchant account and be part of a payment system such as the MasterCard Automated Point-of-Sale Program (MAPP). If you already have an online store, and you want your customers to be able to make purchases there as well as on eBay, this is a convenient way to do it.

Whether you use a bank or another service, credit card merchants are assessed a number of fees for being able to process their customers' credit cards. Typically, the fees look like the ones shown in Table 9-4.

Keep in mind that the fees listed in Table 9-4 vary quite a bit depending on what financial institution you decide to use. Banks tend to be more expensive than

| Fee | What It Is | Amount |
|---|---|---|
| Discount rate | Usage fee charged by banks and merchant account companies | 1 to 4 percent of the transaction |
| Monthly premium | Monthly charge for having a merchant account | $30 to $70 |
| Per-transaction fee | Charge for each transaction | 10 to 30 cents |
| Monthly statement fee | Fee charged for sending the merchant a monthly account statement | $15 minimum |
| Internet fee | Fee charged for conducting credit card transactions on the Internet | 2 to 3 percent of each transaction |
| Monthly minimum processing fee | A minimum charge for using the financial institution's services | $15 to $30 |
| Gateway processing fee | A fee charged by a gateway service for processing transactions online rather than via a POS terminal | $20 to $40 per month |
| Chargeback fee | Fee charged by a credit card company if you process a fraudulent purchase—a purchase using a stolen credit card | $15 or more |

**TABLE 9-4**   Typical Merchant Account Fees

companies that specialize in providing merchant accounts to online merchants. Companies like 1st American Card Service (**http://www.1stamericancardservice .com**) or Merchants' Choice Card Services Nationwide (**http://www.swipethecard .com**) don't charge an application fee. But they do charge Internet fees, discount fees, and so on.

 *When you enter the world of merchant accounts, the term* discount rate *gets thrown around a lot. This term is quite misleading. It sounds like you're saving money on something, but actually it's just a discount from your revenue that goes to the bank or credit card company—in other words, a fee.*

## Consider Merchant Account Alternatives

The procedures and fees described in the preceding section definitely add a new level of complexity to your eBay sales. There must be an easier way to accept credit card payments, right? Happily, a number of services are available that streamline the process of accepting credit cards, and some suggestions are described here:

- **ProPay (http://www.propay.com)**   This service enables you to process credit cards online for a $35 annual fee, 3.5 percent and 35 cents for each transaction, and 35 cents for each transfer to your checking account. There's also an interesting add-on feature that sets ProPay apart from other payment services: for an additional $24.95 per year, your customers can phone in their credit card data.

- **Costco Internet Card Processing (http://www.costco.com/)**   Costco, the warehouse store my kid and I enjoy regularly, offers a variety of membership packages. If you obtain an Executive Membership, you can obtain credit card processing status through NOVA Information Systems. You are charged 1.65% per Visa or MasterCard transaction plus 20 cents. Not only that, but you can process transactions through an Internet gateway as well. Find out more by going to **http://www.costco.com/**, clicking **services**, and clicking **Merchant Credit Card Processing**.

- **VeriSign Payflow Link (http://www.verisign.com/products/payflow/ link/index.html)**   Once you obtain a merchant account from a financial institution, you can use Payflow Link as a gateway service that enables you to process credit card transactions online. You add a link to VeriSign's web site that enables customers to fill out forms in order to make purchases. The service costs $179 to set up, with a monthly fee of $19.95.

In addition, if you sign up for an account to sell online with Microsoft Small Business Services (**http://www.microsoft.com/smallbusiness/bc/default.mspx**), you pay $12.95 for monthly hosting. For an additional $24.95 per month, you can sign up for Commerce Manager, which enables you to sell on eBay and in other marketplaces and accept credit card orders as well.

# Verify Credit Card Data

If you accept credit card payments only for Internet-based transactions, you don't need to purchase and set up a POS terminal to communicate with the credit card network—after all, people aren't going to be sending you their actual credit cards to swipe, and you aren't going to be printing receipts for them to sign. Both of these things—receiving the actual credit card, and having the customer sign the card in front of you so you can compare his or her signature to the one on the card—are safeguards for you, the seller. They enable you to verify that the person making the purchase is actually the cardholder and not someone who has stolen the card.

How do you process transactions and verify the cardholder's identity in an Internet transaction? You're at a disadvantage because you never see who you're dealing with, and you don't get a signature to verify someone's identity. In that case, you need to use credit card processing software to do the verification for you. The software compares the cardholder's billing address to the shipping address that the customer gives you. IC*VERIFY* (**http://www.icverify.com**), shown here, performs such verification and processing.

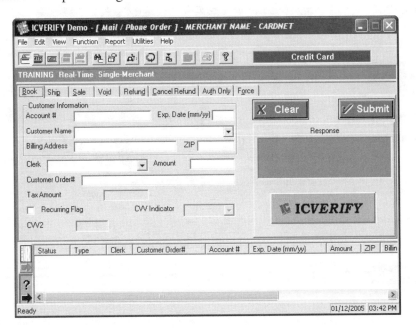

If the two addresses are different, of course, that doesn't necessarily mean the card is being used fraudulently. Someone might be purchasing a gift for someone else, or the cardholder might have moved recently. But if the addresses vary dramatically (for instance, if the billing address is in Oregon and the shipping address is in Bolivia), you should call the cardholder to verify that the transaction is legitimate. If there's no problem, the cardholder will be glad you checked. If there is a problem, you save the cardholder a fraudulent purchase and yourself a chargeback fee.

# Convert Currency

The question of what currency to use when you sell isn't one you need to be overly concerned about. You should pick the currency that is easiest for you to use: your own country's. However, if you do need to calculate different currencies, keep in mind that each one of eBay's international sites has its own currency conversion utility. (And if you use PayPal to accept international payments, the money is converted automatically for you.) They all use the same basic program, but by picking the version that is specific to your own country, you immediately see your native currency highlighted. If that doesn't seem like a big enough advantage to you (it doesn't to me), use the eBay Universal Currency Converter (shown in Figure 9-6) on the U.S. eBay web site, **http://pages.ebay.com/services/buyandsell/currencyconverter.html**.

**FIGURE 9-6**   eBay's Universal Currency Converter

## Where to Find It

- **PayPal**
  **http://www.paypal.com**
  Home page of eBay's payment service, where you can sign up for a seller's account.

- **BidPay**
  **http://www.bidpay.com**
  A service that enables buyers to mail Western Union money orders to auction sellers.

- **eBay Universal Currency Converter**
  **http://pages.ebay.com/services/buyandsell/currencyconverter.html**
  Online utility that enables you to quickly convert different types of currency.

9

# Chapter 10

# Make Sure Your Goods Reach Their Destination

## How to…

■ Pack your merchandise with care for extra safety

■ Pick the right shipping options

■ Ship your items internationally

■ Be aware of language differences

■ Calculate time-zone differences

■ Observe customs and export requirements

Packing and shipping are among the least glamorous aspects of selling on eBay (they rank right up there with accounting and taxes), but they're among the most important as well. A poorly packed item that is broken in transit, or something that gets lost, can effectively destroy a sale and damage your reputation as well.

To be a successful eBay seller, you need to be a successful eBay shipper. eBay is making the process easier than ever by enabling sellers to print their own postage and shipping labels. However, if you don't pack your items correctly, they can break in transit, which can force you to give refunds to your buyers and possibly to get negative feedback as well. It's easy for new sellers to underestimate the time and care they need to take when packing and shipping, whether across the state or across the globe. Often, sellers don't realize that they need to be doing things differently until trouble occurs. One goal of this chapter is to help you avoid packing and shipping problems before they arise.

Another goal is to make you aware of issues surrounding selling and shipping to foreign buyers. You *can* decide you're going to sell only domestically, but you'll cut off a large part of your potential market in the process. One of the strengths of selling on eBay is the ability to reach across national boundaries. Along with that power, though, comes additional responsibility: you need to be aware of language, time-zone, and other differences that apply when you deal with a worldwide auction audience. Understanding customs and other requirements you may need to observe when shipping your goods internationally is also a good idea, so I discuss those considerations in this chapter, too.

# Pack 'n' Ship Like a Pro

I have to confess that I wasn't originally planning to include detailed information about packing in this book. But almost every eBay seller I interviewed included the admonition "Pack carefully!" among their list of tips for new sellers like you. This section passes along the tips I've gleaned on packing and shipping across town or across the globe.

## Pack It Right

You'll find that the more you sell on eBay, the more time you'll be spending with boxes, tape, and labels and heading back and forth to the post office or private shipping companies. It's *good* to spend a lot of time on packing, in fact, though you probably won't think so at first. The packages you send to your customers are the only tangible form of contact you're going to have with them. If your package is going internationally, it's almost certainly going on an airplane. It'll be traveling not in a plush first-class reclining seat with a cocktail on its tray table, but in a crowded cargo hold, buffeted by lots of luggage. It may get wet and battered before it reaches its destination.

When you're packing, pretend that your customers are looking over your shoulder, and that you're going to hand the package to them in person. Packing and shipping are two of the criteria sellers usually consider when they leave feedback. As you are packing, keep in mind the principle that good packing = good feedback, and keep the following in mind:

■ *Use strong boxes.* Don't skimp by using boxes that have already been used and are falling apart, which makes you look cheap and which may fall apart in transit.

■ *Use the U.S. Postal Service's Priority Mail service.* Many sellers use this option so that they can take advantage of the high-quality Priority Mail boxes, which the U.S. Postal Service (USPS) provides free for you to pick up at a postal facility or order by calling 1-800-610-8734. You can also order the boxes through the USPS Postal Store web site (**http://shop.usps.com/cgi-bin/vsbv/postal_store_non_ssl/home.jsp**). But the best place to get Priority Mail boxes is on the USPS eBay page (**http://ebaysupplies.usps.com**), where you find boxes bearing both USPS and eBay logos (see Figure 10-1).

■ *Use lots of packing material.* Make friends with bubble wrap and those little white packing peanuts, and fill all available empty space.

■ *Put a protective barrier between separate pieces.* If what you're shipping comes in separate pieces, insert a slab of cardboard in between them.

**10**

**FIGURE 10-1**    If you ship via Priority Mail, you can obtain these eBay/USPS boxes for free.

- *Double-pack if necessary.* For especially fragile and precious items, surround a box with packing material and put it within another box for extra protection.

- *Include a note.* Some sellers include notes pointing out any flaws that were on the merchandise before it was shipped, so it's clear to the buyer that that particular damage did not occur in transit. Be sure to include the URL for your eBay Store, if you have one, as well as your eBay User ID, to encourage customers to return. A list of upcoming promotions or a coupon that provides a discount on a subsequent purchase will encourage return visits.

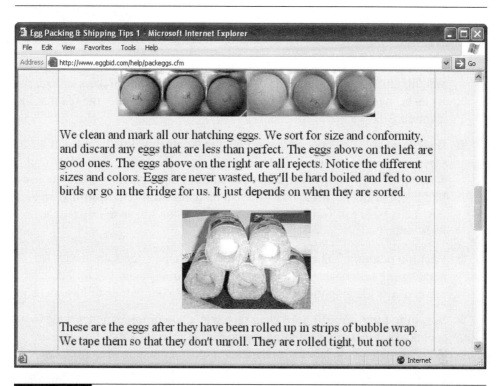

We clean and mark all our hatching eggs. We sort for size and conformity, and discard any eggs that are less than perfect. The eggs above on the left are good ones. The eggs above on the right are all rejects. Notice the different sizes and colors. Eggs are never wasted, they'll be hard boiled and fed to our birds or go in the fridge for us. It just depends on when they are sorted.

These are the eggs after they have been rolled up in strips of bubble wrap. We tape them so that they don't unroll. They are rolled tight, but not too

**FIGURE 10-2** If you can ship eggs safely, you can probably ship just about anything.

If you want some suggestions on how to ship some *really* delicate items, look up another, very different type of online auction site: Eggbid.com. You'll find detailed instructions on how to ship eggs via Priority Mail (see Figure 10-2) so they arrive safely and are even able to hatch chicks (**http://www.eggbid.com/help/packeggs.cfm**).

## Find Packing Material

When you conduct an ongoing business, you're going to need a lot of packing materials. eBay sellers are pretty resourceful when it comes to packing material. They find boxes from any number of sources. The busier sellers that I know scrounge for recycled packing materials. Some budget-conscious sellers look for paper, bubble-wrap, and peanuts wherever they can be found—even in the trash. Here are some suggestions for the kinds of materials that are sure to come in handy:

- **Goo Gone**   You'll probably need to remove old mailing labels at some point, and this stuff is great at removing adhesive residue from stickers and labels. It can be messy, however. You can also tape white paper over the old mailing labels.

- **Bubble wrap**   This is a plastic product that contains little bubbles of air that protect what you pack. Bubble wrap can be expensive if you buy it in small quantities. Shop around on eBay and at online packing supply houses like Fast-Pack.com (**http://www.fast-pack.com/bubblewrap.html**) and buy the biggest roll you can afford so that you don't have to buy it again for a while.

- **Packing peanuts**   These little white peanut-shaped items are handy for packing irregularly shaped objects in boxes. Storing them can be a pain, but consider hanging them in trash bags around your garage or basement.

- **Shipping tape**   You'll need clear tape that's two or three inches wide to seal boxes if you use a shipping method other than Priority Mail. Be sure to cover the mailing label with the clear tape to protect it from the rain.

- **Plastic bags or paper**   Use these to wrap the merchandise inside the box. The plastic bags, in particular, will protect an item from any moisture that seeps inside.

- **Bubble envelopes**   If you ship out flat merchandise such as magazines or posters, these bubble-wrap-lined envelopes are terrific for protecting your goods.

A trip to the local office supply store will suggest many other kinds of tubes, triangle-shaped containers, and specialty boxes you can use to ship odd-shaped items.

NOTE   *Packing material such as the usual "peanuts" piles up in garbage bins and landfills. Consider using ecologically friendly materials such as biodegradable peanuts made from rice. You can also find plastic bags that you inflate with air, which saves money on shipping.*

Many sellers simply use USPS Priority Mail for all of their shipping needs. They have packing boxes, labels, and envelopes shipped to them for free in bulk; they take the finished boxes to the post office on a regular schedule, and they even make friends with the employees who get to know them well. It's a quick and economical shipping method that's hard to beat. eBay has a Shipping Center (**http://pages.ebay.com/services/buyandsell/shipping.html**) that gathers convenient links so sellers can calculate postage, order supplies, and track shipping costs (see Figure 10-3). Or you can order supplies from USPS's own Postal Store (**http://shop.usps.com**).

**FIGURE 10-3**    eBay's Shipping Center makes it easy to calculate postage, print labels, and track shipments.

## eBay Bestsellers
## Don't Skimp when You Ship

A highly experienced eBay seller (User ID: decoray), who has a feedback rating of more than 3400, is known for unusual items of high quality. "I try to get things that are uncommon or one of a kind in order to stand out from the other listings and attract bidders." At the time we spoke, he was selling, among other things, a Royal Copenhagen porcelain bowl with a figure of a lobster on it; many old "magic lantern slides" depicting Native Americans and cowboys from the Old West; and a cardboard store display depicting several bottles of Kingsbury beer.

"decoray" has been in the antique business since 1976: "All those things that never sold in my antique store, I can sell on eBay," he laughs. He has been on eBay for five years. He is not a full timer, yet he still puts in about 40 hours, part time, six days a week. Much of that time is spent packing and doing other post-sale activities, he points out.

"decoray" is also known for taking care with his shipping. That doesn't mean that everything he wants to sell should be shipped, however. "Ask yourself: Is the item actually suitable for eBay?" he advises. "If it is bulky, if it has flaws that are difficult to describe, or if it is of purely regional interest, you might want to sell it in your own area through a live auction rather than anywhere else. For instance, if I had a lamp with a stained-glass shade worth $2000, I wouldn't want to ship it in the first place. I'd try to sell it locally rather than deal with the trouble of packing and potentially having to make an insurance claim if something happened in transit.

"Prospective eBay sellers should realize that you will spend a lot of time on each item: producing good photos or scans, writing descriptions, following up on e-mails, as well as shipping and packing. A good rule of thumb is it will take you an hour per item from start to finish. There are five steps to any eBay sale: You procure the item, you photograph it; you list it; you complete the auction; you ship the item out. I like to do some really creative packing. If you sell 50 items a week, you can estimate that it will take you 50 hours to sell and ship everything out.

"When you are packing, assume the worst. Try to imagine what you need to prevent happening to your item. Take as much time and use as much packing material as necessary to send it to the buyer. Don't skimp on anything.

"If you sell books or records or tapes, the post office offers the Media Mail rate, which used to be called Book Rate. You can use it to send a very heavy book very inexpensively. You should note in auctions that you have the option of a low shipping price. I tell people that I can ship by Media Mail or Priority Mail.

"When an item doesn't attract any bids, try relisting it and lowering your opening bid. If I feel it should have sold for my opening price, I relist it at 20 percent lower. Everybody has things that don't sell, but I tend to sell 60 to 85 percent of the things I list, depending on the time of year.

"Only about 1 percent of my customers turn out to be deadbeat bidders. That's due to the beauty of the feedback system. When I sell something to somebody who has good feedback, I send one e-mail and don't worry about it until quite a bit of time has gone by with no payment. But if the high bidder is someone who has low feedback, I word my initial e-mails so they have to reply. If I don't get a prompt reply, I know I might be in for some problems."

Because he spends so much time and care on preparing sales listings and on packing and shipping, "decoray" is selective about what he puts up for sale. "When you have something to sell, do a search for it on eBay first and see if it is really worth listing. If there are already 30 or 40 of the same things up for sale, don't bother. Take it to the resale shop; give it to your uncle; donate it to the church rummage sale. Don't waste your time. Junk is junk wherever it is, on eBay or wherever. On the other hand, if you have something really good, it doesn't really matter what the minimum bid or reserve price is—you'll sell it on eBay, usually for close to what it's worth."

**10**

# Choose Your Shipping Options

Before you start to sell anything on eBay, give some thought to how you are going to ship it out after you sell it. Scout the nearest postal facility and private mail stores. If you have such a facility right around the corner and there's a convenient parking lot, you might prefer to travel there for shipping. If your post office is small and parking is a problem, it might be better to set up an arrangement with United Parcel Service or Federal Express to provide pick-up service. You can even print out postage at home and call the United States Postal Service for a pickup, without ever having to leave the comforts of home.

The following sections compare the services and suggest things to think about when it comes to setting up accounts, obtaining insurance, and the like. Since the rates and requirements are changing all the time, you're best off visiting the shippers' respective web sites to determine current costs and procedures.

## The Big Three Shippers

Most eBay sellers settle on one of the big shipping services to handle all of their needs: Federal Express (FedEx), United Parcel Service (UPS), or the United States Postal Service (USPS). There's nothing wrong with other shippers, like DHL. Most sellers just find it simpler to get one set of shipping statements because they're using one shipper, for one thing. For another, having to travel to only one facility at a set time each day or each week simplifies the whole week's activities—which can be pretty busy if you are selling dozens of items each week, and some of your time is spent shopping to build up your inventory (see Chapter 3).

### United States Postal Service

One big advantage of using the good old USPS is convenience. You don't need to open an account to start shipping; anyone can go into a postal facility, order supplies, obtain stamps, and ship out merchandise. Another is the fact that eBay has aligned itself with USPS as its shipper of choice, and has set up convenient links that enable you to obtain your own supplies and postage if you so choose.

The most popular form of shipping used by eBay sellers is Priority Mail. It's popular not because of cost, but because shipments only take a couple of days, and USPS gives out free shipping supplies if you use this service. Priority Mail is ideal for one- and two-pound packages. At higher weights, Priority Mail gets more expensive—unless you can fit your item inside the relatively new Priority Mail Flat Rate box, which costs $7.70 to ship. However, you have to pay extra fees if you want tracking numbers or delivery confirmation—services that FedEx Home Delivery and UPS provide for free.

NOTE  *You pay for delivery confirmation if you go to your local post office to ship something Priority Mail. If you use eBay's system for printing out labels, you can also buy your own insurance online and get delivery confirmation for free. Find out more at the eBay Shipping Center (**http://pages.ebay.com/ services/buyandsell/shipping.html**).*

If you are shipping out books, cassettes, videos, or computer-readable media and want to help your customers really save some bucks, give them the option of shipping out Media Mail. You'll have to provide your own packing materials, and the time to ship can be six to seven days, but the cost savings can be huge at weights of 10 to 20 pounds or more. (Find out more about Media Mail at **http://www.usps.com/ mediamail**.) If you've got something that doesn't fit into the Media Mail categories and that weighs up to 70 pounds, you have to send it parcel post, but the rates are much more expensive than FedEx Home Delivery.

> NOTE   *Items weighing more than 70 pounds can be shipped by FedEx Ground or by UPS. UPS requires special "heavy package" stickers (see UPS's suggestions for heavy packages at **http://www.ups.com/content/us/en/resources/prepare/exceed_weight.html**).*

## Federal Express

FedEx is regarded as being more expensive than USPS, and for one- or two-day service, it generally is. But some services that were created when FedEx acquired Roadway Package Service (RPS)—FedEx Ground and its subdivision, FedEx Home Delivery—provide good, cost-effective alternatives to USPS for eBay sellers. In fact, for items that are more than two pounds in weight, FedEx Ground and Home Delivery are actually less expensive than USPS Priority Mail. Along with cost, an advantage is that FedEx gives you software called Ship Manager that you can use to print out labels.

You do need to set up an account to use FedEx, but it's easy to do so through the FedEx web site (**http://www.fedex.com**). Your package can be delivered right to someone's doorstep in one to five business days, depending on where it's going (deliveries to Alaska and Hawaii take three to seven business days). Packages up to 150 pounds for Ground service and 70 pounds for Home Delivery are allowed. If you use FedEx Ground or International Ground, you can have the shipper collect the money from your customers when the items are delivered—FedEx even accepts cash. Extra service options for evening delivery or signature delivery (requiring someone to sign for the package so you have proof it was delivered) are available for additional charges.

## United Parcel Service

UPS is the shipper of choice for at least one of the big-time eBay sellers I profiled because, for an extra fee of $7 to $16 per week, you can arrange for UPS to make a daily stop to pick up your outgoing packages. (Even if you only shipped occasionally with UPS, you could have a driver pick up an individual package or two for an extra fee of $4 per package.)

You can drop off packages at a UPS shipper without opening an account if you want to, but opening a simple Internet account (**http://www.ups.com/content/us/en/bussol/smallbiz/internet_shipping.html**) enables you to print out your own bar-coded labels so that you can save some time. To get started, go to the UPS home page (**http://www.ups.com**), select your country from the drop-down list presented on the home page, and click one of the links under the heading Quick Links.

## How Much Will It Cost?

It's a good idea to give buyers a couple of shipping options rather than just one, so that they feel they have a choice in the matter. Very few eBay sellers give customers the option of sending packages overnight. FedEx Home Delivery, UPS residential, USPS Priority Mail, and USPS ground mail are the among the most common options. Table 10-1 compares shipping costs for a package being sent from my ZIP code in Chicago (60657) to one in Los Angeles, California (90011). Insurance is not included; nor is a delivery confirmation.

eBay's shipping calculators, which sellers specify when creating listings, enable buyers to enter their ZIP code and get a quote that corresponds to their geographic location. All you have to do is enter the shipping method and the package weight when you create your listing.

As you can see from Table 10-1, while Priority Mail is convenient in terms of packaging, and economical for 2- or 5-pound packages, don't overlook FedEx Ground (see Figure 10-4) and FedEx Home Delivery services, which take a couple of days more but provide an excellent value for larger packages. On the other hand, if you are shipping books, Printed Book Rate is a good choice. For media such as DVDs, videotapes, or CD-ROMs, USPS Media Mail is a good value as well.

| Delivery Service | 2 lbs. | 5 lbs. | 10 lbs. | 20 lbs. |
|---|---|---|---|---|
| USPS Priority Mail (2 days) | $5.40 | $11.00 | $16.30 | $28.75 |
| USPS Media Mail (6 days) | $1.84 | $3.10 | $4.84 | $7.84 |
| USPS Parcel Post (6 days) | $4.49 | $8.64 | $14.17 | $20.05 |
| UPS Ground (4–5 days) | $7.45 | $8.87 | $11.42 | $19.48 |
| UPS 3-Day Select (3 days) | $18.94 | $18.94 | $27.81 | $45.11 |
| UPS 2nd Day Air (2 days) | $26.17 | $26.17 | $42.60 | $71.07 |
| FedEx Ground (1–5 days) | $4.88 | $5.87 | $7.52 | $12.82 |
| FedEx Home Delivery (1–5 days) | $4.78 | $5.75 | $7.37 | $12.57 |

**TABLE 10-1**    Shipping Costs Compared

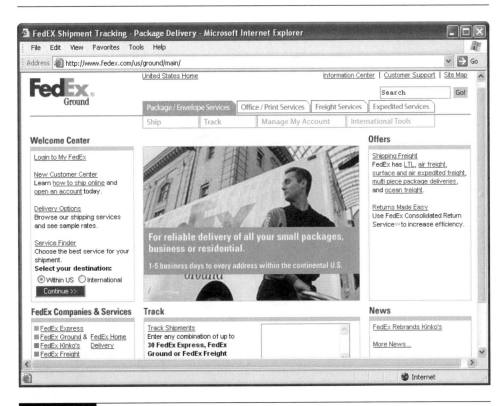

**FIGURE 10-4**   FedEx Ground is an economical choice for many packages.

**NOTE** *You can use a variety of online calculators to quickly determine the most economical way to send your package. USPS's Postage Rate Calculator is at **http://pages.ebay.com/usps/calculator.html**. The UPS Service Center online calculator is located at **http://www.servicecenter.ups.com/ebay/ebay .html#qcost**. FedEx's Rate Finder is at **http://www.fedex.com/ratefinder/ home?cc=US&language=en**.*

One way to get an accurate calculation is to obtain a postal scale that you can use at home. Make sure the model you buy can handle the weight you expect to ship; the one in Figure 10-5 handles packages up to ten pounds.

FIGURE 10-5   Get an accurate postal scale so that you can estimate shipping costs for your customers.

With all this talk about packing materials, you might well ask how much the packing costs and whether you can pass the cost along to your customers. To the latter question, the answer is yes, you can pass along the cost, but don't gouge buyers by tacking on a big "handling fee." You should add your handling fee to your shipping costs—for instance, you should include a phrase such as "$8.95 for shipping and handling" in your descriptions rather than spelling out that you're charging $6 for shipping and $2.95 for handling. But you don't want someone to have to pay $15 in shipping costs for an item that only costs $10 to $20 to begin with, for instance.

TIP    *You can go directly to the USPS Priority Mail Shipping Supplies Online page (http://www.usps.com/shipping/prioritymail.htm) for more information.*

# Obtain Insurance

Suppose you send something to a buyer and, despite your best efforts to pack it carefully, it somehow gets damaged in transit. If you did not insure the item beforehand, you would probably have to work out something with the buyer—you might have to give the buyer a discount on the purchase price, or perhaps a total refund. Insurance coverage can help defray the cost of such refunds. Insurance procedures vary depending on the shipper you use:

- ■ If you ship with USPS, you have to pay extra to insure your item. Fees have risen dramatically in recent years, too (see Table 10-2).

- ■ If you ship with UPS or FedEx, your merchandise is automatically insured for up to $100. You pay extra if you want to insure an item for a higher amount.

An attractive alternative to the insurance provided by the three big carriers comes from Universal Parcel Insurance Coverage (U-PIC), a company that regularly insures packages. U-PIC offers two types of coverage: an Online Ordering program and an Offline Standard program. The Online Ordering program is for occasional shippers who send out a single package once in a while. The Offline Standard program is for sellers who average 100 packages per month. You can realize big savings over the USPS insurance costs, as shown in Table 10-2. The table shows the insurance fees that USPS charges for Priority Mail and other types of mail at this writing. These fees are in addition to the regular shipping charges. They don't include delivery confirmation, registered mail, or other add-on services.

| Insurance Coverage | USPS Fee | U-PIC Online Ordering Program | U-PIC Offline Standard Program |
|---|---|---|---|
| $0.01 to $50.00 | $1.30 | $1.00 | $0.75 |
| $50.01 to $100.00 | $2.20 | $1.00 | $0.75 |
| $100.01 to $200.00 | $3.20 | $2.00 | $1.50 |
| $200.01 to $300.00 | $4.20 | $3.00 | $2.25 |
| $300.01 to $400.00 | $5.20 | $4.00 | $3.00 |

**TABLE 10-2**   USPS and U-PIC Insurance Fees

## Pack and Ship Without Leaving Home

In 2004, eBay established a program with USPS, UPS, and the postage meter manufacturer Pitney Bowes to create a system for purchasing postage and shipping out packages yourself. Without having to establish an account with the post office or purchasing special hardware (other than a postal scale), you can calculate and purchase postage, print labels, obtain insurance, and pack your merchandise. You can even call for a pickup from a postal carrier from your home or office. The result: as long as you have a printer and a PayPal account, you can handle all aspects of packing and shipping from home without ever having to go to a post office. Here's how to do it:

1. Calculate shipping costs, if you need to, by going to the USPS Shipping Center (**http://pages.ebay.com/usps/home.html**) and clicking Calculate Postage. (If you use UPS, use the calculator at **http://www.servicecenter .ups.com/ebay/ebay.html#qcost**.)

2. If you plan to send a shipment by Priority Mail, order boxes and other supplies by going to the USPS | eBay page (**http://ebaysupplies .usps.com**).

3. When you have your postage cost and packing materials ready, you can pack your item and then buy postage and print a shipping label. Follow the general instructions for printing labels at **http://pages.ebay.com/services/ buyandsell/shippingcenter9.html**. As stated on this page, you can initiate the postage/label printing process either from My eBay or from PayPal. For this example, let's assume you are using My eBay; go to your My eBay page and move on to Step 4.

4. Click **Items I've Sold** under the All Selling heading in the My eBay Views column.

5. Check the box next to the item you want to ship, then click the Print Shipping Labels button.

6. In the next window, choose the shipper and shipping method you want to use, enter the To and From destinations, and click Print. You can print either to your home-office printer or to a special Zebra LP 2844-Z label

printer. The postage amount is deducted from your PayPal account. Also, an e-mail message is automatically sent to both you and your buyer, informing both of you that postage has been purchased, and providing instructions on how to track the shipment.

7. After you affix your label, call for a pickup. If you are shipping with UPS, you can have them pick up for an extra charge. USPS offers a Carrier Pickup program for Express Mail and Priority Mail packages. You can request a pickup by 2 A.M. CST, and the package will be picked up later that day. Fill out the form at **https://carrierpickup.usps.com/ cgi-bin/WebObjects/CarrierPickup.woa** to arrange for pickup.

Along with convenience, the system allows you to purchase insurance from USPS along with postage, and you get delivery confirmation as well.

> TIP *You can contact U-PIC through a toll-free number (1-800-955-4623) or by visiting its web site (**http://www.u-pic.com**). U-PIC suggests that you include a copy of your policy in each box you send out, so buyers know the merchandise is insured and that the insurance cost is included in the total fee you charge them. By all means, read the terms of insurance when you insure an item. The terms may restrict liability if you don't package the item according to the insurance company's guidelines.*

**10**

Many eBay sellers print their own postage and save time performing other packing and shipping tasks with the help of a postage service such as Endicia Internet Postage (**http://www.endicia.com**). The big advantage of Endicia is the ability to print your own postage with your home printer. But Endicia also offers free delivery confirmation, custom printed envelopes, and online package tracking. It has a Standard and Premium level of service; Premium-level customers can print with "Stealth Endicia" labels, which hide the postage amount. This enables you to charge shipping and handling fees without worrying about complaints from buyers.

# Reach International Buyers

One of the most exciting moments for many online merchants occurs when they receive their first order from outside their own country. That's when a host of new concerns pops up, too: How do you ship this order to Australia, Norway, Mexico, Japan, or other countries?

## Shipping to Canada

Shipping to Canada from the U.S. might seem straightforward because it's just over the border. Not so. Although the North American Free Trade Agreement (NAFTA) made trade between the United States, Canada, and Mexico flow more easily, it doesn't mean it's less expensive. In Canada, buyers are responsible for paying duty fees, a Goods and Services Tax (GST), and applicable customs brokerage fees in addition to the cost of the merchandise you sell them. Buyers generally pay these fees upon receipt of your shipment (although you can arrange to have UPS bill them beforehand). It's a good idea to tell your Canadian buyers that they may be charged additional fees once they receive your package.

If you expect to sell frequently to Canada, you may want to call UPS at 1-800-PICK-UPS to obtain a Non-Resident Importer (NRI) Account. The U.S. seller can then bill the customer up front for duties and taxes, as well as shipping and handling.

To find out more about Canadian customs charges, visit the Canada Border Services Agency at **http://www.cbsa-asfc.gc.ca/menu-e.html**.

Generally, high bidders and buyers on eBay pay additional costs that may apply, such as duties, taxes, and customs clearance fees. For example, international rates may or may not include pickup and door-to-door delivery with customs clearance. Some carriers will offer customs and brokerage services to help you learn more about what you need to tell your buyers about additional charges, duties, and taxes. An "extended area surcharge" may also apply to your buyers depending on their international locations.

 *Beware of international sellers who ask you to FedEx something they buy with a credit card. Occasionally, they will want you to ship FedEx so the item arrives before the stolen credit card number is canceled.*

To get started with shipping to international buyers, check the appropriate options in the Ship-to Locations section of the Sell Your Item form. You don't have to ship to every country in the world. Going with the Will Ship Worldwide option forces you to accept potential purchases from everyone in the world. If you do not choose this option, you limit the number of potential buyers, but you may want to stick with countries to which it is particularly easy to ship from the United States, such as Canada, to which USPS will ship.

CAUTION

*Before you decide to check Will Ship Worldwide, read "Be Aware of Export Restrictions," later in this chapter, especially if you sell computer software that uses encryption or other potentially sensitive items. You may be prohibited from selling to certain nations. Also, check out the eBay Global Trading message boards, which indicate that some countries are more prone to have fraudulent sales than others (for instance, Indonesia).*

## Language Considerations

Your ability to reach bidders in Japan, Chile, and other countries is greatly enhanced by the use of simple, clear language in your auction descriptions. After all, the important thing is that your buyers understand exactly what you have to offer and what its best features are. Your use of slang may give the residents of your own country a chuckle, but it can leave many more people scratching their heads and clicking on to the next auction listing. (Consider what a translation of "putting someone in stitches" might look like.) Keep your language simple so people from all parts of the world can understand you.

If you do not speak the same language as one of your bidders and you get e-mail that seems garbled or that is in a foreign language, you may want to use an online translation service to translate key phrases. You can also use such a service to translate your English into someone else's language. Some translation services are available free on the Internet, but they are not 100 percent accurate. If you use such a service, provide simple, grammatically correct phrases free of abbreviations to maximize the chance of an understandable translation.

## Use One of eBay's Global Sites

For the most part, you'll probably want to use the main (U.S.-based) version of eBay (**http://www.ebay.com**) to create your auction listings, but if you live in a country where eBay has a Global Site or you want to reach potential buyers in that country, consider listing on that version of eBay. At this writing, eBay has over twenty local sites, which are listed at the bottom of the eBay home page.

One advantage of using such sites is that some members may accept payment in their own currency. Another is that if you are fluent in Spanish and you have an object of national interest (such as an antique version of that country's flag, or a book

10

**Use Babel Fish to Communicate with Foreign eBay Users**

Babel Fish Translation, a service of the search site AltaVista, is particularly easy to use. You don't always get a high-quality translation, and if you have to translate anything complex or dealing with financial information, you're better off with a human translator. But the service is free and works for very simple statements. Follow these steps to get your own instant translation:

1. Enter the address for the Babel Fish Translation web site (**http://babelfish.altavista.com**) in your browser's Address box and press ENTER to connect to the site, as shown here:

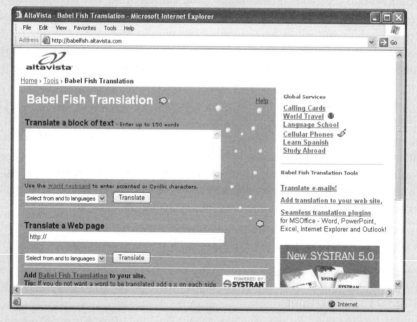

2. Type or paste the text you want to translate in the Translate a Block of Text box. To have the service translate an entire web page, enter the URL in the Translate a Web Page box. (Remember, the shorter and simpler the text, the better your results.)

3. Choose the translation path (that is, *from* what language *to* what language) from the drop-down menu beneath the text box. At this writing, Chinese,

English, French, Japanese, Korean, Spanish, German, Italian, Portuguese, and Russian-to-English (but not English-to-Russian) are covered by the service.

**4.** Click the Translate button.

**5.** As quick as you can say, "Welcome to the new Tower of Babel," a new web page appears onscreen with the translated version of your text.

describing that country's history in the local language), you'll be able to reach local bidders through the Global Site. You might sell on, say, MercadoLibre Mexico, the Mexican affiliate of eBay (shown in Figure 10-6).

**FIGURE 10-6**    If you live in a Spanish-speaking country, you may find it more convenient to sell on MercadoLibre Mexico.

## Observe Time-Zone Etiquette

If you are trying to attract bidders from around the world, try to schedule your auction so that it ends at a time when the largest number of potential bidders are available. Although it's true that proxy bidding (in which a bidder enters a maximum bid amount rather than the minimum increment, so that eBay automatically places bids until the specified maximum amount is reached) makes it unnecessary for bidders to be present at the end in order to place a last-minute winning bid, it's often the last hour or two of an auction that sees the most action.

I once had to schedule a chat event so that the largest number of participants around the globe would be able to participate easily. The company that provided the chat software suggested Saturday around 2 P.M. Central Standard Time as an optimal time for the event. That way, in Europe, it's Saturday evening, while on the West Coast and as far west as Hawaii, people can still participate without having to stay up until the "wee hours." You can determine the difference between eBay's official time and time zones around the world at the Time Zone Conversion page, shown in Figure 10-7.

## Observe Customs Requirements

When you sell to a customer who lives in another country, you or your customer will be subject to customs charges before the shipment can be completed. Customs comes into play whether items are valued at $10 or several hundred dollars. In addition, you may need to fill out a variety of documentation, including:

- A commercial invoice, a form that a shipping company needs you to fill out if the item you're shipping is bigger than a printed document and is going internationally. You can find a sample on the UPS web site (**https://www .ups.com/content/us/en/shipping/international/documents/intl_forms/ comm_invoice.html**).

- A Shipper's Export Declaration (SED), which is required by U.S. Customs if the item you are planning to ship by mail is valued at more than $500 (or, for items that are to be shipped by other means, more than $2500).

The SED requires you to fill out your name, address, and either your Social Security number or Internal Revenue Service Employer Identification Number (EIN), if you have one. You also have to report what you're shipping and where it is going to. You'll find detailed instructions on how to fill out the SEC on the U.S. Census Bureau's web site (**http://www.census.gov/foreign-trade/www/correct.way.html**).

eBay Premier: Help : Basics : Time Zone Conversion - Microsoft Internet Explorer

File   Edit   View   Favorites   Tools   Help

Address http://pages.ebay.com/internationaltrading/timezones.html

Time Zone Conversion

To find out the difference between your local time and eBay offical time , please refer to the table below:

|  | Difference with eBay Time in hours (PST) | Difference with eBay Time in hours (PDT) | Difference with Greenwich Mean Time in hours (GMT) |
|---|---|---|---|
| US/CA Pacific | +00 | +00 | -08 |
| US/CA Central | +02 | +02 | -06 |
| US/CA Eastern | +03 | +03 | -05 |
| Hong Kong | +16 | +15 | +08 |
| Australia (Sydney) | +19 | +18 | +11 |
| Austria | +09 | +08 | +01 |
| France | +09 | +08 | +01 |
| Germany | +09 | +08 | +01 |
| Great Britain | +08 | +07 | +00 |
| Italy | +09 | +08 | +01 |
| Japan | +17 | +16 | +09 |
| Sweden | +09 | +08 | +01 |

Done                                                          Internet

**FIGURE 10-7**   How close are you to eBay time? Find out on this page.

Because such requirements can be complex, it's best to rely on a shipper to act as a customs broker and handle the requirements for you—or at least tell you what forms you have to fill out and what you have to pay. You can find out about Global Priority Mail and USPS's other worldwide delivery options at **http://www.usps .com/global/sendpackages.htm**. FedEx's worldwide delivery services are popular with eBay sellers, and are described at **http://www.fedex.com/us/about/overview/ worldwide**. UPS's international shipping section is at **http://www.ups.com/using/ services/intl/intl-guide.html**. DHL's International Shipping section is at **http:// www.dhl-usa.com/IntlSvcs/IntlSvcsHome.asp**.

CAUTION   *You might run into international buyers who ask you to identify the package as "Gift" on the customs form to avoid paying customs/duty fees. This is a common problem; you should know, however, that it is against the law to mark "Gift" on a customs form when what you are sending is really paid merchandise. You, not the buyer, will get in trouble if you incorrectly identify the package.*

# Be Aware of Export Restrictions

If you are planning to sell your goods and services internationally, you need to be aware of any trade restrictions that may apply to your business. You need to be careful if you trade in foodstuffs or agricultural products (such as seeds or plants), or if you sell software that uses some form of encryption. If you sell computer equipment, and any of your buyers live in a country with which your own country has imposed trade restrictions, you might get in trouble, too.

It pays to take a few minutes to read the U.S. government's export restrictions. You could incur a sizeable fine for exporting to a Denied Person, Specially Designated National, or Restricted Country. You'll find a current list at the Bureau of Industry and Security web site (**http://www.bis.doc.gov/ComplianceAndEnforcement/index .htm#LTC**).

# Where to Find It

- **eBay's International Trading discussion board**
  **http://forums.ebay.com/db1/forum.jsp?forum=31**
  Discussion board devoted to tips and problems associated with selling or buying internationally.

- **eBay's Global Trade web page**
  **http://pages.ebay.com/globaltrade/index.html**
  A welcome page devoted to users who are interested in buying or selling internationally.

- **eBay Shipping Center**
  **http://pages.ebay.com/services/buyandsell/shipping.html**
  A page full of links to shippers, calculators, and information on printing labels and buying postage online.

- **eBay's gateway page for USPS services and supplies**
  **http://ebaysupplies.usps.com**
  Provides you with information on how to obtain USPS/eBay co-branded boxes.

- **USPS Shipping Zone**
  **http://pages.ebay.com/usps/home.html**
  Links to the USPS postal calculator and to the Priority Mail site.

■ **United Parcel Service online rate calculator**
**http://www.servicecenter.ups.com/ebay/ebay.html#qcost**
Calculate rates online for ground and other shipping options.

■ **FedEx Rate Finder**
**http://www.fedex.com/ratefinder/home?cc=US&language=en**
Calculate rates for FedEx Ground, FedEx Home Delivery, and other
shipping options.

# Meet Other
# Auction Hounds

## How to...

- Use feedback to your advantage as a seller
- Support your business with effective e-mail
- Get help and advice on message boards
- Meet other sellers in the eBay Café
- Create or moderate an eBay Group
- Share your wares at eBay "Street Faires"
- Give to charitable causes and help out fellow members

Many web sites, particularly those that depend on selling goods and services to the public, proclaim that they have a community of visitors. By attracting a set of regular visitors and providing ways for those visitors to interact with one another, they keep those individuals on their site longer than they otherwise would. The longer visitors stay on site and the more they see the site as a resource, the better the chances that they will spend money on the site or use the site's resources in some way.

eBay frequently describes the group of people who buy and sell on its site as a community, and for the most part, this is an accurate description. Perhaps the most surprising thing about eBay—the thing that keeps it running smoothly—is the fact that it depends on people behaving in a trustworthy and courteous manner and helping one another.

By becoming a fully participating member of the eBay community, you gain all kinds of benefits. You can get questions answered by experienced buyers and sellers who are happy to pass along their experiences, both positive and negative. You become a better and more effective seller. Like the sellers I know, you can meet some wonderful and interesting people, some of whom may turn out to be friends with whom you interact outside of eBay's world. This chapter describes how to interact with the people you meet on eBay, and how to take advantage of eBay's community-building features to make your time on eBay more fun and, hopefully, more profitable as well.

# Use Feedback to Your Advantage

Feedback makes the world go 'round—in this case, the world of eBay—and it's especially important when you set up shop as an eBay seller. You're probably at least somewhat familiar with the feedback system, and you got some general information about feedback in Chapter 4. This section passes along some tips for using feedback in a way that contributes to eBay's community while helping you succeed in your eBay business.

## Be Courteous, Be Specific

When you give feedback on buyers, remember that your comments are likely to remain online for many months—if not years. The feedback you leave reflects on your reputation as a seller, just as does the e-mail you send to customers. Which of the following examples makes you look better as a seller:

- Jerk did not pay up despite 20 emails!!! I curse you!

- Super-fantastic speedee payment!!! Wonderful buyer!!!

- Buyer's check received in three days; smooth transaction.

The third example is without doubt the most boring. It's also the most businesslike and factual, however.

NOTE    *You can't simply change your original feedback comments once you post them. However, if you ever have different thoughts or want to add to the feedback comments that you leave initially, you can always add some new comments to clarify what you said. You can also make a rebuttal to feedback that others leave for you. You can find out how to do so at **http://pages.ebay .com/services/forum/feedback.html**.*

11

## Encourage Positive Feedback

When you buy on eBay, feedback is important because it has a bearing on how much sellers can trust you to come through and complete your part of a transaction. But when you sell on eBay, feedback becomes even more important. For example, sufficient positive feedback enables you to do the following:

- *Set up an eBay Store.* You can't create a Store until you have a feedback rating of at least 20, unless you have gone through the ID Verify program (see Chapter 16), or have a PayPal account, in which case the feedback rating is not considered.

■ *Become a PowerSeller.* A PowerSeller is someone who has generated at least $1000 of income from eBay sales averaged over a three-month period, who has at least 100 different feedback results, 98 percent of which are positive, and who contacts buyers within three business days after a sale closes. (Other PowerSeller requirements are listed at **http://pages.ebay.com/services/ buyandsell/powerseller/criteria.html**.)

■ *Get more business.* A number of sellers who make a full-time living on eBay told me that when you get to a very high feedback level—around 1200—you start to get more bids. People are drawn to that big feedback number next to your name.

Your goal as a seller, then, should be to get everyone who buys from you to submit feedback. How do you induce buyers to do this? People's natural inclination is often to speak up only when they have a complaint, not when things go smoothly. You may need to insert in the box with each piece of merchandise a slip of paper that says something like this:

I hope you are completely satisfied with your purchase and that it arrives in good condition. If it does not, or if you are unsatisfied for some reason, please contact me. If you are satisfied, please leave feedback for me at your earliest convenience.

You can tailor such a message to fit your own Terms of Sale. If you decide to offer a refund in case someone is dissatisfied, state as much. Also add a reminder to send feedback in the e-mails that you send to your high bidders/buyers.

> **NOTE**   *Don't leave feedback for a buyer until you are paid for your merchandise and until the buyer leaves feedback for you. But don't withhold feedback under a threat, either. Withholding feedback unless someone leaves you positive feedback (which eBay calls "feedback extortion") is prohibited. If you want to encourage buyers to leave feedback, include the following link in your post-sales e-mail messages: **http://feedback.ebay.com/ws/ eBayISAPI.dll?GetAndShowTransactions&item=0&page=1&nflw=1**.*

## Defend Negative Feedback

eBay sellers guard their feedback ratings zealously. They'll do anything to avoid getting negative comments—even refunding merchandise when a refund isn't technically warranted. An antique store owner who sells on eBay proudly told me he has a 99.6 percent positive rating. In the next breath, he told me that he occasionally accepts returns and gives out refunds just to keep customers happy.

While you do need to maintain a high positive feedback rating, you don't need to be a doormat, either. If someone leaves feedback that you think is unwarranted, you have a couple of options:

- *Respond to feedback.* If you feel comments are unjustified, or if you only want to clarify the comments that were left about you, go to **http://pages .ebay.com/services/forum/feedback.html**, click **Reply to feedback received**, and follow the steps shown on subsequent pages.

- *Take advantage of eBay's Mutual Feedback Withdrawal process.* If two eBay members agree that some feedback that was left is no longer accurate or appropriate, and if both agree to withdraw the feedback, the comment is removed from the feedback score of the user who received it. But the comment itself remains posted.

- *Have feedback withdrawn.* If you want to dispute feedback, pay a $20 fee to SquareTrade (**http://www.squaretrade.com**) and ask them to mediate the feedback for you. If you reach a settlement, the feedback comments are withdrawn; they don't count in your feedback rating, though they remain on your feedback page. Sometimes, those who left the feedback don't respond to the request for mediation and, if eBay approves, your feedback is withdrawn and your rating improves. Many sellers would say it's worth the expense.

Even if you use one of the aforementioned options, there's no guarantee that you'll actually get feedback removed. eBay has to approve the removal. If you receive a negative feedback comment that you can't get removed, don't panic. If you have lots of positive feedback comments and one negative one, most buyers aren't likely to focus on the single negative remark.

# Observe Good E-Mail Manners

The Web allows you to sell your items and to contact other users through message boards, but e-mail is arguably the most important way you can establish close connections with buyers and sellers alike. When I buy on eBay, I always try to send an e-mail inquiry to the seller just to let the person know I am a serious bidder, and to evaluate the seller's level of responsiveness. I know others do this, too. The way you present yourself via e-mail has an effect on your sales.

Because e-mail is such an important part of your eBay business, it pays to take some simple yet effective steps to make your e-mail communications more effective. The following sections describe some easy-to-implement techniques for maintaining contact with prospective bidders and current customers.

## Say Hello and Goodbye

E-mail is so convenient that it's alarmingly easy to overlook the basics—the kinds of things your mother told you to do when speaking to people on the phone. I may be overly sensitive, but omitting a salutation such as Hello or Hi at the beginning of an e-mail makes me feel that the sender doesn't really respect me. Also, don't forget to say Best Wishes, Sincerely, or whatever at the end of a message, or someone might think you're mad at them. You can't convey emotions by gestures or facial expressions when you're using e-mail. You need to depend on a little extra effort to build goodwill.

*If you send out e-mail with misspellings or grammatical errors, it indicates that you were in a hurry and didn't think it was worthy of your highest level of attention. Outlook Express and Netscape Messenger both include spell-checkers that you should use before you send a response to a bidder or buyer. In Netscape Messenger, click the Spell button in the Compose toolbar before you click Send. In Outlook Express, select Tools | Options, click the Spelling tab, and click the box next to Always Check Spelling Before Sending.*

## Add a Signature File

A *signature file* is a bit of text that is appended to the bottom of your e-mail messages (as well as the messages you post on Internet newsgroups). It gives the recipient detailed information about who you are, where you work, and how to reach you. A signature file (commonly called a *sig file*) can be as simple as your name and phone number, or as long as your eBay User ID, a link to your eBay Store or About Me page, the street address for sending in that all-important check, and so on.

If you save your sig file as a separate text document, you don't have to type it every time you send e-mail. Your e-mail software lets you specify the sig file to append to your e-mail.

# How to ... Save a Unique Signature File

1.  Open a text editor such as Notepad or WordPad (for Windows users), SimpleText (for Mac users), or Microsoft Word.

2.  Type the hyphen or equal sign key a few times to make a dividing line between the body of your e-mail message and your signature.

3.  Type some information about yourself, such as your name, your eBay User ID, your business name, your phone number, your web site URL, and so on. Press RETURN or ENTER after each line. Signature files are anywhere from three to seven lines long.

4.  Choose File | Save. When the Save As dialog box opens, name the file and save it in a folder on your hard disk. Make sure the name ends with the .txt (plain-text) filename extension so you can locate it more easily.

5.  Start your e-mail program. (This example uses Outlook Express.) Choose Tools | Options, and click the Signatures tab.

6.  Click the File radio button, and then click Browse. When the Open dialog box appears, locate your signature file on your hard disk. Click the file, and then click Open.

**11**

7. When the Open dialog box closes, the path leading to the signature file appears in the File box. Check the Add Signatures to All Outgoing Messages box.

8. Click OK.

Now, when you compose an e-mail message, your signature file appears automatically at the bottom (see the following illustration). This signature file tells other eBay participants who you are and how to reach you. You can delete the message if you don't want it to appear with the particular message you are preparing to send.

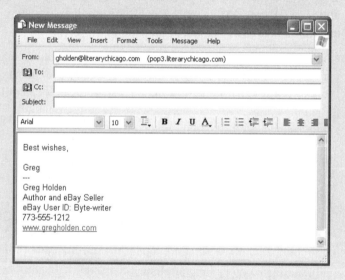

## Use Emoticons

As I just mentioned in the section "Say Hello and Goodbye," registering emotion in e-mail is difficult. That's not totally true—it's easy enough to register negative emotions like anger and disgust with ALL CAPS, or lots of exclamation marks!!!! But it's difficult to register other emotions like amusement, surprise, or sadness.

As time goes on, I see fewer and fewer *emoticons*—graphic images created by typing keyboard characters—and I think it's a shame. Emoticons are typographical representations of things like smiling faces used to annotate a text with a suggestion of how you feel about what you're writing ("That was meant to be a joke." "What a surprise!"). Used sparingly, they can add a personal touch to your e-mail.

TIP

*You can find an extensive list of emoticons at **http://www.computeruser .com/resources/dictionary/emoticons.html**. Some of the emoticons are little-used, and the more obscure ones should probably be avoided: It's hard try to figure out what you can say to legitimately use "starry-eyed angel" or "hats off to you!" for instance.*

## eBay Bestsellers
## She Gets by with a Little Help from Her eBay Friends

Sheila Schneider (User ID: buy-o-sphere) checks her e-mail "six or seven times a day" and takes the time to respond to each inquiry she receives from her bidders, no matter what the question is. She once took the time to explain to someone how to leave feedback for her. She knows how important it is to be a helpful member of the eBay community.

"I find that people really appreciate you helping them through things," comments the Portland, Oregon resident, who has been selling on eBay since November 2002. Schneider, herself, has received some helpful answers from the eBay message boards, so she is no stranger to how eBay members support one another.

"I use the message boards for questions that come up, and I have found them to be very helpful. After the holidays, I posted a message asking if I should try to sell anything in the week after Christmas and before New Year's. Several people answered who are PowerSellers, saying that yes, people are visiting their families and have time on their hands. It turned out to be my most productive sales period ever."

The product-specific message boards attract committed collectors who are only too eager to share their often-encyclopedic knowledge, she adds. "I went on the glass board asking about a particular pattern I wasn't familiar with. One person not only told me about the pattern, but sent me four photos of it. The people who have answered my questions are extremely nice. There's a group of friends who 'meet' there every day, and they seem to know each other."

Sheila also exchanges daily e-mail messages with her friend Jo Stavig in Chicago, whom she describes as her "co-worker." The two exchange tips and tricks about selling. Like her friend Jo (who is profiled in Chapter 2), Sheila used to sell collectible pottery and glass in antique malls, but she's having so much fun selling on eBay that she's beginning to make it her full-time occupation.

**11**

"Some of the items I've sold on eBay were things that sat on the shelf in the antique mall for a year. Some sold far beyond the prices they were tagged with in the antique mall. Your audience on eBay is just so much greater. It's kind of cool to think that people all over the world can see your stuff. My eBay business is allowing me to a) pay my own bills and b) purchase more stuff to sell. Not raking in the dough just yet, but I'm beginning to see that I could make a lot of money."

Sheila passes along the following tips for sellers:

- "I only leave positive or negative feedback, never neutral. The one time I left neutral was when I bought a cookie jar which came to me broken in the mail; the seller turned around and gave me a negative feedback."

- "Never use a flash when photographing items; leaves too much glare. I have a couple of cheap spotlights I bought at the local fix-it store; I use those, and my backdrops are scraps of material I've picked up at garage/estate sales for 25–50 cents."

- "I almost always include a Gallery picture in my auction listings unless the item is super inexpensive and it just doesn't make sense to pay the extra quarter."

- "I learned a great deal from attending the eBay University when it came to my area. It was inexpensive and fun."

- "Priority Mail is the best and safest method I have for shipping breakables. You get the boxes for free and they handle what they ship with care."

Her most exciting sale? A tiny chrome table that had been sitting in the basement for 16 years, and that she hoped to sell for $50. "The night before the sale ended I checked it and it was at $50, and I was happy. The next morning I looked and I thought I was seeing things—the final bid was $350."

# Frequent eBay's Discussion Boards and Cafés

Aside from books like this one, the best places to learn insider secrets about eBay are through the extensive message boards eBay provides to its members. Message boards provide to eBay users with similar interests a place to hold online discussions. On a message board, communication doesn't occur in real time as it does in a chat room. You have a bit more lag time between posting a message and viewing it. You'll find several types of boards listed on the Discussion Boards page, shown in Figure 11-1.

**FIGURE 11-1**    Discussion boards give eBay members a place to meet and greet and post questions and comments.

Some of the most useful selling tips are presented in eBay Member Workshops, which are found by doing one of two things:

■ Click **Workshops** near the bottom of the Boards or Community Overview page.

■ Go directly to **http://pages.ebay.com/community/workshopcalendar/ current.html**.

Workshops are conducted not only by eBay staffers but occasionally by experienced sellers. The one shown in Figure 11-2 provided a variety of tips on spicing up sales descriptions without having to learn HTML. The really nice thing about these workshops is that they are archived; you don't have to be present at the time they were originally held in order to read what was discussed.

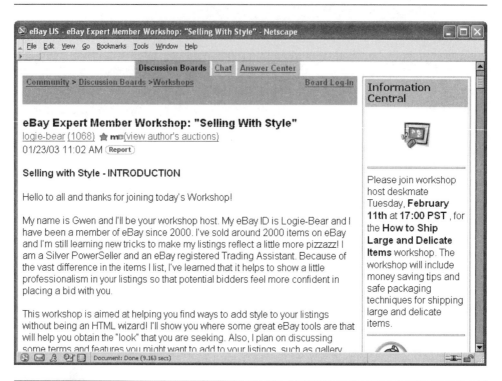

FIGURE 11-2    Individual users sometimes conduct workshops on topics related to eBay selling.

NOTE    *You have a couple of ways to search through several years of past workshops held by eBay. If you go to the Workshops main page and scroll down to the bottom of the current list of workshops, you'll see a set of page numbers. Click on those page numbers (or click Next) to browse through past workshop titles. You can also click the blue Search button and enter search terms in order to find a workshop on a particular topic.*

The discussion boards are divided into several general categories. The Community Help Boards include many subjects of interest to sellers. The Packaging & Shipping board might sound boring, but not if you've recently had an item returned because you didn't ship it carefully enough. The Category Specific Discussion Boards are great if you have a question that only an expert seller of dolls, comics, or needle arts and vintage textiles can answer. The General Discussion Boards (or the well-known eBay Café, **http://chatboards.ebay.com/chat.jsp?forum=1&thread=1**) are the place to go to get to know people and talk about anything that's on your mind. Lots of people visit these boards every day and greet one another like the old friends they are.

NOTE    *eBay uses the term "chat room" to describe many of its discussion areas, but this is misleading. Chat rooms, which are well known to teenagers around the world, enable participants to type messages to one another in real time. eBay's discussion boards function like message boards found on America Online and on the Internet. There's a lag time between comments. The discussion doesn't move as fast as it does in chat rooms, but it tends to be more focused.*

## eBay Bestsellers
## The Good, the Bad, and the Neutral

There are a few bad apples in every barrel, and the eBay barrel is no exception. Another seller, Steve Brothers of Silk Road Trading Concern, has this to say about the people he's met on eBay:

"We have made some good friends through eBay. The majority of our clients are good people and interesting too, but there are a handful of individuals who we have become very close with. eBay has good, bad, and neutral people. We have been quite fortunate to have had very few bad experiences. I think the nature of our items attracts people with a spiritual orientation and those folks are generally conscientious folks who are making efforts to evolve and cultivate compassion, gentleness, and positivity in general.

"We haven't really become close with other sellers, but we have become great friends with a couple of clients. Two in particular come to mind. One doesn't shop on eBay anymore but though we may not be in frequent contact like we were previously, we do stay in touch and have met in person. The second is a gentleman (and his wife) from Atlanta. First-class people, and here again, though he doesn't buy from us very regularly any more, we are in e-mail contact a couple times a week on average. We are very close and indeed our relationship 'outgrew' the confines of eBay.

"But frankly, eBay is not always such a pleasant place. We are grateful for the opportunity it has provided us, but eBay and the clientele have changed a bit over the past couple of years. More neutral-to-unpleasant individuals and experiences seem to have come to the community but, nonetheless, it is a great venue where one is still apt to meet some of the real gems of humanity. That sounds a bit extreme I realize, but really interacting with a couple of these top-notch personalities really does make it all worthwhile."

11

Sometimes, events are staged on discussion boards by eBay members themselves. For instance, under the General Discussion Boards, you'll find a board called The Park. Click on its link and look for a message topic called either eBay Street Faire or Share-Your-Wares. These are announcements of scheduled sales in which eBay members can sell and shop together. During a Street Faire, eBay sellers from specific categories (sometimes, from all categories) get together and list items for sale. For instance, in a Street Faire held just before St. Patrick's Day, members were encouraged to post anything they had for sale that was green. Listings of green ties, turtle bracelets, and even a green-colored juicer were offered, and members had great fun commenting on one another's merchandise.

## Learn Newsgroup Etiquette

The eBay Café and other message boards aren't the same as the newsgroups that populate the area of the Internet known as Usenet (short for User's Network, the system of discussion groups that you access through your account with your Internet Service Provider). The set of rules called "Netiquette" that is widely employed on Usenet can help you use eBay's message boards more effectively. The following sections give you some tips on how to do good messaging.

### Messages Don't Go Away Quickly

It's so easy: You only need to click Send, and that message board posting is on its way to one or more individuals, carrying all of your emotion with it. But stop and think before you click. An angry message that you regret later can invite angry responses and possibly unwanted interactions from other eBay participants.

### Stay on Message

Simply staying "on topic" by reading other messages and getting a feel for a group before you start participating is always a good idea. Often, the discussions on a message board have little or nothing to do with what eBay has stated as the purpose of the board. Members decide what *they* want to talk about instead. In general, it's a good idea to post messages that offer something in the way of advice or personal experience to other participants. If you're able to be helpful, you'll generate goodwill, and your presence in the group will be welcomed.

TIP     *When you sign up for an account on AOL, you can create multiple screen names. The screen names are used to identify you, not only in chat rooms but in your AOL e-mail addresses. If you want to maintain some privacy and separate your social time in the chat rooms from your business time on eBay, consider creating two or more User IDs, one for chat and one for selling.*

# Participate in an eBay Group

eBay Groups—groups that are created and moderated by eBay members themselves rather than eBay—are among the best-known and popular resources in the auction site's community. For sellers, eBay Groups are invaluable for gaining tips and solving problems. Those who choose to either manage or participate in an eBay Group have considerably more freedom than members in eBay's own discussion group and chat rooms: they can decide how many members to admit (some are public, while others are invitation only) and exactly what each group will discuss.

To join a group, connect to the Groups home page (**http://groups.ebay.com/ index.jspa**, shown in Figure 11-3). Find a group that suits your needs (for instance, you may want to find eBay members in your state or your geographic area, or people who sell the same things you do) through the available categories of groups, or enter a ZIP code or keyword in the search box to locate the one you want.

**FIGURE 11-3**    eBay Groups are the perfect place to get support from other sellers.

11

When you first click on a group's link on the eBay Groups home page, you access the group's Welcome page. Click the big Join Group button, then log in with your User ID and password. Click Sign In, and you view the group's Home page. After logging in, you are able to view photos that members have posted, learn about upcoming events, and join discussions.

## Moderate a Group

Although eBay Groups give members freedom, they also give members more work. Moderators need to run them closely and manage discussions. You don't have to do all the work yourself: a group can have a single administrator as well as one or more moderators. Once you know what's involved, it's easy to get the process started: just click the link **Start Group** near the top right of the eBay Groups home page. But before that, you should join a group called the eBay Groups Information Center. This group contains all the instructions you need on how to operate a group after you have formed it.

# Send Emergency Messages

eBay's Emergency Contact board (**http://chatboards.ebay.com/chat.jsp?forum=1 &thread=81**) is the place to go if you need to contact someone and you haven't been able to do so through the eBay e-mail system. Surprisingly, very few if any of the messages posted on Emergency Contact are actually from one individual attempting to contact another one, which is the message board's stated purpose. Users themselves have turned it into a place where they can get help if they're in a hurry.

Suppose you are in the process of uploading image files in order to list an item for sale and something goes wrong. Suppose you've tried over and over to change your User ID, your password, or your e-mail address, and nothing seems to work, and you're at your wit's end. Many users who don't want to contact eBay for one reason or another turn to Emergency Contact.

TIP    *If you really need help, contact eBay directly by clicking the Live Help! button that appears on many eBay pages or by going to **http://pages.ebay .com/help/basics/select-support.html**.*

The Emergency Contact board can be an unsettling yet eye-opening place because it frequently contains messages about the many ways in which eBay users can be scammed by unscrupulous individuals who are attempting to "take over" their user accounts or trick them into giving out their PayPal passwords; yet, it's a good way to learn about the many pitfalls and problems you can run into on eBay.

*Emergency Contact frequently posts messages by users who have been tricked, or almost tricked, into giving out their eBay or PayPal passwords. Don't be fooled by any e-mails that ask for such information.*

# Give to Charitable Causes

eBay regularly conducts a variety of charity auctions, and your organization can sell on eBay as a way of raising funds. You can list charity auctions at **http://pages .ebay.com/givingworks**. You can gain considerable goodwill for your eBay business by helping your own community, either by arranging a town "garage sale" or by lending your expertise to help others sell for their local organization. In summer 2004, the town of Atchison, Kansas raised more than $100,000 for its library and other public institutions. In December of the same year, the city of Chicago held a "Great Chicago Fire Sale" on eBay and raised nearly a quarter of a million dollars for arts groups by auctioning off tours, mementoes, and other offbeat items of local interest.

There's also a Giving Board (**http://chatboards.ebay.com/chat.jsp?forum=1 &thread=59**) where people can give to other eBay members in need. When I checked, there was a long series of messages in response to a plea from a user who needed money for diapers and diaper wipes. Some users were skeptical, but some offered advice as well as monetary support.

## Where to Find It

- **eBay Discussion Boards home page**
  **http://pages.ebay.com/community/boards/index.html**
  Links to all of eBay's discussion boards.

- **eBay Emergency Contact board**
  **http://chatboards.ebay.com/chat.jsp?forum=1&thread=81**
  Supposed to be a place where members can find one another in an emergency, but it's commonly used as a problem-solving forum.

- **eBay Giving Works**
  **http://pages.ebay.com/givingworks/**
  List of current auctions being conducted to benefit charitable causes.

- **eBay Contact Us form**
  **http://pages.ebay.com/help/contact_inline/index.html**
  A form you can fill out to submit a question to eBay's Customer Support staff.

**11**

# Part IV

# Sell Specialty
# Items on eBay

# Chapter 12

# Drive Home the Deal on eBay Motors

# How to...

- Make your vehicle more attractive to bidders

- Determine a reserve or Buy It Now price

- Write descriptions and take photos that sell

- Arrange for inspections

- Transfer the title

- Deal with deadbeat bidders

- Receive the money and ship the vehicle

- Have eBay manage the sale for you

It's downright easy to sell and ship small-scale treasures such as a Beanie Baby or an antique tablecloth on eBay. You take some photos, receive bids, pack the item in a box, and ship it out to the lucky winner. But what if you need to unload a family sedan, a sailboat, or that spare jet airplane that's cluttering up your runway?

There are a few steps involved to auction off a car or other motorized vehicle, but sellers use eBay every day to market their wheels, not to mention related parts and accessories. In fact, eBay Motors is one of the most successful areas on eBay: according to a July 26, 2004 *Detroit Free Press* article (**http://www.freep.com/money/tech/mwendland26e_20040726.htm**), $4.5 million worth of vehicle-related items were sold on eBay in 2003, with $7.5 million projected for 2004. eBay has come up with some services and shortcuts that are designed to streamline the process on a specialized auction site called eBay Motors (**http://motors.ebay.com**). You'll find everything you need to handle the special challenges involved in selling motor vehicles online, including answers to questions such as these:

- How can you induce a buyer to bid thousands of dollars for a vehicle when they can't take it for a test drive?

- How can you be sure you are going to get paid by a customer you may never meet in person?

- How do you get the vehicle to an out-of-state buyer? Who pays for shipping? What happens if the item is damaged in transit?

Did you know?

## eBay Motors: Motors and All That Jazz

eBay itself reports that, on any given day, more than 30,000 vehicle parts and accessories are bought and sold on eBay Motors. Automobiles, trucks, SUVs, and motorcycles are the types of items people think about when they think about selling on eBay Motors. But anything that has a motor and that moves can be put up for sale there. That includes boats, houseboats, yachts, toy cars, airplanes, scooters, and mopeds. Even if you don't have an entire motor vehicle to sell, you can still attract buyers by acquiring and reselling accessories, parts, and repair manuals, which are often hard to find for older and unusual vehicles. Every three seconds, a vehicle part or accessory is sold on this part of eBay (**http://66.139.75.240**).

In this chapter, you'll learn how to drive smoothly through such roadblocks with the help of eBay Motors. As one long-time seller commented on the eBay Motors message boards, the trick is to "sell yourself...the rest is easy."

# Avoid the Used-Car Lot

eBay Motors has become a popular sales channel on the world's most popular auction site. Both amateur sellers and automobile dealers frequent the site. Many of the vehicles you see advertised on eBay Motors are new and have low mileage; they're probably demo cars being put online by traditional used-car dealers. These are especially good deals; the dealers are experienced and reputable and offer warranties and financing.

> NOTE    *eBay reports that an average of eight bids is received for every vehicle listed on eBay motors. This is far more than the number of offers an auto dealer would receive for a car on a lot.*

Some vehicles sell better than others, however, and some sellers tend to get better sales results. Knowing what to expect and what you can gain by auctioning off your vehicle on eBay (as opposed to one of the other long-established sites such as Autobytel and Cars.com) can decrease the chances that what you hope to be a smooth sale will turn into a bumpy ride.

12

The big benefit of selling a car online is the ability to gain a nationwide audience for that vehicle. If your car is a collectible or rare item, you might even attract buyers from other countries. You also get the benefit of eBay's built-in inspection, shipping, payment, and buyer protection services, which make bidders feel at ease.

## Experience Not Required (But It Helps)

Who should sell on the world's largest vehicle auction site? eBay Motors is a good choice if you are an established seller who has accumulated good feedback ratings. An established auto dealer who already has experience with financing and selling cars and who has successfully completed sales also inspires confidence. But you don't need to be an auto dealer already. The whole point of eBay is that it puts buying and selling in the hands of everyday individuals like you and me. If you can, mention any business experience you have, even if it isn't directly related to automobile sales; bidders will want to know that you are someone who is already aware of the need to build and maintain trust among a group of customers.

If you are an existing auto dealer, you can build an extra level of trust by obtaining a seal of trust from SquareTrade (**http://www.squaretrade.com/cnt/jsp/index.jsp**). If you qualify, you can obtain a graphic seal icon that appears next to your eBay auto listings. Anyone who sells on eBay can obtain a SquareTrade seal, and any eBay user can use SquareTrade for dispute resolution, as described in Chapter 16.

> TIP
>
> *For some easy-to-follow instructions on selling vehicles, visit eBay Motors Canada's Simple Guide to Successful eBay Motors Selling page at **http:// pages.ebay.ca/ebaymotors/help/education/selling/tutorial_1.html**. Or you can consult the main eBay Motors Help page at **http://pages.ebay.com/ ebaymotors/help/sellerguide/sell_vehicles.html**. If you are looking for more complete instructions that encompass buying as well as selling cars, click the "How To" Center button in the toolbar near the top of any eBay Motors page to access audio tours, interactive tutorials, and other resources.*

## Selling One Singular Sensation

What you sell on eBay Motors also has a bearing on whether bidders meet your reserve price or Buy It Now price. If you can, pick a *marketable* car to sell. A marketable car is not a "dime a dozen" model. It is unusual, rare, or notable for some other reason (such as its superb condition, its age, and so on). eBay has always been the perfect place to market rare, collectible, or one-of-a-kind items. Things like a Batmobile from a Batman movie, a tiny Corbin Sparrow of the sort seen in the Austin Powers series of movies (shown in Figure 12-1), or a Lamborghini Countach sports car are bound to get bids.

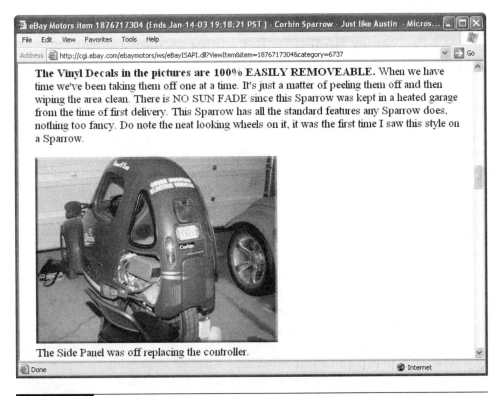

The Vinyl Decals in the pictures are 100% EASILY REMOVEABLE. When we have time we've been taking them off one at a time. It's just a matter of peeling them off and then wiping the area clean. There is NO SUN FADE since this Sparrow was kept in a heated garage from the time of first delivery. This Sparrow has all the standard features any Sparrow does, nothing too fancy. Do note the neat looking wheels on it, it was the first time I saw this style on a Sparrow.

The Side Panel was off replacing the controller.

**FIGURE 12-1**     Unusual or collectible vehicles sell best on eBay Motors. This one's description is especially complete and honest.

12

eBay may be just about the only place where eager collectors or automobile enthusiasts can locate antique or limited-edition vehicles. You won't have any trouble getting bids on them. For autos that are widely sold and readily available at local auto dealerships or through local newspapers, you need to take care writing extra-good descriptions and taking plenty of photos to make your vehicle stand out from the crowd.

TIP

*eBay keeps track of "hot items"—items that are selling especially well at the current time. Go to the Seller Central page (**http://pages.ebay.com/ sellercentral**), click **What's Hot**, and click the link **Hot Items by Category**. You'll have to scroll through the entire contents of this Portable Document Format (PDF) file; it details all categories on eBay including eBay Motors.*

## eBay Bestsellers
## Be "Super Honest," eBay Motors Seller Advises

You don't have to sell tons (and I do mean *tons*) of vehicles or other items on eBay Motors to turn a profit. (In fact, your state regulations may limit the number of vehicles you are actually able to sell in a given year, as mentioned later in this feature.) If you choose wisely, you can make a profit without having to turn around a large number of vehicles.

That's one of many tips provided by Tom Hergert (User ID: tallgazauctions), who specializes in selling older Detroit-made vehicles on eBay Motors along with parts, manuals, and Mopar accessories related to those vehicles. "I sell everything I can get my hands on," comments the Bellevue, Washington resident.

Tom got serious about selling on eBay in October 2003, when he needed a heater control for his 1972 Dodge Polara. He realized eBay was the only place to find such a part, and that other car enthusiasts needed to find auto parts on the auction site as well. He estimates that he's sold a few hundred auto-related items on eBay Motors. "I like to average 10 listings a week and 10 to 15 things in my eBay Store (**http://stores.ebay.com/Tallzag-Auctions-Mopar-Disc-Brake**). I like to stock items in the store that are related to what I sell, such as service manuals for Mopars."

Tom sells on eBay on a part-time basis, when he's not at his full-time 40-hours-per-week job. "I have tons of sources for items, such as older Mopars, which I collect," he says. "I am a Trading Assistant for friends who are in the same hobby. I go to junkyards and buy parts on the cheap and then resell them. I've bought inventory from a parts shop that went out of business, and I sometimes part cars out. I'll pick up another 72 Polara for parts for my own Polara, then pay for it by selling items on eBay that I don't need."

Tom doesn't see much difference between listing eBay Motors items and items to be sold on other parts of eBay. You always need to take a variety of photos, for instance. There are some important differences when it comes to shipping and finalizing transactions, however. "Shipping is only trickier with the big items, like sheet metal. I generally avoid selling this on eBay because of the hassle in packing it up. I've found that I can easily spend way too much time on packing and was not making much profit for the work involved. I am trying a new service called UShip, which might make this much easier."

Selling a car or a boat is a whole different matter entirely, Tom adds: if the vehicle doesn't function properly after it's delivered, you'll have to deal with complaints and possible negative feedback. Returns and refunds are far more difficult than with smaller items such as collectibles.

"The only negative feedback comment I've gotten so far was from a Sea-Doo powerboat I sold. It was a boat that had not been used in a year. It ran well when I sold it, but when it got to its destination the motor decided to let go. The buyer was not too happy and with something like a boat or a car, it is hard to give a refund, especially when you are selling the item on consignment. He gave me a negative feedback and threatened a lawsuit (which happens a lot with these purchases)."

Because Tom is not a licensed auto dealer, he is limited by law in his home state of Washington to selling only five autos in a given year. (You should check with your own state so you are aware of similar limitations.) He does act as a Trading Assistant, charging a flat fee to help clients sell cars under their own User IDs as well: he verified with his state's Department of Motor Vehicles beforehand to make sure this was legal.

"I once sold a very valuable car for a friend on my account (one of my five a year). This car was restored and cosmetically almost perfect. The person who ended up buying the car got stuck in rush-hour traffic in 100-degree heat and the car overheated. This guy got real mad, threatened negative feedback, and my seller eventually gave in to the guy and paid for the tow truck (which I advised him against). I just mention this as an example of how hard it can be to finalize a deal when you sell a car (or other vehicle) on eBay. You have to be super, super honest and pray nothing bad happens with the vehicle, because if something does, even if it's a 30-year-old car, you can be accused of hiding something and told it's your fault."

Of course, most of Tom's transactions on eBay Motors go right rather than wrong. He fondly remembers the time he dragged home a 1970 Plymouth Satellite wagon that he got for nothing. He listed some of the vehicle's parts on eBay and sold a wood-grain radio dash piece for $300.

Tom advises would-be eBay Motors sellers to work with what they like already. "I always have piles of old car parts lying around, so I sell them on eBay. I also sell anything else I can make a profit on too. Even if you do not want to look for things to sell, then become a Trading Assistant. That is how I started. I sold a pair of football tickets for a friend for three times the face value and thought to myself, 'I could make some money doing this.'"

# Get Your Bankroll Rolling

eBay Motors sales are "big" in terms of the sale items themselves—which, after all, might weigh a couple of thousand pounds and span ten feet or more in length. The sales price of your vehicle will (hopefully) be as big as you want as well. What about other money matters, such as the fees you pay to eBay to conduct and complete a sale? These and other big money matters are discussed in the sections that follow.

## Price Research That Pays Off

Before you can sell, you need to have an idea of the vehicle's value so you can set a reserve price or Buy It Now price. One way is simply to search completed auctions on eBay itself, as follows:

1. Go to the eBay Advanced Search page (**http://search.ebay.com/ws/search/AdvSearch**).

2. In the Search box, enter a keyword or two that describes the kind of vehicle you're hunting for. (Adding the year of the vehicle in the form YYYY will help narrow down your search.)

3. Choose eBay Motors from the In this Category drop-down list.

4. Check the Completed Listings Only box.

5. Choose Time: Ending Soonest from the Sort By drop-down list.

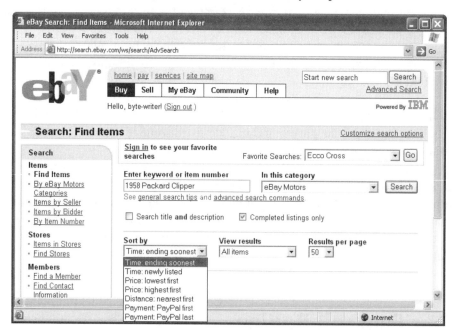

6. Select any other options you want to specify, such as a geographic region or sorting option.

7. Click Search.

You can scan the list of completed sales for cars that match the one you want to sell. Hopefully you'll have enough results to be able to take an average and get a reliable value.

As an alternative, you can have an eBay Trading Assistant handle the sale for you. You fill out a registration form, and you provide detailed information about cars you wish to sell. After that, someone will contact you by e-mail or phone to ask you questions about the car. The service will then help you to determine the value of the car you want to sell.

The advantage of selling an auto on eBay through a Trading Assistant, rather than doing it all yourself, is that the auction site takes responsibility for how the sale is conducted. It costs more to use a listing service but it shows the buyer that you really care about selling the car to a satisfied customer.

*You can also hire an eBay Trading Assistant to handle the sale for you from start to finish. Many assistants specialize in automotive sales. Search for an assistant in your area at* **http://pages.ebay.com/tradingassistants.html**.

## All Sales Formats Are Not Created Equal

The classic eBay sales—the ones with which everyone is familiar—are auctions that last for one, three, five, seven, or ten days. But at the end of the auction, the highest bidder wins if there is no reserve price. If a reserve price has been set, the high bidder wins if his or her bid matches or exceeds the reserve.

However, you may want to dispense with the auction format altogether and simply set a fixed price for your vehicle. If someone offers to meet the price, they agree to purchase it immediately. Or you may want to sell cars or related accessories through an eBay Store like Auto Body Parts, shown in Figure 12-2 (see Chapter 14 for more details on how to set up an eBay store).

There are several advantages to selling vehicles or vehicle-related items through an eBay Store:

- Listings stay up for sale for 30 days or longer.

- You don't have to deal with the uncertainty of an auction or the question of whether to relist the item if the sale ends without a winning bid; when someone commits to paying your price, the sale is done.

- When listed with a range of other vehicles and other automotive products, the item helps to build your reputation as a seller.

12

**FIGURE 12-2** You can gain more attention for your vehicle-related sales by presenting them in one place—an eBay Store.

The options available to you for conventional eBay sales listings are described in the sections that follow.

## Reserve Price

If you want to obtain a minimum amount for the vehicle you are selling, by all means specify a reserve price. Suppose, for instance, you specify a reserve price of $5000 for a car. If the high bidder reaches $3999, you aren't obligated to complete the sale. You can relist or try to sell the vehicle at a later date.

## No Reserve

A no reserve (NR) auction is one in which the high bidder wins no matter what the bid is. That's because the seller has not specified a reserve. Such sales have an air of excitement about them; they typically attract attention on eBay from bidders looking for rock-bottom prices.

Auto sellers frequently choose a no reserve format because they are unsure of how much a vehicle is worth. They simply want to see how much they can get for a vehicle. Many let the sale end and take the high bid, no matter what it is. However, when the close of the auction approaches, some sellers have been known to evaluate the current bidding and decide to end the sale immediately if it seems like the high bid is going to be lower than they were hoping for. Just before the auction ends the sale is stopped, leaving everyone out in the cold. They sometimes remove their eBay listings abruptly just before the final bids come in. Such behavior, while technically legal, frustrates bidders. eBay has been cracking down on this practice; if it notices particular sellers ending sales early on a regular basis, it takes disciplinary action against those sellers. Also, don't choose no reserve unless you are truly prepared to sell your vehicle for whatever the market will bring at the time the sale occurs.

## Buy It Now

A Buy It Now sale is frequently abbreviated as BIN and is also called a Fixed Price sale on the Sell Your Item form. The BIN format is one with which auto dealers should be familiar: the seller chooses a fixed price for the vehicle, which stays in place until the first bid is made in a no reserve auction. In a reserve price auction that includes the option of a BIN price, the BIN price can last for several days. Until the reserve price is met, any bidder can match the BIN price and purchase the vehicle immediately.

NOTE

*Each version of eBay has its own eBay Motors area. eBay Canada, for instance, has one at **http://pages.ebay.ca/auto-index.html**. You should sell in the eBay version that covers the country where you live. That doesn't mean you have to sell only to individuals who live in your own country, however. As a Canadian, you can sell to U.S. buyers or people in other countries, but you have to figure in the exchange rate. If you're looking for a French, German, or other car that's hard to find in the U.S., you should look through the appropriate international version of eBay Motors: you'll find a list of worldwide eBay sites on the home page (**http://www.ebay.com**) under the Global Sites heading and along the bottom of the home page. Many of these sites have an eBay Motors area. However, you'll have to pay high shipping costs, and you'll need to make sure the seller is willing to ship to your part of the world.*

## eBay Store Sale

If you're not comfortable with a sale that lasts ten days or less, create an eBay Store and advertise your vehicle there. You specify a set price for the vehicle, so there's no bidding and no reserve. You can have the vehicle for sale for 30, 60, 90, or 120 days. You can even leave the item online indefinitely if you prefer.

## Spotlight on Marketing Add-Ons

eBay Motors is a popular area of the eBay marketplace, and it can be difficult to get your vehicle to stand out from the crowd. If your vehicle isn't noteworthy because of its manufacturer, age, speed, or other desirable qualities, consider some formatting add-ons that eBay provides to get extra attention.

### Gallery Featured

Gallery Featured items can appear in any number of places. Your vehicle will certainly appear in a special featured area at the top of the general set of Gallery images in eBay Motors. It might also appear on the home page of a particular category, or randomly be chosen to appear on the eBay Motors home page itself. (The rotation of listings on the eBay Motors home page changes several times a day, however.) A Gallery Featured item might also be chosen for inclusion on the Enthusiast or Car Collectors' pages, though there's no guarantee this will happen. Often, sellers feature vehicles that are especially desirable and expensive. If the sale price is $30,000 to $40,000, for example, what's a few extra bucks to get the added attention?

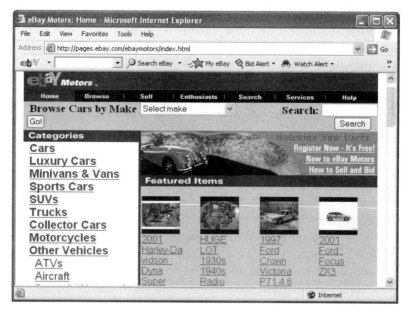

You pay extra for such exposure: the Gallery Featured fee is $99.95 for vehicles, and $24.95 for items that aren't vehicles, such as automobile memorabilia.

## Category Featured

With Category Featured, the listing appears at the top of the specific category in which you want to sell it. For instance, if you are selling a motorcycle and you want to feature it at the top of the eBay Motors Motorcycles listings, you pay a Gallery Featured fee. However, if you are selling a Yamaha motorcycle and you want it to be included in a "short list" of Yamahas that appears at the top of the first page listing all the Yamahas that are currently up for sale, you pay a Category Featured fee of $14.95.

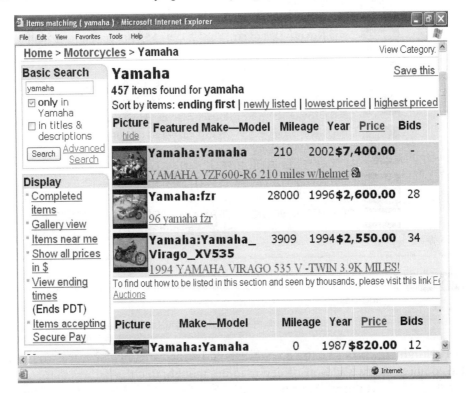

## Highlighting

To my mind, Category Featured listings are difficult to read and don't really call attention to sellers who search by using eBay's Search feature. On the other hand, if you highlight your listing, you can make your listing stand out in a sea of other listings. Vehicle listings are highlighted in a bright color (for instance, purple). Another option is to make your listing stand out in bold type. Both highlighted and bold listings are shown in Figure 12-3.

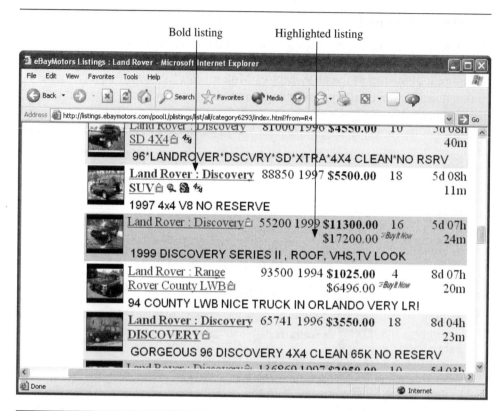

FIGURE 12-3    You can make your listing stand out from the crowd with inexpensive add-ons.

Highlighting costs an extra $5, while bold listings are only $2 extra. You can also combine the two add-ons. Keep in mind, though, that the listings that appear on either side of yours might be bold and/or highlighted, so they may not stand out as much as you hoped.

## Read the Fine Print

You may not know what your item will sell for before you start an eBay auction, but you can calculate the seller's fees you'll have to pay. Some costs are fixed, while others depend on the type of sale you want to conduct. The fixed fees are listed in the table that follows.

| Vehicle | Insertion Fee | Transaction Services Fee |
|---|---|---|
| Cars, boats, airplanes, RVs, snowmobiles, and items listed in Other Vehicles category | $40 | $40 |
| Motorcycles | $30 | $30 |
| Powersports (snowmobiles, jet-skis, scooters, mopeds, and ATVs) | $30 | $30 |

*You don't have to pay the transaction services fee if you held a reserve auction and either you didn't receive any bids or the bids on your vehicle did not meet your reserve price. You can review the current fees for selling on eBay Motors at **http://pages.motors.ebay.com/help/sell/motorfees.html**.*

## Insertion Fee

The insertion fee is the fee eBay charges you for putting your sale online. The insertion fee is nonrefundable; you pay it even if your item gets no bids, if your reserve price is not met, or the high bidder does not pay you for the item. Insertion fees range from $30 for motorcycles and powersports vehicles to $40 for passenger and other vehicles.

*The charge for the insertion fee doesn't apply to items sold on eBay outside of eBay Motors. On other parts of eBay, you can relist the item for free if you are able to sell it the second time around.*

## Transaction Services Fee

If you have sold on other parts of eBay, you are familiar with a final value fee—a fee that eBay charges you if an item is successfully sold. If you sell parts and accessories on eBay Motors, you are charged a final value fee if an item sells.

However, if you sell a vehicle on eBay Motors, you are charged a *transaction services fee* instead. The fee is charged if you receive a bid (on a standard auction), if you receive a bid that meets your reserve (on a reserve auction), or if someone pays your Buy It Now price. If the vehicle listing does not attract any bids or is not sold, you aren't charged a transaction services fee. The transaction services fee is charged to you if you have a successful high bid or Buy It Now price placed on your vehicle. The fee is still charged whether or not the deal is actually consummated. For example, if someone is the high bidder but doesn't follow through with a deposit or doesn't like the car when it is delivered and refuses to pay, you are still charged the transaction services fee.

12

The transaction services fee ranges from $30 for motorcycles and powersports vehicles, to $40 for passenger vehicles and other vehicles.

*After you've completed a number of sales of automotive parts or other vehicle-related items, you might want to take advantage of eBay's new Sales Reports feature. eBay will supply you with data summarizing your own activities so you can easily see which products sell best. You have to subscribe to receive sales reports, but the subscription to receive the basic data is free. A Sales Reports Plus version provides more detailed information on the best time to end sales, the best categories, and the types of sales that work best. The Plus version is free for eBay Store owners. For others, it's free for a 30-day trial period, after which the service costs $4.99 per month.*

# Get Your Auction in Gear

You've registered with eBay (as described in Chapter 2). You've cleaned and serviced your vehicle, and taken some clear digital photos (as described in Chapter 8). You've chosen an auction format and picked some marketing add-ons. Now, you can create your auction listing and publish it online, as described in the following sections.

## Did you know?

### Muscle Car Enthusiasts Are Enthusiastic about eBay

eBay assigned to a Manteno, Illinois custom auto builder named Troy Trepanier the enviable job of purchasing and restoring a classic American muscle car—using some rare parts purchased on eBay and some custom-made parts. The car, a 1967 Mustang Fastback, was purchased for $10,100 at an auction from a St. Paul, Minnesota seller. The Mustang was then completely stripped and replaced with new parts. The employee who picked up the car was greeted with a plate of warm cookies and a glass of milk provided by the seller's mother. You can read about the construction of this one-of-a-kind "project car" at **http://66.139.75.240**.

# Sweet Talking Descriptions That Lead to Sweet Deals

Some cars sell themselves because they're rare. Most, though, need some help from you in the form of clear photos and good descriptions. Bidders go into eBay Motors with a skeptical attitude. They are accustomed to buying autos or boats through newspaper ads or brick-and-mortar dealerships. You have to convince people they should trust you by providing accurate, honest descriptions of what you have to offer.

**TIP**    *Include lots of photos with your descriptions. You can hardly include too many. Make sure they are sharp and well-lit. Be sure you photograph your vehicle from all different sides, so prospective buyers know there aren't any hidden dents or scrapes. If the color isn't quite right in a photo, say so ("the color in the photo has a reddish cast but the real color is purple"). You don't want people to be surprised in any way when the vehicle is delivered.*

Honesty is the best policy when it comes to descriptions of vehicles on eBay Motors. Telling your bidders about any problems with your vehicle and describing both the good and not-so-good aspects of the vehicle helps you as well as your potential customers. Take at least two photos of each car you sell: one from the front left, and one from the right rear. This shows the vehicle from all angles. Also include photos of the instrument cluster, including the odometer, to show how many miles the vehicle has on it. Interior shots of the vehicle make your presentation more complete. If there has been damage to the vehicle, be upfront about it by showing the damage in photos and talking about it in the description. Such completeness helps you because it reduces the chances that buyers will be stricken with "buyer's remorse" after the sale ends (as explained in the section "Buyer's Remorse," later in this chapter).

Of course, your descriptions shouldn't all be about problems. You need to emphasize everything that's positive about your vehicle. Be an enthusiastic booster and try to generate some excitement among your bidders. Here are some examples of the good points you might emphasize:

- Low mileage

- Special options like leather upholstery or extra seats on SUVs

- The fact that you're the only owner, if that's applicable

- If the vehicle has an extended warranty

- If the vehicle has been certified by an organization such as Carfax (**http://www.carfax.com**)

**12**

Buzzwords like "Sporty," "Like New," and "Sharp" aren't specific and descriptive; they're overused. Facts about the vehicle count for much more.

All the buzzwords in the world can't match a guarantee that the vehicle is in the condition you describe, however. If you participate in the Condition Guarantee by Seller Program (**http://pages.motors.ebay.com/services/conditionguarantee .html**), you guarantee that the condition is accurate, and you agree to work with a buyer to make sure they're satisfied, in case they have complaints. Both buyers and sellers have to meet conditions to participate in this program. Only sellers who have a minimum feedback rating of 50 can offer such assurance. You don't have to pay anything to provide the guarantee, however; you just have to pledge that, in case of a dispute, you'll work with a mediator to resolve the problem.

TIP    *Before you start the sale, check your vehicle's warranty information to verify that the warranty may be transferred to the next owner. If the warranty information is transferable, that makes your vehicle more desirable, and you should mention this in your description. Even if the factory warranty is not available, your vehicle may be eligible for eBay's own Short Term Service Agreement (STSA). Based on the make, model, mileage, and year in your description, eBay determines whether the STSA is available. If it is, buyers have an extra level of protection against failure of power train components. It's up to buyers to apply for the coverage if it is available; you don't have to do anything to make the STSA available.*

## Get Inspector Gadget on the Scene

Bidders who don't live near you need to trust you when it comes to an accurate description of your vehicle, or verify your description with an inspection by a third party. You can either pay for an inspection yourself and include the inspection results with your auction listing, or allow the high bidder/buyer to conduct an inspection before the sale ends.

If you include a vehicle inspection report with your listing, you are more likely to get serious bids. You can schedule an inspection either yourself, by taking the vehicle to a local car dealer, or by contacting the inspection service that's affiliated with eBay, SGS Automotive (**http://pages.motors.ebay.com/services/inspection/ inspection.html**). SGS Automotive will do a 150-point inspection for about $99.50.

A less expensive inspection service is provided by Pep Boys (**http://pages.motors .ebay.com/services/inspection/PepBoysinspection.html**). For $24.99, the well-known automotive service will prepare an 89-point Vehicle Condition Report and post it online for you.

*You don't have to have eBay do an inspection. If you are a dealer and you are already affiliated with an inspection service, you may use it instead.*

### Drive Home the Deal

Once you have chosen the sale format, created your description, and taken photos, you put your listing online, as described in Chapter 3. During the sale, be sure to answer questions from bidders promptly and thoroughly. Based on the questions you receive, you may want to add further descriptions or new photos to your auction listing.

*Even while the sale is continuing, if you have second thoughts about your reserve or Buy It Now price, you can lower the selling price. You might want to do this if your vehicle doesn't seem to be attracting much attention.*

## Complete the Transaction

After the sale ends, you should contact your high bidder within three business days. Check your e-mail or phone messages on a regular basis. If you don't get an e-mail message from the high bidder within the three-day period, you can move on to the next-highest bidder—or place the vehicle up for auction again.

### What if You Run into Problems?

There's a reason for the inspection, warranty, insurance, escrow, and other services provided by eBay for vehicle sales. The reason is simple: fraud. Since you're an honest seller, I won't go into the fraudulent, inaccurate descriptions that buyers sometimes encounter. Sellers, too, can run into problems completing a sale.

**12**

### Be Up-Front about Fees

Auto sales require purchasers to handle more fees than are required for other, smaller-scale items sold on eBay. You need to be up front about explaining those fees so the buyer isn't surprised when it comes time to close the deal. For instance, your state probably requires the buyer to pay a fee for documentation, administration, a temporary license tag, and notary services. Besides that, the buyer may have to pay tax and license fees in his or her home state. It's a good idea to mention that buyers are responsible for researching and paying such fees—not you.

## Nobody Meets Your Price

Normally, if none of your bidders meets your reserve price, you don't have to sell. You withdraw the item and resell it some other time. On eBay Motors, however, you have another option. You are allowed to lower your reserve price or your Buy It Now price so you don't have to resell. Suppose you work at an auto dealership, and you have to pay a monthly fee to keep a car on your lot. Relisting the item means you have to pay another monthly fee; by selling right away at a lower price, you not only save yourself some time and trouble, but you might save a little money as well because you don't have to pay that extra month's rent.

## Buyer's Remorse

Buyer's remorse occurs when someone places the high bid or pledges to pay a Buy It Now price, but then decides to back out of the deal. Sometimes, buyers back out before they pay anything. Other times, they pay a deposit, but then fail to pick up the vehicle. The new eBay Motors message board occasionally receives messages

# Underbidders Can Be the Underdogs

The term *underbidder* refers to anyone other than the high bidder. An underbidder, in other words, is someone who just didn't bid high enough. Usually, you can't sell to an underbidder if the deal falls through with the high bidder. But eBay has a new Second Chance Policy in which you can sell to underbidders if the high bidder can't complete the purchase. You can pick any or all of your underbidders; you can also set your price for the Second Chance Offer. If you have two identical items for sale and you offered only one for sale on eBay, you can use the Second Chance Offer to sell the other item to someone else. You can do this up to 60 days after the auction ends. After you are certain that the high bidder is not going to complete the deal, go to your closed auction listing on eBay and click **Bid History**. Then choose the underbidders to whom you want to send the Second Chance Offer listing. (It's unlikely that you have two identical cars for sale, but you might have identical owner's manuals or accessories, for instance.)

from people who sell a car and receive a deposit from a high bidder, and then still run into problems. Examples include:

- Someone who actually drove hundreds of miles to pick up a car and who was unhappy with its condition upon seeing it, and who stalked away angrily without paying.

- One person who threw a fit, kicked the door of a 1953 Buick, and said he would forfeit the deposit.

- Another person who never showed up at the appointed time to pick up the vehicle.

If you run into trouble or need to contact eBay Motors about something, you can send an e-mail message to motors-support@ebay.com. Or, post a message on the eBay Motors discussion board. If you are so inclined, you can take a buyer to small claims court. Many problems with completing transactions are covered by Uniform Commercial Code section 2-708, so you could conceivably sue buyers who refuse to pay a deposit or at least part of the purchase price.

## Drive Your Money to the Bank

You pretty much need to assume that you are going to use a payment or escrow service (see Chapter 9) to handle the transaction because such a large amount of money is involved. Also, you have taken the time and effort to prepare the vehicle for sale, so you need to safeguard that the sale will be transacted successfully and you won't become a victim of fraud.

### Require a Deposit

It's the rule, rather than the exception, for auto sellers on eBay to ask the high bidder or purchaser for a deposit. A deposit is considered "earnest money." It demonstrates that the buyer is serious about wanting the vehicle and will be likely to follow through. You have two options:

- *Require a deposit right in the listing.* That way, you can require any deposit you want. Deposits range anywhere from $200 or $250 to 25 percent of the purchase price.

- *Automatically require a $200 deposit from the seller through PayPal.* You need to be a member of PayPal to use this service, and so does your high bidder.

12

## Use a Payment or Escrow Service

Payment services like PayPal give you a good opportunity to receive payment for vehicles you sell on eBay Motors. Not only that, but some services will also handle the transfer of title and registration for a small fee. You are required to disclose the accurate odometer reading, and in California, you have to provide a certificate stating that the vehicle has passed smog checks as well. An escrow service such as eBay's affiliate Escrow.com will handle the paperwork along with handling payments. Escrow.com, in fact, provides a set of services, collectively called Secure Pay, that is designed to protect eBay Motors buyers and sellers alike. It's up to you and the buyer to determine who will pay the $22 transaction fees (and any extra fees for wire transfers), or whether the fees should be split between the two of you.

## eBay's Financing Center

If your buyer attempts to talk down your price, saying that they can't afford the whole purchase price all at once, don't get mad. Just refer them to eBay's own Financing Center, **http://financing-center.ebay.com**. In this program, eBay has partnered with several lenders to provide auto loans to auction buyers. Buyers can actually arrange financing before they make a purchase, not after. Rates at this writing are 3.79 percent for new autos purchased on eBay and 4.45 percent for used autos.

If you receive any questions about financing, refer your buyers to the Financing Center. There's a tangible benefit for doing this: if you include a link to the Financing Center in your listing and one of your buyers obtains a Financing Center Loan, you get a referral fee of $50 or $75. You have to register with the Financing Center beforehand; find out more at **http://financing-center.ebay.com/HTML/SellerDetails.shtml**.

# Transfer Title

Once payment is received, you need to transfer title to the vehicle to the seller. Check with the state where the buyer lives to determine how quickly this needs to be done. Many states require titles to be transferred within 21 days after purchase; however, Minnesota requires title transfer within 10 days. Check with your own state's Department of Motor Vehicles to verify the current requirements.

> **TIP**    *You'll find a state-by-state list of links to Department of Motor Vehicles web sites at **http://www.magnatize.com/magnatize/dmv.html**.*

If you are able to meet with your buyer in person to receive payment and transfer title, it is obviously the best way to seal the deal. If you can't, you can then require that the seller pay you in full before you sign over the title.

## Let Buyers Decide How to Ship

Shipping is getting to be more and more popular among people who buy cars. eBay is affiliated with Dependable Auto Shippers (DAS): **http://www.dasautoshippers .com**. You can visit the company's web site for an instant quote.

Before you prepare to ship, you need to prepare the vehicle. As with any eBay sale, your goal is to ensure that the customer will be satisfied when the vehicle arrives. You don't want the customer to have any unpleasant surprises—especially with such high-priced items. You need to do some simple but obvious things:

- *Wash the vehicle.* Before you deliver the vehicle to the shipper, make sure it's in good condition so the shipper can inspect it easily.

- *Keep the fuel level low.* Make sure the fuel level is less than half of a full tank to keep the weight of the vehicle down. The lower the weight, the lower the shipping cost.

- *Clean out your personal items.* This keeps the weight down and ensures that you won't end up missing anything important.

- *Keep the vehicle profile compact.* Retract antennas, remove luggage racks. Be sure to turn off car alarms as well.

*Many auto dealers that sell on eBay handle shipping with their usual provider but pass the cost on to the customer. As an alternative, you can suggest that customers get their own quote from a site like the Internet Directory of Automobile Transporters (**http://www.movecars.com**) and give them the option to arrange for shipping themselves.*

## Pay Unto eBay What Is eBay's

When all is said and done, you need to pay your eBay fees and settle up with the purchaser or with your payment or escrow service. Remind your purchaser to send feedback about the sale so you can develop a good feedback rating, which encourages all auto buyers to place bids with you.

CAUTION

*Most states allow you to sell up to five autos per year. However, if you sell more than five autos per year, you may be required to obtain an auto dealer's license. Check with your state to make sure you're operating within the law.*

12

# Where to Find It

- **eBay Motors portal page**
  **http://www.motors.ebay.com**
  Links to all categories on eBay Motors, as well as links to the Help area.

- **Fees for eBay Motors**
  **http://pages.ebay.com/help/sell/motorfees.html**
  How to calculate insertion fees and final value fees; when and how to pay your eBay seller's fees.

- **eBay Motors Simple Guide to Successful Motors Selling**
  **http://pages.ebay.ca/ebaymotors/help/sellerguide/sell_vehicles.html**
  A link to a Seller's Checklist and other tips on how to sell on eBay Motors.

- **Contact support for eBay Motors**
  **motors-support@ebay.com**
  E-mail address for the eBay Motors support staff.

- **eBay Motors Services page**
  **http://pages.motors.ebay.com/services/overview.html**
  Links to inspection, vehicle protection, shipping, insurance, and other services that will streamline transactions for both buyers and sellers.

# Chapter 13

# Auction Off Business Goods and Services

# How to...

- Score business supplies at bargain rates

- Get rid of inventory you don't need

- Limit sales to nearby purchasers

- Put wholesale lots up for sale

- Purchase government surplus materials

- Make a living as a freelancer

- Post projects on eLance

I've set my clock radio to wake me up every morning to the soothing sounds of a classical music station. One of its primary sponsors is featured in a set of commercials that sets up scenarios for missed business connections. Two vendors with intersecting needs are standing in line at an amusement ride, exercising together at the health club, or shopping at a boutique, unaware that each has what the other lacks. All they need is a way to make a connection. eBay's Business & Industrial category and Business Marketplace both provide just such a place to meet and do business.

eBay isn't just for individuals who want to auction off personal goods to other individuals. The eBay marketplace can work just as effectively for businesses that need to connect with other businesses, which, as you might expect, are called business-to-business (B2B) transactions. If you want to cut costs by procuring supplies at more reasonable prices than before, or if you want to easily buy supplies that are usually difficult to locate, you might find just the right supplier through eBay. This chapter discusses five eBay resources that enable businesses to trade more effectively: the Business & Industrial category, the Business Marketplace portal, the Wholesale Lots category, eBay Local sites, and eLance.

Through the Business & Industrial category (**http://business.ebay.com**, shown in Figure 13-1), eBay is already functioning as a B2B marketplace. According to a January 28, 2003 article on eWeek.com (**http://www.eweek.com/article2/0,3959, 849126,00.asp**), business transactions account for more than $1 billion in sales on eBay each year. The 2003 Procurement Managers Survey conducted by the Internet analysis company IDC concluded that eBay was one of the most popular destinations among purchasing managers for buying office equipment and business supplies online.

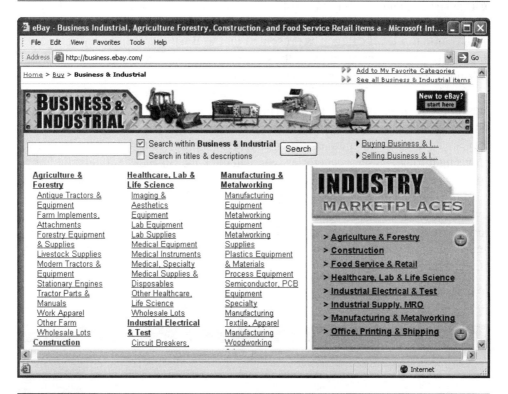

**FIGURE 13-1**   eBay's Business & Industrial category

**13**

*The findings of the 2003 Procurement Managers Survey are summarized at **http://www.northbaybiz.com/archives/2003-07-column-levini.html**. The latest version of the survey is described at **http://www.idc.com/getdoc .jsp?containerId=IDC_P1329**.*

A B2B marketplace is a place where companies can trade every kind of equipment—everything from laser interferometers to Ginsu knives—with other companies. You're likely to find tractors and other agricultural equipment, building and construction materials, restaurant supplies and food services, electronic components, health care supplies, lab equipment, printing, metalworking supplies, retail fixtures, and myriad other items.

eBay actually gives businesses that want to buy and sell supplies two entry points that collect all the business-related items for sale as well as other information of interest to purchasing agents and business managers. Along with the Business

& Industrial category, eBay also offers the Business Marketplace portal (**http://www.ebaybusiness.com**). As you can see in Figure 13-2, this page presents many of the same top-level categories presented on the Business & Industry category opening page, with the addition of the Office Technology set of categories and an expanded set of subcategories within Wholesale Lots.

Besides having different URLs and graphic designs, the two eBay business portals present the same information in different ways. The Business Marketplace page is simpler and designed for visitors who have encountered the page from outside eBay; they aren't already shopping on eBay. If you are already familiar with eBay and browsing through its sales categories, you will click the Business & Industrial link to go to this category's opening page (refer to Figure 13-1). It includes a Top 10 List of most frequently purchased items in the category, and a Popular Searches list of the top five most popular searches. You'll also find a link to the Business & Industry Seller Newsflash newsletter (**http://pages.ebay.com/newsletter/Business.html**). These items are all of interest to business managers who are seeking to purchase on eBay, but they don't have links on the Business Marketplace page.

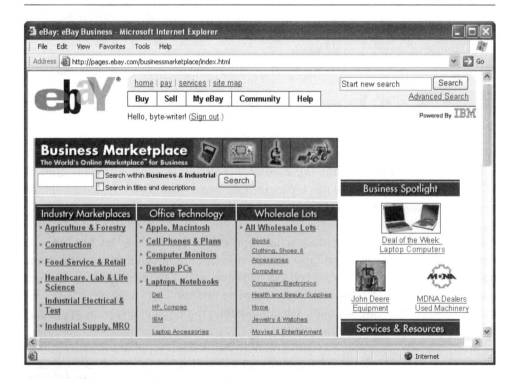

**FIGURE 13-2**    Another portal to eBay's B2B merchandise: Business Marketplace

# Buy or Sell What You Need to Run a Business

Many companies have professionals, or even entire departments, who specialize in purchasing. They save money for many large organizations, and they ensure that quality goods are obtained at reasonable prices. For small-scale purchases of essential supplies or services that a business needs to order periodically (or smaller companies that don't have purchasing agents on staff), however, it can be faster and more cost-effective to put some level of control in the hands of individual employees and let them procure goods over the Internet. In fact, purchasing professionals also commonly save time and money for their companies by doing supply procurement online through venues like eBay.

> **TIP** *If you have questions about eBay's Business & Industrial area, you have two options. Visit the Business & Industrial discussion board (look for a link to the board on the Wholesale Lots or Business & Industrial home page, or go directly to **http://forums.ebay.com/db2/forum.jsp?forum=5**), or e-mail business@ebay.com.*

Did you know?

## E-Procurement Saves Time and Money

13

Businesses have actually known for years that they can save time and money by conducting B2B e-commerce: online transactions between companies rather than individuals. *E-procurement* is a flashy term that describes one of the most popular uses of the Internet for B2B transactions, especially those in which a company purchases supplies over the Internet rather than using traditional paper purchase requests. Most of the companies that do procurement online are obtaining indirect goods—maintenance, repair, and operations (MRO) items they use internally—as well as commodity-type or direct goods they can process and resell. E-procurement can save your company both time and money while maintaining approval and oversight to push costs down and efficiency up. B2B transactions accounted for more than 94 percent of all e-commerce in 2000, according to a March 2002 U.S. Census Bureau report (**http://www.census .gov/eos/www/papers/estatstext.pdf**).

# Buying Business Supplies Online

Going online to procure stock can add up to significant cost savings. The e-marketplaces you use can charge lower prices because they're aggregating purchasing volumes. E-procurement gives you these additional advantages:

- **Control** Your employees can make their own approved purchases of supplies online.

- **Streamlining** Conducting paperless procurement saves the cost and time involved in generating the traditional purchasing documents.

- **Savings** You can find bargains on supplies at auction.

- **Automation** Your preferred suppliers can set up automatic inventory control systems to help you to replenish stock and set up packages of supplies based on previous orders.

- **Reliability** Following standard ordering procedures and filling out forms at electronic marketplaces prevents human errors that can occur by entering data by hand.

Businesses frequently need to sell off equipment because they have ordered too much, remodeled facilities, or shifted the line that they offer. Just like at a garage sale, one person's garbage is another person's treasure.

Table 13-1 lists actual final auction prices taken from eBay's Completed Auctions listings. They indicate the kinds of office equipment deals that bidders have secured for their companies. (You aren't guaranteed to get the same prices yourself.)

# The "How Tos" of Selling Off Excess Inventory

Are you unsure about what price to set for items that you have never sold before? Consider letting the market decide the price by posting your sale on eBay.

| Item | List Price | Business & Industrial Price |
|---|---|---|
| Herman Miller Aeron chair size B black | $800.00 | $476.51 |
| Topcon RLS1B Self-Leveling laser level | $1995.00 | $705.77 |
| Turbotorch self-lighting swivel head torch tip | $139.60 | $32.03 |
| Tektronix TDS744A oscilloscope | $7695.00 (refurbished) | $5825.00 |

**TABLE 13-1** Business & Industrial Auction Examples

The Business & Industrial area can give your company a way to unload stock it may have had trouble selling previously. If you are already a registered eBay seller, the steps involved in selling business supplies are the same as on other parts of eBay. The advantage of selling on Business & Industrial is that buyers go there looking for office supplies, tools, and manufacturing equipment. The best items to sell are commonly used supplies that are in good condition and that you don't mind selling at a fraction of the original list price (though you may get a price higher than the list price, depending on the marketplace). Heavy equipment like forklifts, lumber, or construction-related items sell well. You also are likely to have more immediate results. It takes less time to sell on eBay than it would to place an ad in a trade journal and wait for a response from a potential buyer.

You can get selling tips in eBay's Business & Industrial Seller's Edge newsletter (**http://pages.ebay.com/sellercentral/sbc/business/sellersedge.html**), shown in Figure 13-3.

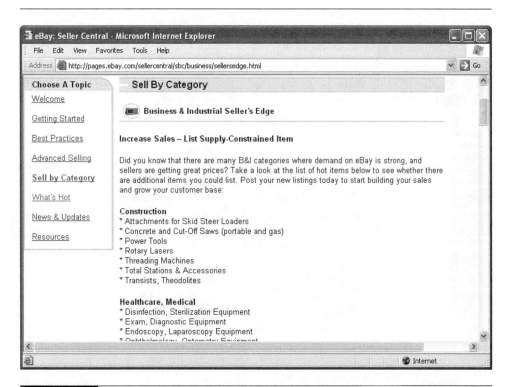

**FIGURE 13-3**    eBay provides this newsletter for companies that sell in the Business & Industrial category.

# "Lots" of Items Mean Lots of Sales

If your store is closing or you are discontinuing a line of merchandise, you are likely to be left with dozens or perhaps even hundreds of items. What can you do? Put them up for auction on eBay's Wholesale Lots area. Wholesale Lots is an area especially designated for companies that need to sell a group of items as a single item (in other words, as a *lot*).

You can find the Wholesale Lots listings on eBay in one of two ways:

■ Go to the Wholesale Lots web page (**http://pages.ebay.com/catindex/ catwholesale.html**), shown in Figure 13-4. If you're looking for a particular type of item, you can click through sets of categories here and hopefully find what you want.

**FIGURE 13-4** You can sell a group of items all at once in Wholesale Lots.

■ Go to the eBay Stores home page (**http://www.stores.ebay.com**), enter **Wholesale Lots** in the Find a Store search box on the left, leave the Store Name and Description radio button selected, and click Search Stores. This presents you with a listing of all current eBay Store listings that have the words "Wholesale Lots" in the title. If you're in a hurry, try this first; if you don't find what you need, go to the Wholesale Lots page listed above and do a lengthier search.

If you expect to deal in wholesale lots frequently, it's a good idea to open an eBay Store. You then get the opportunity to list your merchandise in two places: in a Wholesale Lots category within your store, along with individual listings in the Wholesale Lots area. Because an eBay Store is essentially a gathering of all of your sales in one set of web pages, you won't have to duplicate your listings. Instead, you'll be getting exposure in two areas.

Many wholesalers (as well as PowerSellers looking for a steady supply of merchandise they can sell cheaply) obtain lots of items at a bargain price and hope to sell the lots all at once on eBay to gain a profit. The most sought-after items in Wholesale Lots are personal items: candles, cosmetics, sunglasses, and collectibles. The primary categories related to businesses that you can find in Wholesale Lots at this writing are the following:

■ **Business & Industrial**   This can include tools, restaurant supplies, and MRO items.

■ **Computers & Electronics**   This category is found in Business & Industrial, Half.com, and the general eBay sales area, so make sure you only sell lots of computer equipment here.

■ **Cell Phones**   You'll find cell phones for the office here as well as cellular service plans.

■ **Home**   You'll find the subcategory Building & Repair Materials here.

Often, companies are left with orders that they can't fulfill, and they need to clear out their inventory to make room for new products to sell. If your company is left with inventory you can't sell and you need to get rid of it to make room for new products, Wholesale Lots is the place to do the selling. If your priority is to unload a group of items all at once, list them with no reserve and see what the market will pay for it. The key is to be prepared to sell for as low a price as possible: buyers come to Wholesale Lots looking for real bargains and deep discounts.

To sell in Wholesale Lots, first go to the category where you want to sell your lot of items. For instance, if you have a leftover batch of 100 teddy bears, follow these steps:

1. Go to the Wholesale Lots home page and click **Dolls & Bears**.

2. Write down the category number in the Address box (see Figure 13-5). It can take a bit of looking, but it's the number that appears after the word "category" and the letter Z. For instance, in Figure 13-5, the category number is 52546.

3. Click Sell in the navigation bar at the top of the page.

Copy the category number, which is buried in eBay's long URLs

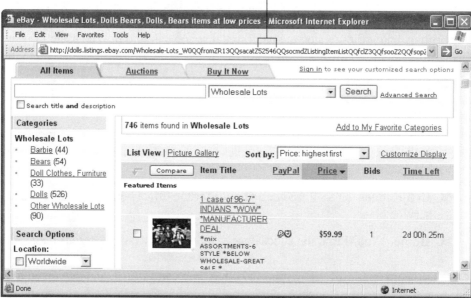

**FIGURE 13-5**   If you have large quantities of identical items to sell, list them in Wholesale Lots.

4. Click Sell Your Item.

5. Sign in with your User ID and password.

6. Choose a selling format and click Continue.

7. When the Sell Your Item: Select Category page appears (see Figure 13-6), type the category number for the Wholesale Lots Dolls & Bears subcategory in the Category # box.

Follow the instructions on subsequent pages to list your own lot for sale.

Type the category number here

**FIGURE 13-6** Enter the Wholesale Lots category number in the appropriate box on this page.

## Discover What's Hot by Exploring Seller Central

If you're interested in selling business supplies on eBay and are wondering if you have the types of supplies that other businesses really want, check out the Hot Items by Category feature of Seller Central (**http://pages.ebay.com/sellercentral/hotitems.pdf**). Hot Items by Category is a detailed report detailing which items are most in demand on eBay based on recent sales figures. The Business & Industrial category is included in the report.

The In the Field and In Demand areas of Seller Central also provide you with information that can inspire and inform you. From the Seller Central page (**http://pages.ebay.com/sellercentral**), click Category Tips, then browse the categories on the Selling by Category page to find these links. In the Field, at this writing, included a detailed profile of a husband-and-wife business selling team with the User ID uBuyWeRush. The In Demand page had a Top 10 Picks list of items to sell that included credit card terminals, construction backhoes, generators, and wide format printers.

# Look for Local Buyers

As even my pre-teen daughter can tell you, the basic assumption is that it's best to attract a wide audience of bidders so that you can get the best price. You can then ship the goods to the buyer. However, if you're trying to sell heavy, bulky items and you are in a hurry, finding a shipper and arranging for transportation can take more time than you have. In such cases it can be practical to locate a buyer in your local area. That way, your buyer can pick up the merchandise and pay you for it in person. Even though you may restrict your potential customer base, you don't have to worry about packaging and shipping. Occasionally, sellers specify in their descriptions with a phrase such as the following that what they are selling must be picked up locally and won't be shipped:

I will not ship this item; it is available for local pickup only...

Such a statement can potentially cause conflicts with bidders, however. Let's say that a bidder really wants what you have to sell and turns out to be the high bidder. The one little detail is that he or she doesn't live in the area you have specified as the one where you either will or not deliver. That individual could possibly claim not to have seen the requirement to live in a particular area. A nasty argument could be the result.

A more reliable method of finding buyers in your area is to click the radio button next to Will Not Ship – Local Pickup Only in Step 4, Payment & Shipping, of the Sell Your Item form. You also need to provide pickup instructions in the Payment Instructions box on the same page.

If you are especially interested in local buyers being able to find and bid on your merchandise, list your item in one of the eBay Local sites. Such sites are specific to a particular metropolitan area or country. They don't restrict buyers to that region; anyone in the world can still bid on your item. However, you give local buyers an additional way to find what you're selling.

If you are looking for supplies and want to locate items in your local area, follow these steps:

1.  If you're looking for an eBay Local site in the United States, click **Advanced Search,** located under the Search button on most pages. You can also go directly to **http://search.ebay.com/ws/search/AdvSearch**. In either case, the eBay Search: Find Items page appears.

> TIP
>
> *If you are looking for an eBay site in a country other than the United States, go to the eBay home page (**http://www.ebay.com**) and click one of the links to international eBay sites listed in the Global Sites drop-down list near the bottom of the page and then click Go. Links to these sites are also provided at the bottom of the home page.*

2.  Enter a word or phrase that describes what you're looking for in the Enter Keyword or Item Number box.

3.  Scroll down to the Items Near Me heading, enter your ZIP code in the appropriate box, and choose the maximum distance you are willing to travel from the drop-down list labeled Within.

4.  Click Search.

You should keep in mind that just because you are selling in, say, the Detroit, Michigan, version of eBay, that doesn't mean you'll get buyers who live in or near Detroit, Michigan. There's no requirement that bidders have to live in a particular region in order to place bids on items that are sold on the local eBay web site. It *does* mean that, if you're shopping for supplies, you'll find sellers who are in or near Detroit. It also means you'll be competing with other sellers in your local area.

*Most people don't restrict their buyers to a particular area because it's possible to ship very large items, including cars and other vehicles such as tractors, anywhere in the world. For some heavy building materials, you might want to specify that you will only ship in the United States, which is a restriction commonly seen on eBay listings.*

# Buy Surplus from Uncle Sam

If you're a bargain hunter like me, you've probably scoured surplus stores and warehouses looking for coats, camping equipment, and other surplus items the U.S. government needs to sell. Now, both federal and state government agencies are turning to eBay to auction off excess property. For instance, the Oregon Division of Administrative Services (DAS) manages auctions for a variety of government offices and reportedly takes in more than $100,000 per week through eBay auctions. You'll find links to its eBay auctions at **http://tpps.das.state.or.us/surplus/auction .htm**. The department reported that it gets higher prices through eBay auctions than through traditional surplus merchandise auctions. For instance, a K2 bike that fetched $300 at a traditional auction sold for $1035.99 online. A Toshiba VCR that sold for $50 at a traditional auction brought $139.05 on eBay.

NOTE  *Even the U.S. Postal Service has, in the past, used eBay to sell items that were found to be undeliverable for some reason or that had been returned to their senders. However, the attempt to unload such merchandise through eBay was suspended and reviewed as a result of deadbeat bidders who never paid for or picked up their merchandise. When I checked, the Postal Service had no items for sale on eBay through its User ID usps-mrc-everythingelse. However, USPS also sells under the User IDs usps-al-pmsc, usps-ne-springfield, usps-orlando, and ms-zip.*

Government entities can sell through the Business & Industrial area on eBay, but they need to follow regulatory procedures for buying and selling goods and equipment. Often, state agencies can't sell directly through eBay, but need to sell through an office such as the General Services Commission (Texas). If you work in a state agency, you may have to make a formal declaration stating what property you are going to declare as "surplus." You may also need to advertise the surplus merchandise locally before you offer it online. Check with your own general services office before you post online.

# Hang Out Your Shingle on eLance

If you're a freelancer or contractor, you probably already use the Internet to look for work. You may have used a service called eLance that enables employers to post projects for which they need freelance help. In response to such postings, freelancers bid on the jobs and the employer chooses a bidder based on price and other considerations.

Like Half.com (see Chapter 14), eLance became extremely popular and is now affiliated with eBay. A story on PR Newswire reported that the number of projects outsourced through eLance grew by more than 55 percent during 2002 as more than 30,000 small businesses used the service. (On eBay, it now goes by the awkward-sounding name eBay Professional Services – eLance, but for the purposes of this chapter, I'll just call it eLance.) If you use eLance, you can buy or provide professional freelance services. eLance brings businesses and service providers together like the want ads or employment agencies, with the help of a few special features:

- **Feedback**   You can check out employers and freelancers to see what kind of feedback has been left for them.

- **Interactivity**   Employers can place their ads before the eager eyes of freelancers in a matter of minutes; freelancers can place bids almost immediately. eLance lets participants communicate and collaborate online, too.

- **Competition**   Freelancers bid on jobs that providers offer, so employers get the best prices, and freelancers have the advantage of being able to find work.

There's another big difference between eLance and more traditional ways of finding work: You have to pay to list yourself as a service provider, if you go over an allotted number of bids per month, and if you get a job, too, as explained in the next section.

*You'll find eLance in two places. You can go to **http://www.elance.com** or **http://pages.ebay.com/business_services/**. If you choose the latter option (the URL for the eBay Professional Services category) and click on a subcategory or a listing, your browser will be directed away from eBay's web site and onto eLance's.*

## Find Freelancers Without Help Wanted Ads

Like the Business & Industrial area, eLance brings businesspeople together. In this case, services such as writing, design, accounting, and consulting are being traded rather than tools, photocopiers, or other objects. Businesses that have projects they need done by outsiders make those projects available on eLance. On the other side of the equation, freelancers who are looking for work market themselves and bid on projects.

Suppose, for instance, you need to have a logo designed for your company. (Web page creation and graphic design are, in fact, two of the most popular services "sold" on eLance.) Here's how the system would work for you:

1. Open an eLance account so you can send payments to service providers or pay transaction fees.

2. Post a description of your project online (see Figure 13-7). You either solicit bids or offer the project at a fixed Buy Now price.

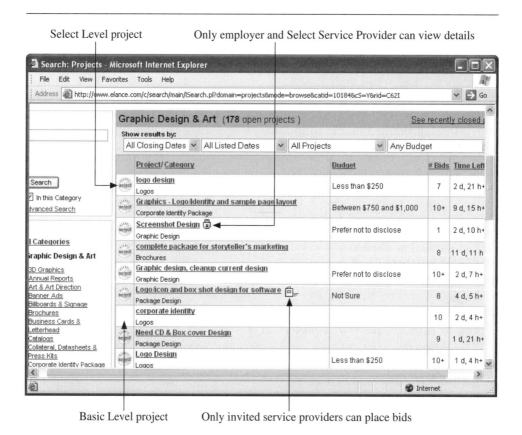

FIGURE 13-7    eLance projects are posted on lists organized by the type of service needed.

3.  Freelance service providers post bids—sometimes, within hours or even minutes of the project going online. You review the bids and check on the providers' bids on past projects, feedback ratings, and sample work.

4.  You can ask bidders questions by posting messages on eLance's private message boards. You then choose the freelancer you want based on the individual's qualifications and the amount of the bid.

5.  The service provider does the work; when the work is done, eLance charges the selected freelancer a transaction fee of 8.75 percent of either the invoiced amount of the job or the original bid amount (whichever is greater). You use eLance's billing and payment services to complete the transaction.

6.  Once the project has been completed to your satisfaction, you post feedback about the quality of the work and of the freelancer. Your feedback then becomes part of the freelancer's overall feedback rating.

For employers, one of the big advantages of using eLance is the fact that you can draw upon a large pool of freelance service providers, and get competitive prices for the project you need done. You don't have to go out and seek professionals yourselves; rather, they come to you. Simply posting a job on eLance is free. When the bids come in, you don't need to pick anyone at all; you can decide not to use anyone's freelance services.

> **TIP** *You can pay an extra listing fee to have your project listed at a Select Level rather than the plain old Basic Level listing. A Select Level listing can be bid on only by providers whose credentials have been verified by one of two third parties, US Search (**http://www.ussearch.com/consumer/index.jsp**) or SquareTrade (**http://www.squaretrade.com/cnt/jsp/index.jsp**), so you're more likely to find someone who's reliable. You gain the opportunity to "prescreen" providers by asking them three questions before a provider can bid on a job. However, you must place a refundable deposit of $25 in order to place a Select Level bid, and projects at the Select Level are subject to minimum bid requirements—$300 for a graphic design job, $550 for web design and development, and so on. See the eLance Help files for more specific information.*

## Use eLance: A Freelancer's Best Friend

If you're a freelancer, eLance has the obvious benefit of listing projects that you can consider and bid on. Once you register with eLance, you need to post background information about your experience and qualifications on a profile page. This page also includes the history of previous projects you've completed on eLance as well as your feedback rating.

eLance is convenient, but it isn't free. You pay an 8.75 percent fee to eLance if you are chosen. If the fee for the job turns out to be $1000, this fee amounts to a not-inconsiderable $87.50. In addition, you must pay a monthly fee to subscribe as a bidder. A Professional Subscription costs between $40 and $95 per month, depending on the type of work you do, and gives you 80 free bids per month. Any bids that go over your number of free bids are subject to bid fees. A Select Professional subscription gives you 120 free bids per month and costs between $75 and $245, depending on the category of the jobs you want to see. As a freelancer, you are rated based on the feedback you receive when you complete a project. The feedback ratings are listed in Table 13-2.

Feedback is calculated by service buyers based on quality of work, responsiveness, professionalism, subject matter expertise, adherence to the budget, and adherence to the schedule. eLance functions as a go-between where payment is concerned; you submit invoices to eLance, the buyer of your services submits payment to eLance, and eLance forwards payments to you.

While you are doing the work, you can make use of a file-sharing area called Work Space that eLance provides, where you can upload files and virtually present them for review. You can also use the Work Space area to exchange messages and do scheduling.

eLance includes a category of freelancers called Select Service Providers. To be given this designation, you have to pay a listing fee and receive "verification" that you are a reputable provider.

| Rating | What It Means |
| --- | --- |
| 5.0 | Extremely satisfied |
| 4.0 | Very satisfied |
| 3.0 | Satisfied |
| 2.0 | Not satisfied |
| 1.0 | Extremely unsatisfied |

**TABLE 13-2**    eLance Feedback Ratings

# Where to Find It

- **eBay Business & Industry Seller Newsflash**
  **http://pages.ebay.com/newsletter/Business.html**
  Lists of "hot items" that sell well in the Business & Industry category;
  profiles of businesspeople who buy and sell supplies on eBay.

- **eBay Business & Industrial area**
  **http://business.ebay.com**
  eBay's B2B marketplace.

- **eBay Business Marketplace**
  **http://www.ebaybusiness.com**
  Another portal leading to eBay's B2B sales.

- **eBay: Professional Services—eLance**
  **http://pages.ebay.com/business_services/**
  Offer your professional services online through eBay.

- **eBay Wholesale Lots**
  **http://pages.ebay.com/catindex/catwholesale.html**
  Lists of items for sale as wholesale lots.

13

# Chapter 14

# Sell at Fixed Price: eBay Stores and Half.com

## How to…

- Set competitive fixed prices for your sales items

- Gather all of your sales in one place with an eBay Store

- Take advantage of Half.com's database of sales images and specs

- Specify shipping options for your customers

- Build positive feedback by providing good customer service

Originally, eBay became famous for its auction sales. But in recent years, more and more shoppers flock to eBay to purchase items immediately at a fixed price, just as they would at any retail store, whether online or off. Buy It Now (BIN) fixed-price sales have advantages for buyers and sellers alike. For buyers, they bring immediate results and the certainty that they'll actually get the item they're interested in rather than face the possibility of being outbid. For sellers, offering items at fixed price through an eBay Store or a Half.com sale enables them to make their merchandise available for weeks or even months at a time.

Sales in either venue can supplement auction sales and provide steady, year-round income. Your eBay Store page, in turn, can list the URL of a full-fledged e-commerce site that enables shoppers to make purchases. The synergy that results from linking eBay auctions to an eBay Store or web site can build credibility for your business and boost your sales, too. This chapter examines two places in which to sell your wares at a price you set: an eBay Store and a marketplace within eBay called Half.com.

# Create an eBay Store

Big-time retailers know that, to maximize income and reach the greatest number of customers, they need to sell in more than one way and use more than one type of sales technique. Auto dealers have known this for years. Look at all the ways you can purchase a new car: you can buy it outright; pay a down payment and finance the rest; or lease it for a fixed period of time with an option to buy at the end of the lease. You can go to an auto dealership, shop online, or visit a place where a number of auto dealers are gathered under one roof, called an auto mall. By marketing your products in a variety of ways, you attract the widest range of customers.

In much the same way, you can supplement your eBay auctions with items you put up for sale for a fixed price in an eBay Store. Setting up an eBay Store is much the same as renting space in a shopping mall, but with two big advantages: eBay is likely to be cheaper, and likely to attract more shoppers than most other malls due to its global reach and enormous popularity.

Shopping malls have never proved very successful on the Web. Early attempts at gathering shops under a single web site umbrella so that people could find them more easily just didn't work. The Web makes it easy to find web-based retailers through user-friendly search engines and easy-to-remember URLs like **http://www.walmart.com**. Only a few web-based malls remain, such as Yahoo! Small Business (**http://smallbusiness.yahoo.com/merchant/**).

Why, then, would you consider setting up an eBay Store in addition to your eBay auctions? I'll give you six reasons:

- eBay attracts more than 36 million home-based and 22 million work-based visitors per month, according to Neilsen/NetRatings' Weekly Top 10 Parent Companies list (**http://www.nielsen-netratings.com/news.jsp?section=dat_to&country=us**).

- You can drive regular buyers to your store with the Stores logo that appears next to your User ID.

- The cost is only $9.95 per month for a basic subscription.

- Listing fees are less than auction sales (only $0.03 per item, including a Gallery image).

- If you really want to sell some items at a fixed price, and you find that Buy It Now doesn't attract buyers, you might have better luck with an eBay Store.

- An eBay Store contains your auction items that are for sale and that are listed in eBay's auction categories, as well as the fixed-price items you list through your store.

**14**

TIP      *You need a minimum feedback score of 20, a PayPal account, or an ID Verify listing to open an eBay Store. (See Chapter 16 for more details on eBay's ID Verify program.) Also keep in mind that eBay Store listings do not show up in eBay searches unless there are 20 or fewer auction-style listings returned in the search results.*

Perhaps the biggest benefit of opening an eBay Store is that you can always have a set of merchandise up for sale. Because eBay Store items can remain online for 30, 60, 90 days or even longer, you can be selling even if you're too sick to create auction listings, or if you're out of town. Many of the experienced PowerSellers I've interviewed report that more than 50 percent of their income comes from their eBay Stores. The following sections discuss these and other advantages in more detail.

## Save a Few Bucks

To set up your own web site with a hosting service might cost $50 a month or more. Even if you rent space in an online mall that attracts a large number of visitors, you'll have to pay a monthly fee, as well as listing fees or fees charged for each item you sell. eBay Stores compare favorably to other malls as indicated in Table 14-1, as far as the basic monthly hosting fee.

## Gain Eyeball Space

The idea behind shopping malls, whether they are down the street or on the Web, is that they help their individual stores gain greater visibility (you might say, eyeball space) than if those stores were situated all by themselves on a street. Malls attract a higher number of visitors just because they gather multiple sales outlets under one roof (or web site). If you pick an online marketplace that is particularly "sticky" (in other words, that has enough resources and services that visitors tend to stay around for a while) you're more likely to get shoppers.

## Attract Your Own Customers

One advantage of setting up an eBay Store is that you can do the marketing in many ways. If you build up a steady clientele through your regular auction sales, you stand a good chance of having those regular customers visit your eBay Store. After all, when you create auction descriptions, you can list your eBay Store's name and publish your logo (if you have one—and you should) at the top of the listing. The more bidders you attract to your auctions, the better your chances that someone will stop by your store.

You should always follow good marketing and business practices, such as printing your eBay Store's name and URL on your business card and letterhead

| Store Host | Monthly Rent | Listing Fee | Final Value Fee |
|---|---|---|---|
| Yahoo! Small Business | $39.95 (Starter site) | N/A | 1.5% of sales price |
| Amazon zShops | $39.99 (for required Pro Merchant subscription) | N/A | 5% (for items priced at $25 or less) |
| eBay Store (Basic Subscription) | $9.95 | $0.02 per item (for 30 days) | 5.25% (for items priced at $25 or less) |

**TABLE 14-1**  Comparison of Online Store Fees

and mentioning your store in the signature file—the text file that is automatically added to the bottom of your outgoing e-mail messages, as discussed in Chapter 11.

## Do Buy It Now One Better

Buy It Now has its pros and cons. On the plus side, it's not a hidden price like a reserve price. You know exactly what the seller wants to charge for an item, and you can buy it immediately without having to wait for the auction to end. Buy It Now is also highly popular and a good way to make sales. eBay, in fact, estimates that as much as 30 percent of its total sales come from Buy It Now offerings.

On the other hand, offering a Buy It Now price on something as well as the option to bid on that same item at auction is a contradiction, in my opinion: it contradicts the original purpose of the sale. People shop for auction items in the hope of getting a good deal. They want to save a few bucks, and they hope to find something unusual or rare at a good price. Buy It Now takes away the feeling that bidders are somehow "beating the system" by making them pay a set price that's not necessarily as much of a bargain as an auction would be.

People want to shop at an eBay Store for many different reasons. Some of them may come to your store because they are already familiar with you or your business and want to see what else you're offering. If they are loyal to you and feel that they can trust you, they won't mind paying a fixed price if they find something that's really desirable. But while it's always good to develop loyalty, eBay has recently made it easier for anyone on the Internet (not just on eBay) to find a store. Such shoppers tend to be bargain hunters. They find a store through the eBay Keywords program, which enables stores to be indexed by Google; listings that contain the keywords you have identified show up in Google searches. And eBay sellers are able to market their stores off eBay (for instance, on their web site) by enabling others to link to their stores; the owners of the sites that contain the links get a store referral credit for visitors they send over.

14

**NOTE** *You pay a per-click fee for each keyword you want to include in the eBay Keywords program; you specify how much you are willing to pay for each click (for instance, 20 cents) a visitor makes on your keyword when it shows up at the top of a set of eBay search results. Visit **https://ebay .admarketplace.net/ebay/servlet/ebay/psp/ebayhome** to find out more.*

If you already sell at auction and have some of your auction sales listed on your About Me page, it's natural to go a step further and sell through an eBay Store as well. Silk Road Trading Concern has a number of items for sale through its store (see Figure 14-1).

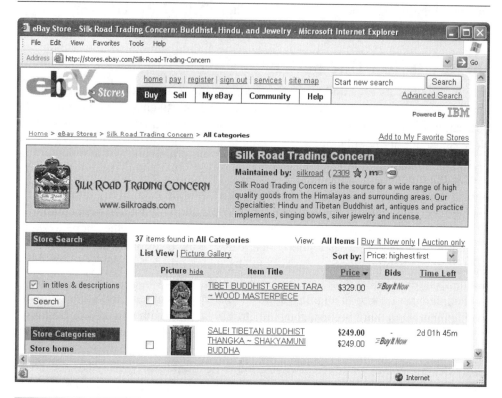

FIGURE 14-1    An eBay Store gives you another way to reach existing customers.

Of course, eBay Stores can help you reach new customers, not just people who have already purchased from you at auction. They might find your store on the eBay Stores home page (**http://www.stores.ebay.com**)—provided you pay $49.95 per month to get yourself placed in that prime real estate.

What, you ask, is the downside to the rosy picture I'm painting? It's the same as with any store: there's no guarantee you'll get enough business to make the store worthwhile, and it takes work, time, and commitment. If you're already spending 30, 40, or 50 hours a week on your auctions, expect to add several hours more for your store. You can't just put your merchandise up for sale and then let it sit there for weeks at a time. People will assume that the selections never change and they'll stop coming altogether. You've got to put new items up for sale regularly and ship items out quickly, just as you do with auctions.

You can close your store if you go on vacation, but you'll have to wait 30 days before you can reopen it. You don't need to close for vacation, anyway; you can turn on a set of "vacation settings" that enables your listings to be hidden for a time.

## Did you know?

## Automate the Construction of Your eBay Store

As this chapter was being revised, the web development company Macromedia announced that it was partnering with eBay to offer an eBay Store creation tool that makes stores better-looking and easier to customize. It's an add-on to Macromedia's software product called Contribute 3, which enables contributors to add content to a web site and edit content. Contribute 3 for eBay costs $99 and is available only for Microsoft Windows computers. If you already have Contribute 3, you can add on the eBay Store formatting functions by downloading a free extension from Macromedia's web site. Find out more about Contribute 3 for eBay at **http://www.macromedia.com/software/contribute/special/ct3_ebay**.

That way, shoppers won't be frustrated if they try to purchase something and you don't respond. But that's only one way to handle your store inventory during a vacation break. You can also add a vacation message to your listings—a standard, prewritten message that states when you will return. You can also choose to add a listing that appears below your store's home page header. Be aware that a vacation message that appears only on your store's home page will be missed by shoppers who find your store inventory listings only through a search, however.

### Set Up Shop

Once you have convinced yourself that an eBay Store is right for you, it's easy enough to get started. If you don't already have a business name, you should decide on a name for your store; it needn't match your User ID. Identify a group of items you want to put up for sale, and settle on the prices you want to list for them. The best title is made up of keywords that are likely to turn up in searches for your store. For example, "Trek Mountain Bikes" is better than "Mike's Bikes." The longer and more specific name will show up better in Google search results.

14

TIP    *You should, in fact, use the same business name and graphics for all of your sales, including your auctions, your About Me page, your eBay Store, and your web site if you create one. A consistent presentation helps you establish an identity and builds trust among your customers, who will be able to recognize you that much more quickly.*

Come to this page to start creating your eBay Store.

Once you've got the preliminaries covered, go to the eBay Stores home page (shown in Figure 14-2), and click the conspicuous Open a Store button.

TIP    *You can always change your store's category or description by clicking the* **Manage My Store** *link on your store's home page.*

## How to ...    Create Your Store

Log in with your User ID and password, if you aren't logged in already, and click Sign In Securely. Read the statement that says you are subject to the same eBay User Agreement that governs your auction sales. Then click I Accept the eBay User Agreement to connect to the first Build Your Store page, where you begin to create your store.

The Build Your Store: Select Theme page presents you with options for your store's layout and color scheme:

1. Scan the Most Popular set of themes, which are shown on the page you view initially. If you don't like the way these pages are designed, click one of the other layout options under Themes: Left Navigation, Top Navigation, or Easily Customizable.

2. Click a radio button or choose a drop-down menu option to select the color scheme you want. When you've chosen the "look" you want, click the Continue button at the bottom of the page.

3. When the Build Your Store: Provide Basic Information page appears, enter your store's "brand name" in the Store name box

4. Write an agonizingly short (300 characters or less) description of your store in the Store Description area. (You can add more information later on if you run out of space.) Make sure your store's description contains keywords that will turn up in searches. Rather than saying "We sell a lot of great camping equipment and provide excellent service," you'll get better results if you say "We sell Coleman, Trek, Columbia, North Face, and Acme camping equipment."

> **CAUTION** *You don't get much room to sell your store—each field in the Store Content page is limited to a small number of characters. If you really want as many words as you need to create your own store, opt for your own web site instead. Otherwise, type your content in any text editor and count the number of characters by using the Word Count feature in Microsoft Word (it's under the Tools menu).*

5. Choose graphics for your store. If you already have an About Me page or a web page, you can simply choose one of your existing image files for your store. Otherwise, you have two choices: create a logo for your store, or use a predesigned eBay graphic. The predesigned images are overused and don't distinguish your store in any way. I strongly suggest that you create a logo as described in Chapter 7. When you're done, click Continue.

6. When the Build Your Store: Review & Subscribe page appears, select the type of store you want to open. It makes sense, if you're just starting out, to choose Basic Store. You can always upgrade later on. When you're done, click Start My Subscription Now.

NOTE *You don't start paying for your store right away. eBay gives you a 30-day trial period in case you change your mind.*

7. At this point, you have created your store. Now, you can customize it. Select one of 14 main categories for your store. Pick the category you use most for your auctions—or choose Everything Else.

8. Fill out some additional information about what makes your store unique in the Store/About Me page.

9. In the Custom Store Categories area, enter the types of sales categories under which your merchandise will be sold. Supposedly, these choices are optional. However, when you want to sell an item, you have to list it under one of the categories you have already defined here. Do yourself a favor and come up with some categories under which your merchandise will be listed. Make the category names searchable keywords to get more traffic to your store: for instance, rather than creating a category called "video games," you should create several more-specific and keyword-oriented names, such as "Gameboy Games," "Playstation 2 Games," "Xbox Games," and so on.

10. Specify your payment methods and ship-to locations, and your sales tax specifications (see Chapter 17).

11. In the Store Customer Service & Return Policy box, type in any money-back guarantee, customer service numbers, return policies, or SquareTrade memberships you can boast of. You have to enter 90 characters or less here; the field is required.

12. Optionally, if you haven't created an About Me page, you get the chance to do so after the Additional Store Information box. The advantage of creating an About Me page here is that, when users click on your About Me logo, they'll be taken to your eBay Store, just as they would if they clicked on your Stores logo.

13. Choose colors for your eBay Store.

Give yourself a pat on the back: you've created your store and now can start selling on it.

TIP *You can find out more about setting up and configuring eBay Stores on the eBay Stores discussion board:* ***http://forums.ebay.com/db2/forum .jsp?forum=21***.

## List Your Sales Items

Once you've made the decisions needed to create your eBay Store, you'll probably find that listing items for sale is a breeze, especially if you are already adept at putting up items for auction on eBay. The principles described in Chapter 3 for creating auction listings and Chapter 8 for creating good images apply. But there's one big difference: you don't have to worry about setting reserve prices or starting bids. You also don't have to worry about monitoring bids as they are placed. There aren't any bids at all; rather, you set a fixed price and the item is listed at that price for 30 days.

### eBay Bestsellers
### Auction Sales from the Top of the World

Selling on eBay and other online venues gives you freedom. You can work where your interest—or your merchandise—lies. That's true for Steve Brothers and his father, Jon, who collect and sell South Asian art and ethnographic items from Katmandu, Nepal, high in the Himalayan mountains. Most of their items are spiritual or religious in nature, with the emphasis on Tibetan Buddhist and Hindu art and jewelry. eBay is only one of several sales venues for Jon and Steve. They sell new items through Silk Road Trading Concern (**http://www .silkroads.com**) and old and ethnographic items through Himalayan Mercantile (**http://www.himalayan-mercantile.com**). They also sell to wholesale clients around the United States and around the world—all without a conventional brick-and-mortar storefront.

The Brothers family has sold more than 3500 items on eBay since 1998, and in that time, they've met some wonderful people who have become their close friends, as well as other sellers who've caused problems.

"eBay is indeed a community, and like all communities it has its saints and its miscreants," says Steve. "Competition is stiff in our genre, but generally speaking, our competitors seem to be very decent folks. I would not describe it as cutthroat, but I would not characterize it as particularly altruistic, either. In the early days of eBay we used to have a lot of trouble with people 'stealing' text from our auction descriptions, and in several instances our photos as well.

If imitation is the most sincere form of flattery, then we were being paid very high compliments, but frankly it was more annoying than anything else. We work hard to present an informative and attractive presentation in the auction context, so it was always a bit disheartening to have someone take what we had gone to considerable effort to create, and use it to compete against us."

Nearly all of the Silk Road images that appear on eBay include an identifying logo that serves as a "branding logo," which makes it more difficult for other sellers to reuse.

This branding logo makes the image difficult to copy and reuse.

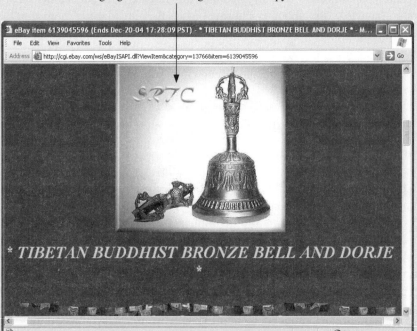

Silk Road Trading Concern, the eBay sales using the User ID silkroad, and Himalayan Mercantile are all family operations. Steve and his wife, who is a native of Nepal, travel throughout the region, collecting sale items and researching the traditions behind them. Steve writes the text and takes the majority of the photos, while Jon Brothers uploads and manages most of the auctions using eBay Seller's Assistant. Jon also handles transaction fulfillment and shipping for the items that are in inventory in the U.S.

Even from the mountains of Nepal, Steve can monitor auctions on eBay with immediacy and directly handle customer queries and special requests.

"There have been innumerable items that have exceeded our expectations in terms of the type of price they might fetch. On the other hand, there have also been great offerings that have flopped from a sales perspective. It's always exciting to watch bidders 'fight it out' in the last minutes of an auction, but the frequency of that has fallen off in the past year and a half or two—partly due to the economy, perhaps, but also due to 'sniping software.'" (Sniping is the process of placing a last-second bid that others cannot outbid because it comes in so close to the end of a sale.)

Steve advises eBay sellers not to follow his example in selling specialty items, however. "My advice for anyone who really wants to make a living on eBay is to sell some mainstream items—something that a good percentage of the general population wants or, better yet, needs. Fringe items that appeal to a subculture like Tibetan Buddhist practitioners are not all that lucrative. There are a lot of sellers but a relatively finite number of buyers. For prospective eBay sellers, I'd say choose some categories of items you are interested in. Research the market and try to gauge demand. If there is a demand, try to determine if the market in question needs or can support another seller of that type of item. If so, try to determine what ways you can set yourself apart from the pack, whether with attractive pricing, customer service, level of expertise, etc. Essentially, try to determine what will make you as a seller into a desirable source for a given item."

# Fix Your Price on Half.com

Half.com is a unique place. You visit Half.com on eBay in order to sell your merchandise at reduced price. But that's not all. You can get in your car and drive to Oregon. There, you'll find the real town called Half.com (a.k.a. Halfway) shown in Figure 14-3. In 2000, Half.com (the company, that is) persuaded the town of Halfway, Ore. (pop. 345) into renaming itself Half.com, Oregon, in exchange for $75,000 and 22 computers. The move made national headlines and made Half.com one of the most popular sites on the Internet. Before long, Half.com (the company) was purchased by eBay.

**14**

NOTE    *There's a reason why Half.com looks and feels different than other parts of eBay. Half.com was started by an entrepreneur named Josh Kopelman. Since you're an online entrepreneur yourself, you may want to read Time.com's full story of Half.com at **http://corp.half.com/pressfiles/time_magazine_02_05_01/time_magazine_02_05_01.html**. eBay had planned to phase out Half.com in 2004, but due to protests from members, it decided to keep Half.com open.*

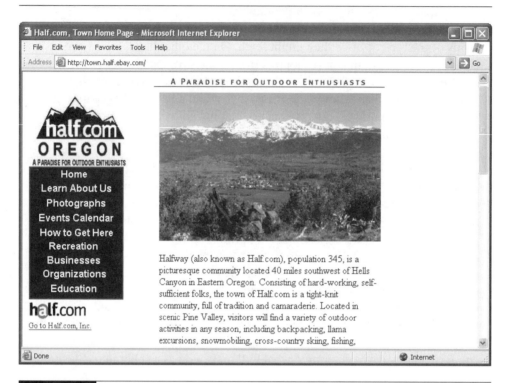

**FIGURE 14-3**     Not just an auction site, but a scenic place to live, too

For sellers, Half.com provides a far different experience than selling on eBay. Half.com's sales are not scheduled to end at a specified time, like eBay's auctions or most eBay Stores sales. Rather than individual listings grouped by time or type of merchandise, Half.com groups on the same page all items with the same book title, game title, DVD title, etc. offered by different sellers. Sellers have very little opportunity to stand out from the crowd, unless they set a price that's slightly less than the other instances of the same item that are already up for sale. They can also write a better description of their item, though only the first few words of that description appear on the sales page.

On the up side, Half.com, unlike eBay, functions as an intermediary with regard to payments. The company bills the buyer and pays the seller, which means there's no danger that a seller will have to deal with a bounced check. If you are looking for certainty and a bit of extra security and don't mind having your sales items look like everyone else's, Half.com (shown in Figure 14-4) is for you.

Buyers can place pre-orders that you can fill          Click here to sell a book, CD, or DVD

**FIGURE 14-4**    Half.com's virtual home on the Web

 *Only U.S. residents (and U.S. military personnel living outside the United States) can buy and sell on Half.com at the time of this writing—a restriction that does not apply to other parts of eBay.*

It's easy to become a Half.com seller—especially if you already have an account to sell on eBay. The following sections lead you step-by-step through the process.

## Step 1: Become a Half.com Member

Some parts of eBay are perfect for businesses (such as Business & Industry, described in Chapter 13), but Half.com is the ideal place for individuals who want to make a few extra dollars by cleaning out books, CDs, or games that are cluttering their shelves.

**14**

As a freelance writer, for instance, I get plenty of sample books from publishers. They tend to languish in boxes unless I sell them. The following sections show how I set up one of my own sales on Half.com.

NOTE *If you are already a member of eBay, you do not have to become a member of Half.com. You can use the same User ID and password for your Half.com account. If you do use the same User ID and password, all your feedback from both sites will be collected in a single set of feedback. However, you may want to keep two different User IDs in case you sell on eBay as part of your business and on Half.com to get some additional personal income, for instance.*

Once you have an account, click **My Account** on the Half.com home page. Then, click **Become a Seller** under the heading My Account. On subsequent pages, you provide Half.com with your address, phone number, and credit card information. As Half.com points out, the credit card information is used to verify your identity. It also might be used to charge you money in case you are found liable as a result of a dispute, or if you have not followed through on a sale.

Next, on the Create Seller's Account: Step 2 of 2 page, you specify how you want to be paid by Half.com when you sell something. This is one of the best advantages of using Half.com for selling—you are paid by Half.com, not the buyer. You can be paid either by a paper check or direct deposit. But if a buyer sends you a check for payment, Half.com requires you to have it direct deposited into your own checking account. Direct deposit from buyer to seller is encouraged in fact, because Half.com charges you a $1.50 handling fee for each paper check. If the item you're selling costs less than $10, for instance, that $1.50 is a substantial part of your profit, after all.

Once you specify a payment option, you choose the default option for how you want your items to be shipped. This might seem confusing at first, because you are the one who will actually pack up your book or CD, take it to the post office or shipping company, and send it out. Keep in mind that, at this point, you're only specifying what you consider your "first choice" shipping option. You and your buyer can work out a different option after the purchase is made. You only have two options: you can specify the U.S. Postal Service's Media Mail (which typically takes 4 to 12 days) or a USPS expedited rate (2 to 8 days). Choose Media Mail if you want your customers to save money and you don't think they'll mind waiting a week or more to receive what they've purchased.

TIP *Half.com charges the buyer and then reimburses you for shipping charges. See the section "Ship Your Goods Promptly" later in this chapter for a more detailed explanation.*

# Step 2: Pick a Sales Category

Once you've become a registered Half.com user, it's time to do some detective work. Look around Half.com and check out the kinds of items that are already up for sale. Do a search to determine whether or not someone else is selling that college textbook or DVD that you need to off-load. If you find that item is already up for sale, you needn't be discouraged. You can still put your own stuff up for sale at any price you want to set. Your price can be the same or even lower than your competitors' price tags; it can also be higher than the price of competing items.

Next, do some scouring around your own house and gather up some goodies you can potentially sell. You can't sell just anything on Half.com. Although the range of items that are put up for sale on Half.com is continually growing, shoppers go there expecting to find new or almost-new books, music, movies, or games. The full range of items sold on Half.com at this writing is as follows:

- **Books**   Half.com started primarily as a place to sell books, and these are still the most common sales items you'll find there. Students selling textbooks, bookstores selling remainders (leftover books that didn't sell), and authors unloading sample copies are ideal sellers. Even eBay's CEO, Meg Whitman, has reportedly sold her old Princeton textbooks on Half.com.

- **Music**   Music is already a popular sales category on eBay and many other online venues. You can only sell CDs on Half.com; music recorded on other media—from LPs, to cassettes, to piano rolls, to laser discs—should be sold on eBay. (You can sell audio books on cassette, though.) When you sell, you list the Universal Product Code of the CD as found on its jewel box. If the CD has an ISBN as well as a UPC, only list the UPC. If you have neither an ISBN or UPC (perhaps because you don't have the original jewel box). You can search for the same item on Half.com and click a link called **Have one to sell?**.

- **Movies**   These can be DVDs or VHS videotapes. Best sellers include boxed sets, recent releases, and tape or disk versions of programs that originally appeared on TV.

- **Games**   These are games that can be played on Game Boy, Nintendo, Xbox, or other players. (PC games are sold under the Computer Software category, however.)

- **Electronics**   This category includes game players such as Game Boy and Nintendo, MP3 players, cell phones, digital cameras, DVD players, camcorders, and the like.

14

- **Computers & Software**   This category includes not only computers but peripheral devices such as scanners, monitors, and printers, as well as software.

- **Sporting Goods**   Half.com isn't all about electronics and books, as this subcategory of the Everything Else proves. You can sell hockey and golf equipment here, as well as skis, football helmets, inline skates, and much more.

- **Everything Else**   This catch-all category includes garden items, jewelry, musical instruments, office furniture.... You'd better scan the list yourself to get an idea of what you can sell here.

Don't turn to Half.com to try to unload antiques, furnishings, heavy equipment, or items that are several years old and more likely to appeal to collectors—you'll have better luck selling those on eBay itself.

## Find the Item Code

Virtually every book published by a commercial publisher has a number code. To begin, you need to look up the ISBN or UPC number code for the book or books you want to sell. ISBN stands for International Standard Book Number. UPC stands for Universal Product Code. They are "standard industry inventory numbers," found on all books, often expressed as bar codes. You'll find examples of ISBN numbers on the back of the book you're reading right now, and on Half.com's Start Selling: Books page (**http://half.ebay.com/help/sell_books.cfm**), shown in Figure 14-5.

## Listing Multiple Items

If you have more than one item to sell, just look up the ISBN or UPC numbers and enter them on the Multiple Listing Form found at **http://half.ebay.com/account/list/multiList.jsp**.

## Research the Competition

In my case, I have a box full of sample books given to me by the publisher of a book I wrote, called *Literary Chicago,* about the literary heritage of Chicago. The books are new, and I can offer them with the author's signature, so I decided to put one up for sale to see what would happen. I did my own detective work beforehand by doing the following:

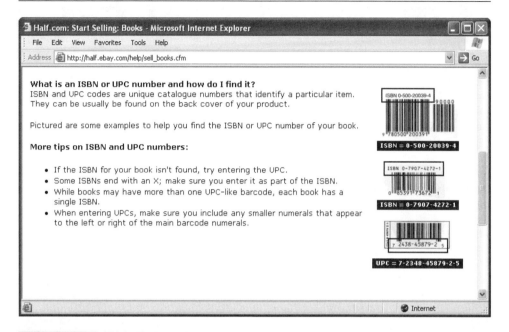

**FIGURE 14-5**    Examples of ISBN numbers

■ I wrote down the ISBN number of the book.

■ I entered the book's title, *Literary Chicago,* in the search box on Half.com's home page to see if anyone else was selling this book. I got 57 listings in the search results with the word "Chicago" in the title; one link was to my own book.

To my surprise, I discovered that more than a dozen sellers had my book up for sale at prices ranging from $8 to $18 (considering that the list price is $15.95, this last price is pretty amazing). I noticed that Half.com did not have an image available for this book. I also noticed that, although the sales form says up to 40 characters of a description might appear on the listing page, as few as 14 characters sometimes appear (refer to the following illustration).

14

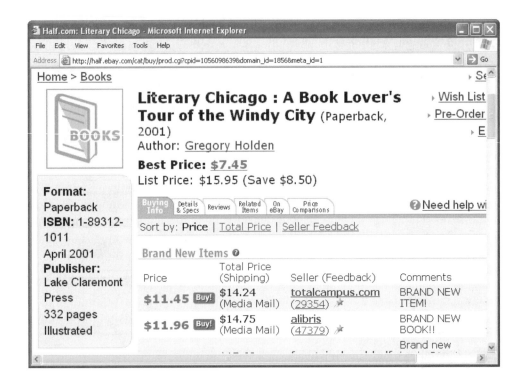

## Set a Sales Price

The original idea behind Half.com was that no book sold on the site would cost more than half its list price. That rule isn't strictly observed today, just as books aren't the only thing you'll find on Half.com. You can sell items for more than half of list price, though eBay doesn't recommend it.

If you find that others on Half.com are already selling what you want to sell, you can get a good idea of what the price should be. If not, you can research the same item on other well-known online retailing web sites such as Amazon.com (**http://www .amazon.com**) or Buy.com (**http://www.buy.com**).

In the case of *Literary Chicago,* I had a new book that was going to compete with other new books selling for between $8 and $18. When prices are close, why does a buyer choose one seller over another? They choose a seller with lots of positive feedback. Since I don't have an eBay feedback rating in the thousands, I can't compete with long-established sellers. I do have a big advantage in that I am the author and I can provide a signed copy, however. I decided to sell my signed copy for $11.99.

*How do you check what constitutes a reasonable price? If you need to compare prices at retail outlets so you can set a Half.com price, check out the Price Checker at the public service site Consumer World (**http://www .consumerworld.org**).*

## Step 3: Fill Out the Sales Form

Armed with a price and the ISBN, and an idea of the competition, I started to fill out the sales form. You get to the Half.com sales form in one of several ways:

- Go to a page that lists the same item you want to sell, and click on the link **Sell Yours Now!**.

- Click the **Sell** link at the bottom of any Half.com web page (you can also reach this page by entering the direct URL **http://half.ebay.com/help/sell .cfm**), then click on the category in which you want to sell.

The form's simple contents are described in the following sections.

### Specify the Condition

The Item Quality ranking on Half.com is very specific and varies depending on what you want to sell. I chose Brand New from the Condition drop-down list. If an item you have for sale isn't brand new, you need to choose the description with care. The categories are listed in Table 14-2.

| Condition | What It Means |
|---|---|
| Brand New | New, unread, in perfect condition |
| Like New | Undamaged cover, no missing or undamaged pages, no writing or highlighting |
| Very Good | No noticeable damage on cover; no missing pages; no damaged pages; no underlining of text, no writing in margins, minimal wear and tear |
| Good | Minimal damage to cover; dust jacket may or may not be present; most pages undamaged, minimal pencil underlining, no highlighting, no missing pages |
| Acceptable | Some cover damage, binding slightly damaged; may be writing in margins as well as underlining or highlighting of text |

**TABLE 14-2**    Condition Categories for Half.com

14

If the condition is worse than acceptable—in other words, if a significant number of pages are damaged and there are missing or stained pages, Half.com does not allow you to sell the item.

 *The condition descriptions vary depending on what you're selling. Refer to the detailed list of options at **http://half.ebay.com/help/index .cfm?helpsection=list#4**.*

## Create a Description

If writing descriptions of sales items is your least favorite aspect of online selling, Half.com is the place for you. Forget about detailed descriptions of the condition or flaws of your book, CD, or movie. Forget about explaining where you found that special something or how many times you used it. You only really need two pieces of information here:

- The ISBN or UPC number

- A standard description that describes the item's condition

That's it. You can add comments of up to 1000 words describing an item, but this is optional. Keep in mind that only the first 40 characters of a description appear on a list of items for sale on Half.com, so these should contain the most important parts of your description. You may receive questions from prospective buyers about the condition of an item, but most of the time, you'll simply receive an e-mail message from Half.com stating that the item has been purchased and providing you with shipping information.

In my case, my biggest challenge was to put, in as few characters as possible, the fact that the book was being sold and signed by the author, and that it was brand new. I tried the following:

New! Signed by author.

I agonized over whether to list the book as Brand New (the official Half.com condition ranking) or simply New. I decided on New to make sure the word "Signed" would appear. This was only 22 characters, so there was a good chance it would all appear on the listing page. I added the following comments:

Sold by author, so signature can be personalized.

## Add an Image

In many cases, you don't have to worry about capturing an image of the item you have to sell. In many cases, Half.com is able to match the ISBN or UPC number you include with the listing to a photo that already exists in its extensive database.

## Did you know?

# Your Listing Can Be Removed

Your listing will be removed from Half.com if you do any of the following:

- List merchandise in the wrong category

- Place ads to your own business within your description

- Place lots of similar listings in a single category, which forces out your competition

- Put imported DVDs up for sale

Although you cannot place an ad to your business within a Half.com description, you can include a link that "points interested buyers to another Internet page that contains only more information (such as pictures, product specifications, or detailed terms and conditions) about eBay items listed by that seller."

Since Half.com did not have an image of *Literary Chicago,* in the Add an Image section of the sales form, I clicked the Browse button and located an image of the book cover on my hard disk. Then I clicked the Continue button at the bottom of the sales form.

## Finish the Listing

After you click Continue, your browser displays a Sell Your Stuff page that prompts you to enter your eBay User ID and password. Enter the information, and click Continue.

The Set Price and List Your Item page appears. Half.com suggests a price based on the average sales price of similar items and the condition you described earlier. In my case, Half.com suggested a price of $12.07. I changed this to $11.99 (which looks slightly less expensive onscreen) and clicked List Item. A page appeared with the heading "Thank You for Listing!"

After your listing is confirmed, be sure to check the listing to make sure the price and description are accurate. If you need to make changes or monitor all of your sales at once, click the **My Account** link at the top of the Half.com home page.

14

Click Manage Inventory, and a list of your current sales appears. Click the link for the sale you want to change, and follow the steps displayed on subsequent screens to make the changes you want.

# Feedback and Customer Service

When you purchase something, whether online or off, you expect good customer service. But when you sell on Half.com, you are the one who has to provide good service, because you are responsible for packaging the items you sell and dealing with your customers. It's not a difficult subject to master: just think about how you like to be treated when you shop, and do the same.

## Build a Good Seller Rating

Feedback is different on Half.com than it is on eBay: only sellers are rated, not buyers. Having a good seller rating not only attracts buyers, but it can bring you more business. You may be called upon to fulfill a pre-order—an order in which the buyer has indicated that they will accept an item as it is described in your sales catalog if you have one, in a specified quality rating, from a seller with a specified feedback score.

 *Don't sell something you don't have the rights to sell. If you burned a CD that you or someone else purchased originally, don't try to sell that copy unless you received permission from the copyright holder to make that copy. Find out more at **http://half.ebay.com/help/index.cfm?helpsection=vero**.*

## Ship Your Goods Promptly

The primary way to build a good feedback rating on Half.com is simple: ship your goods out promptly and be thorough. Half.com suggests that all sellers insure and track their shipments. Packages shipped via Media Mail should have the words "Media Mail" written on the outside.

### First-Class Service Pays Off

Andy Noise is the owner of a small brick-and-mortar music shop in Bakersfield, California. Half.com has helped to transform Andy Noise (that's the name of the store, too) from a local music outlet to a national supplier. He says he does twice the amount of business on the Internet as he does through the physical store.

The store's web site (**http://www.andynoise.com**) contains links to his auctions on eBay as well as Half.com.

At this writing, since becoming a member of Half.com, Andy had sold 7068 items for a total of $72,770.27. Andy (who is well known by this name, but whose real name is Paul Anderson) reports that, currently, his best-selling items on Half.com are textbooks. However, he also regularly scans CD bins to find bargain CDs he can resell. He emphasizes the need to describe an item's condition accurately and to ship out promptly. In fact, he employs a little "trickery" when shipping that helps improve his level of customer service. "My customers pay for Media Mail, and they pay for media but I always ship first class. So they get the stuff faster," he says.

As far as shipping, he uses the e-mail message he receives from Half.com as a mailing label. "Many of the home postage systems require you to enter the address to get the postage and this is a waste of time. I just cut the address off the e-mail and tape it to the bag. That way if the address is incorrect, it is not my error." He uses 6×6.5-inch CD bubble mailers that he buys in lots of 50 on eBay. The best thing about selling on Half.com, he says, doesn't have to do with feedback or money: he's able to spend more time with his sons because he can do much of his work from his home computer. (His 11-year-old son Nicholas created the artwork on his web site, by the way.)

*If you plan to be out of town, be sure to send Half.com a vacation notice so your listing is taken off the site until your specified return date. That way, anyone who purchases your items won't experience long days until you respond.*

If your item is sold, you pay the shipper to send the item out, but the buyer has to pay shipping costs. Half.com then reimburses you for the shipping based on the scale shown in Table 14-3.

*The shipping reimbursement amounts have decreased substantially since the first edition of this book was written.*

For instance, if my book sells for $11.99, the following occurs:

1. The buyer pays a total of $14.98 ($11.99 plus $2.79 for Media Mail shipping).

2. Half.com charges me a 15 percent fee on the $11.99 sale price, or $1.80.

3. Half.com reimburses me $1.94 for shipping this paperback book.

4. Half.com pays me a total of $12.13.

| Item | USPS Media Mail | Expedited Mail |
|---|---|---|
| Hardcover books | $2.33 for first book<br>$0.90 each additional book | $4.70 per book |
| Paperback books | $1.94 for first book<br>$0.69 each additional book | $4.70 for first book<br>$1.50 each additional book |
| Audio book | $1.94 for first book<br>$0.69 each additional book | $4.70 for first book<br>$1.50 each additional book |
| Music | $1.89 for first CD<br>$0.65 each additional CD | $4.70 for first CD<br>$1.50 each additional CD |
| VHS movies | $1.94 for first movie<br>$0.69 each additional movie | $4.70 for first movie<br>$1.50 each additional movie |
| DVD movies | $1.89 for first movie<br>$0.65 each additional movie | $4.70 for first movie<br>$1.50 each additional movie |
| Games | $1.89 for first game<br>$0.65 each additional game | $4.70 for first game<br>$1.50 each additional game |

**TABLE 14-3**    Half.com Shipping Reimbursement

*If you and your buyer have a dispute, Half.com reserves the right to make adjustments to your seller account balance in the event of a member dispute, fraud, or a lack in seller performance. If insufficient funds exist in the seller account balance, Half.com will deduct funds from your checking account, or charge your credit card.*

## Where to Find It

■ **eBay Stores home page**
**http://www.stores.ebay.com**
The welcome page for eBay Stores—the place where customers go to shop.

■ **eBay Storefronts: Seller Landing page**
**http://pages.ebay.com/storefronts/seller-landing.html**
The place where sellers go to create or edit their eBay Stores.

■ **Half.com Help**
**http://half.ebay.com/help/index.cfm**
General instructions on how to buy and sell on Half.com.

■ **Multiple Item Listing page**
**http://half.ebay.com/account/list/multiList.jsp**
A form in which you can enter the ISBN or UPC numbers of multiple books you want to sell.

■ **Start Selling page**
**http://half.ebay.com/help/sell.cfm**
Links to major categories (books, music, movies, games, computers, electronics, sporting goods). Each link leads you to a form that enables you to put up an individual item for sale.

14

# Chapter 15

## Get Instant Results with eBay Live Auctions

## How to...

- Play the Live Auctions game
- Watch the action and place a live bid
- Place an absentee bid
- Register to sell at Live Auctions
- Find a licensed consignment seller

Standard auction listings on eBay have become successful, in part, because they enable you to sell or buy from the comfort of your home; they allow you to track bidding over a period of three, five, seven days or more; and because ordinary people do the selling rather than professionals.

When you buy or sell on eBay Live Auctions, sales proceed much differently than they do in the standard auction listing system. A sale may be announced on the site, and items may be listed several weeks in advance, but the actual sale is conducted in a matter of an hour or less. It's a type of auction conducted in traditional auction houses like Sotheby's and Christie's. If you're a buyer, you find merchandise that you don't usually see up for sale on other parts of eBay, such as fine art, memorabilia associated with a show business personality, or objects that have historical significance.

Because Live Auctions tends to be overlooked, it can also be a good place to sell because there's less competition. There are also stringent requirements for both buyers and sellers, which is good for you as a seller because buyers are less likely to disappear without paying after the sale ends. This chapter will explain how Live Auctions sales work and help you get started with this exciting sales venue that's unique to eBay.

# Get Acquainted with eBay Live Auctions

Regular eBay auctions are great for moderately priced collectibles and merchandise of all sorts, but they might not be the best place to find a certain type of collector. Suppose, among the salt shakers and antique marbles you usually sell, you find a real treasure: a painting from the 1850s hidden behind what seems like a run-of-the-mill print, or a dresser made in Philadelphia in the 18th century? If you've uncovered a really valuable piece of art or furniture and you want to attract worldwide bidders who are looking for maximum reliability and authenticity, you can go to an authorized eBay Live Auctions seller to put it up for auction—or become a Live Auctions seller yourself.

**FIGURE 15-1**  Live Auctions is a great place to auction off high-quality art and other especially valuable objects.

What's the difference between Live Auctions and the rest of eBay? You can get an idea of the difference the moment you visit the Live Auctions home page (**http://www.ebayliveauctions.com**), shown in Figure 15-1.

As indicated by its home page, Live Auctions is a more orderly and dignified place than most of the rest of eBay (or most e-commerce web sites, for that matter). Some live auctions are conducted by auction houses and professional art dealers; others are run by individual antiques store owners. (Some general merchandise is sold through Live Auctions, but the emphasis is on collectibles, antiques, and estate sales.) Each Live Auctions event contains a group of items to be sold, which is called a *catalog*. Each listing in the catalog is designated by the old-style auction term *lot*. A lot can consist of a single item or a group of items.

## Browse Through Catalogs

You can browse through catalogs by looking through the list of upcoming sales on the eBay Live Auctions home page, which lists a half dozen or so upcoming auctions.

15

But these are by no means the only auctions scheduled. If you click on the tiny link **all auctions** just to the right of the Upcoming Auctions heading, you view a page that lists all the auctions scheduled; when I checked, there were more than 50. Any auctions that are currently being held live have to their right a flashing paddle icon as well as Bid Now and View Live buttons. Upcoming auctions have a Sign Up For This Auction button to their right.

You can also browse by clicking on one of the top-level categories listed on the left side of the home page, then clicking on subcategory links until you find the sale that has a catalog you are interested in.

## Search Through Lots and Catalogs (and Lots of Catalogs)

If you or your customers are looking for a specific object among all the upcoming sales on Live Auctions, you can search for individual lots by entering keywords in the Search Live Auctions box on the home page. There's also an Advanced Search page (**http://pages.ebay.com/liveauctions/search/items/search.html**). As you can see from Figure 15-2, the Advanced Search page lets you search individual lots by title.

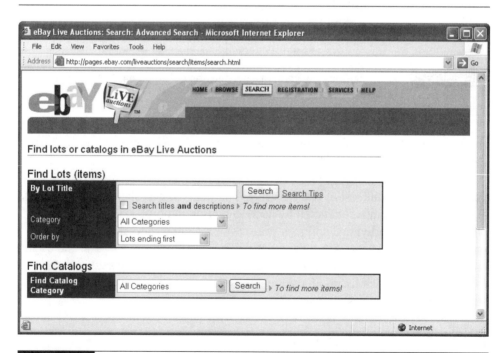

**FIGURE 15-2**    Advanced Search lets you focus a search through individual lots or sales catalogs.

A separate box enables you to restrict your search by catalog. There may be so many catalogs listed that you may want to narrow your search to only those sales focusing on jewelry or fine art, for instance.

*You can combine search terms using commas or other operators, just as you can in the Search boxes on the rest of eBay. But you can't save your searches and reuse them, as you can using My eBay.*

Live auctions have been held for many decades by traditional auction houses. eBay's live auctions attract dedicated collectors and other dedicated buyers who are looking for high-quality merchandise. As you can see from your own searching and browsing, shoppers can shop at leisure, bid without encountering sniping or the heated competition that is found in many traditional eBay auctions, and get instant results, too.

## Participate in Live Auctions

There's nothing quite like a live auction—an auction in which bidding occurs in real time and the whole sale is over in a matter of minutes rather than days. Selling at Live Auctions enables you to have bidders compete in real time both online and in real-world auction houses in locations such as New York and London. In other words, as bidders on the Internet place bids on an item, their bids are announced to bidders assembled in the auction house's brick-and-mortar location (if there is one), who then have the chance to counterbid. Their bids are posted on the catalog's Live Auctions web page, which enables online bidders to place counterbids, and so on until the sale is made.

You can participate in live auctions in one of three ways:

- **Just watch**   This is a good way to get acquainted with what's going on.

- **Place bids**   You compete not only against other bidders who are online, but against individuals who are physically present in the auction seller's brick-and-mortar auction house.

- **Place absentee bids**   Live auctions take place at specific times, and you may not be able to be present at your computer when the sale occurs. In that case, you can place an absentee bid before the start of the sale. You register for the auction, go to the web page where the sale item (or "lot") is described (such as the one shown in Figure 15-3), and place your bid as you would with a conventional eBay online auction.

**15**

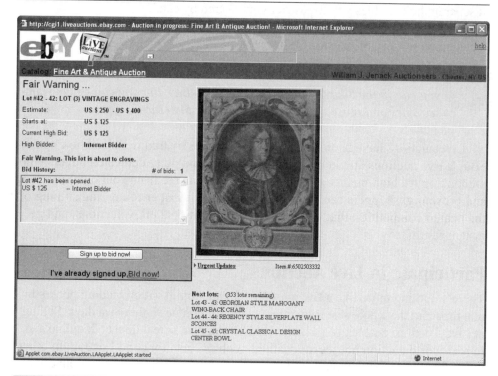

**FIGURE 15-3** Bidders in the auction house compete against Internet bidders with lightning speed.

*To participate in Live Auctions, you can use any computer that is reasonably fast and that works with the rest of eBay. If you plan to place live bids yourself, your computer has to meet some system requirements. At minimum, you need to have at least 64MB of RAM, Windows 95 or later, Internet Explorer 4.01 or Netscape 4.03 or later, and a Pentium II processor or later running at 350 MHz at least. Your web browser has to have Java enabled. If you use the Macintosh or Linux, you can't place live bids—rather, you have to place absentee bids. Find out more at **http://pages.ebay.com/liveauctions/ help/before/lasystem.html**.*

## Begin by Watching

If you've never seen a live auction, it can be great fun. You inspect the lots beforehand and pick out the ones on which you want to bid. Then the action starts. The tension mounts as you wait for your special items to come up. Your heart pounds as you place the bid and wait for counterbids.

It's just as exciting to be a "live" auction participant from the comfort of your home, sitting before your computer screen, as it is to be on the real brick-and-mortar auction floor. It's easy to check out a live auction as an observer without actually bidding in it. Follow these steps:

1.  Go to the eBay Live Auctions home page (**http://www.ebayliveauctions .com/**).

2.  Click **Watch & Bid** on the left side of the page, under Learn About, to get an overview of the process of participating in live auctions.

3.  Click Browse to browse through the Live Auctions sales coming up, and find one that interests you.

4.  Click **Sign Up for This Auction** to the right of the auction in which you are interested.

5.  Read the terms of the auction carefully, check the box that says you accept the terms and conditions, and then click Continue.

6.  Read the Live Auctions User Agreement, check the box stating that you accept the terms of the User Agreement, and then click Submit.

You'll receive an e-mail message telling you that you have signed up for the sale. This message contains links that enable you to place absentee bids, if you want. Otherwise, you wait until the auction begins, then go to the Live Auctions site and click on the auction to view what's going on.

## Place a Live Bid

When the sale you are interested in begins, go to the eBay Live Auctions home page and click **Bid Now** next to the sale's listing. Sign in with your username and password, and pay attention to the system requirements for live bidding, so you make sure you can watch the auction action occur live and can place bids. When you're ready, click Continue. A new window opens, displaying the items in the auction lot as they are put up for sale, one after another. When the item you are interested in appears, click the **Bid Now** link (see Figure 15-3) and place your bid.

## Place Absentee Bids

Absentee bids go against the purpose of live auctions. After all, live auctions are supposed to bring bidders together at the same time so they can compete against

15

one another. Absentee bids give you a chance to beat the time constraints that those auctions impose, however. Here is how absentee bids work:

1.  You register to participate in a live auction, as outlined in the previous section. After you're approved, go back to the lot page and input the maximum amount you are willing to pay for that lot—that is your absentee bid.

2.  You and any other approved bidders place absentee bids up to one hour before the live event begins. Suppose you bid $750 for an item, another bidder named Jill bids $450, and Frank bids $300. The bid increment is $50.

3.  When the auction starts, eBay calculates all the absentee bids and determines the winning absentee bid: the winning absentee bid equals the second highest bid plus one bid increment. In this example, you are the winner at $500.

4.  When the live bidding starts, the auctioneer is told that there is an Internet absentee bid of $500. Other bidders in the auction house can then bid against you during the time period of the live auction.

If the live auction bids do not exceed your maximum bid of $750, you are the winner. However, if someone in the live auction period bids more than your maximum of $750, they win, not you.

 *Read the requirements for the live auction carefully if you plan to bid. Some sellers require you to provide credit references or place a deposit of as much as 20 percent of your likely bids before you can even begin to participate.*

## Become a Live Auctions Seller

If you are already "in the trade"—in other words, the business of buying and selling fine art, antiques, or collectibles—you are eligible to become an authorized seller on eBay Live Auctions. One of the advantages of doing so is the ability to prescreen buyers: bidders are required to register and have their ID verified before they participate. Your chances of running into a nonpaying bidder are far lower than with conventional eBay sales. Another is the fact that sellers put the contents of an estate up all at once, because they can be sold in their entirety in a single day.

Live Auctions has its own set of requirements for sellers. Most notably, sales are restricted to sellers who are already licensed auction sellers or those who are using a licensed auctioneer. Dealers who are "old school"—those who are more comfortable with traditional auction sales than selling online—will be happy to sign on and sell through this venue. If you want to sell on eBay Live Auctions, you need to follow its rules, including:

- You must be a manager or employee of an auction house.

- You must be a licensed auctioneer.

If you already run an auction house, fill out the application form at **http://cgi1 .liveauctions.ebay.com/aw-cgi/eBayISAPI.dll?LAApplicationForm** and submit it to eBay. If you aren't a licensed auction house or auctioneer, you need to arrange with one to sell your items on Live Auctions. Of course, you can apply for an auctioneer's license, but that is a time-consuming process. The exact requirements vary by state, but in general, you have to enroll in an approved auction school, and take a class that lasts from several weeks to a semester; alternately, you can serve as an apprentice auctioneer for a period of time.

If you do decide to sell on Live Auctions, make sure you have a lot (I mean, a large quantity, not a single item) of things to sell, because Live Auctions charges you $1500 as an insertion fee for selling an entire catalog of items. For each item you sell, you also pay a 5 percent final value fee based on the sales price. Live Auctions isn't the place to sell a single item at a time, in other words: it's designed for professionals who want to sell hundreds of items in an estate all at once.

## Guaranteeing Authenticity

When you are preparing a description for eBay Live Auctions, keep in mind that you need to provide a guarantee, as stated at **http://pages.ebay.com/liveauctions/ help/welcome/laguarantee.html**. One of the advantages of using Live Auctions is the structure that it imposes on sellers, and the requirements it places on both sellers and buyers. Buyers are likely to be serious, because they are required to pay a substantial Buyer's Premium along with a winning bid. They also have to place a credit card on file or have their ID verified with Live Auctions before they can bid at all.

Here are just a few examples of the kinds of requirements that live auction sellers need to observe with respect to the items they sell:

- **Authenticity**   The authenticity of an item is the accuracy with which its date and place of origin can be verified.

- **Condition**   The condition needs to be accurate.

- **Refunds**   If the condition and authenticity are found to have been inaccurate, the seller (eBay) will be required to provide a refund to the buyer.

*Guarantees of authenticity aren't the only requirements for selling on Live Auctions. The winning buyer pays a Buyer's Premium of perhaps 15% of the sale price (you can decide on the premium that you want to charge). Sellers pay the additional $1500 catalog listing fee and 5 percent final value fee (which is calculated on the sale price but does not include the premium). In other words, if you sell something to a high bidder for $1000 and you charge a 15 percent Buyer's Premium, that bidder actually pays you $1150. However, you pay eBay 5 percent of $1000, or $50.*

# The Longer the Description, the Better

You have to follow Live Auctions' rules for creating listings and buying and selling, which tend to be more stringent than those on other parts of eBay. On the plus side, this means that you create listings that are of better quality, more accurate, and more reliable than others. They are listings that will make people feel they can invest many thousands of dollars in an item. On the down side, they make you go through more work. The elements of a Live Auctions listing are described in the following sections.

## Main Description

The main description is a short summary of the estimated value of the item being sold and a brief summary of the item's main features. This initial description should tell prospective bidders at a glance what the item is, how big it is, and its condition.

Before you list the item, you need to make sure it does not violate the eBay sales restrictions. Be sure to check the What Items May Not Be Sold On eBay? Help page (**http://pages.ebay.com/help/community/png-items.html**) for a current list.

## Additional Information

You can add information to your Live Auctions listings after the sale goes online, just as you can on eBay. However, eBay encourages Live Auctions sellers to include a "captivating additional note" with each entry when you first create it. Just what does this mean? Each auction description is divided into three main sections:

- **Estimate**   An estimate of the item's value

- **Description**   A brief summary of the item

- **Notes**   Detailed notes that describe the item's origin and authenticity and why it is distinctive and valuable

For example, take a look at the bottom half of the description of a guitar up for auction shown in Figure 15-4. At the top, you have a brief description of the item's features. The Notes section is far more extensive, and provides information about the seller, payment method, and rules for bidders, as well as the item itself.

If you don't have a great deal to say about an item, don't feel obligated to include lengthy notes about it. Also, don't assume that everything you sell on Live Auctions has to be extremely expensive. You'll find moderately priced wristwatches on the site for less than $200 or $300, just as you would on eBay, for example. The difference is that dealers and authorities in the field sell on Live Auctions, so they are more likely to get serious bidders, or bidders who are most concerned with getting what they paid for: buyers who don't want to be swindled, in other words. Another big difference: you find buyers who are willing to pay the 15 percent Buyer's Premium

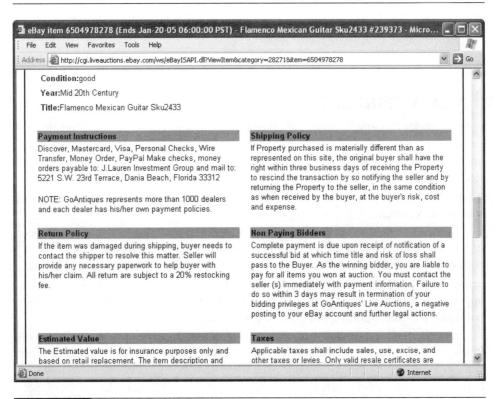

**FIGURE 15-4**    Sellers tend to present more information—and restrictions—on Live Auctions than on eBay.

15

that is added to the winning bid price and that is paid to the seller, ostensibly to cover the cost of the sale. In my opinion, this fee (which is standard procedure in traditional auction sales, but not on eBay) discourages bidders, many of whom prefer to look for bargains on regular eBay auctions.

## Make Your Images Worth a Thousand Words

To sell through Live Auctions, you have to play by the rules. Presentation and appearance count for a lot. That means you need to have at least one clear image of an item, preferably more. You need to make sure your images are clear and close up. Take the time to photograph the item from several angles, if possible, just as you would in a conventional auction. I suggest you browse extensively through the Live Auctions listings to see what other sellers do, and gather ideas for your own presentations.

 *You'll find tips and suggestions for selling rarities in the Antiques Selling Guide at **http://pages.ebay.com/sellercentral/sbc/antiquessellerguide/ index.html**.*

# Find a Consignment Seller

eBay's standard auction listings and eBay Stores are so popular and well-traveled that chances are you aren't going to want to sell exclusively on eBay Live Auctions unless you're already a dealer of art, antiques, or the like. You can still sell on Live Auctions when the occasion arises, however. You can consign some of your merchandise to a Live Auctions dealer rather than go through the application process and learn to run such a sale yourself.

If you do want to consign, make sure you get adequate background on the level of experience of your chosen seller. If possible, get references and talk to them personally either by e-mail or on the phone. Get all the seller's fees spelled out in advance. (You might encounter "hidden" or unexpected fees for photography, appraisal, insurance, and the like.) Make sure you get a written contract from the consignment seller spelling out all the fees that apply.

Be wary of a Live Auctions seller whose representative entices you to allow them to auction your collection without a reserve or a high opening bid. Sometimes this strategy produces spectacular results, but there have been many instances in which consignors were heavily disappointed when they received their checks from the auction company.

You should look around and find an approved seller who can sell the item for you on consignment. Scan the list of current and upcoming auction sales for an Associate who deals in what you want to sell. Be sure to review the seller's previous sales and pay attention to the way the business is presented online. Make sure the Associate's sales are presented the way you would want your own to appear. Look at the seller's feedback in the Live Auctions Feedback Forum (**http://pages .ebay.com/liveauctions/services/forum/feedback.html**). You can also get a quick link to the seller's feedback by clicking the **Read feedback comments** link in the Seller Information box on any one of the auction site's lots for sale. Then approach the seller to see how well you get along.

The Seller Information box also contains a Me icon next to the seller's User ID if an About Me page is available. In some cases, the seller's About Me page has a selection of feedback presented. In other cases, the About Me page contains background information about the seller and links to upcoming sales the seller has scheduled, as shown in Figure 15-5.

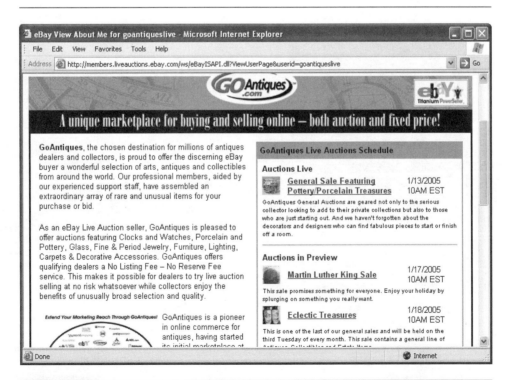

**FIGURE 15-5**   Live Auctions sellers have About Me pages and feedback ratings, the same as other eBay sellers.

Typically, the feedback is gushingly positive, but it can still give you an idea of whether the seller can do a good job for you.

## Where to Find It

- **eBay Live Auctions**
  **http://www.ebayliveauctions.com**
  Links to upcoming live auctions on eBay.

- **Live Auctions Feedback Forum**
  **http://pages.ebay.com/liveauctions/services/forum/feedback.html**
  Instructions on how to leave feedback or look up feedback for a Live Auctions seller.

- **Advanced Search page**
  **http://pages.ebay.com/liveauctions/search/items/search.html**
  A simple form that lets you limit searches to catalogs or keywords.

# Part V

# Keep Your eBay Business Running Smoothly

# Chapter 16

## Protect Yourself and Your Customers

## How to…

■ Control your sales by creating a list of pre-approved bidders

■ Reduce chances of trouble by investigating first-time bidders

■ Build your own credibility with ID Verify

■ Give your sales a "seal of approval"

■ Use encryption to verify your identity

■ Encrypt your e-mail messages

■ Offer a warranty to your customers

■ Steer clear of prohibited items

■ Shy away from shill bidding

As a seller, you might think at first glance that bidders are the ones who are in control of eBay auctions, not you. On the surface, at least, it seems like your job is to present the items for sale and simply wait until the bids come in. You can't control who places the top bid, and you can't ensure whether the purchaser is a reputable individual or not.

Or can you? Actually, as an eBay seller, you probably have more control than you think. You can "ban" from bidding on your current sales any members who have burned you in the past. You can choose the individuals you want to bid on your items. You can insure what you sell. You can tell potential buyers you care about their safety by entering the SquareTrade program or by obtaining an icon from eBay that verifies your identity. If you're looking for an extra measure of security, you can even encrypt your communications with your customers. You can also keep sales running smoothly by avoiding the sale of items that are prohibited or questionable. This chapter discusses different ways in which you can control who bids and buys what you put up for sale, and how you can ensure that the transaction goes smoothly.

# Control Who Bids and Buys from You

Most auctions work by attracting as many interested bidders as possible to gain the highest purchase price. When you cast a wide net, however, you attract both not-so-good bidders and good bidders. The bidders who fall into the not-so-good category are ones who turn into deadbeats and don't follow through with purchases. To avoid the deadbeats and attract purchasers who have bought from you in the past and whose qualities you are familiar with, you may want to add a note to your auction description, or create a pre-approved list of buyers, as described in this section.

## Add a Note to Your Description

One of the most effective ways to avoid attracting bidders who are likely to cause problems (to retract their bid at the last minute or simply fail to follow through with a transaction) is to include an advisory note in your auction description. Such a note might read as follows:

> Bidders with overall negative feedback, no feedback, or more than *x* [fill in the blank] negative feedbacks in [fill in a period of time] will be removed from the auction.

Such a note isn't terribly friendly. But some sellers who have had problems with deadbeat buyers believe such a message is effective in discouraging bidders you don't want. If the final bidder is someone who ignored that part of your Terms of Sale, then you can just offer the item to the second bidder instead, because the final bidder ignored your terms. On the other hand, opinions differ about whether such restrictions actually discourage or actually serve to *attract* deadbeats. Carol Hearn, the seller quoted in the "Did You Know?" sidebar that follows, doesn't set such restrictions, for instance. It's up to you to decide which approach is best for your needs.

## Create a List of Approved Buyers

In their quest to get the highest price possible, most sellers don't think about ways to limit the number of bidders who try to win their auctions. In fact, you do have the ability to create a list of approved individuals—people you have identified as being eligible to bid on your items. The feature works like this:

- You specify the pre-approved list of eBay members who can bid on your item or purchase it using the Buy It Now feature.

- Anyone who is not on your list must e-mail you for approval before they can bid; you can screen bidders by asking questions about their background or what they plan to do with your item.

**16**

- You can create a pre-approved list for each item individually, so your other sales can be restricted if you wish.

- While a sale is ongoing, you can add and delete pre-approved bidders or buyers.

The practice of limiting who can bid on your sales might seem to contradict the concept behind auctions, where you want to attract as many customers as possible. But creating a pre-approved list does have an important purpose. For one thing, if the items you want to sell are special in some way—such as objects that are used in religious worship—you might want to screen bidders beforehand to make sure they're going to respect the intended purpose of the object. Some eBay sellers use a pre-approved list for bidders who express an interest in purchasing two or more of their sales items at the same time, as described in "Join Sales with a Pre-Approved Bidder/Buyer List" later in this chapter.

# Be Specific, But Don't Scare Bidders Away

When you spell out in your auction descriptions exactly which bidders you won't accept, you protect yourself. But you affect your image, too. You might scare away new eBay members who are eager to build up good feedback.

"I try not to turn customers off with a list of requirements they must meet in order to buy from me," says Carol Hearn, a PowerSeller who is profiled in the eBay Bestseller sidebar later in this chapter. "Many sellers don't realize how it sounds to tell people 'You can't buy from me unless you: have a certain number of positive feedbacks; live in the U.S.; contact me within so many days; pay me within so many days; go through my special checkout,' etc. Instead, I make my requirements as simple as possible and state them in language that a new user can understand. I have had many successful transactions with low-feedback customers; everyone starts with zero feedback."

In other words, just because someone has zero feedback, that doesn't mean they're out to place a high bid and then not follow through. It's a balancing act: you need to protect yourself by specifying your most important requirements, while letting newcomers bid along with long-established members.

CAUTION

*The obvious problem with creating a pre-approved list of buyers is that you won't get as many bids as you would otherwise. eBay users, for the most part, don't like to be told what to do. They prefer the freedom of being able to bid or sell without restrictions. Some will be completely turned off by the pre-approval requirement and not e-mail you. On the other hand, those who do e-mail asking for approval are likely to be serious purchasers rather than deadbeat bidders.*

## Create the List

To create a list of pre-approved bidders, you first offer your item for sale on eBay. Then, follow these steps:

1. Go to the login page for creating a set of pre-approved buyers (**http://cgi3 .ebay.com/aw-cgi/eBayISAPI.dll?PreApproveBidders**).

2. If you are prompted to (in other words, if you aren't already logged in), enter your eBay User ID and password, and click the Sign In Securely button.

3. When the eBay Pre-Approve Bidders/Buyers page appears, read the brief introduction, then click **Add a new item**.

4. When the next page appears, enter the eBay item number of the sale item you want to restrict in the Item No. box.

5. In the box labeled Add or Remove Pre-Approved Bidders/Buyers, enter the User IDs of the bidders or buyers you have pre-approved, as shown in Figure 16-1.

6. Click Submit Item.

When the list has been created, the notice shown in Figure 16-2 appears in the area where bidders would normally begin the bidding process.

When prospective bidders click on the link shown in Figure 16-2, they are asked to sign in with their eBay User ID and password. Bidders who are not pre-approved are prompted to contact the seller to bid on the item. When you receive that e-mail, you can evaluate whether the bidders are ones you want to permit. You can ask them to register with eBay's ID Verify program (see the section "Use ID Verify" later in this chapter). You can also click on their User ID, check their feedback history, and ask why they are interested in your item. If they seem serious and trustworthy, you can add them to your list. Only then will the individual be able to bid.

16

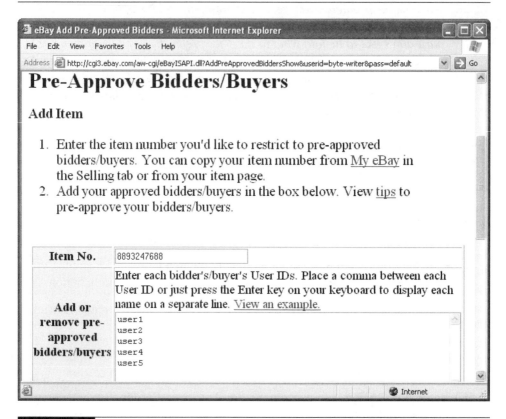

**FIGURE 16-1** You create a list of pre-approved bidders or buyers after your sale has gone online.

Even if you have already created a list of pre-approved bidders, you have the option of adding or removing names at any time while the sale is ongoing. To add a name, go to your list of pre-approved bidders and add the User ID of the new bidder on a new line. Or, you can separate each of the names on the list with a comma, colon, semicolon, or even a single blank space.

TIP *It's a good idea to explain in your item's description that you are pre-approving bidders, and to describe the criteria for approving new bidders.*

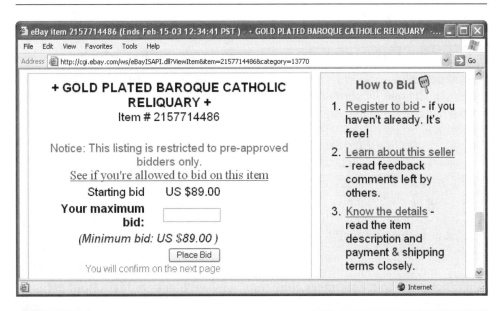

**FIGURE 16-2**   If you want to restrict access to a sale, eBay adds this note to your description.

You can also change your mind and open up your sale to all bidders rather than a selected list while the sale is still going on. You might want to open up the sale if your item is attracting more interest than you expected, for instance. You do this by clicking the **Deactivate** link on the web page that lists your pre-approved bidders.

## Join Sales with a Pre-Approved Bidder/Buyer List

You might also want to use a pre-approved bidder's list to combine two or more of your sales so that you can ensure that those items will go to a particular bidder. I've seen this done by a seller who specializes in Laura Ashley items. This seller charges $22 for shipping domestically; however, this is a flat rate and doesn't depend on weight. If someone expresses an interest in several different items, the seller will take those items and create a pre-approved bidder's list that includes only the interested buyer. That way, the buyer can buy two, three, or more items at once and save on shipping charges. The point of using a pre-approved bidder's list in this

**16**

## eBay Bestsellers
## Block Buyers Who've Burned You, Seller Advises

As an active PowerSeller on eBay, Carol Hearn (User ID: wanderingcreekantiques) occasionally runs into problems with bidders. She takes steps to prevent problems from recurring, and to protect her investment, too. "I add every nonpaying bidder and a few other difficult customers that I don't want to deal with again to my banned bidder list," Carol says. "This doesn't help if they choose to bid under another User ID, but it does prevent most repeat problems with the same bidder. I *always* file for my fees back, which gives the bidder a strike against them from eBay. And I leave negative feedback saying, 'Auc ended 2/1-no contact or pmt as of 2/22 despite reminders fr seller and eBay.' I have only gotten one retaliatory negative and am sure my feedback has helped other sellers in dealing with the same bidder."

You, too, can block buyers who have turned out to be non-paying bidders in the past. Go to **http://pages.ebay.com/help/sell/block_bidders.html** to find out how to create a list of such members.

Hearn, who lives in Bothell, Washington, began selling antiques and collectibles part-time while she still had a full-time career as a government manager. After she retired, she opened an antique store in a shopping mall. "When I was introduced to eBay in 1997, I became a part-time auction seller. Later, when we closed our shop, I became a full-time eBay seller. I will never generate the income on eBay that I did in the shop, because I sell miscellaneous merchandise on eBay rather than the estate fine jewelry I used to sell in the store. But eBay has still given me the opportunity to continue to operate my own business as long as I'm physically able and interested."

Carol says her biggest challenge has not been selling online, but in getting up to speed with computers and, as she says, "learning to use technology to my advantage." Here too, eBay offers fantastic resources in its user groups. Unlike running your own physical business, there's free help available 24/7 at the touch of a button.

Carol's biggest tip is one that can help sellers protect themselves in many different situations: "Treat customers the way you like to be treated," she says. "If you've made a mistake and an item needs to be returned or a refund given, do it graciously and quickly, pay shipping (both ways, if you are at fault), and move on. On the other hand, if you have a disagreement with a buyer and you've followed eBay's rules and haven't done anything wrong, don't be a doormat."

> She also advises sellers to make their profit when they purchase an item, not when they sell it. "If you pay too much for your merchandise or buy the wrong thing, no amount of bells and whistles and fine customer service will make up for the poor buying decision. Whether you're buying new, overstock, or used items, do research on eBay (and, if necessary, on web sites as well) before you buy. You may lose a few wonderful buys this way, but you'll avoid a bunch of *stinkers* and an overflowing garage as well."

case is that it ensures that one person will get the items, since that person is the only bidder on the list. This is an unorthodox—and clever—way to use the pre-approved bidder's list feature to boost sales. At the same time, the sales go through eBay, so they are subject to eBay's protection systems for both buyers and sellers. The more common and easier way is to combine shipping charges for multiple items, or create a Buy It Now listing and tell the buyer to click on the Buy It Now option and buy the other items immediately.

## Contact Buyers Who Make You Nervous

Suppose you are nearing the end of a sale and the current high bidder is someone who has negative feedback or appears to be a first-time buyer. You might reasonably be concerned as to whether the individual is really serious about following through with the sale and really understands how the auction process works (keeping in mind that new users with zero feedback are usually trustworthy, because they want to build a good reputation and develop a good feedback rating). You don't want the buyer to turn out to be a deadbeat. What can you do?

Rather than waiting for the sale to end and crossing your fingers in the hope that the buyer will complete the transaction, take a proactive approach. Don't come right out and ask if they are serious about their bid. You might be perceived as confrontational and unfriendly, and you may provoke exactly the response you're trying to avoid. Rather, ask the person if he or she needs any help or advice. Simply remind the person that you will be happy to answer any questions they have about the object, such as shipping options. Their response may well indicate how serious they are. At the very least, you will convey that you are in charge of your sales and that you care about how they proceed.

16

*Keep in mind that if a buyer does fail to complete the transaction, you can make a Second Chance Offer to the next highest bidder. A Second Chance Offer is a feature of eBay that enables sellers to sell to a bidder at the bidder's highest bid amount, even if that bid amount did not meet the reserve price. Keep in mind, though, that some bidders intentionally bid low in the hope that you'll lower your price through a Second Chance Offer. Find out more in Chapter 4 and at* **http://pages.ebay.com/help/sell/ personal_offer.html**.

# Build Your Credibility

eBay bidders are hopeful, but they don't take for granted good deals or descriptions that they read online. Every bit of documentation that you provide helps induce them to bid. The more effectively you can convey that you are a reliable businessperson, the more bids you'll get. How do you prove you are who you say you are? Feedback helps, but what if you don't yet have a lot of feedback? You can't show your state ID or passport to someone online, but you can display a seal of approval from a third party that verifies that you are a reputable business, and you can give buyers or other sellers you meet an electronic document called a *personal certificate.*

## Obtain a Seal of Approval

Some eBay businesspeople stand out from the crowd and indicate their commitment to good customer service by adding a seal of approval to their descriptions, their About Me pages, and their eBay Stores. The Better Business Bureau Online (BBB*OnLine*) and SquareTrade are two companies that provide seals of approval. In the case of both the BBB*OnLine* and SquareTrade seals, you need to spend some money to obtain and keep displaying the symbol, but you can take advantage of the organization's dispute resolution services. When you have an independent organization verify your identity and your reputation, you increase the chances that someone will bid on your items rather than those of your competitors.

### BBB*OnLine*

The BBB*OnLine* Reliability Seal (which is described at **http://www.bbbonline .org/business**) is intended for existing businesses that are already members of their local Better Business Bureau. The seal tells prospective customers that you will handle complaints and returns fairly and promptly, that you will use the BBB's dispute resolution services if needed, and that you observe the BBB's Code of Online Business Practices. The Code states that you will not use deceptive or misleading practices, that you won't disclose details of your transactions with your customers, and that you'll answer questions and resolve complaints in a timely and responsive manner.

Replacements, Ltd.'s About Me page includes a BBB*OnLine* reliability seal along with a privacy statement, as shown here:

**TIP** *You can read a summary of the Code of Online Business Practices at **http://www.bbbonline.org/reliability/code/code.asp**.*

To apply for the BBB*OnLine* seal, you need to provide the BBB with your company's street address and telephone number, you need to have been in business for at least one year, and you need to pay a licensing fee that varies by location. If you run an e-commerce web site that's a spin-off of an existing brick-and-mortar business and you also sell on eBay, the BBB*OnLine* seal is perfect. If you are an individual who sells on eBay on a part- or full-time basis and you don't own your own business, turn to the SquareTrade seal of approval.

## SquareTrade

SquareTrade is an organization that provides dispute resolution and other services for individuals and companies that buy and sell online. One of SquareTrade's most useful services, online dispute resolution, is a resource you should definitely know about. Dispute resolution is discussed in Chapter 19. Keep in mind that, if you ever

16

run into a disgruntled buyer or seller, you should go to the SquareTrade home page (**http://www.squaretrade.com**), shown next, and click the eBay link.

To build credibility, you can also apply to obtain a SquareTrade Seal. SquareTrade claims that as many as 10,000 eBay users display such a seal on their auction listings, About Me, or eBay Stores pages. An example is shown in Figure 16-3.

You can try SquareTrade free for 30 days. During that time, you can see if you receive more bids when your auctions display the SquareTrade logo, as SquareTrade claims. If you decide to stay in the program, you pay a $7.50 monthly fee. Of course, you have to fill out an application form and go through an approval process first. During the approval process, SquareTrade does the following:

- Verifies your identity
- Reviews your selling history
- Checks your feedback
- Checks for dispute resolution problems

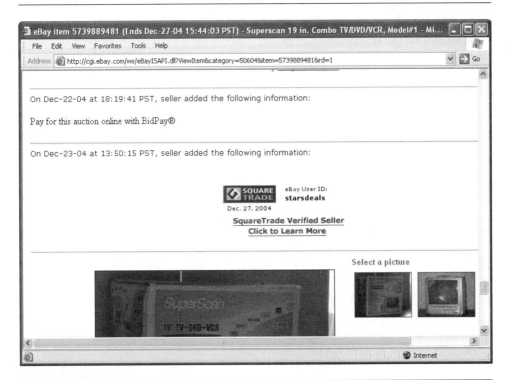

On Dec-22-04 at 18:19:41 PST, seller added the following information:

Pay for this auction online with BidPay®

On Dec-23-04 at 13:50:15 PST, seller added the following information:

**FIGURE 16-3**   The SquareTrade Seal tells bidders you are committed to providing good customer service.

TIP *You might consider signing up with SquareTrade for free for 30 days and conducting a pseudo-scientific test. Place the logo on some of your sales and leave other sales logo-free. You can then compare the response.*

SquareTrade and other "seal of approval" services like BuySafe (**http://www .buysafe.com**) usually claim that negative feedback is reduced when you add their logo, and that you not only receive more bids, but the purchase price goes up as well. Take these claims with a big grain of salt. It's hard to quantify the benefits of added credibility. Enrolling in the Seal Program, however, does bring you tangible benefits, including the ability to receive seller activity reports from SquareTrade that graphically depict your sales activity over a period of time. As a Seal holder, you also give your buyers $250 worth of fraud protection from SquareTrade.

16

## Use ID Verify

How do you know who is actually placing a bid on your merchandise? By the same token, how do your bidders know who *you* are? You can use the ID Verify program to confirm to bidders that you are who you say you are. ID Verify is an identity verification service available to eBay users (but only to residents of the United States and U.S. territories, not to international users). Your personal information is checked against databases of consumers and businesses for consistency. The company that does the checking, VeriSign, verifies your identity only against existing information in its files, not by performing a credit check. ID Verify isn't just an option for telling people who you are. eBay requires that you use ID Verify before you can offer anything for sale on a Buy It Now basis.

To initiate the verification process, go to the ID Verify: Accept Terms page (**http://pages.ebay.com/services/buyandsell/idverify-terms.html**) and click I Agree.

TIP

*Along with getting a SquareTrade Seal, which carries monthly fees, it's also a good idea to follow through with eBay's ID Verify program, which has only a one-time fee of $5. You need to go through ID Verify to buy an item through Buy It Now, or to sell anything in the eBay Mature Audiences category. Plus, your ID Verify status enables you to bid on items that cost more than $15,000.*

## Obtain a Personal Certificate

A *certificate,* also known as a Digital ID, is an electronic file that verifies your identity to others on the Internet. A certificate is issued by a third party called a *certification authority (CA),* which takes responsibility for verifying the owner's personal information. The owner's identity is verified by the use of encryption. Like the seals described in the preceding section, you need to purchase and maintain your certificate by paying a licensing fee.

### Understand Personal Certificates

Your friends know who you are because they recognize your voice, your face, and other unique characteristics. When you make a purchase from a brick-and-mortar store, the salespeople can verify your identity by viewing a photo ID card you present to them. How, then, do you verify who you are online, where people can't see you in person?

When you obtain a certificate, the CA gives you a license to use a mathematical formula it owns, called an *algorithm.* You use the algorithm to generate a very long series of encrypted characters called a *key.* This initial key is called a *private key* because you are supposed to keep it secret and never share it with anyone. Once you have the private key, you use it to create a new key, called a *public key*. The public key is freely exchanged with people who want to verify your identity; it's what verifies your identity to customers or others you meet online.

Certificates are commonly used by businesses to verify their own identities and to provide information about where they are located. You just have to remember to keep your certificates up to date by paying the regular license fee.

## Acquire Your Own Personal Certificate

You may want to obtain a certificate if you operate a business web site in addition to your eBay auctions. You can include a link to your web site on your About Me page. Visitors to your site can elect to receive your certificate to verify that your business is real and that you are who you say you are.

It's surprisingly easy to get your own certificate. You apply to and pay a license fee to a CA such as VeriSign. A VeriSign Class 1 Digital ID, which you can use to authenticate yourself in e-mail, news, and other interactions on the Internet, costs $19.95 per year, and you can try it out free for 60 days. To get a VeriSign certificate, follow these steps:

1. Launch your web browser and go to the VeriSign Digital IDs for Secure Email page at **http://www.verisign.com/products/class1/index.html**.

2. Click Buy Now. It's confusing, but you need to click Buy Now whether you want to pay for a Digital ID or try one out for free.

3. Read the introductory information on the Digital ID Enrollment page, then click Buy Now.

4. A new window opens prompting you to choose your browser.

5. If your browser displays a dialog box asking if you want to download a certificate installer, click OK. If your browser displays an Enrollment page listing different browsers, click your browser's name.

6. Fill out the form on the first Enrollment page. Click the I'd Like to Test Drive a 60-Day Trial Digital ID for Free radio button. Read the Subscriber Agreement, and then click Accept.

7. Click OK when asked to confirm your e-mail address. Then, type a password in the dialog box that appears and click OK. The password is used to generate your private key.

16

**8.** Check your e-mail inbox in a few minutes for a message entitled Trial Class 1 VeriSign Digital ID Pickup Instructions.

**9.** Click and hold down your mouse button and scroll across the PIN to select it; then choose Edit | Copy to copy the PIN.

**10.** Go to the URL for the Digital ID Center that is included in the e-mail message, and paste your PIN in the text box next to Enter the Digital ID Personal Identification Number (PIN).

**11.** Click Submit.

**12.** When the Digital ID Installation and Registration page appears, click Install. The certificate is downloaded to your computer.

To view the certificates you obtain using Internet Explorer 6, choose Tools | Internet Options, click the Content tab, click the Certificates button, click the certificate you want to view, and then click the View button. VeriSign's certificate is shown here. If you use Netscape Navigator, choose Edit | Preferences to open the Preferences dialog box, click the arrow next to Privacy & Security, click Certificates, and click Manage Certificates.

**NOTE** *VeriSign is well known, which means that its Digital IDs are widely trusted, but it has drawn complaints for its aggressive marketing techniques and the way it manages customer information. VeriSign isn't the only CA around, though. Also look into RSA Security (**http://www.rsasecurity.com**) and thawte Consulting (**http://www.thawte.com**).*

## Secure Your Communications

Once you have obtained a Digital ID, you can use it to verify your identity to those with whom you do business. You may want to do one of two things:

- *Send a digital signature.* You can attach your Digital ID to your e-mail messages so that you can assure the recipients that the message is really coming from you.

- *Encrypt your e-mail messages.* You can use the personal key that is part of your Digital ID to ensure that only the intended party can read it.

*You can only encrypt or digitally sign messages that you send using your e-mail software, such as Outlook Express, Netscape Messenger, or Eudora. You can't attach your Digital ID to e-mail you send through eBay's usual system for contacting other eBay members, because such messages are sent through a web page interface rather than e-mail software. If you want to send encrypted communications to someone, you'll have to first contact the individual (go to the member's profile page by clicking on his or her User ID, then click the Contact Member button). When the message arrives in your e-mail inbox, you can use your regular e-mail software to compose a digitally signed or encrypted message.*

Once you obtain your Digital ID, you can follow these steps to send encrypted or digitally signed messages with Outlook Express:

1. Open Outlook Express, then choose Tools | Address Book to open the Address Book.

2. Right-click the name of the person to whom you want to send a signed or encrypted message and choose properties to open the Properties sheet for that individual. (If the person is not yet included in your Address Book, you need to create a new listing.)

3. Click the Digital IDs tab and then click Import.

4. Locate your Digital ID file on your hard disk, click its name, and then click Open.

5. Your certificate appears in the Digital IDs Associated with the Selected E-Mail Address box. Click OK. The Properties dialog box closes.

**16**

6. In the Address Book, highlight the recipient's name, click the Action toolbar button, and choose Send Mail from the menu that appears.

7. When the New Message window appears, click either Tools | Encrypt (to encrypt the message) or Tools | Digitally Sign (to digitally sign it).

8. Finish composing your message, and click Send to send it on its way.

NOTE    *You can also use a popular program called Pretty Good Privacy (PGP) to encrypt your e-mail messages. However, the recipients also have to have PGP installed so that they can exchange public keys with you. You then attach the public keys to the e-mail messages you exchange. (This is the best way for Mac users to be able to encrypt e-mail messages and files.) Pretty Good Privacy is available in two versions: freeware and commercial. The freeware version is distributed by the Massachusetts Institute of Technology at **http://web.mit.edu/network/pgp.html**. The commercial version is available from PGP Corp. at **http://www.pgp.com**.*

# Keep Your Transactions Trouble Free

It isn't possible to eliminate all problems from eBay auctions, because you can't always predict what your bidders will do. However, you can minimize the number of disputes or problems you encounter by following a few simple practices.

For instance, if you sell items such as computers or electronics equipment, you can point out to your customers that warranties are available for eBay purchases if they want to pay a nominal fee to obtain one through eBay Warranty Services, as described in the section that follows. You can also avoid trouble for yourself by avoiding the sale of items that are prohibited by eBay or by state or local laws. You can protect your buyers by avoiding illegal attempts to artificially drive up the price of the items you sell (a practice known as *shill bidding*—see "Steer Clear of Shill Bidding," later in the chapter) and by not selling questionable items that can get your purchasers in trouble at some point after the sale.

## Offer a Warranty

A warranty is a contract or guarantee to perform specified duties or services. In terms of consumer products, a warranty is a guarantee that a product will perform satisfactorily during a specified period after purchase. eBay sales items come in a virtually limitless range of ages and conditions, and most are far from new. Your high bidders or buyers, however, aren't necessarily looking for merchandise in perfect condition. They just want what they purchase to be in the condition you described.

Anyone who purchases a computer- or electronics-related item, a video game, or a musical instrument on eBay has the opportunity to purchase a warranty, or *Service Plan,* through eBay's Warranty Services program. The Service Plan includes one year of coverage on most new, used, or refurbished items. It is provided not by eBay itself but by a partner organization, N.E.W. Customer Service Companies, Inc. Buyers aren't the only ones who benefit from this program. If you display a Warranty Services banner on a sale, like the one shown in Figure 16-4, and your high bidder or buyer purchases a warranty, you earn a cash bonus. For items that sell for $200 or less, you get a bonus of 25 percent of your eBay final value fee; for items that sell for more than $200, your bonus amounts to 50 percent of your eBay final value fee.

**TIP** *Residents of Maine, Oklahoma, Alaska, Guam, and Puerto Rico cannot have the items they sell covered by Warranty Services due to state regulations. You can find out more about eBay's Warranty Services and how they can benefit sellers at **http://pages.ebay.com/help/warranty/seller_overview.html**.*

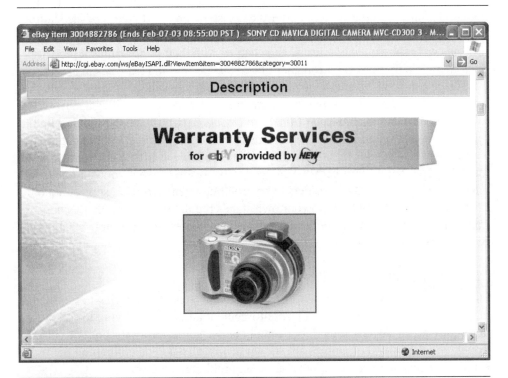

**FIGURE 16-4**   If you offer a warranty, you can add this banner to your sales description.

16

The cost of a warranty (which is paid by the buyer) depends on the final purchase price of the item you are offering. But it's up to buyers to decide if they want to purchase the plan and, if so, the amount of coverage they want. You offer the warranty as an option; for many buyers, this makes your item more desirable. If the item is computer-related and the purchase price is between $200 and $600, coverage costs $99.99.

You can add a Warranty Services graphic to your sales page by going to the How to Offer Warranties page (**http://pages.ebay.com/help/warranty/how_to_offer.html**), reviewing the types of graphic banners that are available, and copying the HTML code for the one you want. You then copy the HTML code into the description for a sales item. You can also add the banner to your About Me and eBay Store pages.

## Don't Sell Anything Illegal

While I was working on the first edition of this book, the space shuttle Columbia broke up while entering Earth's atmosphere, dropping wreckage over several states. Incredibly, only a matter of hours after the disaster, supposed pieces of the shuttle were offered for sale on eBay. Those items were quickly removed by eBay. Two Texas residents were subsequently arrested and charged with theft of government property. Such charges carry maximum penalties of a $250,000 fine and ten years in prison.

This is a dramatic example of what can happen if you sell, or attempt to sell, the wrong things on eBay. Other items that might not obviously seem illegal can get you in trouble: on July 10, 2004, the *Charlotte Observer* (Charlotte, North Carolina) reported the attempted sale of songbird nests and eggs—a practice that can earn a seller prison time and a $250,000 fine (report available at **http://www.hiltonpond.org/eBayNestSalesMain.html**). You need to be aware of what you can't sell, and what your own home state considers to be prohibited items. You are subject not only to federal regulations but also to your own state's regulations governing business transactions. The following sections describe how to keep out of trouble by simply being aware of what you can't sell on eBay.

### Stay Away from Prohibited Items

Prohibited items are banned from sale from eBay. In some cases, trying to sell illegal items can get you in trouble with law enforcement authorities. Trying to sell other items may not be strictly illegal, but can get either you or eBay (or both of you) in trouble in other ways. Examples are shown in Table 16-1. The column on the right lists some items that you might not realize are prohibited on eBay.

| Obviously Prohibited Items | Not-So-Obvious Prohibited Items |
| --- | --- |
| Alcohol. However, you can sell alcohol on eBay if the container has not been opened, the buyer is over the age of 21, and the container is considered collectible, with a value exceeding the alcohol's retail price. In other words, rare bottles of wine or cans of beer that aren't available in retail stores can be sold. | Human parts and remains. Just about the only thing you can sell that contains human body parts on eBay are lockets or other jewelry that contain human hair, or skulls and skeletons that are used for educational purposes. Everything else is prohibited. |
| Counterfeit currency and stamps | Travel. Don't try to sell airline tickets, vacation packages, or lodging unless you're licensed to do so and are in the Seller Verify by SquareTrade Program. |
| Credit cards | Catalog sales. You can't list sales catalogs or web sites that sell items directly—unless you're trying to sell a 1901 Sears, Roebuck catalog or other collectible item, for example. |
| Drugs and drug paraphernalia | Postage meters. These are available only from licensed manufacturers. |
| Firearms, ammunition, replicas, and militaria | Stocks and other securities. These are regulated by the U.S. Securities and Exchange Commission; leave any selling to a broker and don't try to sell it yourself. However, you can sell business inventory, information on how to start a business, or domain names. You *can* sell old or collectible stock certificates for business entities that no longer exist. |
| Fireworks | Mailing lists and personal information. This includes not only the information itself but any software designed to send spam e-mail, too. |
| Satellite and cable TV descramblers | Plants and seeds. Some plants that are considered "exotic" or "noxious" are prohibited from sale by federal, state, or local laws. (See **http://www.aphis.usda.gov/npb/statenw.html** for a state-by-state list.) |
| Tobacco (however, you may be allowed to sell collectible tobacco packing on eBay if the package is unopened and your description states as much). | Animal and wildlife products. No, you can't sell your baby bunnies or kittens on eBay. You can't sell stuffed migratory birds such as ducks, geese, or owls, either. You can't sell animal pelts, bear-related products, or items that are made from genuine tortoise shell. The latter includes guitar picks, combs, or jewelry made from genuine tortoise shell. |

**TABLE 16-1**     Items Prohibited to Sell on eBay

16

*In addition to the items mentioned in Table 16-1, you cannot include links on your eBay listing to pages or web sites that offer merchandise for sale that is not permitted on eBay.*

Each of the categories in Table 16-1 has specific dos and don'ts that are too detailed to list here, and that change occasionally. Also keep in mind that the table only describes regulations that apply to eBay's U.S. site; regulations are different in other countries. Go to the Help page entitled What items may not be sold on eBay? (**http://pages.ebay.com/help/sell/questions/prohibited-items.html**) and click on the link for the item you're considering to see if it falls into the banned or questionable category.

*Even if your item containing alcohol falls within one of the exceptions to prohibited items on eBay, many states have regulations that prohibit the shipping of alcohol either to or from the state by an individual. Check with your state's commerce commission or Department of Commerce to make sure.*

## Stay Away from Questionable Items

eBay lists a type of sales item as "questionable" if you can sell it under certain narrowly defined circumstances. You'll find links to each item on the same Help page listed earlier (**http://pages.ebay.com/help/sell/questions/prohibited-items .html**). If you want to be really safe and steer clear of trouble, avoid selling these

## eBay Corners Market on Outrageous Sales Items

Some truly outrageous (and illegal) items have been put up for sale on eBay over the years. For instance, during the year 2000 presidential election, someone allegedly attempted to auction off votes on eBay as a political protest, which prompted an investigation by the U.S. Justice Department (read about it at **http:// www.cnn.com/2000/TECH/computing/08/18/internet.vote**). One California man attempted to sell his own family (**http://www.signonsandiego.com/news/ state/20030111-0449-ca-ebayfamily.html**). Human kidneys, used dentures, and souvenir debris from the World Trade Center and Pentagon have also gone up for auction (**http://abcnews.go.com/Technology/story?id=98268&page=1**). You can find out what your own home state does not allow you to sell by contacting your state's Department of Commerce.

items as well as the Prohibited Items mentioned in the preceding section. Some of the examples that I personally found surprising are listed here:

- **Artifacts**  Be especially careful if you describe a work of art or a craft item as being of Native American origin. You must be a member of a state or federally recognized Indian tribe yourself, according to the Indian Arts and Crafts Act.

- **Autographed items**  Autographs are frequently sold on eBay, but make sure the autograph you sell is genuine. You may want to contact one of the experts at **http://pages.ebay.com/help/community/auth-overview.html** to authenticate it.

- **Electronics equipment**  Scanners or radios that can receive cellular transmissions cannot be sold on eBay.

- **Used clothing**  Used clothing can be sold as long as it has been "thoroughly cleaned according to the manufacturer's instructions."

- **Weapons and knives**  Many types of knives can be sold on eBay. However, other weapons such as blackjacks, brass knuckles, or even metal replica hand grenades are prohibited.

## Get Notified of eBay Policy Changes

eBay's policies aren't written in stone. They change from time to time. If you sell a large quantity of items in a variety of categories, you need to know when the policies change. You have to change your user preferences to receive e-mail notifications of policy changes. Just follow these steps:

1. Go to the Change Notification Preferences page (**http://pages.ebay.com/ services/myebay/optin-login.html**).

2. Enter your User ID and password, and click Sign In Securely.

3. When the eBay Change Your Notification Preferences page appears, scroll down to the Legal and Other Emails section. Check the boxes next to User Agreement Changes and Privacy Policy Changes.

4. Click the Save Changes button.

The User Agreement Changes option tells you of any changes to the list of prohibited or questionable items. The Privacy Policy Changes option lets you know of any changes in the way you handle customer information, or in the way your own information is handled by eBay.

16

## Steer Clear of Shill Bidding

In 2004, three men were sentenced to prison terms for placing bids to artificially increase interest in paintings for sale on eBay. In one case, a Dutch bidder was induced to place a winning bid on a work by American abstract painter Richard Diebenkorn. One bidder was induced to place a winning bid of more than $135,000 by the fake or "shill" bids placed by the conspirators. To add insult to injury, the painting itself turned out to be fake. In February 2002, three individuals were arrested and charged with intentionally driving bids up to more than $1.3 million on some highly desirable René Lalique glass that was being auctioned on eBay, in an effort to inflate the final price.

Shill bidding occurs when individuals bid against one another with no intention of actually buying the item in question but rather with the goal of forcing serious buyers to bid higher and higher. Such activity, known as *shill bidding,* not only is prohibited on eBay, but is a federal offense as well. Breaking the Federal Wire Fraud statute is a serious offense involving the use of interstate commerce to defraud. The individuals were charged with wire fraud and could face five years in prison.

Shill bidding is one of the biggest threats to eBay's operation. Besides being illegal, it can destroy the trust that keeps online auctions running successfully. It might seem easy to set up shill bidding with a friend or relative, or even by setting up multiple User IDs, but the practice is so well known that savvy bidders can spot it readily. Bidders who consistently bid and never win are suspicious, and a bidder's history can be easily checked to reveal such patterns. In addition, even though you might use multiple User IDs, if you use the same computer to place bids, that computer has a unique identifier called an *IP address* that it uses to connect to the Internet, and eBay can use the IP address to determine who is actually placing the bids. If you think you have been the victim of shill bidding yourself, go to **http://pages.ebay.com/help/tp/programs-investigations.html**. Click the link **Shill bidding** under Selling Offenses to access a form you can use to report the offense.

 *A related activity, shill feedback, occurs when a seller who has been conducting shill bidding wins his or her own auction. Before quickly relisting the item, the seller leaves positive feedback for him or herself in an effort to inflate feedback ratings. Such activities mislead buyers and erode the level of trust and community spirit that keeps eBay going.*

## Lloyd's of London Insurance

Another eBay feature that helps to make transactions proceed smoothly is the Fraud Protection Program, which covers the transactions of all legitimate buyers.

The prestigious insurance company Lloyd's of London covers the high bidder/purchaser for $200 of the final auction price, after a $25 deductible.

For sellers, the Fraud Protection Program doesn't do anything. It doesn't protect you from bounced checks or nonresponsive buyers. It's just good to know the program exists, especially if a dispute occurs. Buyers, though, are only covered if they file a claim with their credit card company beforehand.

## Where to Find It

- **eBay User Agreement**
  **http://pages.ebay.com/help/community/png-user.html**
  Information on what you can and can't do on eBay, either as a buyer or seller.

- **Login page for creating a pre-approved buyers list**
  **http://cgi3.ebay.com/aw-cgi/eBayISAPI.dll?PreApproveBidders**
  Enter your User ID and password, then click Sign In, to begin the process of creating a list of pre-approved buyers for one of your sales items.

- **ID Verify Accept Terms page**
  **http://pages.ebay.com/services/buyandsell/idverify-terms.html**
  Start the process of having your identity verified by a third party so you can have an ID Verify logo added to your User ID.

- **BBB*OnLine***
  **http://www.bbbonline.org**
  Go here to obtain a BBB*OnLine* Reliability Seal.

- **SquareTrade**
  **http://www.squaretrade.com**
  Go here for dispute resolution or a SquareTrade Seal.

- **VeriSign's Digital IDs for Secure E-Mail page**
  **http://www.verisign.com/products/class1/index.html**
  Go here to obtain a Digital ID from VeriSign.

- **eBay Warranty Services**
  **http://pages.ebay.com/help/warranty/seller_overview.html**
  Information for eBay sellers on the Warranty Services program.

- **eBay Prohibited and Questionable Items**
  **http://pages.ebay.com/help/sell/questions/prohibited-items.html**
  Lists of items that eBay either has prohibited or considers "questionable."

# Chapter 17

## Fulfill Your Accounting and Tax Requirements

## How to…

- Organize your eBay business's back-office finances

- Track and meet your income and sales tax requirements

- Deduct your auction-related expenses

- Computerize your tax and accounting needs

- Locate professionals who can keep taxes from being taxing

As I write this, tax time is fast approaching. I'm dutifully gathering pay stubs, receipts, and slips of paper in order to present them to my accountant. Chances are you're doing much the same thing. But what about the profit you realize from your sales on eBay—the income that isn't documented by W-2s or Form 1099s? The truth is simple: income from your eBay business is subject to tax just like income from any other type of business activity. It doesn't matter whether eBay sales are your sole source of income or just a sideline. You are required to report money you make from auctions just as you would any other income.

The good news is that because you have income from your eBay business, you can deduct the expenses associated with that business. That includes the camera you use to photograph the items you sell; the computer you use to prepare the sales; the fees you pay to eBay; and much more. It's all a matter of keeping appropriate financial records. It can actually be fun to keep track of where your eBay business is at financially and save a few bucks at tax time as well. I'm neither a tax expert nor an accountant; I am a self-employed individual who is used to paying business taxes and accounting for business expenses. This chapter is intended to give basic advice on the kinds of tax and accounting issues you need to know about; you should consult a tax professional or accountant to get specific advice that applies to your own situation.

# What's Different about Being Self-Employed?

When I became a freelance writer, lots of things changed. Keeping track of money was one of the biggest changes—not only the source of the money, but how I make sure Uncle Sam gets his share. First of all, I have to pay taxes not once, but four times a year. I need to make an estimated tax payment based on the amount of taxes I think I'll have to pay at the end of the year. My tax accountant calculates how much this should be, and even sends me the proper vouchers to send in on a quarterly basis.

I run a sole proprietorship (a legal type of business classification described in Chapter 18), so I have to report income and investments on Schedule C of Form 1040, Profit or Loss from Business. I need to document both my income and all my business-related expenses.

A sole proprietorship is relatively simple to run. Some eBay entrepreneurs, like Bob Kopczynski (who runs Maxwell Street Market, and is profiled in Chapter 4), have chosen to incorporate or form a limited liability company, and they have employees as well. Things get far more complicated in terms of tax and accounting when you run a corporation: you need to withhold payroll tax from paychecks, pay payroll tax, issue W-2 forms, and much more. Bob has an accountant do the heavy lifting, though his wife, Katy, does day-to-day bookkeeping as well. There are, of course, benefits that go along with the extra work: you are shielded from personal liability in case one of your customers causes legal trouble; you can deduct some insurance costs; and because you have a team of employees, you can do more work and generate more income, too.

Doing my own bookkeeping and handling expenses and payments is more work than when I was a full-time office employee, but it's more satisfying, too. It's all part of running your own business. Whether you are a full-time eBay seller or make only a handful of sales a month, you can benefit by taking charge of your own bookkeeping and tax responsibilities.

*There are all kinds of formulas you can use to calculate your quarterly estimated tax payments, and all kinds of rules about what kinds of deductions you can take. I strongly recommend you hire an accountant to file your taxes for you. My accountant continually comes up with new ways to lower the taxes I have to pay.*

# Perform the Basic Accounting Practices

As eBay grows in popularity, the fact that many entrepreneurs like you are making good money by selling online is also becoming well known. In addition, eBay keeps records of all of your sales income. It's wise to establish some sort of regular record-keeping procedure, whether that procedure simply involves gathering all of your receipts and stuffing them in an envelope, entering data in your hand-held device, or writing your mileage down when you're driving to the post office.

By doing business online, you have a big advantage: You can print out a list of your sales from eBay at tax time so you can add up exactly what you've sold. It's a little more work to keep records of your expenses, and the prospect of doing accounting and

17

paying business taxes can seem intimidating. But it's not that hard, either. (If I can do it, anyone can, believe me.) It's a matter of keeping and storing receipts so you can add them up at tax time.

 *You don't have to take my word for all this. Consult the Internal Revenue Service's Publication 334,* Tax Guide for Small Business, *available at* **http://www.irs.gov/pub/irs-pdf/p334.pdf.**

## Cash-Basis vs. Accrual-Basis Accounting

Do your eyes glaze over when you see the terms "cash-basis" and "accrual-basis"? They're just two different ways of describing when your business was paid. Chances are you'll simply use the cash-basis method, but it's good to know that the two options exist, if only so that you can discuss them in an informed way with your accountant:

- **Cash-basis accounting**   You report income when you actually receive it and write off expenses when you pay them. This is the easy way to report income and expenses, and probably the way most new small businesses do it.

- **Accrual-basis accounting**   This method is more complicated than the cash-basis method, but if your online business maintains an inventory, you must use the accrual method. For instance, suppose your eBay business sells an inventory of surplus items. You report income when you actually receive the payment; you write down expenses *when services are rendered* (even though you may not have made the cash payment yet). For example, suppose 25 of your eBay sales are completed on June 31, and you ask your customers to get their payments to you by July 8. The payments don't all arrive, however, until July 15. You still record the income as having been received on July 8, when the payment was originally due. Accrual-basis accounting creates a more accurate picture of a business's financial situation. If a company is having cash-flow problems and is extending payment on some of its bills, cash-basis accounting provides an unduly rosy financial picture, whereas the accrual-basis method would be more accurate.

For eBay sellers who don't have a steady inventory, the cash-basis method is the one to use. But if you run a full-time eBay business and have a steady supply of stock from a wholesaler, ask your accountant if you should the accrual method.

NOTE   *You probably assume that the accounting period you're going to use is the same as the calendar year: January 1 to December 31. When you're running a business, however, you don't have to stick to the calendar necessarily. In this case, the business picks a date other than December 31 to function as the end of the fiscal year. Many large organizations pick a date that coincides with the end of their business cycle. Some pick March 31 as the end, others June 30, and still others September 30. If you use the fiscal-year method of accounting, you must file your tax return three and a half months after the end of the fiscal year. If the fiscal year ends on June 30, for example, you must file by October 15.*

## Practice Good Record-Keeping

It pays to be meticulous about keeping financial records. After all, the better your records are, the more accurate your estimated tax payments will be, and the more deductions you'll be able to take. In the long run, keeping good records can actually save you money. Besides that, you won't have a realistic picture of how your business is doing—whether all your effort is worthwhile, in other words—unless you can accurately compare how much you're making to how much it costs to generate that income.

When you record how much you pay for supplies, how much you pay in fees to eBay, and how much you are paid by your bidders and buyers, you're doing the same thing Bob Cratchit did in the Dickens story "A Christmas Carol"—it's called bookkeeping. Even if you hire someone like Bob to do the work for you, it pays to have at least a passing familiarity with bookkeeping terms such as assets, liabilities, income, and expenses.

You might think of the financial side of your eBay business as consisting of different financial accounts. Every time a financial event occurs, an account's balance either decreases or increases. When someone purchases one of your auction items and you deposit the payment, your bank account increases and the money people owe you decreases. The dual activity—one account goes up while another goes down—is known as *double-entry accounting*. This type of accounting makes use of standard types of business accounts:

- **Bank account**   Your income from sales—the good stuff.

- **Accounts receivable**   The amount that people owe you and that you expect to receive at some point—those checks that are in the mail, and that money in your PayPal account that hasn't yet been transferred to the bank.

17

- **Asset account**  The value of your business assets—your inventory, your equipment, and the items you currently have up for sale.

- **Expense account**  The amount you have allocated for expenses.

In double-entry accounting, any one business transaction affects two or more accounts, as illustrated in Table 17-1.

These somewhat dry concepts become more understandable if you take an online workshop such as the interactive presentation created by the Bank of America and provided on its online Resource Center (**http://www.va-interactive .com/bankofamerica/resourcecenter/**).

> TIP
>
> *Since you're already familiar with computers, you might want to use an accounting program to record your records, as described later in this chapter. You can also record expenses in a hand-held computing device if you have one. (The cost of purchasing such a device counts as a deductible business expense, of course.) Otherwise, one of the printed books that is specially designed for maintaining financial records can help. Go to your local office supply store and get a financial record book called a journal, which is set up with columns for income and expenses.*

## Record Income

Brick-and-mortar businesses receive invoices for their income. As an eBay businessperson, you're likely to get income from any number of sources: personal checks, PayPal transfers, or direct deposits to your bank account from credit card companies. This is probably the most enjoyable thing you can record in your accounting software or booklet.

| Event | Bank Account | Accounts Receivable | Asset Account | Expense Account |
|---|---|---|---|---|
| You make a sale | Increases | Decreases | No change | No change |
| You purchase supplies or equipment | Decreases | Increases | Increases | Increases |
| You buy inventory you plan to sell | Decreases | No change | Increases | No change |
| You incur a business-related expense | Decreases | No change | No change | Increases |

**TABLE 17-1**    A Double-Entry Accounting Example

*I've seen estimates (which probably aren't very scientific) to the effect that as many as 60 percent of eBay sellers don't pay taxes on what they make from auction sales. If you have income that you didn't pay taxes on, the IRS will label it unreported income, and you will have to pay taxes and possibly fines and penalties on it.*

The best way to record your income is to be systematic about it: Just how should you record your revenue? You can print out all the statements that PayPal sends to you and the records from your eBay auction management service, such as eBay Selling Manager or Marketworks, if you use one. For each item, write down a brief, informal statement that describes what was received and when it came in. This is a personal record that you may make on a slip of paper or even on the back of a canceled check. Be sure to include the following information:

- The date of the transaction

- The type of payment (PayPal, credit card, or check)

- The amount you were paid

- The name of your high bidder or buyer

## Don't Forget Your Business Assets

Every business has equipment of one sort or another that it uses to produce its goods or services. Such business equipment goes by the name *assets* in accounting jargon. As an eBay seller, you probably have assets such as:

- Your computer

- Your digital camera, scanner, or both

- Modems, hubs, cables, speakers, printers, and other computer-related equipment

- Packing materials: boxes, tape, packing peanuts, and the like

- Postage machines

You might have to *expense* (in other words, spread out over time) the original cost of the equipment that is expected to help you generate income over its useful life. Expensing the cost of an asset over the period of its "life span" is called *depreciation*. In order to depreciate an item, you estimate how many years you're going to use it

17

and then divide the original cost by the number of years. The result is the amount that you report in any given year. For example, if you purchase a digital camera that costs $1000, and you expect to use it in your business for five years, you expense $200 of the cost each year.

> TIP  *Also ask your accountant about the 179 deduction, which in 2004 enables you to recover up to $102,000 of equipment put in service that year.*

You need to keep records of your assets that include the following information:

- Name, model number, and description

- Purchase date

- Purchase price, including fees

- Date the item went into service

- Amount of time the item is put to personal (as opposed to business) use

File these records in a safe location along with your other tax-related information.

## Record Payments

If you scour flea markets and estate sales, you pay for the collectibles you sell on eBay. If you purchase from wholesalers, you pay (hopefully) a nominal fee for what you purchase, with the goal of making a profit by reselling on eBay. Such payments should be recorded for accounting purposes. In addition, like any online businessperson, you probably need to make regular payments to the company that gives you Internet access, and possibly to web page designers and computer technicians. If you hire employees to help you, the payment system becomes more involved.

Suppose you hire your cousin to handle shipping and packing and a neighbor to create auction listings. Your accountant is likely to bring up the question of how you pay such employees. You have two options: you can treat them either as full-time employees or as independent contractors. The IRS uses a stringent series of guidelines (see Publication 15A, *Employer's Supplemental Tax Guide,* available at **http://www .irs.gov/pub/irs-pdf/p15a.pdf**) to determine whether your helper is a contractor or a full-time employee. Hiring independent contractors rather than salaried workers is far simpler for you: you don't have to pay benefits to independent contractors, and you don't have to withhold federal and state taxes. Just be sure to get invoices from any independent contractor who works for you. If you have full-time employees whom you pay an hourly wage, things get more complicated, and you had best consult an accountant to help you set up the salary payments.

## Business Expenses

When you spend the day at the flea market or at a government auction, do you chow down at the local burger joint? Be sure to get a receipt for that lunch and file it away in your receipts envelope at the end of the day. Print out that receipt at the gas pump, and save receipts for meals and postage. They're all business expenses—costs that you incur in order to produce revenue—and you can deduct them at tax time.

Pulling together evidence of expenses doesn't have to be a high-tech matter. If you have a tablet PC or hand-held device, great. Otherwise, get a big folder and use it to hold any receipts, canceled checks, or credit card statements. Be sure your records include basic information such as:

- Date the expense occurred

- Name of the person or company that received payment from you

- Type of expense incurred (equipment, utilities, supplies, and so on)

# What about Sales Tax?

The question "Should I charge sales tax?" is one I hear all the time from people who conduct business online. There's no simple answer, because the question is continually being discussed by legislators and advocates of free commerce on the Internet. The question of whether sales tax should be assessed on out-of-state sales that occur online is continually being debated by legislators. The Internet Tax Freedom Act is still in effect at this writing, having been extended by the Internet Tax Non-Discrimination Act, which was signed into law in December 2004. It provides for a freeze on new taxes related to Internet access and e-commerce. It does not mean that states cannot collect sales tax on Internet sales—only that they can't enact new tax requirements.

At this writing, you are required to add sales tax only to in-state transactions—unless, of course, you hang your hat in one of the five states that doesn't collect sales tax at all: Montana, Alaska, Delaware, New Hampshire, and Oregon. If you live in one of the states that does require you to collect sales tax, you need to collect only from your customers who live in the same state where you reside.

17

*Most states require their merchants to charge sales tax not only on the purchase price but on shipping and handling charges as well. Check with your state to make sure. You'll find a list of links to state tax agencies at http://www.tannedfeet.com/state_tax_agencies.htm.*

## Deduce Your Business Deductions

All of the work required to keep your books, collect taxes, and prepare your taxes pays off at the moment when you add up your deductions. You can reduce your tax payments substantially by taking all of the deductions for which you are eligible (check with your accountant to make sure which ones qualify as deductions). These include the computer equipment you use to prepare your auction sales, the spaces where you do your computer work and store your inventory, and the fees associated with going online and completing transactions.

## If You Don't Report, You Can't Deduct

I know that many eBay sellers like to stay "under the radar." They don't want to talk publicly about how much they're making on the auction site because they don't want to report their income on their tax returns. I can understand the desire to have some tax-free income. However, this practice is not only risky and illegal, but it may not make sense fiscally, either.

Businesses don't always turn a profit. eBay businesses are no exception. When you report your eBay income, you gain the ability to deduct your eBay business expenses, too. You might well find that, at tax time, even though you made some income from your auction sales, your expenses might turn your overall picture into a loss. This is most likely to happen when you're starting out and you purchase new equipment such as a printer, computer, fax machine, second phone line, and the like. Even though you depreciate that equipment over time, you still might come out with a net deficit and not end up paying taxes on your eBay business—or if you do pay taxes, you might find that they're less than you think. To my mind, it's better to stay legal and take some deductions than to try to take your eBay business "off the tax rolls."

## Computer Equipment

It used to be that you had to depreciate computer equipment, but now you can deduct the cost all at once. Be sure to keep all of your receipts from the computer or electronics store or from the repair shop. If you buy digital cameras or computer-related components on eBay, be sure to print out the web page that shows your high bid or Buy It Now price (or the e-mail from the seller that shows the total cost, including shipping) so you have it for your records.

## Your Home Office

If you work principally at home, you can deduct part of your mortgage and home-related expenses—specifically, the part that's related to your business. If you work out of a home office and your office is, for example, 100 square feet in a 2000-square-foot house, you can deduct 5 percent of your home-related expenses.

 *If you intend to deduct your home office, the space must be used exclusively for work purposes. You can't mix personal computing activities there. Ask your accountant to explain the requirements to you in more detail.*

Don't forget the miles you drive to the post office, the trade show, the merchandise mart, the wholesale outlet, the estate sale or flea market where you buy things to sell, and other business-related driving. Postal fees definitely apply, as do the cost of subscribing to collector's magazines you use to research what you sell.

 *Keep a notebook in your car so you can record your mileage as you make trips to the post office or shipping store.*

## Internet Connections and Other Fees

Without some form of access to the Internet, you wouldn't have an eBay business at all. The monthly or yearly charges you pay for Internet access are deductible. So are these others:

- Part of your phone bill, if you use a dialup modem connection to get online, or if it includes DSL connection fees
- Part of your cellular phone bill, if you use your cell phone to check your eBay transactions or talk to customers
- Web hosting charges, if you run an online business web site

17

- Fees paid to a photo hosting service, if you use one that's different from your web hosting service

- Charges to an auction management service such as Marketworks or SpareDollar

- PayPal and eBay fees

# Find Accounting Help Online

If going to math class made you want to jump out the nearest window, maybe dealing personally with expenses, accounting periods, and income isn't your thing. Luckily, there are plenty of reputable professionals who would be delighted to have you as a client. Even luckier, the professional's services not only count as a business expense but can help you reduce your taxes as well. What's more, the time you save will enable you to give your undivided attention to running and promoting your online business.

On the other hand, you may be the ultimate do-it-yourselfer. Chances are, you won't have to enroll in a single business class. The following web sites offer the free instruction and advice that can make you into your own accountant before you can say, "one, two, three":

- **Accounting for everyone**    This site (**http://www.accountz.com/afeintro .html**) includes three free chapters of a longer instructional work that you can order on CD-ROM. The free content covers double-entry accounting, and recording debits and credits in a journal or ledger book.

- **The Entrepreneurs' Help Page**    As its name suggests, if you have your own business, this site is especially for you. It includes a Financial Records page (**http://www.tannedfeet.com/financial_records.htm**) that covers what you need to know about small business accounting.

- **EZ Accounting**    The CPA who set up this web site (**http://www .ezaccounting.com**), Timothy C. Stewart, charges $19.95 a year if you want to examine the site in detail. You can peek at a preview page, however, for free. His goal is to make it easy for beginning entrepreneurs to grasp the basics of accounting.

Where better to go to find accounting help than on eBay itself? Actually, you won't find accountants on eBay, but you will on its professional service partner, eLance. Just go to **http://www.elanceonline.com** and click **Accounting & Bookkeeping** (under Management & Finance). When I visited, more than 300 accountants were listed all

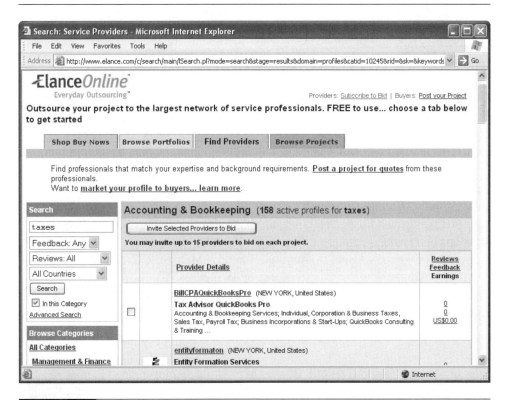

**FIGURE 17-1**    Get accountants to bid on your tax preparation or bookkeeping needs

over the world (see Figure 17-1). Many offer tax help and other business services. You post your project and get these tax preparers to bid on your job. (See Chapter 13 for more information on how eLance works.)

*The Tax and Accounting Sites Directory (**http://www.taxsites.com**) is a good starting point if you are looking on the Web for information related to tax requirements and links to accounting firms.*

# Use Accounting Software

Whether you use a shoebox, filing cabinet, envelope, or a messy spot on your shelf, you've got to keep copies of all of your auction transactions. I can hear you saying, "But eBay keeps all the records for me on its site." There are two flaws in this argument. First, you can't depend on eBay to maintain your sales records for years at a time. Second, if you are audited, there's no guarantee the IRS will consider a web

17

## Take Your Business Questions to the eBay Community

You can get help with just about every aspect of running an eBay business if you turn to one of the many discussion forums and user groups that comprise the eBay community. Accounting and taxes are no exception. In eBay Groups, you'll find a forum called Accounting & eBay (**http://groups.ebay.com/forum .jspa?forumID=8166**). It's a great place to turn if you have tax or bookkeeping-related questions, keeping in mind that the members offering advice most likely are not professional accountants.

Another group, the Excel & Accounting Software Support Forum (**http:// groups.ebay.com/forum.jspa?forumID=100004054**), has been set up by the eBay seller with the User ID katiyana. She sells Microsoft Excel templates that help eBay sellers track their income and expenses. You'll find them in her eBay Store (**http://stores.ebay.com/Katiyanas-Collectibles**) by clicking the category link **New eBay Seller Services**.

page an adequate financial record. Be sure to print out receipts related to your sales, including postage, shipping, and insurance. Also track all of your eBay final value fees and other fees you have to pay to get online and do business. Print out your eBay sales summary so you have a record on hand in case eBay servers go offline or the information is archived.

What, then, do you do with all of those facts and figures when you need to calculate your taxes? For many people, the best alternative is simply to push a few buttons, choose a few menu options, and let an accounting program do the heavy lifting. Accounting software can definitely make that part of your financial life easier.

A good software package can help save time when it comes to accounting and tax preparation for small businesses. All such packages let you record income and expenses and prepare business reports. For instance, QuickBooks by Intuit is also highly recommended by many accountants and small business owners, as are the packages described in the section that follows.

## Pick the Package That's Best for You

Accounting programs are among the most highly competitive types of software on the market today. Each year, it seems, Microsoft, Intuit, and MYOB come out with new, souped-up editions of their software, each designed to have more features than the last. On top of that, most of the products come in several versions, each with a different set of features. Which program is right for you? Keep in mind that you're not simply trying to balance your checkbook, but you need to track accounts receivable and possibly employee salaries and payroll taxes. It's a good idea to pick the version of an accounting program that enables you to track business finances. Table 17-2 provides you with some features to compare.

The well-known packages described in this section have plenty of features and add-ons. Programs such as Microsoft Money and Quicken, for example, let you create customizable home pages that you can configure to provide up-to-the minute reports on your stock holdings. They also help you with financial planning.

| Product | Web Site URL | Features |
|---|---|---|
| Quicken Premier Home & Business | **http://www.quicken.com** | Oriented toward home and personal finance needs. Gives you a place to track mileage and receivables. Includes a merchant account service so that you can receive credit card payments. |
| QuickBooks Basic | **http://www.quickbooks.com** | Oriented toward small business needs. Helps you back up your data; gives you access to an online Help & Support Center. Lets you track your inventory. |
| Peachtree First Accounting | **http://www.peachtree.com** | Specifically designed for home users who are starting up a small business. Integrated to work with Microsoft Office products. Provides a variety of business services you can use online, such as payroll, tax filing, and bill payment. |
| Microsoft Money Small Business | **http://www.microsoft.com/ money/default.mspx** | Ideal for users who do online banking. Enables you to track payroll, prepare taxes, and integrate database information with Microsoft Outlook. |
| MYOB AccountEdge | **http://www.myob.com** | AccountEdge is especially designed for Mac OS X users. Versions specific to the financial requirements of different countries are available, including the United States, United Kingdom, Australia, New Zealand, and Malaysia. |

**TABLE 17-2**   Accounting Software Features

17

Since I find the prospect of doing my own accounting downright intimidating, I don't use accounting software myself. The only program that doesn't scare me half to death is a simple shareware product by OWL Software called OWL Simple Business Accounting 2 (**http://www.owlsoftware.com/sba.htm**). It doesn't have a lot of automated gimmicks; it doesn't connect to a web site automatically to get new features; it doesn't coordinate with your bank account online. All it does is provide you with a way to create accounts and enter income and expenses, and then generate reports that you can use to prepare your taxes.

## Keep Your Books Online

In addition to purchasing and installing individual software programs, many of the commercial accounting programs have an online version. A site like QuickBooks Online Edition enables you to keep all of your books online. Although it costs $19.95 per month for this service, the advantage is that you don't have to download new versions of the software as they become available—and accounting programs are so highly competitive that new versions tend to appear virtually every year. You can try out the service for 30 days before you actually commit to buying it. Just follow these steps:

1. Connect to the QuickBooks Online Edition web site (**http://quickbooks .intuit.com/commerce/catalog/product.jhtml**).

2. Click Online Edition on the left side of the page.

3. Click Buy Now—even if you only want to try the online version rather than purchase it.

4. Click Try It For Free.

5. The next page instructs you to log in by creating a username and password, and describing your business. When you are done, click **Create Company**. When the Startup Interview page appears, click **Start Free Trial**.

6. When the next page appears, click **Install Active X File Now**.

7. If an alert dialog box appears asking if you want to download files, click **Yes**. You need the files to run QuickBooks Online Trial Edition.

8. When the files have been downloaded, click **Continue**. Your home page on the QuickBooks Online Edition web site appears (see Figure 17-2).

**FIGURE 17-2**    For a monthly fee, you can keep your accounting information online.

CAUTION    *QuickBooks Online Edition or any online accounting service works best if you have a broadband connection and are connected to the Internet all the time. You also need to realize that, when you use an online service to keep your financial records, you put a big level of trust in the web site that you use. After all, it is holding your financial data on its web site, not yours. Although such sites should and do protect your information, if a hacker manages to break in, your information could be compromised. In contrast, if you install and use accounting software on your computer, you control where it's located and how it's stored. It's also up to you to protect your files and make sure hackers can't break into your computer.*

17

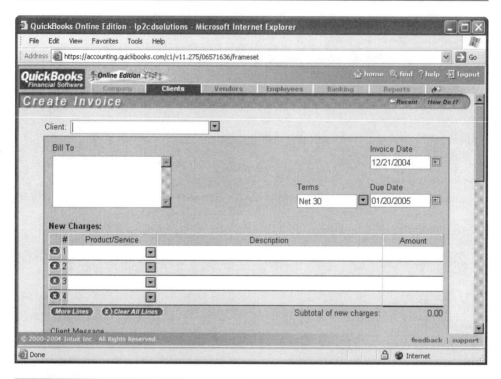

**FIGURE 17-3**   The QuickBooks Online site can provide you with tax forms and help with day-to-day accounting, too.

Once you have an account established online, you can use the site to print tax forms, handle payroll records, or print invoices, as shown in Figure 17-3.

## How Long Should You Keep Your Records?

The short answer to this question is: as long as you can. If you have the room to keep ten years' worth of tax records and receipts, do so to be on the safe side. However, the IRS, in its Publication 583, *Starting a Business and Keeping Records,* has more specific recommendations, shown in Table 17-3.

TIP    *You'll find Publication 583 online at **http://www.irs.gov/pub/irs-pdf/p583 .pdf**. In fact, you can view and print out a wide variety of tax forms and informational brochures from the IRS web site at **http://www.irs.gov/ formspubs/index.html.***

| Situation | How Long to Keep Records |
|---|---|
| You owe employment tax (if you have employees) | 4 years after tax is due or paid |
| You receive property | Until the year in which you dispose of the property |
| You did not report income that you should have reported, and it amounts to more than 25 percent of your gross income | 6 years |
| You filed a fraudulent tax return | No limit |
| You failed to file a tax return | No limit |

**TABLE 17-3**    Guidelines for Keeping Business Records

# Where to Find It

■ **IRS Small Business and Self-Employed One-Stop Resource**
**http://www.irs.ustreas.gov/businesses/small/index.html**
Tax requirements, forms, and information especially for small business owners.

■ **IRS** *Tax Guide for Small Business*
**http://www.irs.gov/pub/irs-pdf/p334.pdf**
A complete publication you can view online or print out that explains how to file taxes when you have business income or expenses.

■ **The Entrepreneurs' Help Page list of state tax agencies**
**http://www.tannedfeet.com/state_tax_agencies.htm**
Links to state tax agency web sites where you can look up sales tax requirements.

# Chapter 18

# Keep Your eBay Business Legal

## How to...

- Avoid violating someone's copyright when listing auctions

- Protect your eBay business's trade name and copyright

- Decide on the right legal form for your eBay business

- Pay your local business licensing fees

- Protect your customers' privacy

Rules of conduct are what make eBay work as well as it does; all members have to play by the same rules. If they didn't, auction chaos would result. Sales could end at any time; bidders could keep bidding after the ending time; people might pay with peanuts rather than dollars. Just as you observe eBay's rules, you need to observe the rules set down by local and federal governments. If you don't keep your eBay business legal, chaos might not result on eBay, but a sort of chaos might hamper your ability to do business at all. You might get sued; you might get negative feedback; you might even be charged with breaking the law.

Chances are you're not a lawyer. You likely started out on eBay in the hope of making a few extra bucks, and you probably don't have experience navigating the legal requirements for businesses. This chapter discusses some commonsense principles to follow to avoid legal trouble. You need to be aware of the laws that govern the type of business you operate, avoid stepping on someone's trademarked or copyrighted material, pay necessary fees, and observe the privacy of those you meet on eBay. If you do these simple things, your business will run not only smoothly but profitably, and you'll be able to head off potential trouble before it occurs.

 *This chapter is just a starting point for understanding the legal requirements of your eBay business. There's no substitute for contacting an attorney who can help you prepare privacy statements, guide you through the incorporation process, and help you register trademarks. Do a search for "e-commerce attorney" on Google or in Yahoo!'s directory to find a lawyer who specializes in doing business on the Internet.*

# Copyright and Trademark Concerns

When you scan the pages and pages of auction listings on eBay, you're likely to see parts of auction descriptions that attract your attention. I've had sellers tell me, "I saw that graphic of a little doll, so I copied it and put it on my page," or, "I thought that description was really good, so I copied it and just pasted it onto my description."

Such copying might seem harmless, and it's certainly easy to do. In most cases, people don't complain if they see something that used to be on one of their web pages now residing on someone else's page. But many people *do* become understandably irritated if they see that their images or text have been "lifted." If someone does complain, you should know that, technically, they have a right to do so—a copyright, in fact. This section examines two legal pitfalls you need to avoid: copyright violations and trademark infringements.

## Don't Do a Copy-Wrong

*Copyright* is a legal term that describes the right of the creator of a creative work (or a person or entity to whom the creator has sold the copyright) to control how it is copied. If someone uses permission covered by copyright without asking the copyright owner, the copyright owner can sue and be compensated for any losses that have been suffered. The owner can even obtain a court order (called an *injunction*) that forces the infringing party to stop.

It often surprises people to learn that everything that is published on the Web, just like everything else that is considered intellectual property, is automatically covered by copyright law, whether it is accompanied by a formal copyright notice (such as the one at the bottom of the eBay auction listing shown in Figure 18-1) or not. So if you're in a hurry and need to create 20 or 30 auction descriptions at a time, don't simply copy something from another auction listing and paste it on yours. Likewise, don't try to sell something like pirated software or entertainment material that, itself, represents an object that infringes someone's copyright.

**FIGURE 18-1**  Images and text published on the Web are protected by copyright law, regardless of whether a copyright notice such as this is posted.

18

# eBay Sellers Can Be Sued

Can you be sued for attempting to sell products on eBay that were created by someone else who holds a copyright or trademark on those items? The answer is yes, depending on the copyright holder and depending on whether the items were copied illegally. Here are three examples of the sorts of legal morasses in which eBay sellers were embroiled in recent years:

- In December 2004, a U2 iPod that had seven albums from a group called Negativland added to it was pulled from sale by eBay after Apple Computer complained that the sale violated its copyright on the iPod—even though intellectual property attorneys interviewed by *Wired* magazine (**http://www.wired.com/news/digiwood/0,1412,65959,00 .html**) saw no reason why any copyright had been violated. The lesson: even if there's a hint of a possible trademark infringement or copyright violation, eBay will end a sale.

- Also in December 2004, the eyewear manufacturer Silhouette Optical Ltd. was awarded $304,554.30 in U.S. District Court in Manhattan after an eBay seller operating as Marina's Boutique Store had a preliminary injunction filed against her to block false advertising of products being sold under the trademarked Silhouette brand. The injunction stopped the store from using any Silhouette trademarks when selling eyewear falsely claimed to have been made by Silhouette.

- In October 2002, the Digital Millennium Copyright Act was cited when eBay tried to prevent a seller from distributing his own band's music on the auction site. George Ziemann certainly holds the copyright to his music (at least, until he signs it away to a publisher). But the problem was that he was using recordable CDs to distribute his band's album. eBay automatically conducts sweeps of its sales to see if music is being sold this way. It was a case of mistaken identity—eBay didn't realize that Ziemann was trying to sell his own music—but a series of warning messages from eBay irked Ziemann and he reportedly decided to stop selling his music on eBay altogether. The lesson is that eBay will contact you if you try to sell music, movies, or other materials on recordable media like CDs or DVDs—even if it's your own material.

If you do sell something that's in violation of copyright infringement, don't expect eBay to be legally liable. In a 2001 legal case, *Hendrickson v. eBay*, a federal judge in Los Angeles held that eBay was protected from secondary liability after a seller sold a pirated DVD at auction. In other words, if you sell something that's been pirated or that is copyrighted, *you're* liable.

*You can read about the copyright infringement case, as reported by* USA Today, *at* **http://www.usatoday.com/tech/columnist/2001/09/13/sinrod.htm**.

# Determine Who Owns the Copyright

If you need to determine who owns the copyright on a printed work or other product, you only have to look at the copyright notice or the trademark. To check someone's trademark, you can go to the Trademark Electronic Search System (TESS) of the U.S. Patent and Trademark Office web site (go to **http://www.uspto.gov/main/trademarks.htm** and click **Search trademarks**), as shown here, and search for the legal owner of the trademark.

18

You can sell used books and records at auction as long as they are legitimate copies rather than pirated or bootlegged versions. But because they are copyrighted material, the way in which you sell those items can possibly get you in trouble. Here are some suggestions for avoiding copyright infringement trouble:

- Don't scan the trademarked logo on a book, record, or product and use it in your auction listing. (However, you can photograph an item, including its manufacturer's logo, and put that in your listing.)

- Don't copy the text or part of a record and include it in your auction listing, or in a link from your auction listing.

- Create your own description of the item, rather than copying promotional descriptions from the dust jacket (if it's a book) or the cover (if it's a record, CD, or DVD).

If you are selling the types of items that are frequently counterfeited, such as an item that bears the autograph of a famous person, it may be to your advantage to describe where you got the property and why you have a right to sell it—in other words, to certify its authenticity by stating how you came to own it. You might say you "bought it at a store, and I can provide the original receipt of purchase." Some eBay business owners pay a licensing fee to sell material that was created by someone else. In Figure 18-2, a seller makes a statement, at the end of a sales description, to tell viewers that the artwork on the item being sold has been licensed from the original artist; in other words, it's not a copyright violation.

If you are accused of violating a copyright, be sure to consult with an attorney before you respond.

## Avoid Trademark Infringement

When you're in business, you are involved in *trade*. A business is known, whether on eBay or in the marketplace, by its *trade name*—for example, the name "eBay" itself. A trade name can also be *trademarked,* which means that the owner has taken the extra step of registering the trade name so it can't be used without permission. Commercial entities protect their trade names and trademarks, and frequently court battles erupt over who can legally use a name or something very close to it (such as the creators of the operating system Lindows, who were sued for trademark infringement by Microsoft, owners of the trade name Windows; Microsoft eventually paid the makers of Lindows more than $20 million to stop using the name).

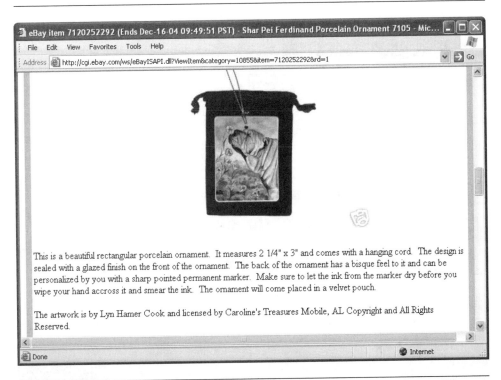

**FIGURE 18-2**   If you sell items containing original art, make sure you have a license to do so.

What, you ask, is the difference between copyright and trademark? Copyright is used to protect the creator's ownership of creative works such as writing, art, software, video, or cinema (but not names, titles, or short phrases). It provides the copyright owner a way to protest or seek damages in case someone copies the works without permission. A trademark is a way of controlling the use of distinctive words, symbols, slogans, or other things that serve to identify products or services in the marketplace.

What does all this mean for your fledgling auction concern? It means you need to be careful when you sell items that bear someone else's trade name or logo. A company can trademark any visual element that accompanies a particular tangible product or line of goods and serves to identify and distinguish it from products sold by other sources. In other words, a trademark is not necessarily just for a business's trade name. In fact, you can trademark letters, words, names, phrases, slogans, numbers, colors, symbols, designs, or shapes. Just look at eBay's home page in Figure 18-3 and see how many trademarked symbols you can spot.

**18**

Registered trademark    This phrase is trademarked

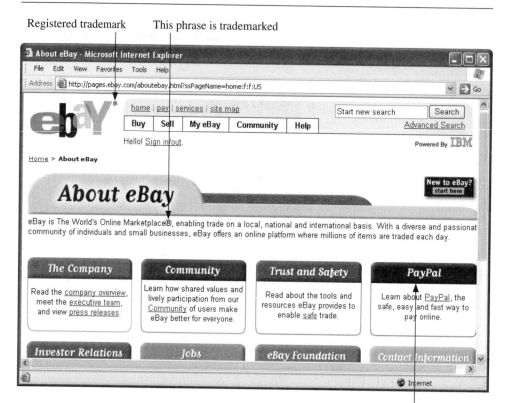

PayPal's name is often trademarked (even though
the ™ designation is not visible in this instance)

**FIGURE 18-3**    Be careful about how you handle trademarks when you sell a trademarked
item.

The lesson for you, the auction seller, is this: you can sell items that are related to
a trademark holder, and you won't be violating eBay's listing policies if you include
the trademarked logo, name, or phrase associated with that item's manufacturer in
your auction description. For instance, eBay's policies state that you can mention that
you are selling "a For Dummies™ book" in the text of your description on Half
.com and you can reproduce the actual For Dummies™ logo as a graphic image that
accompanies your textual description. The policy states that you can't use another
brand name or domain name that's not related to the item you are actually selling. But
I would go a step further and urge you to be careful about reproducing a trademarked

logo as a graphic image in your description. You might find that trademark owners frown on anyone but them using their logo(s) in *any* situation.

*For more details, read eBay's Brand Name Misuse Policy at* **http://pages .ebay.com/help/policies/brand-name.html***.*

Because eBay cannot check every one of the items sold on its site for copyright or trademark infringement, it created the Verified Rights Owner (VeRO) program. VeRO enlists the help of eBay members themselves, who report sales that infringe upon the copyright, trademark, or other rights of third parties. VeRO program participants and other rights owners can report infringing items and have such items removed. You can become a member of the VeRO program yourself by filling out the application for membership at **http://pages.ebay.com/help/community/notice- infringe2.pdf**. You can view a list of VeRO members' About Me pages at **http:// pages.ebay.com/help/community/vero-aboutme.html**. The members listed are companies and individuals who are concerned about protecting their trademarks and copyrighted items; you should be careful about trying to sell anything associated with any company or individual included on the VeRO list, because they are especially likely to complain.

## Add Digital Watermarks

You can protect your auction images and graphics through a process called *digital watermarking*. This process involves adding copyright or other information about the image's owner to the digital image file. The information added may or may not be visible. An application called ImageBridge by Digimarc (**http://www.digimarc .com**), which functions as a plug-in application with the popular graphics tools Adobe Photoshop (**http://www.adobe.com**) and Paint Shop Pro (**http://www.corel .com**), is one of the most widely used watermarking tools.

## Acceptable Use Policies

You should always be aware of acceptable use policies set up by agencies that control what goes out online. Usually, the company that hosts your web site has a set of acceptable use guidelines spelling out what kind of material you can and can't publish. For example, America Online has its own policies for its members who create home pages through AOL.

In the case of auction listings, the policy that matters is eBay's User Agreement (**http://pages.ebay.com/help/policies/user-agreement.html**). Have you actually read this agreement? Some pertinent acceptable use policies in the eBay User Agreement are provided here:

■ **Section 6.2(c)**   You agree that what you sell shall not "infringe any third party's copyright, patent, trademark, trade secret or other proprietary rights or rights of publicity or privacy."

■ **Section 6.2(i)(cc)**   You agree that the descriptions of the items you sell shall not "link directly or indirectly to or include descriptions of goods or services that...are concurrently listed for sale on a web site other than eBay's (this does not prevent linking to or advertising an eBay item from another web site)."

■ **Section 7(ii)**   You agree that you will not "copy, reproduce, alter, modify, create derivative works from, distribute or publicly display any content (except for Your Information) from the Site without the prior expressed written permission of eBay and the appropriate third party, as applicable."

 **File an Application with the U.S. Patent and Trademark Office**

Once you have made sure no one else is using the word, phrase, or graphic image you want to trademark, you can file an application with the U. S. Patent and Trademark Office online by following these steps:

1. Start up your browser and go to the Trademark Electronic Application System (TEAS) Home Page (**http://www.uspto.gov/teas/index.html**). The page contains instructions on how to either fill out your application online or print out the application form and mail it in to the Patent and Trademark Office.

2. Click **Apply for a NEW mark** under Forms.

3. A page with a list of application forms appears. Click **Trademark/ Servicemark Application, Principal Register**.

4. Fill out the Trademark/Service Mark Application Form Wizard page, read the Privacy Policy Statement at the bottom of the page, and then click Next.

**5.** Fill out the Trademark/Service Mark Application form, shown here. Note that this form asks for the legal form of your business; the options are described in "Decide on a Legal Form for Your Business," later in this chapter. Be sure to include your credit card data (so that you can pay the $335 per form application fee) and the electronic signature fields at the bottom of the application.

**6.** If you want to trademark an image of a symbol or logo, click the **Attach an Image** link. A new page appears that lets you specify the image.

**7.** Click **Validate Form**. If you filled out all the fields correctly, a Validation screen appears. If not, you return to the original form page so that you can correct it.

**8.** Print out the form for your records, and then click Submit.

If the process is successful, you see a confirmation screen and receive an e-mail acknowledgement of your submission. Do not be discouraged if months pass by without a response; such delays are common, and the process can take 24 months. Trademark applications are often returned without approval for one reason or another because the Trademark Office has raised a question about part of the application form. If that happens, you probably need to go to a lawyer who knows trademark law and can complete the application process successfully.

18

*In addition, be sure to review the Listing Policies for Sellers (**http://pages .ebay.com/help/policies/ia/listing_policies_for_sellers.html**) for more dos and don'ts of which you need to be aware when creating your auction descriptions.*

## Protect Your Own Trade Name

To avoid getting sued for trademark infringement and having to change your trade name or even pay damages if you lose, you should conduct a trademark search before choosing a name for your business. A trademark search is an investigation whose goal is to discover any potential conflicts between your trade name (the name by which your business is known in a marketplace such as eBay) and someone else's. Ideally, you should do the search before you actually use your trade name or register for an official trademark.

*You can determine whether someone has already trademarked the name you want to use. Just visit one of the U.S. Patent and Trademark Depository Libraries (which are listed at **http://www.uspto.gov/go/ptdl/ptdlib_1.html**). This approach can be time consuming, but the price is right (it doesn't cost anything). You can also pay a professional search firm to research a trademark for you. Professional search firms are listed in the Yellow Pages under Trademark Consultants or Information Brokers and typically charge between $25 and $50 per trademark searched.*

Just to make things a little more complicated, a trade name can be a trademark even if it hasn't been registered with the U. S. Patent and Trademark Office. Not only that, but each state has its own set of laws establishing when and how trademarks can be protected in addition to federal trademark law. You can obtain trademark rights in the states in which your trademark is actually used, but you also need to file an application with the U. S. Patent and Trademark Office.

# Decide on a Legal Form for Your Business

*You* know that you run an eBay business. So do your customers. To describe your business to city and county agencies, however, you need to formally declare its legal form. The legal form of a business is a designation that is recognized by taxing and licensing agencies. You have a number of options to choose from, and the choice can affect the amount of taxes you pay and your liability in case of loss. The following sections describe the alternatives.

# Should You Incorporate?

Many eBay sellers have decided to incorporate to reduce personal liability in case of business debt or other obligations, such as Bob Kopczynski, who was profiled in Chapter 4, and Mike Morin of Wooden Nickel Trading Company, who is profiled later in the chapter. Forming a corporation isn't straightforward. You *can* file the necessary papers yourself, but do you really want to? You'll almost certainly want a lawyer to lead you through the process. Plus, you have to comply with the regulations made by federal and state agencies that oversee corporations.

Despite these downsides, you may want to consider incorporation for the following sorts of reasons:

- When you incorporate, you separate your business from the people who own and operate it. As a result, the company's managers (including you) are shielded from personal liability in terms of debts and obligations.

- If you run a big-time auction operation and hire employees to help you get sales online and out the door, you can set up retirement and health insurance plans for those individuals (including yourself).

- It's easier to transfer ownership from one shareholder to another.

Once you decide to incorporate, you next have to pick one of two options: a C corporation or a subchapter S corporation. The latter is the most likely choice for small businesses, whether they are auction concerns or not.

## Subchapter S Corporations

Liability protection is the big benefit of forming a subchapter S corporation. This form of incorporation enables start-up businesses that encounter losses early on to offset those losses against their personal income. Subchapter S is intended for businesses with fewer than 75 shareholders. Another advantage: the income the S corporation gains is subject only to personal tax, not corporate tax.

Sounds great, doesn't it? Before you start looking for a lawyer to get you started, consider that in an S corporation, like a C corporation, you must pay an annual corporate tax, and the process of filing for S corporation status can take weeks or even months. You also have to elect shareholders and officers of your company, such as a secretary, hold an annual meeting, then file the notes from that meeting. For many small businesses run by a single individual, the "officers" and "shareholders" are family members. A quick conversation between you and your attorney might suffice for the "notes" taken at a "meeting." In any case, the prospect can be daunting

18

for a lone entrepreneur who's just starting out and has only a few dozen sales a month, so it's advisable to wait until you have enough income to hire an attorney and pay incorporation fees before you seriously consider incorporating, even as an S corporation.

## C Corporations

Big-time businesses, rather than small auction sales operations, choose to become C corporations. I mention C corporations only in passing so that you know what they are. Profits are taxed at the corporate level and at the shareholder level. (The fact that double taxation occurs means that you need a tax professional to handle your finances.) C corporations tend to be large and have lots of shareholders. In order to incorporate, all stockholders and shareholders must agree on the name of the company, the choice of the people who will manage it, and many other issues.

## Limited Liability Corporations

The limited liability corporation (LLC) combines aspects of both S and C corporations. Limited liability corporations have a number of attractive options that make them good candidates for small businesses. These options include the following:

- Income and losses are shared by the individual investors, who are known as *members.*

- Members are subject to limited liability for debts and obligations of the LLC.

- LLCs receive favorable tax treatment.

The disadvantage is that it is neither cheap nor easy to create an LLC. The forms needed to create this entity cost $500, and an attorney's fees to prepare those forms and file them are in addition to that cost. The responsibilities of LLC members are spelled out in an operating agreement, an often complex document whose preparation requires hiring an attorney who is knowledgeable in LLCs.

# Consider a Sole Proprietorship

When I started employing myself, I had to pay a $10 fee to the Secretary of State to register my business as a sole proprietorship. In return, I received a certificate that made me feel like I had "arrived."

In a *sole proprietorship,* you're the only boss. You make all the decisions and you get all the benefits. On the other hand, you take on all the problems that arise, too. You don't have liability protection; if you are sued, you may be 100 percent liable if a judgment is made against you. This is the simplest and least expensive type of business because you can run it yourself. You don't need an accountant

## eBay Bestsellers
## Seller Finds That "Inc." Reduces Red Ink

Mike Morin is the owner, operator, and president of Wooden Nickel Trading Co., a brick-and-mortar store located in Bakersfield, California with a presence online (**http://wntconline.com/**). The initials of his company's name translate into his eBay User ID (wntc). The business sells "anything from video games to diamonds and gold" on eBay. A member of eBay since 1997, Morin has chalked up a feedback rating of more than 10,000 and PowerSeller status.

As the owner of both a physical storefront and an eBay business, legal concerns are naturally important to Morin. Each of wntc's listings on eBay bears the following unobtrusive copyright notice buried in the green border that encloses his descriptions:

© Wooden Nickel Trading Co. All Rights Reserved 2003

Early on in his eBay business career, Morin did encounter other members who reused his images and violated his copyright. He says this has become less of a problem since digital cameras have become so affordable.

Mike decided to incorporate for both the liability and the tax benefits. He does have an attorney with whom he confers two or three times each year. But he points out that he was able to obtain California S corporation status for his company with the help of his accountant for about $800.

Morin also had to apply for several licenses in order to do business in California. He obtained a City License and a Fictitious Business Name License from the city of Bakersfield (the latter is required if a business's name does not contain all the names of its owners) and a Second-Hand Dealers License from the state.

or lawyer to help you form the business (though it helps), and you certainly don't have to answer to partners or stockholders. To declare a sole proprietorship, you may have to file an application; check with your local county clerk.

## Opt for a Partnership

I don't have to tell you how much work it is to buy antiques or other items, take them home, describe and photograph them, sell them at auction, and complete the transaction. It makes sense to share the work (and the benefit) with another person. You might want to draw up a formal partnership agreement that spells out how business decisions are made and how any disputes that arise should be

18

settled. You're well advised to have an attorney prepare this and other papers that are needed to create a partnership, and do clarify procedures to be followed in case one partner wants to leave.

In a partnership, all partners are held personally liable for losses. The partners share the risk and profit with each other. Ideally, your partners bring skills to the endeavor that complement your own contributions. One obvious advantage to a partnership is that you can discuss decisions and problems with your partner. The rate of taxes that each partner pays is based on his or her percentage of income from the partnership.

# Comply with Licensing and Trade Restrictions

Even if you decide not to turn your auction business into MyVeryOwnAuction, Inc., you'll probably have to process paperwork of one sort or another. Every online business has to pay license fees to local agencies and observe restrictions that limit what it can buy or sell.

## Pay Your License Fees

Sure, you can set up shop in your basement and start hauling boxes of collectibles in and out. To be on the safe side, check with your city, county, or state licensing and zoning offices to make sure you aren't breaking a rule by doing so. Trade associations for your profession often have a wealth of information about local regulations as well. Also, check with your local chamber of commerce. If you fail to apply for a permit or license, you may have to pay a fine.

A small business—even a one-person operation that makes a few extra bucks each month on eBay—may need to conform to various local regulations, including:

- **Taxes**  This shouldn't surprise you. Some cities tax small businesses as well as business assets such as office furniture and (uh-oh) computer equipment.

- **Zoning**  Your city or town government may have *zoning ordinances* that prevent you from conducting business in an area that is zoned for residential use, or it may charge you a fee to operate a business out of your home. This policy varies by community; be sure to check with your local zoning department.

- **Doing Business As**  If your business name is different from your own name, you may have to file a Doing Business As (DBA) certificate and publish a notice of the filing in the local newspaper. Check with your city or county clerk's office for more information.

## Sales Permits

As you learned in Chapter 17, you need to collect, report, and pay sales tax on sales you make to individuals who live in the same state where you do business. In addition, you may need to obtain a sales permit for each place where you do business.

## Reseller Certificates

Chances are you are not the original producer of the items you sell on eBay. Like so many other eBay sellers, you are reselling things that were made by many different manufacturers at widely varying times in the deep dark past. If that's the case, you may need to obtain a reseller certificate. Usually, you only need a reseller certificate if you sell large numbers of items to wholesale distributors—but check with your local agencies to make sure.

## City Business Licenses

In addition, you may need to obtain one or more licenses to operate legally. If the business is located within an incorporated city limits, a license must be obtained from the city; if it is outside the city limits, then from the county. For more information, contact the county or city office in your area.

## Certificate of Occupancy

If you plan to occupy a new or used building for your office space or to hold your auction inventory, you may need a certificate of occupancy. For more information, contact the county or city office in your area. Also check out the Small Business Administration web site (**http://www.sba.gov**), which includes licensing information for individual U.S. states as well as tips and advice on business planning, taxes, and legal aspects of starting a business.

# Maintain Your Own and Your Buyers' Privacy

Any businesses with a Web presence need to address the issue of customer privacy. A web-based business targeted at consumers may face more stringent requirements with regard to privacy issues and a higher level of scrutiny by federal agencies (such as the Federal Trade Commission) and state agencies. Furthermore, federal and state statutes limiting the collection and use of information from children, like the 1998 Children's Online Privacy Protection Act, may also come into play, more so for B2C-oriented businesses than for B2B-oriented businesses. In other words, if you sell something to a child and you collect that child's personal information,

18

you could technically be in violation of the Online Privacy Protection Act. If you sell things that kids might buy, you may want to tell people that they have to have their parents present, or remind them of the existing eBay requirement that they have to be more than 18 years of age.

A privacy statement is an important part of many web sites. You may want to add one to your own. If you already have an attorney to handle legal matters for you, ask the attorney to help you with such a statement, too. Any statements that you put in writing on the Web have to be carefully worded because, the moment they are published, they become statements you have to observe. If you don't, you'll get in legal trouble. It's important to get contracts and privacy policies in writing, but be sure that, whatever statements you publish on your web site, you are prepared to honor them fully.

## Where to Find It

- **Trademark Electronic Search System**
  **http://www.uspto.gov/main/trademarks.htm**
  Go here and click **Search trademarks** to conduct a search for the legal owner of a trademark.

- **eBay User Agreement**
  **http://pages.ebay.com/help/community/png-user.html**
  Here you'll find lots of restrictions about what you can and can't do on eBay, including the prohibition against infringing on someone else's copyright or trademark.

- **eBay Listing Policies for Sellers**
  **http://pages.ebay.com/help/policies/ia/listing_policies_for_sellers.html**
  This page lists requirements for creating auction descriptions that don't violate eBay rules.

- **Trademark Electronic Application System (TEAS)**
  **http://www.uspto.gov/teas/index.html**
  This site has instructions on how to apply for your own trademark.

- **VeRO Members' About Me pages**
  **http://pages.ebay.com/help/community/vero-aboutme.html**
  Links to About Me pages of individuals and organizations that watch for trademark and copyright infringement.

# Chapter 19

# What to Do in Case of Trouble

# How to…

- Respond to nonpaying bidders
- Avoid post-transaction confusion
- Avoid scams and tricks played on eBay members
- Handle complaints when the merchandise is received
- Recognize and head off potential trouble before a sale ends
- Try to resolve a dispute yourself
- Turn to third-party mediation when all else fails

The great fear of people who start using eBay is that something will go wrong with a sale. This, I think, is what makes people reluctant to start selling online: because you can't actually see the person you're dealing with, you have to trust that they'll follow through with their end of the bargain. If you buy something and send the payment, you're never sure the merchandise will actually arrive. If you sell something, you're never quite sure the high bidder will send the payment. Or the bidder might complain about something even after he or she does receive it.

Such problems do occur on eBay. I have heard reports (which seem to appear frequently in comments on eBay's message boards) that as many as 15 percent of eBay transactions turn out bad in some way. That might be true for some buyers and sellers, but I have heard figures that were far less—ranging from 1 to 5 percent—from the sellers I interviewed. On the other hand, eBay claims that less than 1 percent of its transactions "go bad." It's hard to tell which figure is really accurate, but I believe that if you are a reputable seller and you function in a professional way, you'll find that disputes occur far less often than you think.

You also need to be aware of problems that occur outside of transactions: scams that attempt to get you to give up your personal information, for instance. These kinds of scams, of course, take place on PayPal and many other web sites. No matter how many problems you do encounter, you have plenty of safeguards and responses you can use to protect yourself and your customers, as described in this chapter.

# If the Transaction Falls Through

Here's some free advice that applies to virtually all eBay transaction problems: remain calm and businesslike at all times. You may not be a longtime businessperson, and you don't report to an employer, so it can be difficult not to get impatient. But remember that it is essential for you to remain in control of the transaction at all times. By getting mad and becoming confrontational with the bidder, you sink down to the level of the bidder and lose control and credibility.

Another piece of advice that applies to problems in general: leave feedback that is specific, brief, and straightforward. Just state what happened ("Person never left payment") and don't be abusive or retaliatory. Also be sure to keep copies of all e-mails pertaining to the transaction until the payment has been received and feedback has been left. Such messages can provide essential evidence in case of a dispute.

*This book's technical editor, Lisa Suttora, suggests the following: "Many eBay sellers keep a paper trail (or an e-mail trail) of all transactions for both customer service and financial record-keeping. I keep an e-mail trail, sorted by month, and have frequently gone back and utilized my archives."*

## Deadbeat Bidders/Buyers

The formal eBay-speak for individuals who don't follow through with a transaction and pay for what they have purchased is *nonpaying bidder.* But most eBay sellers call them deadbeat bidders (or worse). You'd think such bidders would read the message eBay sends before placing a bid:

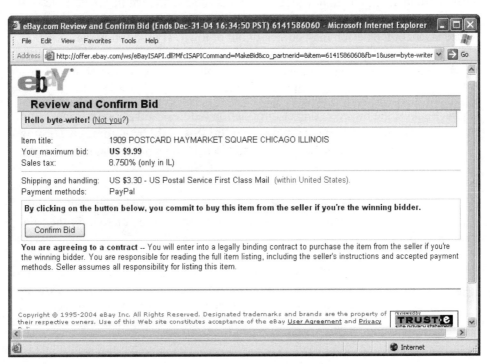

Here's what typically happens in a nonpaying bidder scenario: At the end of the sale, eBay sends its automatic notices telling you that the sale has ended, and notifying the high bidder that he or she has won. You send an e-mail to the bidder with payment information. The buyer either does not respond or says he or she will pay, but never sends payment.

When you run into a problem with a nonpaying bidder or other buyer, it can be helpful to take things in an orderly, step-by-step fashion.

> **TIP**   *You're not alone, so don't take it personally. Deadbeat bidders are a common problem on eBay, though they're not as widespread a problem as you might think. eBay has developed a process to help you deal with deadbeat buyers, at **http://pages.ebay.com/help/tp/unpaid-item-process.html**.*

## Step 1: Don't Overreact

If you do not receive a response to your initial e-mail notification that the individual has won the merchandise (or any subsequent e-mail), don't immediately assume that your buyer is a deadbeat. For one thing, you can check the person's feedback for similar occurrences that would indicate whether the person is a deadbeat. For another, the person may be having legitimate troubles with e-mail, which is by no means a trouble-free communications medium. The e-mail host may be flooded with other traffic, the individual's e-mail or Internet access account may be suspended for some reason, or the person may be sick or out of town. Try the following:

- Contact the person from another e-mail address, in case something is wrong with your mail server, not the buyer's.

- Request the buyer's contact information (address and phone number) from eBay (**http://cgi3.ebay.com/aw-cgi/eBayISAPI.dll?MemberSearchShow**). After you enter the item number and User ID, both buyer and seller will be e-mailed one another's contact information.

Simply receiving the e-mail from eBay will flush many buyers out of the woodwork. However, if you don't hear from someone a week or so after the sale ends, go to Step 2.

> **NOTE**   *eBay's sales software Selling Manager and Selling Manager Pro streamline the process of contacting buyers. They help you contact the buyer through eBay's communications system rather than through e-mail servers that might stop messages due to their spam e-mail filtering systems.*

## Step 2: Initiate an Unpaid Item Process

An Unpaid Item Process is a formal set of steps you can use to try to contact someone who hasn't responded to eBay's notice that they are the high bidder, or to e-mails from you telling the person where and how to send the payment. Filing an Unpaid Item dispute is not optional if you want to receive a refund of your final value fee and have a negative mark, called an Unpaid Item strike, filed against the nonresponsive buyer.

You can start the Unpaid Item Process between 7 and 45 days after the end of the sale. But the 7- to 45-day rule is hardly a hard-and-fast rule, however. One longtime eBay seller, "decoray", told me that when someone with a substantial amount of positive feedback purchases one of his items, he'll wait as long as one or two weeks before sending a "reminder" e-mail. If the purchaser is someone with little or no feedback, however, he sends an e-mail with a very different tone that requires the buyer to respond as soon as possible. You might send a reminder such as the following:

> I'm happy that you are the high bidder on my item #XXXXXXXXXX. Now that the sale has ended, it's important that you acknowledge that you have received notification from eBay that you're the high bidder, and that you let me know that payment is on the way. Please do this as soon as possible. My payment requirements follow, etc.

Once you start the Unpaid Item Process, eBay takes the pressure off you with regard to reminding your recalcitrant buyer. First, eBay sends the buyer an e-mail notification that the process has begun. Not only that, but if the buyer in question signs into eBay within two weeks after you filed the Unpaid Item Report, a pop-up message appears stating that payment has not been received and giving instruction on how to pay.

If your buyer does contact you and asks to cancel the transaction, eBay gives you the option to formally agree through the Mutually Agree to Cancel the Transaction option. By using this option, you receive a final value fee credit. You might agree to do this, for example, if the buyer informs you that the purchase was made without permission by a child.

## Step 3: Request a Final Value Fee Credit

If you still haven't received payment within seven days of filing the Unpaid Item dispute, you can take the final step: request a final value fee credit from eBay. You also get a credit that enables you to relist the item without having to pay an insertion fee. Unless the buyer reaches an agreement or disagrees with your assessment of the situation, he or she receives a black mark called a "strike." Another two such strikes and the individual will be suspended from eBay.

19

If, after receiving your final value fee credit, you work things out and receive payment after all, the buyer can appeal the Unpaid Item strike and have it removed.

If the bidder never pays, you have two options: you can make a Second Chance Offer to someone on the original list of bidders for the item by filling out the form at **http://cgi3.ebay.com/aw-cgi/eBayISAPI.dll?PersonalOfferLogin**, or you can relist the item.

## Have eBay Contact a Nonresponsive Buyer

If you can't contact a buyer, it might not be that person's fault. There might be a problem with an invalid or inactive e-mail address; the buyer's inbox could be full, preventing any new messages from being received. There may be a problem with the buyer's ISP (America Online users have been known to have problems with communications from eBay members). Or the buyer's spam e-mail filter might be blocking your messages for some reason. If you don't want to take it upon yourself to phone the buyer, you can get eBay involved.

"When I get e-mails from a buyer asking for information I've already sent more than once, I send an e-mail and an invoice through eBay's system," advises Carol Hearn, a seller who is profiled in Chapter 16. "At the same time, I write to PowerSeller support (if you aren't a PowerSeller, you'd write to the regular support address) and report that e-mail to the winner of item number *[fill in the blank with the eBay item number]* isn't getting through, and to please take necessary action," she adds. "This generates an e-mail to the buyer from eBay asking them to reply to the message to confirm their address."

To contact eBay's support staff, follow these steps:

1. Click Help in the eBay navigation bar.

2. Click **Contact Us**.

3. In the first of the three Contact Us boxes, select Report Problems with Other eBay Members.

4. In the second box, click Problems with Buyers.

5. In the third box, click Buyer's Email Address/Contact Information Is Invalid.

6. Click Continue.

**7.** When the next Contact Us page appears, click the **Email** link.

**8.** Sign in with your User ID and password.

**9.** When the e-mail form appears, enter the buyer's User ID, and type a description of your problem in the space provided. Then click Send Email to contact eBay.

If eBay does not receive an answer from the buyer after it tries to contact the person, an Unpaid Item strike is placed against the person. This helps you avoid getting negative feedback from a buyer who wasn't able to contact you.

## Bounced Checks

The problem of checks being returned for nonsufficient funds doesn't happen terribly often to eBay sellers, as far as I can tell. It's more common that someone won't follow through with a sale at all. If someone does follow through, they are likely to send payment promptly and have enough money in the bank to cover their check.

The simplest way to avoid running into a problem with a bounced check is to simply hold delivery of your merchandise until the buyer's check clears the bank. (Be sure to state in your auction Terms of Sale that you will do so.) Another way to prevent the problem is to specify that you'll only accept payment in the form of a cashier's check or postal money order. Or use the escrow service Escrow.com, which waits until checks clear before it notifies you that it's safe to send out merchandise to a buyer.

If you do have a check returned, deal with it in a courteous and businesslike manner. After all, chances are the buyer made an honest mistake and will be embarrassed that the problem occurred at all. Request that the buyer pay you in the form of a cashier's check or money order, and pay any fees the bank charges you for depositing a check that is returned. Be sure to hold on to the returned check in case you have a dispute and you need evidence. If you still don't receive payment, you can follow Steps 2 and 3 in the preceding section: start an Unpaid Item Process with eBay and then, if seven or more days go by without payment, close the Unpaid Item and request a final value fee credit.

## Problems with the Seller (Yes, I Mean You)

This heading refers to you, the eBay seller: problems can occur at your end that either delay the sale or prevent it from finishing altogether. Sometimes, the problems occur unintentionally. For instance, you advertise that you will accept credit cards on your

19

auction listings, but either your approval hasn't come through from the bank or you have been approved but haven't set up your point-of-sale hardware or software. You have to tell bidders that you need to wait for such approval and run the risk of unhappy buyers and negative feedback.

I've said this elsewhere, but you shouldn't plan to go on vacation or be out of town when your sale ends. If your buyers have to wait a week or more just for you to respond, they're going to begin to suspect that you're a deadbeat seller and initiate action against you through eBay.

## Don't Be a Deadbeat Seller

Sometimes (I shudder to say this) sellers don't follow through. For some reason, they decline to accept payment from the winning bidder or purchaser, or they never respond to the purchaser. This not only damages their reputation, but it detracts from the entire network of trust that keeps eBay going. If you're not going to follow through, don't sell at all.

*eBay may warn or suspend you if you don't follow through with a sale and don't have a good reason for not doing so. Read the notice at **http://pages .ebay.com/help/policies/non-selling-seller.html** to find out more.*

## Make Sure You Tell All in Your Listings

It's hard to remember every single detail about a sale, especially when you are attempting to process dozens of sales at a time. That's why you should come up with a template for your sales that clearly lists your accepted payment methods and shipping options as well as any extra charges for credit card transactions or other things. Your auction template should include the standard information that buyers want to know and that you want them to know, such as:

- Charges for using credit card systems.

- Reminders that buyers should not send any payment until you have e-mailed them a message listing the amount required (the purchase price plus shipping or other charges), if you are not using the eBay shipping calculator provided in the Sell Your Item form.

- If you encourage buyers to obtain multiple auction items from you in order to save on combined postage, put in a reminder statement saying postage charged will be reduced, but not necessarily by half (if two items are purchased), by one-third (if three items are involved), and so on. After all, the additional weight and additional packing required to ship multiple items may increase shipping charges. At the very least, you want to cover yourself if they do.

■ A statement indicating by when you expect the buyer to contact you and then send payment: "Buyers must contact me/us within three working days of the end of the auction, and payment must be received within __ days."

■ If you have a policy of not accepting bids from sellers with no feedback or with a negative feedback rating, state that as well.

■ If you don't want to ship internationally, state that in your auction terms. (Or, if you do ship internationally, you may want to include a separate shipping charge.)

■ If, like many sellers, you wait for personal checks to clear before shipping out items, make that clear.

■ Your refund policy, if you have one, such as "If you are unhappy with your purchase for any reason I will fully refund your purchase but only if the item(s) is returned in the original packaging and in the condition in which it was purchased."

All of these policies and statements are collectively called the *Terms of Sale.* By taking the time to create an accurate and comprehensive Terms of Sale template, you decrease (though not eliminate) the number of questions you get from buyers, and you "cover yourself" in case someone complains.

Many of the options mentioned here, and some other useful specifications, are included in eBay seller "decoray"'s Terms of Sale, shown in Figure 19-1.

NOTE    *In other chapters, I discuss problems that can crop up with eBay transactions. In Chapter 16, you learn how to make sure what you want to sell isn't illegal or prohibited on eBay. In Chapter 17, you learn for which sales you need to collect sales tax, and that you need to pay income tax on your eBay sales. In Chapter 18, you learn how not to infringe on someone's copyright or trademarks.*

# If Problems Occur after You Ship

You might think that, after you receive payment and either ship the merchandise or it is picked up in person, your problems are over. Not necessarily. For one thing, the buyer may claim that the item was never received and was lost in the mail, unless you get some form of delivery confirmation from the U.S. Postal Service (USPS), UPS, FedEx, or other shipper. (In the U.K., such confirmation is called a Certificate of Posting.) Or, the buyer may claim that the item is damaged or that you did not disclose defects with the item.

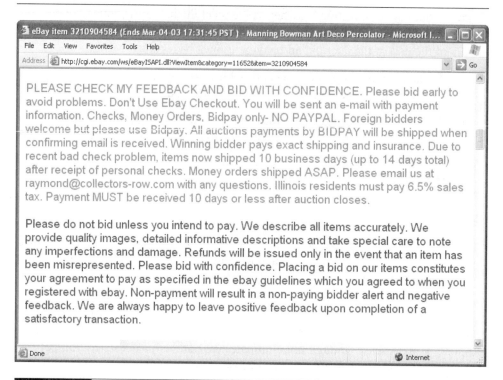

**FIGURE 19-1** Spell out your Terms of Sale as clearly as possible in your auction listings to eliminate disputes after the auction closes.

## The Buyer Claims Damage

One post-shipping problem that can occur is that the buyer claims the item was damaged when received. You can prevent this by inspecting the merchandise thoroughly when you pack it. Thorough packing is one of the most important parts of an eBay transaction. Make sure you pack as carefully as possible and follow these tips that were passed along to me by eBay seller "decoray":

- Buy good boxes, either from USPS (it will deliver the boxes to you in lots of 25 if you use Priority Mail) or from an office supply store.

- Use plenty of bubble wrap and packing "peanuts."

- If you have items that include multiple separate pieces, put pieces of cardboard between each piece.

- For extra valuable or delicate items, pack a box inside another box.

NOTE

*Shipping boxes requested from USPS are free as long as they are used for Priority Mail shipments. If you use Priority Mail, you can also obtain free labels and envelopes. (The nice wrapping tape with the Priority Mail logo is no longer offered for free, unfortunately.) But it's a criminal offense to use any of these shipping materials for any purpose other than Priority Mail.*

Leave a note with the item describing any damage that was present when it was purchased—for example, a sticky note or typed statement on your letterhead with the words "This chip was described in the auction listing." You may also want to write down any serial numbers or identifying codes on the item itself so buyers can't claim it was damaged and return it while substituting another, similar (possibly counterfeit) item for the original.

You can obtain insurance for what you ship from USPS or from private shippers. However, all the indications I've heard are that it's very difficult to get reimbursed if you make a claim. (It's up to you, the shipper, to make the claim, not the recipient.) All shippers stipulate that they won't pay claims if your packaging is judged by them to have been insufficient in some way.

TIP

*You can get confirmation of delivery from USPS if you send a package using Delivery Confirmation, Signature Confirmation, Certified Mail, or Registered Mail. Delivery Confirmation can be used with First-Class Mail, Priority Mail, Parcel Post, Media Mail, and several other types of shipping. Typically, Delivery Confirmation costs only $0.55 if you purchase it from a retail post office, and only $0.13 if you order shipping labels electronically. It's well worth the minimal expense. The options are explained at **http://www.usps.com/shipping/trackandconfirm.htm**.*

## The Buyer Just Isn't Satisfied

Most people are happy with what they have purchased on eBay. The vast majority are overjoyed when they receive their package. Once in a while, however, someone just isn't satisfied. They claim that your merchandise isn't as big/clean/colorful as you said in your description. In one memorable posting I spotted on the eBay Motors message boards, someone who came in person to pick up the auto just purchased on eBay—and who had already submitted a deposit—expressed great dissatisfaction at the condition of the car, kicked the door in anger, and left in a huff.

That's an extreme example, of course, but if someone just isn't happy, you have two options. You can follow the letter of the law and state that the sale is final, and you don't have to accept the returned item because it wasn't damaged in transit. You'll probably receive negative feedback, however. Or, you can take the "big picture" view and think of your business's long-term well being, and

19

simply let the customer return the item and get a refund. You can resell it later on. Yes, you lose your final value fee, and you have to go through the extra effort of reselling. But in the long run, you avoid a conflict, and you don't have a dispute, either.

# If Problems Occur During the Sale

It's hard to pay attention to all of your sales all of the time, but try to check in once a day, or once every other day, to see who the high bidder is on each of your sales. Lots of things can happen while the sale is going on. The overwhelming majority of the time, bidding will progress smoothly. You may, in fact, never run into an instance of "interference" during an auction, but it's good to be aware of such incidents in case they do occur.

The fact that eBay buyers and sellers can all contact one another by e-mail means that some types of interference can arise before a sale ends. In theory, bidders are supposed to place their bids, perhaps pose some questions to you before the sale ends, and nothing more. In practice, eBay bidders can interfere with the sale by telling other bidders:

- That the seller is not to be trusted because of past transgressions against the person making the complaint.

- That they can sell to the other bidders the same object they're bidding on—at a lower price. They then direct bidders to one of their own sales or someone else's.

Both types of bidding interference are prohibited by eBay. If you detect such interference (or, hopefully, if one of your bidders tells you about it), report the incident to eBay's Investigations team (**http://pages.ebay.com/help/tp/programs-investigations.html**).

# How to Resolve a Dispute

What should you do if you and a buyer have a dispute that you just can't resolve through negotiation? First, realize that you aren't alone. As a first resort, turn to the eBay message boards and chat rooms if you are having trouble with a bidder and ask other sellers' advice. Sometimes, just hearing from others who have gone through similar troubles calms you down. One of the best resources available to you as an eBay seller is the dispute resolution service offered free of charge by

# Avoiding Scams and Shams

Some of the most notorious types of problems to plague both buyers and sellers on eBay have nothing to do with specific transactions. They occur when unscrupulous individuals go "phishing" for the personal information of eBay members. All too often, they find it—and the members pay a price.

> **NOTE** Phishing *refers to the practice that's similar to real-world fishing: you throw some bait into the water and hope some unfortunate creature will get hooked. On the Internet, phishing involves an e-mail message that tempts you into clicking on a link and visiting a web site, where you are then encouraged to "verify" your information.*

The "phisher" can make use of your credit card information to ring up some fraudulent purchases. A valid eBay User ID and password can be used to create some fake sales: when the supposed items are sold, the money is collected and the goods are never delivered. The criminal gets the money, and the legitimate owner of the User ID and password gets his or her reputation tarnished.

You might think it's difficult for someone to trick you into giving out sensitive information like your Social Security number, checking account number, and other details you normally keep to yourself. But online criminals are both clever and devious. When they approach eBay members, they send messages that claim there's an urgent problem. They try to instill panic in the members. The messages might claim that the member has been suspended from eBay and needs to "verify" his or her information by going to a special web page and resubmitting it. Or perhaps the message will claim there's been a security breach; "eBay" suspects that your account has been hijacked, and you need to send your information in again.

Whatever the reason, you need to ignore any of these spoof e-mails. eBay will never contact you by e-mail asking for your account details or other personal information. You should also go a step further and forward such messages to an address that eBay has set up to deal with such scams: **spoof@ebay.com**.

**19**

SquareTrade (**http://www.squaretrade.com**) as long as you and the buyer work together in the process. (If you hire a SquareTrade mediator to negotiate, a $20 fee is charged.) eBay's own Rules & Safety area (**http://pages.ebay.com/help/community**) simply directs you to SquareTrade for dispute resolution services.

Keep in mind the helpful advice that one eBay seller (who prefers to be anonymous) wanted me to pass along: "For me, one of the most anxious parts of selling on eBay is the whole feedback system, and the potential that people will be ugly to you if something goes wrong. It seems to me that people can be more volatile or nasty by e-mail than they ever would face-to-face. If their claim or complaint seems legitimate, I offer them their money back. If I feel that they are lying or getting angry or might get abusive, I never answer their e-mail immediately. I always give myself a day to calm down before I respond. It's not worth it to get into an argument."

*If you do have to leave negative feedback for someone, just state the facts without being abusive. Just say, "Person never left payment" and leave it at that.*

## Where to Find It

- **Find a Member form**
  **http://cgi3.ebay.com/aw-cgi/eBayISAPI.dll?MemberSearchShow**
  A form you can fill out to obtain the contact information for individuals with whom you have had transactions.

- **Overview of Unpaid Item Process**
  **http://pages.ebay.com/help/tp/unpaid-item-process.html**
  A description of the steps you need to follow to file an Unpaid Item dispute if a buyer fails to respond.

- **eBay Investigations Team**
  **http://pages.ebay.com/help/tp/programs-investigations.html**
  Descriptions of offenses eBay investigates and links to a form you can fill out to report trouble.

- **The U.S. Postal Service's Track & Confirm page**
  **http://www.usps.com/shipping/trackandconfirm.htm**
  Information on options for obtaining Delivery Confirmation on merchandise you ship to buyers.

# Glossary

**About Me**    A page that you can create on eBay's web site that provides some brief personal information about you, showcases your business and customer service policies, and displays a sampling of your current sales.

**as is**    An item that you sell in its advertised condition and with no other warranty, either implied or stated.

**bid increment**    A predetermined amount by which bids are increased as they are placed. The increment varies depending on the current high bid.

**bid retraction**    The process of canceling a bid that has already been made. Retractions are only allowed in exceptional circumstances, such as the entry of the wrong bid amount, or if the description of the item changes "significantly." Such retractions are only allowed before the last 12 hours of a sale. See **http://pages.ebay.com/help/buy/bid-retract.html** for more information.

**bid shielding**    A process in which two bidders conspire to defraud a seller out of a high bid. The high bidder retracts the bid at the last minute, so the partner's lower bid can win.

**blocked bidder**    Someone who has specifically been excluded from bidding on an item, usually because of problems with previous transactions.

**Buy It Now**    A way to sell your item on eBay for a fixed price. Buy It Now auctions can be conducted in either of two ways. In a Fixed Price auction, you offer an item at a fixed Buy It Now price and the buyer purchases it immediately at that price. In an Online Auction, the buyer can buy the item at the Buy It Now price only before the first bid is placed; after a bid is placed, the Buy It Now option disappears.

**category gouging**    A condition that occurs when one seller lists numerous similar items in one category, thus forcing their competition off of the main page and eliminating fair comparison for the buyers.

**changed User ID icon**    An icon added to a User ID if the individual has changed that User ID within the last 30 days.

**chargeback**    A fee charged to a seller by a credit card company for accepting a credit card number for a purchase that turns out to be fraudulent.

**Chat**    Normally used as a shorthand term for Internet Relay Chat (IRC), a real-time communications method on the Internet. eBay regularly uses Chat to describe its Community Boards, which are really message boards.

**Checkout**   A way of streamlining the end of a transaction in which the seller specifies how much to pay for shipping, insurance, and sales tax when the item is listed. The buyer then receives an e-mail at the end of the auction that automatically lists the total and where the item should be shipped. You also receive an e-mail describing the buyer's shipping address and preferred method of payment. Find out more at **http://pages.ebay.com/help/sell/checkout.html**.

**consignment**   The process of selling something for someone else. The seller who offers the merchandise and who conducts the sale usually collects a fee for his or her services.

**cookie**   A small bit of information that is placed on a visitor's computer by a web site and that provides the site (such as eBay) with information when you revisit, so you don't have to log in again.

**corporation**   An organization established for the purpose of doing business.

**counter**   A utility that tracks the number of visits that have been made to a web page.

**Dutch auction**   An auction format that enables a group of identical items to be sold to a group of bidders at once rather than in separate sales. Also known as a multiple-item auction.

**eBay Motors**   An auction area on the eBay web site where participants can buy and sell motor vehicles, including cars, boats, and planes.

**eBay Stores**   A feature that enables sellers to sell a group of items, including your Fixed Price format store listings and your regular auction listings, on a web page they publish on eBay.

**escrow**   A way of completing transactions through the use of an intermediary. The buyer sends payment to the escrow company, the seller ships the item to the buyer, the buyer inspects and approves the item, and the escrow company releases funds to the seller.

**feedback**   A system of communication that enables eBay users who have been involved in transactions with other users to leave comments that describe their level of responsiveness, the quality of the transaction, or related (and sometimes unrelated) issues.

**fink**   Someone who turns out to be a fraudulent buyer or seller.

**Fixed Price format**    A sales format in which eBay users can purchase an item for a fixed price specified by the seller; an alternative to an auction.

**gallery**    An eBay feature that enables sellers to post small, thumbnail-size photos of their items that buyers see next to the auction title when they browse or do a keyword search.

**Half.com**    An area of eBay where sellers can offer books, CDs, or other items at a discount.

**hijacked account**    An eBay account that has been taken over by someone who has stolen the owner's information.

**HTF**    Short for *hard to find,* a descriptor used frequently by participants in eBay's message board, or in auction listings.

**HTML**    Abbreviation for HyperText Markup Language, the set of instructions that is used to present text and images on web pages (as well as eBay auction descriptions).

**ID Verify**    A program in which sellers or buyers have their personal information verified against consumer and business databases so others can trust that they are who they say they are.

**keyword spamming**    The practice of including brand names or other keywords that aren't related to the item being sold, in an effort to get extra attention for the item.

**live auction**    An auction held in real time. eBay users can find out more at **http:// pages.liveauctions.ebay.com/help/welcome/overview.html**.

**MIB**    An abbreviation for *mint in box* that occasionally appears in auction listing titles. The item in the box is in mint condition; the box may not be, however.

**MIMB**    An abbreviation for *mint in mint box.* The item in the box is in mint condition, and the box is, too.

**My eBay**    A starting page you can configure to track and manage all the items you are currently selling, the ones you have sold, and the items you have obtained recently, or on which you have bid. You can also set messaging and account preferences using this page.

**NIB**    An abbreviation for *new in box*; *see* MIB.

**nonpaying bidder**    Someone who qualifies to obtain an item by being the high bidder, but then fails to complete the transaction by not paying for the item.

**NR**    Abbreviation for *no reserve*; used to describe a sale for which a reserve amount has not been specified. The high bidder will win the item.

**pink**    Someone who works at eBay. When they post on message boards, their name is highlighted with a pink background. Whenever they post, you also see the eBay logo next to their name.

**proxy bid**    A bid that eBay places for you automatically based on the maximum amount you are willing to pay for an item. If someone outbids you, eBay automatically places proxy bids up to your maximum amount.

**relist**    To put an item up for sale again after a sale has ended.

**reserve price**    An amount specified by a seller as the minimum price the seller is willing to accept in order to purchase it. The reserve price is kept secret until a bidder meets it. The seller is not obligated to sell an item if the reserve price has not been met.

**Second Chance Offer**    An eBay feature in which, if a winning bidder fails to buy an item or if the seller has a duplicate item for sale, the seller can offer the item to any one of the underbidders.

**shill bidding**    An illegal practice involving the use of family members or friends to drive up the bidding on an item. (Sometimes called "bid padding.")

**Unpaid Item Process**    A series of steps that sellers should follow when a winning bidder or buyer fails to respond, or fails to send payment, after a sale ends. Find out more at **http://pages.ebay.com/help/tp/unpaid-item-process.html**.

**Verified Rights Owner (VeRO) Program**    A program in which owners of brand names, copyrights, or trademarks, or their authorized representatives, work to make sure that eBay sales do not infringe upon those intellectual property rights.

# Index

# INTERNATIONAL CONTACT INFORMATION

**AUSTRALIA**
McGraw-Hill Book Company
Australia Pty. Ltd.
TEL +61-2-9900-1800
FAX +61-2-9878-8881
http://www.mcgraw-hill.com.au
books-it_sydney@mcgraw-hill.com

**CANADA**
McGraw-Hill Ryerson Ltd.
TEL +905-430-5000
FAX +905-430-5020
http://www.mcgraw-hill.ca

**GREECE, MIDDLE EAST, & AFRICA
(Excluding South Africa)**
McGraw-Hill Hellas
TEL +30-210-6560-990
TEL +30-210-6560-993
TEL +30-210-6560-994
FAX +30-210-6545-525

**MEXICO (Also serving Latin America)**
McGraw-Hill Interamericana Editores
S.A. de C.V.
TEL +525-1500-5108
FAX +525-117-1589
http://www.mcgraw-hill.com.mx
carlos_ruiz@mcgraw-hill.com

**SINGAPORE (Serving Asia)**
McGraw-Hill Book Company
TEL +65-6863-1580
FAX +65-6862-3354
http://www.mcgraw-hill.com.sg
mghasia@mcgraw-hill.com

**SOUTH AFRICA**
McGraw-Hill South Africa
TEL +27-11-622-7512
FAX +27-11-622-9045
robyn_swanepoel@mcgraw-hill.com

**SPAIN**
McGraw-Hill/
Interamericana de España, S.A.U.
TEL +34-91-180-3000
FAX +34-91-372-8513
http://www.mcgraw-hill.es
professional@mcgraw-hill.es

**UNITED KINGDOM, NORTHERN,
EASTERN, & CENTRAL EUROPE**
McGraw-Hill Education Europe
TEL +44-1-628-502500
FAX +44-1-628-770224
http://www.mcgraw-hill.co.uk
emea_queries@mcgraw-hill.com

**ALL OTHER INQUIRIES Contact:**
McGraw-Hill/Osborne
TEL +1-510-420-7700
FAX +1-510-420-7703
http://www.osborne.com
omg_international@mcgraw-hill.com

# Sound Off!

Visit us at **www.osborne.com/bookregistration** and let us know what you thought of this book. While you're online you'll have the opportunity to register for newsletters and special offers from McGraw-Hill/Osborne.

*We want to hear from you!*

# Sneak Peek

Visit us today at **www.betabooks.com** and see what's coming from McGraw-Hill/Osborne tomorrow!

Based on the successful software paradigm, Bet@Books™ allows computing professionals to view partial and sometimes complete text versions of selected titles online. Bet@Books™ viewing is free, invites comments and feedback, and allows you to "test drive" books in progress on the subjects that interest you the most.

Mc
Graw